The Database Expert's Guide to IDEAL

The Database Expert's Guide to IDEAL

Earl H. Parsons, Jr.

Intertext Publications
McGraw-Hill Book Company

New York St. Louis San Francisco Auckland Bogotá
Hamburg London Madrid Mexico Milan Montreal
New Delhi Panama Paris São Paulo
Singapore Sidney Tokyo Toronto

Library of Congress Catalog Card Number 88-83060

10 9 8 7 6 5 4 3 2 1

ISBN 0-07-048550-X

IDEAL is a trademark of Computer Associates, Inc.
Data Dictionary is a trademark of Computer Associates, Inc.

Intertext Publications/Multiscience Press, Inc.
One Lincoln Plaza
New York, NY 10023

McGraw-Hill Book Company
1221 Avenue of the Americas
New York, NY 10020

Dedication

I would like to dedicate this book to my wife, Lynn,
who diligently read it again and again to find all of
my spelling, grammar, and typing mistakes,
of which there were many.

Contents

Prologue

As with many new concepts, the main problem in learning how to work efficiently in IDEAL is finding a place to start.

The purpose of this text is to provide that starting place. It is designed to serve first as a textbook, for either a self-study project or a classroom environment. Then readers can use it as a reference book when they begin working in the field.

Because of this design, we spend most of our time discussing the whys, hows, and whens of the language. It has also been organized in such a way that each concept builds upon the previous concept.

We hope to show the reader how to make the most of the strong points of the language, while avoiding the problems that we found in our experience.

In this way we hope that this book will be helpful in providing a means by which more users can create successful systems in IDEAL.

The original release of this text was based on the 1.3 version of the language. In April of 1988 we incorporated the features of IDEAL 1.4.

1

The Beginning

As we recall the history of the development of programming languages, we can see the entire emphasis has been the simplification of communication between the user and the machine. We began coding in the binary language of the machine. The next step was the development of assembler macros, which the machine would translate into binary. The next step was the design of the "higher-level" languages such as COBOL, which had specific commands, that were compiled into a series of assembler macros. These macros were in turn translated into the required binary code.

The purpose of a fourth generation language like IDEAL is to further reduce the degree of detail that the programmer must face. In his book, *Fourth Generation Languages*, James Martin states that they should be designed with the following principles in mind:[1]

1. The principle of minimum work
2. The principle of minimum skill
3. The principle of avoiding alien syntax and mnemonics
4. The principle of minimum time
5. The principle of minimum errors
6. The principle of minimum resistance
7. The principle of minimum results

Of course this is accomplished at the cost of more machine overhead, but when we start comparing the falling cost of machine time to the rising cost of programmer time, we can easily see the justification.

In this chapter we will begin our study of IDEAL by discussing what a *relational database* is, how it is designed and used, and the advantages of using it over the more traditional data structures.

When the average person learned how to program, he began with what was then the nearly insurmountable task of reading in a collection of data and producing a report line for each piece of information. This collection of data was called a file. The *file* was made up of a series of records, each with the same length and the same arrangement of fields. Each *field* was a specific piece of information which either described, or was described by, another field on the record.

For example, we could have had an employee file, with the following layout:

```
01   EMPLOYEE-FILE
     05   NUMBER          X(05)
     05   NAME            X(24)
     05   STREET-ADDRESS  X(24)
     05   CITY-ADDRESS    X(15)
     05   STATE-ADDRESS   X(02)
     05   ZIP-CODE-LOC    X(05)
     05   SOCIAL-SECURITY X(09)
```

The employee number uniquely identifies each employee. All of the other information describes some aspect of the employee's individuality, but we cannot identify the specific employee from a single field without knowing the unique employee number. It is quite possible to have two John Joneses working for the same company. We can then produce a report showing the identity and address of each employee in the company.

However, there is often more information pertaining to an employee than his name and address. While the personnel department is maintaining the personnel file, the payroll department has the all-important payroll file.

```
01   PAYROLL-FILE
     05   NUMBER          X(05)
     05   ACTIVITY-CODE   X(01)
     05   ACTIVITY-STATUS X(01)
     05   CURRENT-RATE    9(06)V99
     05   YTD-WAGES       9(06)V99
     05   YTD-COMMISSION  9(06)V99
     05   YTD-TAX         9(06)V99
```

While this file has some of the most important information in the company, it is not sufficient to produce the payroll checks. We also need the employee's name and address so that we know to whom to issue the check.

We can get this information for the check writing program in one of two different ways. We can keep it in the payroll file in addition to having it in the employee file, or we can merge the two files together with program code. Both of these solutions have distinct disadvantages. If we keep the data separate, then each time we need a new report, a programmer has to write a new match merge routine. If we do this, we will find ourselves falling further and further behind the work load. We will also soon find ourselves buried in a heap of programs, job streams, parameters, etc., that push the same pieces of data around from dataset to dataset in a seemingly endless set of combinations. We then find ourselves with a massive maintenance headache, trying not only to keep the programs running, but also to assure the integrity and accuracy of the data. We know of one bank that has a separate file for each type of account; savings, checking, loan, IRA, mortgage, etc. Each account on each file contains the customer's name and address. If the customer moves to a different part of the city, the address on each of these flat files needs to be changed individually. This becomes especially difficult as each file is "owned" by a different department, and hence each has its own update routine. Thus it takes a couple of months to get one's address straight on all of the files after a simple move.

The other solution, to keep everything on a massive file, also has its drawbacks. The first problem is the massive size of the resulting file. We know one company that has all of its pension plan data on a single file. This file has over a million records on it, and each record is 1600 bytes long. To make a simple change to a single account requires that they read in and rewrite the entire file, catching and changing the single record as it goes through the merge logic between the master file and the transaction file. The six-hour run time is nearly overwhelming, let alone the size of the reports that it creates, and the cost of magnetic tape to store it. The second problem is that each of the programs that has anything to do with the file must be changed and recompiled whenever a change is made to the layout of the file.

Thus a way was needed to consolidate all of the data into a single repository, while allowing access to either inquire on or update a single unique record. The great salvation was the database.

In many cases we simply took the small files, identified the unique keys, and loaded them into the new data structures. We could then write programs where we "typed in" the desired employee number and the program would get the corresponding employee and payroll records and display the information on the screen. The operator would then change the current rate on the screen and the program would change the information in the current rate field on the database for that employee without touching the other records.

This was all well and good until things started to get complicated (as they often do in DP). We got away from having a single record type in each database and we started building hierarchical databases. This was done because the equipment that we were using did not have the power to handle all of the overhead required to run multiple databases. A *hierarchical* file is one in which some records are subordinate to other records.[2]

In our employee file example, we would have the following hierarchical structure:

```
-------------------------------------


    EMPLOYEE

-------------------------------------


        ADDRESS


        -------------------------------------


        PAYROLL


        -------------------------------------
```

We would have an employee record which would have the employee name and number. The address record would have the employee's address, and the payroll record would have the same payroll data that we had in the flat file above. We would then have to "navigate" through the data structure, establishing our position on one record, and reading all of the records that were either subordinate or superior to the record that we found. For example, if we wanted to find all of the employees that had a certain wage rate, we would locate each employee record, then find the corresponding payroll record, and then test to see if the RATE was greater than the desired rate. If it was, we would write out the report line. Thus we have an extra input/output (IO) transaction to get data that we might or might not need. Still this wasn't too bad until our hierarchical structures started getting out of hand. For example, an invoice history file could look like this:

```
-------------------------------------
INVOICED CUSTOMER
-------------------------------------
        BILL-TO-ADDRESS
        -------------------------------------
        SHIPMENT 01
        -------------------------------------
                SHIP-TO ADDRESS
                -------------------------------------
                LINE 001
                -------------------------------------
                LINE 002
                -------------------------------------
                        LINE 002 - SPECIAL CHARGE 001
                        -------------------------------------
                        LINE 002 - SPECIAL CHARGE 002
                -------------------------------------------------
                LINE 003
                -------------------------------------
                        LINE 003 - SPECIAL CHARGE 001
                        -------------------------------------
                        LINE 003 - SPECIAL CHARGE 002
                -------------------------------------------------
                FREIGHT CHARGES
        -----------------------------------------------------------
        SHIPMENT 02
        -------------------------------------
                SHIP-TO ADDRESS
                -------------------------------------
                HEADER SPECIAL CHARGES
                -------------------------------------
                LINE 001
                -------------------------------------
                LINE 002
                -------------------------------------
                        LINE 002 - SPECIAL CHARGE 001
                        -------------------------------------
                        LINE 002 - SPECIAL CHARGE 002
                -------------------------------------------------
                LINE 003
                -------------------------------------
```

```
              LINE 003 - SPECIAL CHARGE 001
           ---------------------------------------
              LINE 003 - SPECIAL CHARGE 002
       ---------------------------------------------
        FREIGHT CHARGES
       ----------------------------------------
```

The first record in the structure contains the customer data that describes to whom the invoice was sent. The next record shows where the shipment was delivered. The third record contains the shipment data for the material that was sent (such as the carrier, the tax codes, the shipping warehouse, etc.). In fact, in this system we have the possibility of having multiple shipments per invoice. The next record that we see is the ship-to address. We then see the line records, which say what was shipped, (part number, quantity, price, etc.), and records for any special handling charges which are being added to the total price (such as handling, labor, non-returnable cable reels).

Trying to find the amounts that we charged a group of customers for a certain special charge item would create a worse navigational problem than Captain Ahab had when searching for Moby Dick.

This problem became even more serious as the user community became more sophisticated, and less patient. They wanted to write their own queries against the data and were tired of hearing the phrase "you can't get there from here." The problem was also complicated by the fact that even a minor database change could cause navigational routines to cease to function.

At about this same time, the machines became more powerful. This meant that they could handle more overhead work without taking resources away from the programs. When this happened, we were able to take a great leap backwards and start building databases that again had the idea of a single record type per file. Each field on these records had a direct relationship to the record's key field. Thus we began the idea of relational databases.

A *relational database* is a database, or series of databases, which appear as two-dimensional arrays, and where each piece of data in the record describes the main field of the record. The main field (or *key*) uniquely identifies some entity.

Each record in the database then defines something in the real world. For example, a *part* database would begin with a field whose value uniquely identifies that part. The rest of the record would contain information that describes the physical attributes of that part, its color, weight, where we buy it, etc.

Thus each record is an entry of a two-dimensional table, which is the simplest way to store and display information.

These databases are designed through a process called *normalization*, in which the basic information that the company has is collected, and each piece is identified with, or related to, the piece of information that it describes. We will not attempt to describe that process in detail here, but simply say that there are three basic levels of normalization. These are

1. FIRST NORMAL FORM — The design is said to be in *first normal form* if all of the data is in atomic form. This means that the data is arranged in such a way that there are no repeating groups in the structure.
2. SECOND NORMAL FORM — The design is in *second normal form* if it is in first normal form and every non-key attribute is fully dependent on the primary key. Thus every field in the record describes some quality of the item that is identified by the value of the primary key. If we had a part database record, and the PART-NUMBER field would identify a specific part (5585590701), the other fields (UM, VENDOR-NO, VENDOR-NAME, WEIGHT, COST) further describe the part (FT, G0701, AUSTIN CABLE TECH., 1LB/FT, .01/FOOT). However we cannot identify the specific part from any of these description fields.
3. THIRD NORMAL FORM — When a design is in second normal form, it is usually already in third normal form. However, in some instances it is a possible to have "transitive dependence" in second normal form. This means that a non-key field is dependent on both the key field and another field in the record. If the value of one field in the record changes, then the value of the second field must also be changed to maintain the accuracy of the data. In our second normal form description, we included both VENDOR-NO and VENDOR-NAME. If we begin buying this part from another vendor, then we must change not only the number on the part record, but the name as well. Also, if the vendor changes his name, we must change the name on each of the PART records with that VENDOR-NO. However, if we broke the VENDOR-NO and VENDOR-NAME relationship out into a separate database, we would only have to change the value of one field in each of these instances. Thus the field VENDOR-NAME is transitively dependent on both the part number and the vendor number. To obtain a third normal form construct we will remove VENDOR-NAME from the PART database, and establish a VENDOR database

that contains this relationship. Then when we want to know the name of the vendor from whom we buy the part, we would read the PART file for the specific part, and get the VENDOR record with the corresponding VENDOR-NUMBER.

The study of this relating of data in different records is called *relational algebra*. With this facility we can build standard procedures into the language itself to obtain data instead of having to design a way to navigate through the data that is unique to each individual database.

Relational algebra is the study of the manipulation of sets of data to create different sets from which we can obtain answers to queries. The eight main relational algebra functions are

1. UNION
2. INTERSECTION
3. DIFFERENCE
4. PRODUCT
5. SELECT
6. PROJECT
7. JOIN
8. DIVIDE

We will discuss the details behind these functions, and the commands that IDEAL has to execute them, in Chapter 5 of this book.

This type of data manipulation of course takes more machine power than other types of data storage, which is why it was not used in the first place. However this consideration is becoming less and less important as the machines become more and more powerful. In addition there are a number of distinct advantages to working with a fully normalized database. James Martin lists these advantages as being[3]

1. **Ease of use** — The easiest way to represent and display data is in the form of a two dimensional table.
2. **Flexibility** — Relational algebra operations allow the easy manipulation of data along the lines of the multiple relationships that naturally occur in the data structure.
3. **Precision** — Precise results of relational mathematics can be applied to the data, instead of relying on the sometimes misleading directed links.
4. **Security** — Certain pieces of a sensitive relation (such as salary) can be placed in its own separate record with a

separate set of security rules. If these rules are met, then the data can be *joined* to the rest of the record.

5. **Relatability** — Maximum flexibility is available in relating the different files together.

6. **Ease of implementation** — This is the easiest way to store data in the machine. It is also comparably easy to make changes to the database structure.

7. **Data independence** — The relational structure is also comparably easier to change. New relations can be added to the structure without changing the rest of the database.

8. **Data manipulation language** — As we said before, we can build the relational algebra functions directly into the language. These structures will not be very complex because the data that they are going after is not very complex.

9. **Clarity** — The relational database structure is the easiest for a new employee to understand and begin using. This is especially important when we start adding additional business functions to the structure. For example, a structure that was originally designed for customer invoicing can be expanded to include the functions of salesman incentive compensation and the general ledger.

One of the keys to the successful development of a fully normalized database is the use of a DATADICTIONARY. A DATADICTIONARY is a catalog of the different types of information used by the corporation, giving their names, structures, and usages. By using a DATADICTIONARY we can create a single repository for the definition of terms used by the different organizations of a corporation. This is important because different people in an organization can use the same term for different ideas, and different terms for the same concept.

Take for example the term *cost of goods sold*. To the finance group, this could refer to the amount of inventory that has been relieved from the warehouse based on a certain accounting method (FIFO, LIFO, etc.). To the marketing group, it could be the quantity sold multiplied by the current price charged by the vendor. To a purchasing group it could be the accumulation of the actual price charged by the vendor on each unit purchased. In the DATADICTIONARY we would create three entries, ACCTG-COST-OF-GOODS-SOLD, MARK-COST-OF-GOODS-SOLD, and PUR-COST-OF-GOODS-SOLD. Each entry would then refer to a specific and an exclusive value, based on the different definitions.

The other side of the problem would have the three groups calling the price that we normally charge our customers for an item by three different names. Finance might call it *base-price*, Marketing might call it *book-price*, and Purchasing might call it both *standard-price* and *floor-price* interchangeably. For the DATADICTIONARY, the three groups would have to agree on a common name, and that name would be used as the DATADICTIONARY entry. The other names could be carried in the description as aliases.

In doing this we improve the accuracy of our communications, by having everyone using the same terms for the same ideas.

Three basic entries are made in a DATADICTIONARY:

1. ENTITY TYPE — These are the general catagories found in the dictionary. In the DATADICTIONARY that is used by IDEAL there are twenty standard ENTITY TYPES:

DATABASE	KEY	SYSTEM	REPORT
AREA	ELEMENT	PROGRAM	JOB
FILE	LIBRARY	MODULE	STEP
RECORD	MEMBER	AUTHORIZATION	DATAVIEW
FIELD	PANEL	PERSON	NODE

2. ENTITY OCCURRENCE — This is a specific occurrence of an ENTITY TYPE that contains the detailed definitions. For example, a FIELD entry would contain the field name, definition, length, standard report header, displacement in the record, type, signed/unsigned, aliases, etc.

3. RELATIONSHIPS — Shows how certain entity occurrences are made up of other entity occurrences. For example, a program (PROGRAM1) could call certain dataviews (employee, payroll). We would then have the following relationship entries:

    ```
    PROGRAM1.EMPLOYEE,PGM-DVW-USE
    PROGRAM1.PAYROLL,PGM-DVW-USE
    ```

    where PROGRAM1 is the *subject* entity type, employee and payroll are the *object* entity types, and the clause PGM-DVW-USE is the relationship type or *name*.

With this information we can

1. Inform people about the data structures in a clear, concise, and consistent manner.

2. Control the definition and representation of the data. By having a single repository of information, we can control how, when, and by whom changes in the definitions of data are made.
3. Determine what entities will be effected by a proposed change. If we wish to change the length of a field on a dataview, we would simply look through the PGM-DVW-USE relationship table and find all of the entries to the programs that reference that dataview.
4. By having everyone agree on definitions and usages, we can gain control of the corporate data structure.

Conclusions

As we review the abilities and structures of the IDEAL language, we will see that each of these principles are employed in its design. The simplicity of the procedure language minimizes the amount of work and time that it takes to produce a program. The panel definition is self-contained so that there is no requirement to align difficult assembler definitions, thus easing the effort required to create a panel. All of the data and program names are easily available to the DATADICTIONARY so that a change to a program or a panel or a report definition requires only a simple program code change instead of trying to "GEN" something into the right format library. The database access statements are built in such a way as to eliminate the possibility of getting most of even the standard DATACOM return codes. The DATADICTIONARY is available to help in the definition and control of the database.

In the rest of this book we will discuss how to use this new language and its associated relational databases in the most efficient manner possible. We hope that you will find it to be the powerful tool that we have found it to be.

Exercises

1. What is a *relational database*?
2. What is the name of the process used to define relational databases?
3. Define the three normal forms.
4. What is *relational algebra*?
5. What are the eight functions of relational algebra?

6. What did we list as the advantages of using a fully normalized database as opposed to using other data structures?
7. Which, if any, of these advantages are lost if the data is not fully normalized?
8. What does Mr. Martin list as the principles that are used to design a fourth generation language?
9. What are the three basic entries in a DATADICTIONARY?.
10. What are the standard DATADICTIONARY entity types?

Exercises — Answers

1. What is a *relational database*?

   A relational database is a database, or series of databases, which appear as two dimensional arrays, and where each piece of data in the record describes the main field of the record. The main field (or *key*) uniquely identifies some entity.

2. What is the name of the process used to define relational databases?

   Normalization.

3. Define the three normal forms.

   FIRST NORMAL FORM — data is in its atomic form, no repeating groups.
   SECOND NORMAL FORM — data is in first normal form, and all non-key fields are dependent on the key field.
   THIRD NORMAL FORM — data is in second normal form, and all of the transitive relations are removed.

4. What is *relational algebra*?

   The mathematical study of how sets of data can be related together to obtain a third set of data.

5. What are the eight functions of relational algebra?

   1. UNION
   2. INTERSECTION
   3. DIFFERENCE
   4. PRODUCT

5. SELECT
6. PROJECT
7. JOIN
8. DIVIDE

6. What did we list as the advantages of using a fully normalized database as opposed to using other data structures?

1. Ease of use
2. Flexibility
3. Precision
4. Security
5. Reliability
6. Ease of implementation
7. Data independence
8. Data manipulation language
9. Clarity

7. Which, if any, of these advantages are lost if the data is not fully normalized?

All of the advantages, if not lost entirely, are at least degraded. If the data is not fully normalized it becomes more complicated and less flexible. Our ability to make easy changes to both the data structure and the value of the data is lost. This in turn reduces the reliability of the data, and complicates the programming task.

8. What does Mr. Martin list as the principles that are used to design a fourth generation language?

1. The principle of minimum work
2. The principle of minimum skill
3. The principle of avoiding alien syntax and mnemonics
4. The principle of minimum time
5. The principle of minimum errors
6. The principle of minimum resistance
7. The principle of minimum results

9. What are the three basic entries in a DATADICTIONARY?.

1. ENTITY TYPE
2. ENTITY OCCURRENCE
3. RELATIONSHIP

10. What are the standard DATADICTIONARY entity types?

DATABASE	KEY	SYSTEM	REPORT
AREA	ELEMENT	PROGRAM	JOB
FILE	LIBRARY	MODULE	STEP
RECORD	MEMBER	AUTHORIZATION	DATAVIEW
FIELD	PANEL	PERSON	NODE

Notes

1. James Martin, *Fourth Generation Languages*, vol. 1, Prentice-Hall Inc., Englewood Cliffs, New Jersey, 1985, p. 15
2. Ibid. *Computer Database Orginization*, Prentice-Hall Inc., Englewood Cliffs, New Jersey, 1975, p. 689
3. Ibid. p. 226

2

Dataviews and Native Database Access

As we saw in the last chapter, a relational database is in reality a large table, which is accessed either on a row by a predefined key, or by reading all the values in a column. Each row (or record) in this relational database table has the same record layout, in that all of the fields are in the same relative position. Thus, we could have a database file that would look like Figure 2-1, where

    MSTK — is the master key of the file
    SECK1 — a secondary access key
    SECK2 — a secondary access key
    SECK3 — a secondary access key
    FLDA — is a datafield in the record
    FLDB — is a datafield in the record
    FLDC — is a datafield in the record
    FLDD — is a datafield in the record
    FLDE — is a datafield in the record
    FLDF — is a datafield in the record
    FLDG — is a datafield in the record
    FLDH — is a datafield in the record
    FLDI — is a datafield in the record

Because each record in a file has the same layout, it is possible for us to define a logical record layout of the physical record, which can

```
MSTK FLDA FLDB SECK1 FLDC FLDD FLDE FLDF FLDG SECK2 SECK3 FLDH FLDI
MSTK FLDA FLDB SECK1 FLDC FLDD FLDE FLDF FLDG SECK2 SECK3 FLDH FLDI
MSTK FLDA FLDB SECK1 FLDC FLDD FLDE FLDF FLDG SECK2 SECK3 FLDH FLDI
MSTK FLDA FLDB SECK1 FLDC FLDD FLDE FLDF FLDG SECK2 SECK3 FLDH FLDI
MSTK FLDA FLDB SECK1 FLDC FLDD FLDE FLDF FLDG SECK2 SECK3 FLDH FLDI
MSTK FLDA FLDB SECK1 FLDC FLDD FLDE FLDF FLDG SECK2 SECK3 FLDH FLDI
MSTK FLDA FLDB SECK1 FLDC FLDD FLDE FLDF FLDG SECK2 SECK3 FLDH FLDI
```

Figure 2-1   Database Sample

contain all or some of the physical fields. This logical grouping is called a "dataview" in IDEAL. (See Figure 2-2.)

Thus, if we created an application that accessed the database by using DATAVIEW 1, the program would only see the master key and fields FLDA and FLDB.

We can also see that it is not always necessary to have the master key within the dataview. This is because it is not always necessary to access the data through the master key. Access to the data can be made through any column in the database. We can build a dataview that does not contain any of the predefined keys, as shown in Figure 2-2A.

In addition, we can see in this example that neither the order nor the position of the fields in the dataview are important, but that they are entirely interchangeable.

We can also see that it is possible for an application to deal with only a small portion of the physical record, and thus only with the data that it needs. There are a number of good reasons for wanting to limit the amount of information that is available to an application. These include

1. SECURITY — it is possible to define dataviews in such a way that an application will not even know of the presence of sensitive data such as the salary of the corporation's president.
2. REDUCTION OF IO PROCESSING AND BUFFER SIZE — by reducing the length of the record, we can place more logical

```
DATAVIEW 1 — MSTK FLDA FLDB
DATAVIEW 2 — SECK1 FLDC FLDD FLDE FLDF FLDG
DATAVIEW 3 — SECK2 SECK3 FLDH FLDI
DATAVIEW 4 — SECK3 FLDH FLDI
```

Figure 2-2   Logical DATAVIEW Creation

DATAVIEW 5 — FLDB FLDC FLDG FLDF FLDD

Figure 2-2A   DATAVIEW Without Keys

records in the IO buffer. Thus we reduce the number of IO occurrences and thereby reduce the wall time required to handle
a request.
3. REDUCTION OF WORKING STORAGE SPACE REQUIRED
— again, by reducing the record length, we reduce the size of
the working storage area required to hold it for processing.
4. REDUCTION OF THE SIZE OF TEMPORARY STORAGE
USAGE — whenever an IDEAL program comes to a point
where a subroutine is called or a screen is transmitted to an
operator, IDEAL writes all of the working storage that it currently has to a "temporary storage" area, so that it can restore
everything when control comes back to the calling program. By
reducing the size of our working storage, we can reduce the
amount of the system's temporary storage we use and the time
required to process it.

Another special dataview that we can create is a "key only"
dataview. As this name implies, this dataview contains only the
master key or the secondary key of the record.
This key dataview is a significant efficiency due to the physical
structure of the DATACOM/DB system. As we examine this structure more closely, we can see that the key records are stored in a
special index file, along with the physical address of the data record.
It is possible to determine the existence of a record without doing an
IO to the full database. For example, if we have an application that
creates customer orders, it is possible for us to enter a customer
number into the program and have it see if that customer exists on
our database by accessing the customer file index, rather than going
to the customer database.
All of the database accesses that are made by an IDEAL program
are made through a procedural command called a FOR statement.
This statement is used to manipulate the data through the use of the
pre-defined dataviews. when this FOR statement is processed by the
IDEAL compiler, it is translated into a series of native database
commands. We will discuss the FOR statement at a later time. It is
prudent that we discuss the basic DATACOM/DB access now, so that
we can use them to build a "logical model" of the FOR statement
processing.

There are a number of access commands available to the DATACOM/DB environment, the combination of which will give the application full and complete access to the database. These commands are

1. LOCATE
2. LOCATE NEXT
3. LOCATE NEXT DUPLICATE
4. LOCATE NEXT KEY
5. LOCATE SEQUENTIAL
6. READ
7. READ AND HOLD
8. READ NEXT
9. READ NEXT AND HOLD
10. READ NEXT DUPLICATE
11. READ NEXT DUPLICATE AND HOLD
12. READ SEQUENTIAL
13. READ SEQUENTIAL AND HOLD
14. INSERT
15. UPDATE
16. DELETE

The dataview that is available to these native commands is defined as the element table. The IDEAL dataview consists of a series of element tables. An element table in turn is any combination of sequential fields. By discussing the logical functioning of the database now we hope to be able to explain the FOR statement more easily and understandably in Chapter 4.

We can see from the above list that there are three basic types of commands: LOCATE, READ, and those that actually update the database (INSERT, UPDATE, and DELETE).

The LOCATE commands are used to position a pointer at a certain value in the index file. As you will remember from above, we said that in reality every database is made up of an index file and a data file. These two files are related to each other through the datafile address which is stored on the index file, as in this example:

CORE		DASD STORAGE						
Key-value	Address	Address	FLD1	FLD2	FLD3	FLD4	SECK1	FLD5
MSK1A	101	101	1AAA	1BBB	1CCC	1DDD	2SK2	1EEE
MSK1B	103	103	2AAA	2BBB	2CCC	2DDD	6SK6	2EEE
MSK1C	105	105	3AAA	3BBB	3CCC	3DDD	3SK3	3EEE
MSK1E	107	107	4AAA	4BBB	4CCC	4DDD	4SK4	4EEE
MSK1F	109	109	5AAA	5BBB	5CCC	5DDD	2SK2	5EEE

```
MSK1G      10b            10b      6AAA  6BBB  6CCC  6DDD  6SK6   6EEE
MSK1H      10d            10d      7AAA  7BBB  7CCC  7DDD  6SK6   7EEE
```

This storage method is used to increase the efficiency of the data searches on the master key. This increase is available because the address is a much smaller piece of data than the actual data records, which allows these records to have a better blocking factor. This in turn eliminates IOs from the search by allowing us to bring in more records at a time.

The LOCATE statement positions itself in the index database at the key value which is equal to or greater than the requested value, depending on the relational operator that is used. If we were to issue the command:

```
LOCATE DATAVIEW-NAME WHERE KEY-VALUE EQ MSK1C
```

it would position our search at MSK1C.

On the other hand, the command

```
LOCATE DATAVIEW-NAME WHERE KEY-VALUE EQ MSK1D
```

would return us an error code, saying that it was unable to establish, or find, the requested position.

To cover this circumstance, we would have to issue the same command with the relative operator of greater than or equal to:

```
LOCATE DATAVIEW-NAME WHERE KEY-VALUE GE MSK1D
```

which would position us at the value MSK1E.

Once we have used the LOCATE statement to establish our position, we can then use the stored address to READ the corresponding data record, and/or to continue processing through the index.

To continue through the index, we have two possible choices, either reading the index sequentially, or obtaining duplicate entries. In DATACOM, these two commands take the form:

```
LOCATE SEQUENTIAL DATAVIEW-NAME WHERE KEY-VALUE REL-OP SRCH-VALUE
LOCATE NEXT DUPLICATE DATAVIEW-NAME
```

and are used to

1. Read each index record individually, in the native key sequence, until the end of the index is reached, or the program is

stopped in another way. This is the normal procedure when processing on the master key.

2. Read each index record that has the same value as the index record on which we were originally positioned. This is the process that is most used for a file that can have a duplicate master key (which should be a very rare occurrence) or on the processing of a secondary index.

A secondary index is a special index dataset which is set up to facilitate search processing, but does not control the actual physical address of the datafile. Like the master key, it points to the address of the corresponding data record. Thus, from the previous example, we would have this resultant secondary key file:

SECONDARY KEY FILE			MASTER KEY FILE	
SEC-KEY-VALUE	ADDRESS	MST-KEY-VALUE	KEY-VALUE	ADDRESS
2SK2	101	MSK1A	MSK1A	101
2SK2	109	MSK1F	MSK1B	103
3SK3	105	MSK1C	MSK1C	105
4SK4	107	MSK1E	MSK1E	107
6SK6	103	MSK1B	MSK1F	109
6SK6	10B	MSK1G	MSK1G	10b
6SK6	10D	MSK1H	MSK1H	10d

In this example we can observe the following properties of a secondary index:

1. The secondary index is ordered by its value first, then the primary index on duplicates.
2. There can be multiple occurrences of the value of a secondary index, but each entry points to only one master key value.
3. All of the master key values are represented on the secondary file.

Let us suppose that we wish to locate all of the secondary index records with a value of 6SK6. To do this we will have to issue the following set of commands.

```
LOCATE DATAVIEW-NAME WHERE SEC-KEY-VALUE EQ 6SK6

LOOP UNTIL NO-MORE-DUPLICATES
        OR END-OF-DATABASE
            LOCATE NEXT DUPLICATE DATAVIEW-NAME
ENDLOOP
```

Here the first LOCATE command establishes our position in the database at the first occurrence of 6SK6. In our database, this occurrence has the master key value of MSK1B. The program will then control the execution of the LOCATE NEXT command, which will be executed until the last of the 6SK6 records is found, or the end of the database is reached (which is what will happen in this case). Each execution of the command will bring into the IO area the next occurrence of the key value, so our command will be executed three times. The first will bring in the record with the master key value of MSK1G, the second with master key value of MSK1H, and the third will tell the program that the end of the database has been reached and to end the loop.

The READ command functions against the index in much the same way that the LOCATE command does, with the additional operation of moving the corresponding datafile record into the program's IO area. It will only function after position has been established within the index database, either by issuing a LOCATE command first, or by including a LOCATE request through the WHERE clause of the READ command.

When a READ command is issued against a key field of a dataview, DATACOM will read the index to determine the address of the datafile that has been requested. For example, if we issued the command:

```
READ DATAVIEW-NAME WHERE SEC-KEY-VALUE EQ '4SK4'
```

DATACOM would find the first occurrence where SEC-KEY-VALUE is equal to 4SK4. It would then look for the corresponding master-file record which in our case is MSK1E. The datafile record at address 107 would then be placed in the IO area of the program.

Then, since we have established position in the database in the same manner that we did in the index with the LOCATE command, we can do either duplicate or sequential processing against the file. Each subsequent call will bring the data record into the IO area for processing.

Another option that we have with the READ command that we do not have on the LOCATE command is to establish exclusive control on a record with the HOLD command. Exclusive control means that no other program can access this record until the current program has released it. This is used as a preparatory step to either an UPDATE or a DELETE function. This is important because if two programs tried to update the same record at the same time without establishing control over the record, the changes that were made to the first rewritten record would not be reflected on the second, because they happened after the second record was placed in the IO area of its program, and so they were never seen by it. Without this feature, it would even be possible for the second program to try to update a record that the first program has deleted.

The release of this exclusive control takes place at the end of the processing of the update command, and is handled automatically by DATACOM. As we pointed out above, there are three types of database update commands, INSERT, UPDATE, and DELETE.

If no update occurs, a RELEASE command can also be issued by the application program.

The INSERT command takes the information in the IO area of the program and loads it into the database. This is done by:

1. Determining if the master-key file already has an entry with this value. If there is, then an error condition is returned to the program.
2. Creating the master-key record in the index file.
3. Creating any required secondary key records.
4. Creating the datafile record at the appropriate address.

For example, if we had a record in our IO area that looked like this:

```
KEY-VALUE FLD1 FLD2 FLD3 FLD4 SECK1 FLD5
  MSK1D   8AAA 8AAA 8CCC 8DDD 3SK4  8EEE
```

and we executed our INSERT command, DATACOM would

1. See that there was no other occurrence of the master key MSK1D
2. Insert a master key entry between MSK1C and MSK1E
3. Insert a datafile record between address 105 and 107 (which would be position 106)
4. Update the master key with address 106
5. Create a secondary key index record between 3SK3 and 4SK4

This would, of course, give us the following databases.

CORE		DASD STORAGE						
KEY-VALUE	ADDRESS	ADDRESS	FLD1	FLD2	FLD3	FLD4	SECK1	FLD5
MSK1A	101	101	1AAA	1BBB	1CCC	1DDD	2SK2	1EEE
MSK1B	103	103	2AAA	2BBB	2CCC	2DDD	6SK6	2EEE
MSK1C	105	105	3AAA	3BBB	3CCC	3DDD	3SK3	3EEE
MSK1D	106	106	8AAA	8AAA	8CCC	8DDD	3SK4	8EEE

MSK1E	107	107	4AAA 4BBB 4CCC 4DDD 4SK4 4EEE
MSK1F	109	109	5AAA 5BBB 5CCC 5DDD 2SK2 5EEE
MSK1G	10B	10B	6AAA 6BBB 6CCC 6DDD 6SK6 6EEE
MSK1H	10D	10D	7AAA 7BBB 7CCC 7DDD 6SK6 7EEE

SECONDARY KEY FILE		MASTER KEY FILE	
SEC KEY-VALUE	MST KEY VALUE	KEY-VALUE	ADDRESS
2SK2	MSK1A	MSK1A	101
2SK2	MSK1F	MSK1B	103
3SK3	MSK1C	MSK1C	105
3SK4	MSK1D	MSK1D	106
4SK4	MSK1E	MSK1E	107
6SK6	MSK1B	MSK1F	109
6SK6	MSK1G	MSK1G	10B
6SK6	MSK1H	MSK1H	10D

The UPDATE command works in a similar manner to the INSERT command, except that instead of creating a new record, it simply changes the values in the datafile record. It is also important to note that only data values and secondary key values can be changed; the primary key value cannot be changed. This is because the physical addresses are all dependent on the primary key.

After a record has been brought into the IO area of the application through a READ AND HOLD command, the application makes updates to the appropriate working storage fields. The UPDATE command is then issued, which in turn updates the database and releases the record.

The DELETE command is the direct opposite of the INSERT in that it removes records from the database. A READ AND HOLD command is issued, and then the DELETE command is invoked, which removes all of the secondary index records, the data record, and finally the master key record.

A log of all changes to the database is being kept throughout this entire process. This log gives the database management system the ability to automatically restore the database to the point where it was before the beginning of the current process. Whenever a database transaction terminates abnormally, this log is read in the reverse order that it was written. Each transaction that has occurred during the process is "backed out" by having the image copy of the record rewritten to the database.

To accomplish this function, this log contains the following information:

1. A before-update image of the record
2. The transaction
3. Date / time stamp
4. Job name and number

It is the before image record that is replaced onto the database in the case of the backout of an UPDATE or DELETE transaction. When an INSERT transaction is backed out, the record matching the after image record is found and then deleted from the database.

As we stated above, this process occurs until the beginning of the current process is encountered. This point can be marked by a number of different occurrences. These are

1. The beginning of the program run
2. The end of a program run
3. The end of the last backout
4. An abnormal termination of the program
5. The transmission of a screen from the program to the operator in an online program
6. Last overflow of the log file

At these points, the log is spilled to the recovery file and the system is ready to start a new log set.

It is also possible to invoke these two functions from our program, rather than waiting for the DBMS to automatically function. For example, if we have a long-running batch job, we can issue a CHECKPOINT command, which will do the same log purge as the beginning of a program. Then, if our job abended near the end of its work, the automatic recovery would only go back to the last time that the CHECKPOINT command was issued, rather than to the beginning of the program. This way only a small portion of work has to be backed out and redone when the problem is corrected. This saves processing time and expense by reducing the time necessary to recover an abending job, and by reducing rework.

The BACKOUT command can be issued for the exact opposite reason when we do not want to save the changes that we have just made. This could be desirable in the case where the program is building a new record, but is missing a piece of critical information. The new record can be automatically removed from the database through the DBMS without requiring logic in the program to accomplish this (which would in all probability cause more problems than it would solve).

Conclusions

In this chapter, we have seen how the DATACOM database is defined to an application, and how that application can and will access that database.

In Chapters 4 and 5, we will discuss the definition and efficient usage of IDEAL's FOR statement, which combines and uses the datacom commands that we have discussed here.

However, let us postpone that discussion and examine the actual IDEAL programming and processing environment in Chapter 3.

Exercises

1. What data structure does a relational database most resemble?
2. What is a dataview?
3. Is it necessary that a dataview always contain the master key of the record?
4. What are the advantages of dealing with a small dataview over working with the entire record?
5. What is a *key only* dataview?
6. What are the basic DATACOM/DB commands?
7. What is the difference between the READ and the LOCATE commands?
8. What is a *secondary index*?
9. What processing is done by the INSERT command?
10. Can the master key be changed by an UPDATE command?
11. When is a CHECKPOINT taken?
12. Why is it neccessary to obtain exclusive control of a record that we wish to UPDATE or DELETE?

Exercises — Answers

1. What data structure does a relational database most resemble?

   A two-dimensional array or table.

2. What is a dataview?

   A logical definition of a physical record.

3. Is it necessary that a dataview always contain the master key of the record?

   No.

4. What are the advantages of dealing with a small dataview over working with the entire record?

   a. Security
   b. Reduction of IO processing and buffer size
   c. Reduction of working storage space required
   d. Reduction of size of temporary requirements

5. What is a *key only* dataview?

   A key only dataview is a special dataview that contains only the key value and the address of the corresponding physical record that it represents. The advantage of using it is that the key is shorted, allowing greater efficiency during a READ because of the improved blocking factor.

6. What are the basic DATACOM/DB commands?

   ```
   LOCATE
   LOCATE NEXT
   LOCATE NEXT DUPLICATE
   LOCATE NEXT KEY
   LOCATE SEQUENTIAL
   READ
   READ AND HOLD
   READ NEXT
   READ NEXT DUPLICATE
   READ NEXT DUPLICATE AND HOLD
   READ SEQUENTIAL
   READ SEQUENTIAL AND HOLD
   INSERT
   UPDATE
   DELETE
   ```

7. What is the difference between the READ and the LOCATE commands?

   The READ command goes against the entire record, and the LOCATE command accesses only the index record.

8. What is a *secondary index*?

A secondary index is a special index which is set up to allow DATACOM access to the database in a way other than through the master key of the record. A secondary index has the following properties.

a. Ordered first by its value, then by the primary index on duplicates.
b. There can be multiple occurrences of the value of a secondary key, but each entry points to a specific and exclusive master key.
c. All of the master key values are represented on the secondary index.

9. What processing is done by the INSERT COMMAND?

a. Determines if the master key already exists on the database
b. Creates the master key record
c. Creates any required secondary key records
d. Creates the datafile record at the appropriate address.

10. Can the master key be changed by an UPDATE command?

No.

11. When is a CHECKPOINT taken?

a. Beginning of the program run
b. End of the program run
c. End of the last backout
d. Abnormal termination of the program
e. Transmission of a screen from the program to the operator in an on-line program
f. When commanded in the application program
g. Log file overflow

12. Why is it neccessary to obtain exclusive control of a record that we wish to UPDATE or DELETE?

So that two different applications do not try to change the same record at the same time. This would cause one of the updates to be overlayed.

3

IDEAL Entities and Facilities

The IDEAL language is a menu-driven fourth generation language which is designed to function completely and exclusively within its own environment. This means that all the work that needs to be done to process data can be accomplished through IDEAL's facilities, without relying on programs or processes written in other languages. In this chapter we will discuss IDEAL's entities, menus, functions, and facilities.

Entities

IDEAL processing consists mainly of drawing data from the database through *dataviews* which are defined in the DATADICTIONARY. This data is processed by the program which either manipulates other data in the database, returns information to the user via an on-line panel, or gives batch results to the user through a printed report. Each of these entities (dataview, program, panel definition, and report definition) is defined as an individual element and dynamically linked at compile time. The program is then executed either as an on-line program with a RUN command, or is submitted as a background batch job utilizing the standard IBM JCL (Job Control Language) that is stored in a member.

Some of these main entities are further broken down into components.

The program definition consists of five parts. These are the *identification, working-storage, parameter, resource,* and *procedure* sections.

The *identification* section contains the program statistics that are used for identification of the program by the DATADICTIONARY and by the index. This consists of the program name, date and time last modified, date and time last compiled, and the short and long descriptions of the program's purpose and functions.

The *working storage* section contains those fields which are used during execution but are not to be stored in a dataview. Six types of data are allowed in this section: alpha-numeric, numeric (which can be Binary, Packed decimal, or Zoned decimal), flags (which have a value Y or N), date structures, conditional name statements, and variable length-fields.

The *parameter* section is the receiving area for any data passed to a called program, whether this call comes from another module or from a JCL passed parameter. This section contains the same six types that are found in the working storage section. In addition, fields can be protected from the called program by marking them as inquiry only, thus allowing the called program to change only those fields that are marked as updateable.

The *resource* section, or table, is used to define all of the different IDEAL entities that are used by the program at execution time. Here we specify the dataviews to be accessed, what sub-routines are to be called, and what panels and reports will be filled with information and given to the user.

The *procedure* section contains the actual source code that will be compiled into object code for later execution. In addition to the normal constructs that are found in a procedural language (conditional, assignment, iterative, and branching statements), there are those statements that are used to access the database, handle IO between the program and its panels, cause report execution, and execute system- defined functions (for example, retrieval of system current time and date, stringing and unstringing of fields, conversion of packed numeric data to display format, etc.).

The *panel definition facility* (PDF) consists of several components also. Each panel has an *identification* section which is similar in use and appearance to that contained in the program definition.

The actual position of the fields is defined to IDEAL through the layout panel, which is used by simply "painting" the layout on the screen using the predefined symbols. The field names and general attributes of those fields (protected, highlighted, alpha, etc.) are specified to the DATADICTIONARY through the *summary definition panel.* In addition to these general attribute definitions the language has the facility to specify other field attributes through the extended field definition panel. These further definitions include edit patterns, decimal alignment, minimum and maximum allowable values, etc. The values on the extended field definitions for all of the fields on the panel are summarized on the IRULES and ORULES screens.

In addition to these screens which concern themselves with the field definitions there is another, the *PARAMETER* screen, which defines to the system the panels processing characteristics. This feature is used to specify attributes such as the default input fill characters, the value of the program function keys, and the name of any help panels that are attached to the panel.

When these screens have all been completed, another feature can be used to test the default processing of the screen. This screen, called the *facsimile*, can be called up and run without the presence of any procedure code. When used it will present the defined panel to the developer as it will appear to the eventual user. Then when the ENTER key is pressed, the facility will execute all of the edits that were defined in the field screen against whatever data the developer has entered. It will then return the screen showing whatever values it defaulted to and highlighting any edit violations it encountered.

The *report definition facility* (RDF) is also broken into components. In the first of these, the HEADING screen, we define the report heading layout that is to appear on the top of each report page.

The *DETAIL* and *COLUMN* screens are used in conjunction to determine the placement and attributes of the report columns. These specify the width, tabbing, and edit patterns that are to be used by the report- generating facility. In addition, the programmer can specify report breaks to occur whenever the value of a selected field changes. These report breaks can also produce a total line on the report. There is also a facility here to choose a sorting order for the records that are released to the reporting facility. This feature works like the output procedure of a COBOL program with an internal sort.

After the *DETAIL* screen is formatted, the programmer will need to complete the corresponding *COLUMN* screen. This screen will appear with the column names, widths, and tabbing already copied from the *DETAIL* screen. The programmer then needs only to type in the desired column headers.

In addition to these fill-in screens, there is a *PARAMETER* screen that is used to define the run-time attributes of the report, much as the *PARAMETER* screen of the PDF does. This screen specifies such attributes as the number of lines per page, the placement and format of the current date and page counters, the underlining of columns, and the placement and selection of control headers and footers. This area can also be used to define simple report headers.

Another entity in IDEAL is the *member*. This entity is an open area, similar to the *procedure* area of a *program definition*. In it an IDEAL user can place standard IBM JCL statements, IDEAL SET commands that affect his session, or notes and documentation.

It is through the JCL contained in a member that IDEAL can access the batch environment.

There are also two specially defined members that each IDEAL user must set up. The first of these is the JOBCARD member. This member contains a jobcard whose syntax is acceptable to the local operating system that the IDEAL session is running on. IDEAL will then use this jobcard for background batch processing.

The second special member is the SIGNON member. This member is used by the IDEAL processor to establish the attributes which the programmer wishes to have in place when the session begins.

Since IDEAL is an interactive processor, there are a number of session attributes that can be set for use at one of three timing levels. The highest level are the global attributes, which are used at all times. These are usually those attributes which affect default values in the PGM, RDF, and PDF coding (for example, all panel values are uppercase). These attributes usually constitute shop coding standards and are put into place by the site's IDEAL administrator.

The second and third levels of timing concern the relationship between the programmer and the processing of his session. Second-level attributes are designated at signon, and third-level attributes are set using the command line.

In Figure 3-1 we see the basic design of an interactive IDEAL screen, and hence some of the attributes that we can control through the SET commands.

First of all we can set the number of *command lines* that we wish to have during our session. We can also set up what value the *separator line* will have.

In addition to reformatting the basic screen, we can override the default values for some of the processing commands. These include the value of the command line delimiter, the REPEAT, and the RESHOW commands. We can also set the scrolling feature from the default of page scrolling to cursor position scrolling.

The detailed syntax of these SET commands is found in Appendix C, but Figure 3-2 shows an example of SET commands in a SIGNON member. When the user signs on, these commands will be executed. This will:

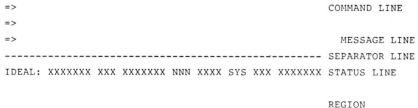

```
=>                                                   COMMAND LINE
=>
=>                                                   MESSAGE LINE
-------------------------------------------------- SEPARATOR LINE
IDEAL: XXXXXXX XXX XXXXXXX NNN XXXX SYS XXX XXXXXXX STATUS LINE


                                                     REGION
            DISPLAY AREA
```

Figure 3-1   Basic IDEAL Screen.

1. Reduce the standard 3 command lines to 1 line
2. Cause all batch foreground job outputs to be held for future release instead of immediate printing
3. Cause IDEAL will route job output to the printer which is defined to the operating system as RMT25
4. Choose the cursor position-scrolling option.

Then throughout the session the programmer can override any of these options. This can be done by

1. Typing in the override instruction on the command line
2. Executing another member which contains the desired commands.

The example shown in Figure 3-3 will

1. Allow all output to go directly to the designated printer
2. Submit the program named BLPGRCY1 to the foreground processor
3. Return the output disposition to its original status of HOLD

```
SET COMMAND LINE 1
SET OUTPUT DISPOSITION HOLD
SET OUTPUT DESTINATION SYSTEM RMT25
SET CURSOR SCROLL
```

Figure 3-2   Sample Sign On Member.

```
SET OUTPUT DISPOSITION RELEASE
RUN PGM BLPGRCY1
SET OUTPUT DISPOSITION HOLD
```

Figure 3-3   Sample Executable Member.

Menus and Menu Processing

As with many on-line development languages, IDEAL is operated through a series of menu commands, leading from the main menu through the lower-level menus to the prompts that build the actual executable commands.

Figure 3-4 shows the main menu as it appears when the developer signs onto IDEAL. As the reader will see, the functions on this menu can be placed into one of two groups. The first group leads to the manipulation of specific IDEAL entities (PGM, DATAVIEW, PDF, and RDF). The second group leads to IDEAL processing (PROCESS, DISPLAY, PRINT, ADMINISTRATION, and OFF).

Figure 3-5 shows the structural relationship between the different menus and prompts.

When we access the entity menus (options 1–4 on the main menu) we see that three of them, PGM, PDF, and RDF, contain the same options. (Samples of these menus are contained in Appendix B.)

This allows us to redraw Figure 3-5 as shown in Figure 3-5A.

```
IDEAL: MAIN MENU          MEM EHP.SIGNON          SYS: DEV  MENU


   ENTER DESIRED OPTION NUMBER ===>  THERE ARE 9 OPTIONS IN THIS MENU:


    1. PROGRAM           DEFINE AND MAINTAIN PROGRAMS

    2. DATAVIEW          DISPLAY DATAVIEW DEFINITIONS

    3. PDF               PANEL DEFINITION FACILITY

    4. RDF               REPORT DEFINITION FACILITY

    5. PROCESS           COMPILE, RUN, SUBMIT

    6. DISPLAY           DISPLAY ENTITIES

    7. PRINT             PRINT ENTITIES

    8. ADMINISTRATION    ADMINISTRATION FUNCTIONS

    9. OFF               END IDEAL SESSION
```

Figure 3-4   Main Menu.

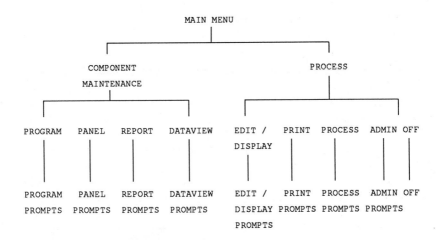

Figure 3-5   Menu Interaction Hierarchy.

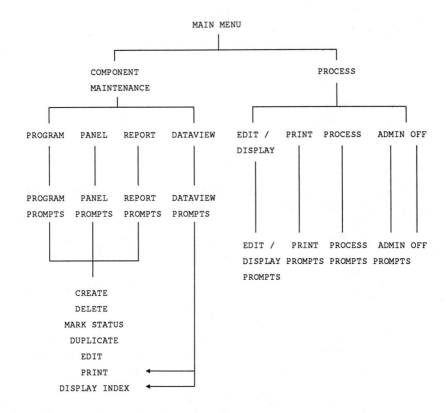

Figure 3-5A   Basic Function Level Diagram.

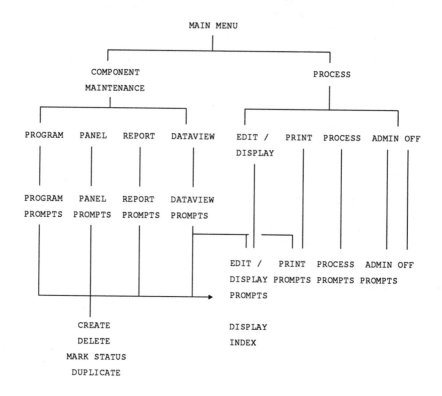

Figure 3-5B   Entity Grouping.

We can also see that two of the main menu options (DISPLAY and PRINT) are available through the entity maintenance menus. This allows us to redraw Figure 3-5A as shown in Figure 3-5B.

As you can see, the maintenance functions of DISPLAY, DISPLAY INDEX, and PRINT can be combined with the process screens.

All of these selections, depicted in Figure 3-5B, lead us to the prompt screens. Here the developer fills in the required fields and the system takes in the information to format and execute the request.

Let us consider an example to better understand this process.

After signing on, we desire to edit the resource section of program BLPGA007. At the main menu we have the choice of two routes, we can go through the program maintenance screens or through the EDIT/DISPLAY complex.

Let us first assume that we chose the program maintenance route. We would enter a "1" in the prompt area of the main menu to enter

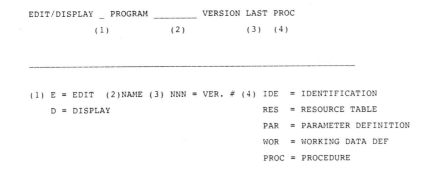

```
EDIT/DISPLAY _ PROGRAM _____ VERSION LAST PROC
            (1)              (2)         (3)  (4)


_____


(1) E = EDIT  (2)NAME (3) NNN = VER. # (4) IDE  = IDENTIFICATION
    D = DISPLAY                            RES  = RESOURCE TABLE
                                           PAR  = PARAMETER DEFINITION
                                           WOR  = WORKING DATA DEF
                                           PROC = PROCEDURE
```

Figure 3-6   EDIT/DISPLAY Prompt Screen.

the program complex. When that screen comes up, we again enter a "1" to select the EDIT/DISPLAY function.

The EDIT/DISPLAY selection presents us with the proper prompt screen, shown in Figure 3-6, which the developer fills in as follows:

1	E	(to select edit)
2	BLPGA007	(the program name)
3	LAS	(to select the most recent version)
4	RES	(to select the resource table of this program)

We could have entered a "6" at the MAIN MENU, which would have sent us to the EDIT/DISPLAY menu (shown in Appendix B). Here we would have entered a "1" to select program processing. This selection would have given us the same prompt screen that we have discussed above.

It is also possible to circumvent the menu processing flow by entering instructions on the command line that correspond to those created by the prompts.

Using the same example, if we had entered EDIT PGM at the main menu command line, we would have skipped the program maintenance menu and gone straight to the EDIT PROMPT screen. In addition, the command EDIT PGM BLPGA007 RES would have called up the *resource table* of the last version of program BLPGA007 to our view.

Thus we can draw our final version of Figure 3-5. (See Figure 3-5C.)

Now that we understand the relationship between the screens and their processing order, we can begin to investigate the individual screens in detail.

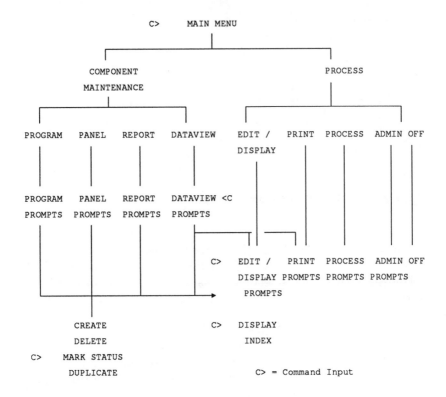

Figure 3-5C   DISPLAY and PRINT Grouping.

The top of the basic screen (Figure 3-7) contains information about the status of the component of which we currently have control.

The IDEAL processor remembers what the last component it processed was, and maintains control of it until a new component is selected. That information is displayed as shown in Figure 3-7, where

1 component type
2 entity type

```
-------------------------------------------------------------------
IDEAL: XXXXXXX XXX XXXXXXXX NNN XXXX SYS: XXX XXXXXXXX
         (1)    (2)   (3)     (4) (5)     (6)    (7)
```

Figure 3-7   Basic Screen.

```
-------------------------------------------------------------------
IDEAL: RES      PGM BLPGA007 001 TEST SYS: DEV      MENU
        (1)         (2)   (3)   (4) (5)         (6)        (7)
```

Figure 3-8   Returned Basic Screen

3 entity name
4 version number of that entity
5 status of that entity
6 system that we are logged onto
7 type of screen we are using

Therefore, if we were to return to the main menu after editing the last example, our entity description would appear as shown in Figure 3-8, where

1 resource section of BLPGA007
2 entity type is program
3 program name BLPGA007
4 version 001
5 status is TEST (as opposed to history or production)
6 we are logged onto the development sub-system
7 we are currently viewing the main menu

This ability also allows us another option in our screen movement. We can return to the entity that we just left by entering the command:

```
EDIT *
```

which will internally build the command:

```
EDIT PGM BLPGA007 V 001 RES
```

We can also use this feature to go to a different component of the same entity:

```
EDIT * WOR
```

which will build the command

```
EDIT PGM BLPGA007 V 001 WOR.
```

```
--------------------------------------------------------------------
IDEAL: PROGRAM MAINTAINCE    XXX                    SYS: DEV   MENU


ENTER DESIRED OPTION NUMBER ==>    THERE ARE  7 OPTIONS IN THIS MENU
    1. EDIT/DISPLAY       - EDIT OR DISPLAY A XXXXXXX

    2. CREATE            - CREATE A XXXXXXX

    3. PRINT             - PRINT A XXXXXXX

    4. DELETE            - DELETE A XXXXXXX

    5. MARK STATUS       - MARK PROGRAM STATUS TO PRODUCTION OR HISTORY

    6. DUPLICATE         - DUPLICATE XXXXXXX TO NEXT VERSION OR NEW NAME

    7. DISPLAY INDEX     - DISPLAY INDEX OF XXXXXXX NAMES IN SYSTEM
```

Figure 3-9   Entity Maintenance Menu.

In Figure 3-5A we saw that the main menu will either bring up entity maintenance or processing screens. We also saw that the entity maintenance menus differed only in the entity type indicator. Figure 3-9 shows the entity maintenance menu.

Here, and in the rest of this chapter, the string XXXXXXXX or XXX indicates the entity type to be processed.

As we saw above, the EDIT/DISPLAY feature leads to the different prompt screens for each of the different entities.

In Figures 3-10 through 3-10C, position 1 is the selection for either displaying or editing the entity. Position 2 is for the DATADICTION-ARY-recognized entity name that we wish to work with. Position 3 is for the version level of the entity. This can be either the three-digit level number if the entity is in test status, the production version (if we have selected the display option), or simply the last test version if

```
--------------------------------------------------------------------
IDEAL: EDIT/DISPLAY PROGRAM     PGM                SYS: DEV PROMPTER


EDIT/DISPLAY _ PROGRAM _____    VERSION  LAST  PROC
            (1)             (2)             (3)   (4)

--------------------------------------------------------------------
(1) E = EDIT      (2) NAME (3) NNN = VER. #  (4) IDE  = IDENTIFICATION
    D = DISPLAY              PROD (DISPLAY       RES  = RESOURCE TABLE
                                  ONLY)          PAR  = PARAMETER DEF
                          LAST                   WOR  = WORKING DATA
                                                 PROC = PROCEDURE
```

Figure 3-10   A EDIT Program Prompt Screen.

```
--------------------------------------------------------------------
IDEAL: EDIT/DISPLAY REPORT      RPT                SYS: DEV PROMPTER


EDIT/DISPLAY _ REPORT _____   VERSION  LAST  DET
            (1)          (2)                (3)   (4)
--------------------------------------------------------------------
(1) E = EDIT    (2) NAME (3) NNN = VER. #  (4) IDE = IDENTIFICATION
    D = DISPLAY              PROD (DISPLAY      PAR = PARAMETERS
                                  ONLY)         HEA = PAGE HEADING
                            LAST               DET = DETAIL
                                               COL = COLUMN HEADING
```

Figure 3-10A   EDIT RDF Prompt Screen.

the user does not want to be bothered with level numbers. Position 4 is used to specify the component that we wish to see first. IDEAL automatically loads this field with the name that it feels is the most common request as a help to the user, as it does by putting 'LAST' in the version field. The operator can change this for any selection by simply typing over the field with the value that they want.


```
--------------------------------------------------------------------
IDEAL: EDIT/DISPLAY PANEL       PNL                SYS: DEV PROMPTER


EDIT/DISPLAY _ PANEL _____   VERSION  LAST  LAY _____.
            (1)          (2)                (3)   (4)     (5)
--------------------------------------------------------------------
(1) E = EDIT    (2) NAME (3) NNN = VER. #  (4)IDE = IDENTIFICATION
    D = DISPLAY              PROD (DISPLAY      PAR = PARAMETERS
                                  ONLY)         LAY = LAYOUT
                            LAST               SUM = SUMMARY
                                               FIE = FIELD
                                               FAC = FACSIMILE
                                               IRU = INPUT RULES
                                               ORU = OUTPUT RULES

                                           (5)FIELD NAME
                                              OR NUMBER
                                              WHEN (4) is FIE
```

Figure 3-10B   EDIT PDF Prompt Screen.

```
---------------------------------------------------------------------
IDEAL: EDIT/DISPLAY PANEL          DVW         SYS:DEV      PROMPTER


   DISPLAY    DATAVIEW  _____     VERSION   LAST
                            (1)                       (2)
---------------------------------------------------------------------
   (1) DATAVIEW NAME        (2) NNN = VER. #
                                PROD (DISPLAY
                                LAST
```

Figure 3-10C   Display DATAVIEW Prompt Screen.

In addition to these fields, the panel maintenance screen has an additional field. when the summary panel option (SUM) is selected it is possible to go directly to the extended field definition screen by specifying either the field name or the field number.

The dataview display panel is noticeably different from the other entity maintenance screens because a user is only allowed to view a dataview definition. All other maintenance is done by the database administrator through other facilities.

The CREATE option of entity maintenance will lead to the following prompt screen. (See Figure 3-11.)

In position 1 we specify the entity type that we wish to create. The system will populate the field (again as a courtesy) with the entity type whose maintenance menu we came from. This can of course be changed by the operator. In position 2 we specify the name by which we wish the DATADICTIONARY to recognize this entity.

```
---------------------------------------------------------------------
IDEAL: CREATE               XXX                SYS: DEV PROMPTER


CREATE  XXX    _____
         (1)      (2)

---------------------------------------------------------------------
(1) PGM=PROGRAM (2) NAME
    PNL=PANEL
    RPT=REPORT
    SYS=SYSTEM
    USR=USER
```

Figure 3-11   CREATE Prompt.

```
IDEAL: DELETE              XXX  (001) TEST        SYS: DEV PROMPTER


DELETE  XXX  _____  VERSION LAS
         (1)      (2)                 (3)



(1) PGM=PROGRAM USR=USER DEFINITION   (2) NAME (3) VER.# ONLY
    PNL=PANEL    SYS=SYSTEM DEFINITION
    RPT=REPORT   OUT=OUTPUT
    MEM=SYSTEM
```

Figure 3-12   DELETE Prompt.

We will discuss the PRINT option with the other process screens. The DELETE option of the entity maintenance panel leads to the following prompt shown in Figure 3-12.

This panel again fills in the entity type as a courtesy and position 2 is the DATADICTIONARY name. Position 3 must be a three-digit numeric field containing the version number we wish to delete. Leaving the system supplied 'LAS' will cause an error.

Marking status consists of setting the entity to either history, test, or production. The production version can no longer be updated through editing or deletion. It can, however, be duplicated to a test version, which can then be modified and marked as production. When this new version is marked as production, the previous production version is retired to a history status. This history version can in turn be deleted.

The MARK STATUS prompt appears as shown in Figure 3-13.

Here position 3 is the version we are working with and 4 is the desired status. Therefore, if we wanted to mark the second version of program BLPGA107 to production, our prompt would be filled in as shown in Figure 3-14.

Entity duplication can be accomplished through the use of the prompt screen shown in Figure 3-15.

As the reader can see, it is possible to duplicate an IDEAL entity either to the next version number of the same name, thus making it the current version of that entity, or to the first version of a new name. This is done by entering NEXT VERSION into positions 5 and 6, or NEWNAME in position 5, and the new program, panel, or report name into position 6.

```
IDEAL: MARK STATUS          XXX  (001) TEST          SYS: DEV PROMPTER


MARK STATUS  XXX  _____   VERSION LAST TO ____
             (1)       (2)                 (3)    (4)


_____

(1) PGM = PROGRAM (2) NAME (3) NNN = VER. # (4) PROD = PRODUCTION
    PNL = PANEL                    PROD            HIST = HISTORY
    RPT = REPORT
    SYS = SYSTEM
    USR = USER
```

Figure 3-13   MARK STATUS Prompt.

The last entity maintenance option leads to a display of the entity index. This index is a listing of all of the entries of an entity that are in the system. As shown in Figure 3-16, they are listed in name order, with the short descriptions, and other information that is obtained from the identification section of the entity.

The prompt screen to display an index appears as shown in Figure 3-17.

Here we can choose to display all or parts of the entity index. We can enter the *entity type*, a string that will serve as a character mask for the search, and the *entity status* that we wish to see. For example, if we wished to see a list of all of the PROD status programs that started with the string 'BLPG', we would enter the command:

```
IDEAL: MARK STATUS          XXX  (001) TEST          SYS: DEV PROMPTER


MARK STATUS  PGM  BLPGA107___   VERSION 002  TO PROD
             (1)       (2)                 (3)    (4)


_____

(1) PGM = PROGRAM (2) NAME (3) NNN = VER. # (4) PROD = PRODUCTION
    PNL = PANEL                    PROD            HIST = HISTORY
    RPT = REPORT
    SYS = SYSTEM
    USR = USER
```

Figure 3-14   Completed MARK STATUS Prompt.

```
-------------------------------------------------------------
IDEAL: DUPLICATE          XXX  (001) TEST       SYS: DEV PROMPTER


DUPLICATE XXX _____ VERSION LAST SYSTEM ___ TO _____ _____
          (1)       (2)              (3)        (4)    (5)    (6)


-------------------------------------------------------------

(1) PGM=PROGRAM (2) NAME (3) NNN=VER.# (4) ORIGIONAL 5-6:NEXT VERSION
    PNL=PANEL           LAST           SYSTEM IDON
    RPT=REPORT          PROD           (DEFAULT     NEWNAME NAME
    SYS=SYSTEM                          CURRENT)    (FOR PGM PNL
    USR=USER                                            RPT)
    MEM=MEMBER
```

Figure 3-15   DUPLICATION Prompt.


```
DISPLAY INDEX PGM 'BLPG++++' VERSION PROD
```

An asterisk (*) can be used to mask around a given string; the plus sign tells IDEAL to find all entries that begin with the given string.

We can also see all of the entities that relate to the selected group. If we wanted to see all of the subprograms called by a group of programs, we would fill in the prompt as follows:

```
-----------------------------------------------------------------
NAME       VER S DESCRIPTION                 CREATED  UPDATED
BLPGA000   001 T MANUAL INVOICE HEADER PROCES 11/18/83 04/10/84 NON-SHR
BLPGA000   002 T MANUAL INVOICE HEADER PROCES 04/10/84 04/10/84 NON-SHR
BLPGA007   001 T ADD INVOICE TO SALES HISTORY 01/25/84 05/09/84 NON-SHR
BLPGA007   002 T ADD INVOICE TO SALES HISTORY 02/02/84 02/16/84 NON-SHR
BLPGA007   003 T ADD INVOICE TO SALES HISTORY 12/16/84 05/30/84 NON-SHR
BLPGA007   004 T ADD INVOICE TO SALES HISTORY 05/30/84 08/22/84 NON-SHR
BLPGA107   001 T LINE DIRECTION PGM           11/18/83 04/10/84 NON-SHR
BLPGBLCU   001 T CLEANUP BILLING DB           07/03/85 09/13/85 NON-SHR
```

Figure 3-16   Screen Print of an INDEX Display.

```
-------------------------------------------------------------------
IDEAL: DISPLAY INDEX         XXX  (001) TEST        SYS: DEV PROMPTER


DISPLAY INDEX XXX  _____  VERSION ____
                (1)     (2)                (3)


   RELATED TO  ___  _____  VERSION ____
               (4)     (5)               (6)
-------------------------------------------------------------------

(1) PGM=PROGRAM  (2) ENTITY NAME (3) VERSION NNNN
    PNL=PANEL                                TEST
    RPT=REPORT                               PROD
    SYS=SYSTEM                               HIST
    USR=USER      DVW=DATAVIEW
    MEM=MEMBER


(4) PGM=PROGRAM  (5) ENTITY NAME (6) VERSION NNNN
    PNL=PANEL                                TEST
    RPT=REPORT                               PROD
    SYS=SYSTEM                               HIST
    USR=USER
    DVW=DATAVIEW
    MEM=MEMBER
```

Figure 3-17   INDEX Display Prompt.

```
DISPLAY INDEX PGM   OEPGCB++ VERSION PROD
              (1)     (2)               (3)


   RELATED TO  PGM   ******** VERSION PROD
               (4)     (5)              (6)
```

For the member selection, the function will display only those members that are associated with the users LOGON-ID.

Process Screens

The main menu options also lead to screens and prompts that interface with the operating system. These include features that submit compilations and program execution requests, print out entities, and provide maintenance to user and system definitions.

```
-------------------------------------------------------------------
IDEAL: PROCESS PROGRAM    PGM XXXXXXXX (XXX) TEST    SYS:DEV MENU


ENTER DESIRED OPTION NUMBER ==>   THERE ARE 3 OPTIONS IN THIS MENU

    1. COMPILE      - COMPILE A PROGRAM

    2. RUN          - RUN A PROGRAM ONLINE

    3. SUBMIT       - SUBMIT A MEMBER CONTAINING A BATCH JOBSTREAM

    4. EXECUTE      - EXECUTE A MEMBER CONTAINING IDEAL COMMANDS

    5. PRODUCE      - PRODUCE A REPORT FACSIMILE
```

Figure 3-18   PROCESS Selection Screen.

The first of these screens, the PROCESS screen (option 5 of the main menu), is shown in Figure 3-18.

This screen shows the two ways that a program can be executed in IDEAL. It can be submitted on-line if it does not need JCL to specify outside files. This is true both for programs that are designed for on-line execution with interactive panels and for batch programs that run quickly and use only IDEAL databases and work areas. If the program requires the use of outside files (for input/output from/to other environments, or writing a report to a dataset for storage, as examples), the JCL can be stored in a batch member. The member is then "submitted" to the operating system, which strips the JCL from the member and spools it into the normal batch input queues for processing.

We will deal with the interfaces to the operating system in more detail in the chapter on the operating environment. Meanwhile, the run prompt screen is shown in Figure 3-19.

Positions 1 and 2 identify the program name and version that are to be executed. Position 3 decides whether or not the database is to be updated permanently by this run, or if changes made to it are to be backed out after execution. (This is a handy option for updating programs because you don't have to rebuild your test data after every run.) Position 4 allows the inputting of any run-time parameters which are defined in the PARM section of the program. Positions 5 and 6 designate the destination of the programs output. It can go either to the IDEAL output library (LIB _____) or directly to a system- defined printer (SYS RMT16). Option 7 determines how many copies are to be made of the output, and position 9 determines the maximum number of lines that can be printed.

```
------------------------------------------------------------------------
  IDEAL: RUN PROGRAM              XXX              SYS:DEV  PROMPTER


  RUN  _____  VERSION  LAST    UPDATE DB?  Y
       (1)                (2)                (3)



  PARAMETER _____
                   (4)


  REPORT OPTIONS:
  DEST LIB _____  COPIES  1  DISP HOL  MAXLINES _____  DESC _____
       (5)   (6)              (7)    (8)             (9)              (10)
  ----------------------------------------------------------------------
  (1) PROGRAM NAME
  (2) VERSION: NNN = VER.#, PROD, LAST
  (3) UPDATE DB?: Y=YES, N=NO
  (4) USER PARAMETER TO THE APPLICATION PROGRAM (MUST BE IN QUOTES)
  (5) LIB = OUTPUT LIBRARY    (6) SYSTEM      (7) # COPIES (8) REL=RELEASE
      SYS = SYSTEM PRINTER        PRINTER NAME              HOL=HOLD
      NET = NETWORK PRINTER                                 KEE=KEEP
  (9) MAXIMUM LINES PER REPORT       (10) DESCRIPTION (MUST BE IN QUOTES)
  NOTE: OUTPUT NAMES WILL BE THE SAME AS REPORT NAMES
```

Figure 3-19   RUN PROGRAM Prompt Screen.

Position 8 designates the disposition of any output created by the program. Release (REL) should be used if the output is to be sent directly to the printer. HOLD (HOL) and KEEP (KEE) should be used if the output is going to the system library. Use KEEP if the output may be printed off later; use hold if the output will remain in the library until it is deleted.

Position 10 is also used in conjunction with sending output to the system library. It is used to define the value of the output description found on the right-hand side of the output library display. This is used to help the developer remember which run the output represents.

The SUBMIT MEMBER screen is much simpler because all of the options for the run are contained in the JCL the developer is submitting. This is shown in Figure 3-20, where all that is required is the name of the member to be submitted.

The EXECUTE MEMBER prompt is the same as the SUBMIT MEMBER prompt.

```
------------------------------------------------------------------
IDEAL: SUBMIT MEMBER      PGM XXXXXXXX (XXX) TEST  SYS:DEV PROPMTER

SUBMIT _____
       (MEMBER NAME)
```

Figure 3-20   SUBMIT MEMBER Screen.

The process screen is also used to submit programs to the IDEAL compiler, which is a quasi-background job. In fact, the prompt screen for compiles (Figure 3-21) is similar to the prompt screen for on-line execution.

Positions on the compilation and run screen line up as follows:

```
------------------------------------------------------------------
IDEAL: COMPILE PROGRAM          XXX            SYS:DEV  PROMPTER

COMPILE _____  VERSION   LAST
          (1)                 (2)


IDE  N   EXD  N   BOD  N   ADV  Y   MEL  Y   PNL  N
     (3)      (4)      (5)      (6)      (7)      (8)


DESTINATION LIB _____ COPIES  1   NAME _____ DISP HOL
                 (9)  (10)         (11)       (12)       (13)
------------------------------------------------------------------
(1) PROGRAM NAME
(2) VERSION: NNN = VER.#, PROD, LAST
(3)-(9): COMPILER LISTING OPTIONS, Y=YES, N=NO
   (3) IDE = IDENTIFICATION
   (4) EXD = EXTERNAL DATA (DATAVIEWS, PANELS, REPORTS)
   (5) BOD = BODY (WORKING DATA, PARAMETERS, PROCEDURE)
   (6) ADV = ADVISORY MESSAGES
   (7) MEL = MARK ERROR LINES IN LIBRARY
   (8) PNL = PANEL LISTING F=FULL S=SHORT N=NO
(9)-(13):COMPILE LISTING DESTINATION INFORMATION:(11) #COPIES
(9) LIB=OUTPUT LIBRARY  (10) SYSTEM            (12) PRINTOUT NAME
    SYS=SYSTEM PRINTER       DESTINATION       (13) REL=RELEASE,
    NET=NETWORK PRINTER      NAME                   HOL=HOLD,KEE=KEEP
```

Figure 3-21   COMPILATION Prompt Screen.

Compile	Run	Meaning
1	1	Program Name
2	2	Program Version
9,10	5,6	Output Destination
11	7	Number Of Copies
12	10	Output Description
13	8	Output Disposition

The other positions are selections of what is to be printed on the compiler output listing. Each selection is yes or no (Y or N).

Position	Action
3	IDENTIFICATION section is to be printed.
4	External entities (DATAVIEWS, PANELS, REPORTS).
5	Main body (WORKING STORAGE, PARAMETERS, PROCEDURE).
6	COMPILER ADVISORY MESSAGES.
7	Mark errors by highlighting fields if error in the copy of the program residing in the source library.
8	Determines how much of the associated PANEL definitions will be displayed.

It should be noted that the output options selected in these screens will override the session setup for the execution of this job.

The last process option is to print a facsimile copy of a report definition. We will delay the detailed discussion of this screen until Chapter 8.

Figure 3-22 shows the PRINT OPTION selection menu.

This menu works in direct conjunction with the jobcard member attached to the user's signon. By accessing the options on this panel the system will automatically submit the request as a batch print job to the printer that the SET attributes are currently pointing to.

Options 2 and 3 of the menu, which execute automatically upon being called, send the options and destinations list directly to the printer. Option 4 shows the index selection screen (Figure 3-17) and then sends the copy of the selected index to the printer.

Figure 3-23 in turn shows the PRINT OCCURRENCE PROMPT screen.

This screen is the same as the other process screens in that the first line designates which entity is to be printed, and the second line of the prompt controls the execution options.

The eighth option of the main menu is for the system and database administrator's use in maintaining the user and system

```
-------------------------------------------------------------------
IDEAL: PRINT MENU              XXX XXXXXXXX (XXX) TEST SYS:DEV    MENU


ENTER DESIRED OPTION NUMBER ==>    THERE ARE 4 OPTIONS IN THIS MENU


1.PRINT OCCURANCE    PRINT A SPECIFIC PGM,PNL,RPT,DVW,USR,SYS,MEM,OUT
2.PRINT OPTIONS      PRINT CURRENT SESSIONS OPTIONS
3.PRINT DESTINATION  PRINT CURRENT PRINT DESTINATIONS
4.PRINT INDEX        PRINT INDEX OF PGMS,PNLS,RPTS,DVWS,SYS,USRS,MEMS
```

Figure 3-22   PRINT Option Selection Menu.

definitions and the DATADICTIONARY, respectively. Further discussions of these screens will be postponed until our discussion of the environment in Chapter 9.

The final option of the main menu is the OFF option. This is simply IDEAL's log-off option, which will take the user back to the CICS system.

```
-------------------------------------------------------------------
IDEAL: PRINT OCCURENCE    XXX XXXXXXXX (XXX) TEST SYS:DEV    PROMPTER


PRINT   ___  _____    VERSION LAST
        (1)      (2)                   (3)


DEST LIB _____  COPIES  1  NAME _____  DISP HOL DESC _____
    (4)   (5)            (6)       (7)        (8)              (9)
-------------------------------------------------------------------
(1) PGM=PROGRAM  SYS=SYSTEM DEFN (2)NAME (3)NNN  (4) DESTINATION
    PNL=PANEL    USR=USER DEFN.            PROD  LIB=OUTPUT LIBRARY
    RPT=REPORT   MEM=MEMBER                LAST  SYS=SYSTEM PRINTER
    DVW=DATAVIEW OUT=OUTPUT
(5) DESTINATION NAME  (6)COPIES  (7) NAME OF OUTPUT (8) DISPOSITION
                                                     REL=RELEASE
(9) DESCRIPTION (MUST BE IN QUOTES)                  KEE=KEEP
                                                     HOL=HOLD
```

Figure 3-23   PRINT OCCURENCE Prompt Screen.

```
------------------------------------------------------------------------

INITIAL PANEL LAYOUT


THE INITIAL LAYOUT FILL-IN CONTAINS NULL-FILLED LINES. FIELDS

CAN BE ENTERED ANYWHERE IN THESE NULL-FILLED LINES. ALL FIELDS

ENTERED DURING THE INITIAL LAYOUT OF A PANEL MUST BE ENTERED WITH

THE "NEW FIELD" SYMBOL AT THE START OF THE FIELD. A FIELD IS

ENDED EITHER BY THE "END FIELD" SYMBOL OR ANOTHER "NEW FIELD"

SYMBOL STARTING ANOTHER FIELD. TO MAINTAIN SPACE (A GAP) BETWEEN

FIELDS, SPACES MUST BE ENTERED IN PLACE OF THE NULL CHARACTERS.

TO LEAVE A BLANK LINE, AT LEAST ONE SPACE MUST BE ENTERED ON THE

LINE.


                                                        ...MORE
```

Figure 3-24   HELP Screen Example.

PF Keys

Another method of navigation through the various entities and menus is through the use of PF keys. We have already pointed out that the PF2 key is the IDEAL system return key. With it we can exit the component or menu that we are in and backtrack through the system until we return to the main menu.

In addition to this, PF1 is always assigned to be the help screen request, which contains instructions on the completion of the panel in which the user is working. For example, if the user was in the layout screen of the panel definition facility, pressing PF1 would result in the display shown in Figure 3-24.

PF3 in its turn is always set up to be a screen print of the viewed panel. When pressed it sets up a background job that routes the contents of the displayed screen to a printer using the JCL contained in the user's JOBCARD MEMBER.

There are also standard PF-KEY assignments during the editing session of any entity or component.

PF-KEYS 7 and 8 are used take care of backward and forward scrolling in the text. PF-KEYS 10 and 11 will also take you to the top or bottom of a text, respectively.

Then each of the entities use the remaining PF-KEYS (4,5,6,9, and 12) for internal navigation during the edit session:

During program editing these assignments are

 4 positions the session at the top of the procedure area.
 5 positions the session at the top of the work area.
 6 positions the session at the top of the parameter area.
 9 repeats the previous find command.
12 opens the area with a section of null lines for inputting.

During panel editing the assignments are

 4 displays the extended field definition for the field that precedes the currently displayed field.
 5 displays the extended field definition for the field that follows the currently displayed field.
 6 displays the panel layout definition screen.
 9 displays the panel field summary definition table.
12 opens the layout panel screen with null lines for definition of more fields.

During report editing the assignments are

 4 positions the session at the top of the parameter area.
 5 positions the session at the top of the report heading panel.
 6 positions the session at the top of the column detail.
 9 reserved — not assigned a value by the language.
12 opens area with nulls.

During the display of a dataview area, these five keys are not assigned values.

Split Screen

Another navigational tool that IDEAL provides is the ability to split the screen into three separate IDEAL sessions.

The SPLIT command can be entered in three ways, each producing a different screen format. In each case the command SPLIT is entered into the command line. If the cursor is also on the command line, the screen will be divided into equal size regions. If the cursor is in the display area, the second region will begin at the cursor's position. The third command format is to define the size of the regions with the command SPLIT N (M), where N will be equal to the number of lines that we wish to see in the first region and M is the optional number of lines in the second region. In each of these cases it is important to remember that the minimum region size that IDEAL allows is nine lines.

When the split occurs, the system establishes a new IDEAL session in the second region using the developers LOGON ID, and executes the SIGNON member. Therefore all attributes in the second region are the same as they were when the developer signed onto IDEAL and executed the SIGNON. It should also be realized that since the second region is an independent session, any IDEAL entity that it is displaying is in its possession, and is not available to the other session. For example if the developer tried to submit a compile in the first region for a program that was being edited in the second region, the compiler would abort with the message that the program was "busy" and would invite you to try again later.

When the second region comes up, the screen will show the command lines at the top as they were when the split command was entered, the top portion of what was on the screen, and the second region positioned at the main menu without a command line. The user now has two options on how to navigate through the second region. He can either select options and flow through the menu processes, or he can access it through the command lines at the top of the screen. This is done by prefixing all commands with the number of the region in which you wish to have the command executed.

For example, suppose we were viewing the output listing of a program compile with errors in it, and we wished to look at the corresponding source code. We would enter the command SPLIT to divide the screen into two equal portions. We would then enter the command   2 EDIT PGM BLPGA107 V 2   which would put the top of the procedure section into the top of the second region, allowing the user to see both his source code and his compiler errors. (Figure 3-25).

We also could have strung those commands together by using a semi-colon (;) as a *delimiter*. In this case, SPLIT ; 2 EDIT PGM BLPGA107 V 1 ; 2 POS 13200 would have split the screen, brought program BLPGA107 into the second region in the edit mode, and brought line number 13200 of that program to the top of the display area of region 2.

It is also possible for the user to change the relative size of the regions after they have been established. This is done with the command REFORMAT N (M), where N is the number of lines of the first region and M is the optional number of lines of the second region. The nine-line minimum also applies to this command.

```
-------------------------------------------------------------------------
IDEAL   DISPLAY OUTPUT        OUT BLPGU602                    DISPLAY
                       ADV: ADVISORY MESSAGES:
                              *** REPORT INTERNAL RECORD SIZE  55 BYTES
                              *** REPORT INTERNAL RECORD SIZE 107 BYTES


PGM  BLPGU602   002  TEST   SYS:DEV    NOVEMBER 12, 1986
ERRORS:
PROCEDURE:      BLPGU602            VERSION 002      STATUS:   TEST
              2100 CMLX   25-E FIELD NAME NOT KNOWN, WK-INVOICE-NO
              7000 CMLX   25-E FIELD NAME NOT KNOWN, WK-ORD-CNTL-NO
             19900 CMLX   25-E FIELD NAME NOT KNOWN, WK-INVOICE-NO
             26400 CMLX   25-E FIELD NAME NOT KNOWN, WK-MEMO-REF-NO
             26500 CMLX   25-E FIELD NAME NOT KNOWN, WK-MEMO-BILL
             26700 CMLX   25-E FIELD NAME NOT KNOWN, WK-MEMO-REF-NO

-------------------------------------------------------------------------
IDEAL: PROCEDURE DEFINITION   PGM BLPGU602 (002) TEST   SYS:DEV


...............................................................COMMAND
==================================T O P============================ ======
<<BLPGU602>> PROCEDURE                                        000100
   DO INITIALIZATION                                          000200
   DO EXTRACT-SH                                              000300
   DO EXTRACT-ARC                                             000400
   DO WRITE-REPORT                                            000500
   DO WRT-DET-TOTAL                                           000600
ENDPROC                                                       000700
                                                              000800
<<INITIALIZATION>> PROCEDURE                                  000900
   MOVE $DATE('YY/MM/DD') TO RPT-CURR-DATE                    001000
```

Figure 3-25   Split Screen Example.

We can also split the second region into a third area, and reformat all three regions with the same commands. This is not recommended, however, because of the overhead lines that IDEAL has and the small size of the resulting regions.

To delete the second and third regions, we simply enter the command COMBINE. If we are displaying three regions, this will release the third and leave two. Executing it again will leave us with one full screen.

IDEAL Editor

The IDEAL editor handles the manipulation of the information within an IDEAL component. When the edit function is accessed, either by a menu-generated prompt or by a command, IDEAL marks the component as not executable, and any program with that version of that component in its resource table must be recompiled before it can be run again.

There are three types of commands that are used by the IDEAL editor. These are line editing commands, commands from the command line, and keyboard commands.

We can define line editing commands as those commands used to manipulate the order or placement of lines within the component. These commands are used by placing the valid symbols into the line command section of the displayed screen. This area is the column of numbers called the *command* area of the screen.

The position of the numbers is determined by the command:

```
SET EDIT MARGIN (RIGHT / LEFT)
```

The valid commands are

R = REPEAT the positioned line
I = INSERT null lines into the component after this line
D = DELETE the positioned line
M = MOVE this line to the marked position
C = COPY this line to the marked position
A = TARGET position of copy or move, place AFTER this line
B = TARGET position of copy or move, place BEFORE this line

These commands are available in three formats, depending on the size of the operation the developer wishes to perform. If a single line is to be manipulated, a single character will be entered into the command area opposite the line to be changed. If multiple occurrences of the same line are desired (for example, repeating a line five times), the syntax of the command appears as (N)I, where N is the number of occurrences and I is the command. (In this example the command would be 5R). To manipulate a range of lines, simply put two occurrences of the command (RR) on the lines at the top and at the bottom of the range.

The side of the command that the multiplier goes on is determined by the command:

```
SET EDIT MULTIPLIER (RIGHT/LEFT)
```

```
IDEAL: PROCEDURE DEFINITION    PGM BLPGU602 (002) TEST    SYS:DEV


..................................................................COMMAND
===============================T O P=============================== ======
<<BLPGU602>> PROCEDURE                                             000100
   DO INITIALIZATION                                               CC0200
   DO EXTRACT-SH                                                   000300
   DO EXTRACT-ARC                                                  000400
   DO WRITE-REPORT                                                 CC0500
   DO WRT-DET-TOTAL                                                000600
ENDPROC                                                            000700
                                                                   A00800

<<INITIALIZATION>> PROCEDURE                                       000900
   MOVE $DATE('YY/MM/DD') TO RPT-CURR-DATE                         001000
   MOVE $DATE('YY/MM/DD') TO RPT-CURR-DATE                         R01000
ENDPROC                                                            001100
                                                                   001200
:***************************************************** D01300
:** EXTRACT AR DATA FROM SALES HISTORY                **           001400
:***************************************************** 001500
                                                                   DD1600
<<EXTRACT-SH>> PROCEDURE                                           001700
   FOR EACH  SALES-HIST-BILL                                       001800
       WHERE SALES-HIST-BILL.AR-EXTRACT-IND EQ 'Y'                 001900
           ADD 1 TO CT-SHIST-READ                                  DD2000
           MOVE SALES-HIST-BILL.INVOICE-NO TO WK-INVOICE-NO        002100
           IF SALES-HIST-BILL.CREDIT-DEBIT-CD EQ 'C'               002200
               DO BLD-MEMO-REC                                     002300
           ELSE                                                    002400
```

Figure 3-26   Line Command Examples.

We can also delete from the position of the cursor to the top of the data (DT) or to the bottom of the data (DB).

Figure 3-26 shows examples of each of these line command formats. In this and all other examples, we have used the commands:

```
SET EDIT MARGIN RIGHT
SET EDIT MULTIPLIER LEFT
```

The RESET command clears the line commands that are pending execution. When a line command is entered it is possible to leave the

```
IDEAL: PROCEDURE DEFINITION    PGM BLPGU602 (002) TEST    SYS:DEV
PENDING: MM(1000) MM(1400)
.......................................................COMMAND
================================T O P============================= ======
<<BLPGU602>> PROCEDURE                                       RESET0
  DO INITIALIZATION                                          000200
  DO EXTRACT-SH                                              000300
  DO EXTRACT-ARC                                             000400
  DO WRITE-REPORT                                            000500
  DO WRT-DET-TOTAL                                           000600
ENDPROC                                                      000700
                                                             000800
<<INITIALIZATION>> PROCEDURE                                 000900
  MOVE $DATE('YY/MM/DD') TO RPT-CURR-DATE                    MM
  MOVE $DATE('YY/MM/DD') TO RPT-CURR-DATE                    001000
ENDPROC                                                      001100
                                                             001200
:***************************************************** 001300
:** EXTRACT AR DATA FROM SALES HISTORY              ** MM
:***************************************************** 001500
                                                             001600
<<EXTRACT-SH>> PROCEDURE                                     001700
  FOR EACH   SALES-HIST-BILL                                 001800
      WHERE SALES-HIST-BILL.AR-EXTRACT-IND EQ 'Y'            001900
            ADD 1 TO CT-SHIST-READ                           002000
            MOVE SALES-HIST-BILL.INVOICE-NO TO WK-INVOICE-NO 002100
            IF SALES-HIST-BILL.CREDIT-DEBIT-CD EQ 'C'        002200
               DO BLD-MEMO-REC                               002300
            ELSE                                             002400
```

Figure 3-27   PENDING and RESET.

screen that we are viewing and scroll through the component. When we do this, the command will be marked as pending, and a reminder message will be displayed (Figure 3-27). We can delete the pending commands by entering the RESET command into the line command area.

The line command RESHOW will refresh the data in the region that we are viewing to its original value. Thus if we make some changes to a screen full of data and decide that we do not like the result, this command will allow us to return the screen to its original status.

The line command IGNORE does for the line on which it is placed what the RESHOW command does for the entire screen.

The last line command is for positioning a line to the top of the screen. This is done by placing an asterisk (*) on the line on which we wish to be positioned on and using the ENTER key.

The command line functions are used for global work within the component, or for accessing information from other components.

The CHANGE command is used to change all occurrences of a given string to a new value, within a certain range. The syntax of the command is

```
CHANGE /STRING-A/STRING-B/

        LINES      START-LINE                              A

        LINES      TOP              BOTTOM        B  A  A
                   CURSOR           END-LINE         B  B
                   * offset         CURSOR           B  C
                                    * offset            D

        COLUMNS    START-COLUMN     MAX           C  A  A
                                    END-COLUMN          B
```

The (/) here serves as the string delimiter and must be closed to allow the command to function. STRING-A is the target string, and STRING-B is what we want STRING-A changed into. Three types of ranges that be specified:

1. Process the data from a certain line to the bottom of the data.
2. Process the data from

   a. the top of the data
   b. the line the cursor is on
   c. a certain number of lines from the top of the displayed region

   To

   a. the bottom of the data
   b. a certain position line number
   c. the position of the cursor
   d. a certain number of lines from the top of the displayed region

3. Process data within the previously defined (or default) line area; changes affect only data within *COLUMN* boundaries:

FROM a specific column

To

   a. the right-hand margin
   b. a specific column

If STRING-B is longer than STRING-A, the line of data containing STRING-A is shifted to the right. If STRING-B is shorter, the line is padded with null characters to the right.

For example, let's suppose that we have the program code

```
MOVE BILLING-HEADER.INVOICE-NO TO SALES-HIST-BILL.BILLING-CNTL
```

and we enter the command

```
CHANGE /BILLING-HEADER/BIL-INVHDR-READ/
```

This will result in

```
MOVE BIL-INVHDR-READ.INVOICE-NO TO SALES-HIST-BILL.BILLING-CNT
```

The command found the string 'BILLING-HEADER' and replaced it with the string 'BIL-INVHDR-READ'. To do this it had to insert an extra character before the string '.INVOICE-NO' because our replacement string was longer than our target. This results in the truncation of the last character of 'BILLING-CNTL'.

Now let us suppose that we have the code line:

```
MOVE BILLING-LINE.LINE-NUM TO SALES-HIST-LINE.LINE-NUM
```

and we enter the command

```
CHANGE /LINE-NUM/LINE-NO/
```

Our result would be

```
MOVE BILLING-LINE.LINE-NO TO SALES-HIST-LINE.LINE-NO
```

Here both occurrences of 'LINE-NUM' were changed and the over-all length of the string was shortened and left-justified. The right-hand side of the line was padded with nulls.

The COPY command works like the C line command, except that it accesses information from another program or member. The command appears as

```
COPY (PROGRAM NAME (VERSION(NNN ))) (NUM-1 (NUM-2 ))(NUM-3 ))
                           (PROD)    (TOP    (BOTTOM))(TOP    ))
       (MEMBER   NAME)     (LAST)                     (BOTTOM))
```

or as an example

```
COPY PROGRAM PROGNUM1 VER 002 TOP BOTTOM 004250
```

Here we are to copy the program named PROGNUM1, version number 2, beginning at the top and going all the way to the bottom, and placing that information after line 004250 of the program we are editing. Thus we see that the first two positions show the range of information we want (either by line numbers or top and bottom), and the third is for the placement in our program or member.

If the command is executed while editing a program, it will draw the data from the corresponding component of the called program.

If we are editing the working data of a program, the above command would have accessed the working data section of program PROGNUM1.

The FIND command is used to position the cursor at a specific string. The syntax and function is similar to the CHANGE command in that the string must be delimited by special characters, and the search goes from the specified begin point to the specified end point. To repeat the command the developer can retype FIND in the command line without a new search string, or hit the PF9/PF21 key.

The POSITION command is used to place a specific line at the top of the display area. This can be used for a line number in programs and members, or a field position on the LAYOUT screen of a panel.

The RENUMBER command is used to refresh the sequence numbers at the right side of the screen. When the lines are moved, added, or inserted the editor simply increments those new lines by one level less than that of the current level. Thus, if the lines were numbered

```
016500
016600
```

```
016700
016800
016900
017000
017100
```

and we entered the command 3R on line 016700, the result would be

```
016500
016600
016700
016710
016720
016730
016800
016900
017000
017100
```

By entering the RENUMBER command, the line numbers would be

```
016500
016600
016700
016800
016900
017000
017100
017200
017300
017400
```

We can also change the incrementation with the second half of the command RENUMBER ((BY) N), where N is the new incrementation level.

The default level is 10.

The commands CHECKPOINT and ROLLBACK are used to protect or eliminate changes made during an edit session. The command ROLLBACK refreshes the component to its appearance at the start of the edit session. The command CHECKPOINT makes permanent the changes since the beginning of the session or the last rollback.

When a component is accessed which was being edited during a system failure, a screen specifying these two choices is presented to the developer. He can either make permanent the changes of the last session or he can refresh the component with a ROLLBACK.

The last edit feature that we need to discuss is the SCROLL feature. In addition to the PF-KEYS, it is possible to specify scrolling commands on the command line. We can scroll either forward or backward by cursor position, by an entire frame, by a specific number of pages (in an output member) or by a specific number of lines.

This command appears as

```
SCROLL (FORWARD ) (CURSOR )
       (BACKWARD) (FRAME  )
       (+        ) (N PAGES)
       (-        ) (N LINES)
```

The characters + and - are the equivalents of forward and backward, respectively.

It is also possible to scroll to the left or right, top or bottom of an output library member.

```
SCROLL (RIGHT   ) (CURSOR )
       (LEFT    ) (FRAME  )

SCROLL (TOP     )
       (BOTTOM  )
```

Keyboard editing commands are the insert and delete keys found on standard IBM keyboards. Changes to specific characters are made by simply keying over the displayed text.

IDEAL editing commands are executed in the following order.

RESHOW
IGNORE
Updated text application
RESET
Then line commands in top down order
    D
    DD
    M
    MM
    (N)R
    RR
    C
    CC

(N)A
(N)B
*
(N)I
IDEAL Templates
Command Line
PF Keys

Conclusions

In this chapter we have learned the basics of navigation through the IDEAL development facility. We have seen how the main menu leads to prompt screens through a series of intermediate menus.

We have also seen the relationships of the entities of the IDEAL language, their components, and how they are maintained. We have also learned how the editor functions.

In the remaining chapters we will examine each of the IDEAL components in detail, and how to get this code to function in the environment.

Exercises

1. Obtain a CICS and an IDEAL SIGNON ID from your supervisor and log-on to the IDEAL development facility.
2. Create and fill-in a JOBCARD member with a jobcard that meets the syntax requirements of your facility. This is done with the command EDIT JOBCARD, which will then establish a JOBCARD member. Then use the editor to fill in the null area.
3. Create and execute a SIGNON member that will

    a. set up 1 command line
    b. establish the job output destination to the IDEAL output library
    c. establish the job output disposition as keep
    d. set the editor scroll to function at the cursor level

4. Name the different IDEAL entities, their respective components, and the use of each.
5. Describe the paths to get from the main menu to

    a. display panel definition index

    b. display a specific program

    c. duplicate a report

6. What are the different statuses that an IDEAL entity can have? What is the purpose of each?

7. Obtain from your supervisor the name of a program, a report, and a panel and navigate through them using both the command line and the PF-KEY commands.

Exercises — Answers

3. Create and execute a SIGNON member that will

    a. set up 1 command line

    b. establish the job output destination to the IDEAL output library

    c. establish the job output disposition as keep

    d. set the editor scroll to function at the cursor level

```
SET COMMAND LINE 1
SET OUTPUT DESTINATION LIBRARY
SET OUTPUT DISPOSITION KEEP
SET SCROLL CURSOR
```

4. Name the different IDEAL entities, their respective components, and the use of each.

```
PROGRAM
        IDE    — Program identification
        PROC  — Contains PDL commands
        WOR   — Working storage definition area
        PARM  — Parameter definition area
        RES    — Resource table
PANEL
        PARM  — Defines panel global PARMS
        LAY    — Define screen layout
        SUM    — Defines panel names and attributes
        FAC    — Shows facsimile of a panel report
        PARM  — Defines panel global PARMS
        DET    — Shows line detail
        COL    — Defines column headers
        HEA    — Defines report headers
```

DATAVIEW — Defines database layouts

MEMBER — Contains batch JCL and IDEAL session commands

The EXTENDED FIELD definition, the INPUT RULES, and the OUTPUT RULES screens are not really components of the panel definition, but are furthur details of the summary screen.

5. Describe the paths to get from the main menu to

    a. display panel definition index
    b. display a specific program
    c. duplicate a report

    a. 1 — DIS INDEX PNL
        2 — MAIN TO ENTITY TO PANEL-MAINTENANCE
        3 — MAIN TO PROCESS TO DISPLAY
    b. 1 — DIS PROGRAM NAME
        2 — MAIN TO ENTITY TO PROGRAM-MAINTENANCE
        3 — MAIN TO PROCESS TO DISPLAY
    c. 1 — DUP RPT REPORT-NAME
        2 — MAIN TO COMPONENT TO PROGRAM-MAIN-TENANCE

6. What are the different statuses that an ideal entity can have? What is the purpose of each?

    TEST — Allow application changes
    PROD — Protected against changes
    HIST — Archived version of entity

4

IDEAL Program Development Facility

Introduction

As we saw in the last chapter, it is the program entity that contains the instructions and logic for IDEAL's manipulation of data. We also saw that this entity is made up of five components, namely the *identification, working storage, parameter, procedure* sections, and the *resource table*. In this chapter we will deal with the first four of these components in detail, and we will see how they relate to one another to create a functioning IDEAL program.

First, we will look at some of the basic terms and data structure rules that we will see in IDEAL.

Naming Standards

Everything, from the largest program to a one-byte field in the working storage area, must have a unique address that the computer can understand and reference when it needs the corresponding piece of information. This address is described to IDEAL and the compiler by means of an *identifier*.

For an identifier name to be valid to IDEAL it must meet the following requirements.

1. All names begin with a letter or a national character ($, @, #)
2. They can be made up of any combination of valid letters, numbers, national characters, or embedded hyphens.
3. A name cannot have spaces in it
4. Reserved words cannot be used as a name (see list in Appendix A)
5. Names must be unique to the entity type (for example, a program and a report can have the same name, but two different programs cannot share the same name)
6. The name must meet the length limit requirements for its type

```
FIELD                15 characters
GROUP                15 characters
DATAVIEW             15 characters
PROGRAM DEFINITION    8 characters
REPORT DEFINITION     8 characters (no hyphens)
PANEL DEFINITIONS     8 characters
```

7. A field or group name must be unique to the entity in which it is found (such as panel layout, working storage, parameter section, dataview, or report). This unique name serves as the identifier.

Because an identifier only needs to be unique within its entity, it is possible for the developer to encounter the situation where the same identifier is used to address two different fields. For example, we may be trying to move the value of a field labeled LINE-NO on a dataview to a field labeled LINE-NO on a panel definition. These fields can be uniquely identified by prefixing the field name with the name of the higher level entity and a DOT. In our example we would see the following command:

```
MOVE DATAVIEW-NAME.LINE-NO TO PANELNM.LINE-NO
```

where DATAVIEW-NAME is the name of the dataview and PANELNM the name of the panel.

It is also possible to place up to three levels of subscripting on an identifier. This subscript must appear in brackets to the right of the identifier. It must always have an integer value between 1 and the occurrence size of the table being referenced. The subscript can be either a numeric literal or another identifier that has a numeric definition.

Data Structures

No discussion of a language would go very far without defining the different formats which the data that it uses can take.

Each field in IDEAL falls into one of two categories. It can either be an *elementary field* (meaning that it does not have subordinate fields), or it can be part of a *group* (meaning it has elementary fields that are subordinate to it). In IDEAL, these groups are further classified as being either *alpha* groups or *non-alpha* groups. IDEAL considers a *non-alpha* group as a group which has an elementary field with a numeric definition. IDEAL restricts the usage of *non-alpha* groups and allows their access only in the following cases:

1. In a SET, MOVE, MOVE BY NAME, MOVE BY POSITION
2. As a PARAMETER in a CALL statement
3. As an OPERAND in an ALPHANUMERIC FUNCTION.

By imposing these restrictions, IDEAL is able to line up numeric fields in a SOURCE group with corresponding numeric fields in a TARGET group. This in turn eliminates the possibility of moving alpha data into a packed numeric field, which would cause an OC-7 type abend. Moreover, IDEAL also has a restriction on the movement of data to numeric elementary fields, in that an alpha value is converted to packed numeric before it is moved. If the field contains non-numeric data the program will abend, showing the offending data in the output listing. A compile time warning is also generated when this situation is found in a program.

These restrictions are also placed on the movement of literal statements. A numeric literal is a literal which contains only numeric characters and an optional leading sign. These are coded in either the value column of the working storage definition or in the actual procedure code without any delimiters. An alpha or alphanumeric literal must be enclosed with matching " or ' characters.

Another type of literal is the Boolean Literal. It is valued as either *true* or *false* and is not enclosed in delimiters. These literals are used in conjunction with the flag structure. The flag is a special structure which is defined in the working storage or parameter area with the TYPE field set to F, and a value of either T (for true) or F (for false). It is then possible to test the value of a flag in the procedure code with the statement:

```
IF DEFINED-FLAG
```

thus allowing more readable code to be written.

```
LEVEL FIELD NAME          T I CH/DG OCCUR VALUE/COMMENT/DEP ON/COPY

_____ _____ _ _ _____ _____ _____

_____ _____ _ _ _____ _____ _____

_____ _____ _ _ _____ _____ _____

_____ _____ _ _ _____ _____ _____

_____ _____ _ _ _____ _____ _____
```

Figure 4-1   Blank Working Storage FILL-IN.

In addition to the flag condition, it is possible to build more complicated condition statements with a greater choice than true or false.

All of these data structures can be in defined the working storage area of the program definition.

Working Storage

In Figure 4-1 we see an example of a blank working storage fill-in.

The first position is for the *field level* number (LEVEL). This position is used to show the grouping relationship of the fields. All independent fields would be level 1. If a group was identified, the highest level would be level 1. The breakdown definition of that field would be level 2. Any furthur definition of the level 2 fields would be level 3, and so on until the elementary field level was reached.

The *name* field (FIELD NAME) contains the name, unique to working storage, that identifies that field to the corresponding procedure definition that uses it. This uniqueness can be made by only using the name once in the program, or by qualifying it with the name of a higher level working storage field of which it is part.

The *field type* (T) designates the data structure type that is used. The valid values are:

```
X   ALPHA NUMERIC
N   SIGNED NUMERIC
U   UNSIGNED NUMERIC
C   CONDITION
F   FLAG
D   DATE
V   VARIABLE LENGTH ALPHANUMERIC FIELD
```

The *date* and the *variable-length alphanumeric* fields are special data structures for IDEAL. The date field is a numeric field containing the number of days since December 31, 1900. It is from five to seven digits in length and has an initial value of zero. We will discuss the specific processing of this feature later in the chapter.

A variable-length field is assigned an initial maximum length. Then when a value is placed within the field, the field shrinks around the literal, saving working storage space. This type of field must always be defined as a level 1 elementary field.

The CH/DG field is used to designate the length of the field. The length of an alphanumeric or integer field is defined by putting a numeric field length in the column. A field with a decimal point is defined by placing a period (.) between the length definitions of the two sides.

The *field internal representation* (I) column is used to furthur define the numeric and the date fields, and can have one of three values:

```
P     PACKED
Z     ZONED
B     BINARY
```

These have the standard IBM references and are used primarily when interfacing with non-IDEAL subroutines. A detailed discussion of their usage is contained in Chapter 6.

The *occurrence* field (OCCUR) is used to define the number of rows in a table.

The last field is used to assign a *value* to a field, to establish a *depending on* relationship, to make a descriptive *comment* about a field, for the placement of the *redefinition* keyword, or for a COPY DATAVIEW command.

The redefinition, or REDEF, command, is used to define a field as another view of the next previous field with the same level number, that is itself not a redefinition. The two fields may have different types, but the redefinition field cannot be longer than the primary field.

The COPY DATAVIEW command allows a copy of a cataloged dataview structure to be placed in the working-storage fill-in. The COPY command must be on a level 1 definition line.

Basic Data Structure Definitions

In Figure 4-2 we see how the basic data structures are defined in an IDEAL working-storage fill-in screen.

LEVEL	FIELD NAME	T	I	CH/DG	OCCUR	VALUE/COMMENT/DEP ON/COPY
1	ALPHA-FIELD	X	_	10	_____	_____
1	SIGNED-NUMERIC	N	P	10.2	_____	_____
1	UNSIGNED-NUMER	U	P	10	_____	_____
1	NUMERIC-LITER	N	P	3	_____	111
1	ALPHA-LITERAL	X	_	3	_____	'XXX'
1	ALPHA-NUM-LIT	X	_	5	_____	'X1X2X'

Figure 4-2   Basic Working Storage Fields.

This figure contains the basic fields, alpha, signed numeric, unsigned numeric, numeric literal, alpha literal, and alphanumeric literals as elementary fields as they would appear in the working storage fill-in after program compile.

Figure 4-3 shows how these fields can be arranged into alpha and non-alpha groups.

Both of these figures (4-2 and 4-3) can be translated into COBOL working storage structures for comparison as shown in Figure 4-4.

Figure 4-5 shows how flags and conditions are defined to an IDEAL program.

As we can see, a flag can have one of two conditions, either true or false, even though the length of the field is one byte. These flags are accessed by using the Boolean conditions of true or false. It is also possible for the developer to build an alphanumeric flag in his working storage area. These are used by querying the actual value of the field with an IF statement.

LEVEL	FIELD NAME	T	I	CH/DG	OCCUR	VALUE/COMMENT/DEP ON/COPY
1	ALPHA-GROUP	_	_	_____	_____	_____
2	ALPHA-FIELD1	X	_	10	_____	_____
2	ALPHA-FIELD2	X	_	5	_____	_____
_____	_____	_	_	_____	_____	_____
1	NONALPHA-GROUP	_	_	_____	_____	_____
2	SIGNED-NUMERIC	N	P	10.2	_____	_____
2	UNSIGNED-NUMER	U	P	10	_____	_____
2	ALPHA-FIELD	X	_	3	_____	_____
_____	_____	_	_	_____	_____	_____
_____	_____	_	_	_____	_____	_____

Figure 4-3   Alpha and Non-Alpha Groups.

```
01  ALPHA-FIELD      PIC  X(10).

01  SIGNED-NUMERIC   PIC  S9(10)V99         COMP-3.

01  UNSIGNED-NUMER   PIC  9(10)             COMP-3.

01  NUMERIC-LITER    PIC  9(03)  VALUE 111 COMP-3.

01  ALPHA-LITERAL    PIC  X(03)  VALUE 'XXX'.

01  ALPHA-NUM-LIT    PIC  X(05)  VALUE 'X1X2X'.


01  ALPHA-GROUP.
    05  ALPHA-FIELD1  PIC X(10).
    05  ALPHA-FIELD2  PIC X(05).


01  NONALPHA-GROUP.
    05  SIGNED-NUMERIC PIC S9(10)V99 COMP-3.
    05  UNSIGNED-NUMER PIC  9(10)     COMP-3.
    05  ALPHA-FIELD    PIC  X(03).
```

Figure 4-4   COBOL Translation of Figures 4-2 and 4-3.

The multiple condition statement works much like an "88" statement in COBOL. In fact the corresponding COBOL definition of the condition definition in Figure 4-5 is shown in Figure 4-6.

We can then query the structure as we would an '88' statement in COBOL:

LEVEL	FIELD NAME	T	I	CH/DG	OCCUR	VALUE/COMMENT/DEP ON/COPY
1	DEFINED-FLAG-F	F	_	1	_____	FALSE
1	DEFINED-FLAG-T	F	_	1	_____	TRUE
1	DEFINED-FLAG-A	X	_	1	_____	'T'
_____	_____	_	_	_____	_____	_____
1	MULTI-CONDITION	X	_	1	_____	_____
	CONDITION-1	C	_	_____	_____	'1'
	CONDITION-2	C	_	_____	_____	'2'
	CONDITION-3	C	_	_____	_____	'3'
	CONDITION-4	C	_	_____	_____	'4'
	CONDITION-5	C	_	_____	_____	'5'
	CONDITION-6	C	_	_____	_____	'6'
_____	_____	_	_	_____	_____	_____
_____	_____	_	_	_____	_____	_____
_____	_____	_	_	_____	_____	_____

Figure 4-5   Flags and Conditions.

```
01   MULTI-CONDITION PIC X(01)
        88  CONDITION-1  VALUE  '1'.
        88  CONDITION-2  VALUE  '2'.
        88  CONDITION-3  VALUE  '3'.
        88  CONDITION-4  VALUE  '4'.
        88  CONDITION-5  VALUE  '5'.
        88  CONDITION-6  VALUE  '6'.
```

Figure 4-6   COBOL Translation of Figure 4.5.

```
IF CONDITION-6
   DO BUILD-REC-6
ENDIF
```

Figure 4-7 shows an example of the REDEFINITION command.

In this example, the field REDEF-COPY redefines the same area that REDEF-TARGET defines. This means that the field REDEF-COPY-1 contains the same data as the combination of the fields REDEF-TRGT-1 and REDEF-TRGT-2.

Table Definition

As with most languages, IDEAL has the facility to define arrays and tables for use in specific programs. These tables are defined in the working storage area, and can be either *fixed length* as defined at compile time, or a *variable length*, which is determined at run time.

LEVEL	FIELD NAME	T	I	CH/DG	OCCUR	VALUE/COMMENT/DEP ON/COPY
1	MASTER-FIELD	_	_	____	____	_____
2	REDEF-TARGET	_	_	____	____	_____
3	REDEF-TRGT-1	X	_	3		_____
3	REDEF-TRGT-2	X	_	1		_____
3	REDEF-TRGT-3	X	_	2		_____
2	REDEF-COPY	_	_	____	____	REDEF
3	REDEF-COPY-1	X	_	4		_____
3	REDEF-COPY-2	X	_	2		_____
____	_____	_	_	____	____	_____
____	_____	_	_	____	____	_____

Figure 4-7   Example of REDEF.

LEVEL	FIELD NAME	T	I	CH/DG	OCCUR	VALUE/COMMENT/DEP ON/COPY
1	DEP-ON-TBL-AREA	_	_	_____	_____	_____
2	NUM-OF-ENTRIES	N		3	_____	_____
2	DEP-ON-TABLE	_	_	_____	100	DEP ON NUM-OF-ENTRIES
3	DEP-ON-FIELD1	X		10	_____	_____
3	DEP-ON-FIELD2	X		5	_____	_____
_____	_____	_	_	_____	_____	_____
_____	_____	_	_	_____	_____	_____

Figure 4-8   Variable Length Table Definition.

A variable-length table is defined by using the DEPENDING ON command in the last field of the fill-in as shown in Figure 4-8.

Here we see that the table DEP-ON-TABLE was defined with an upper limit of 100 entries. The field NUM-OF-ENTRIES is used to keep the size of the table under that value. If at any given time the value of the field NUM-OF-ENTRIES was 25, the table would only be 25 rows long, and any access to the table with a subscript greater than 25 would cause a TABLE EXCEEDED abend.

The field that determines the table length must be an elementary numeric field with no decimal places. It must also be defined prior to the table, and within the same structure. Thus both examples in Figure 4-9 are incorrect for one of these reasons.

The length of a table can also be permanently fixed at compile time by use of the OCCURS area of the FILL-IN screen. (See Figure 4-10.)

In this figure we can see that there are many alternative ways to structure a table. They can be either an elementary item within a group, a stand-alone elementary item, or they can be further refined by placing elementary items under them.

Not only can we assign the length of a table at compile time, but we also have the ability to assign values to the table. (See Figure 4-11.)

Here we can see the two ways to establish a table with specific values and how they can be used. In each case the designated occurrence of the table contains the specified information, i.e., the third occurrence of the table contains the value '035 PENNSYLVANIA'.

We can then access the field directly through a subscript, or we can move the entire occurrence to a working storage area and access it there.

It is important to note that only the specified occurrences will have a value. In our example above, the last four occurrences will be

LEVEL	FIELD NAME	T	I	CH/DG	OCCUR	VALUE/COMMENT/DEP ON/COPY
1	DEP-ON-TBL-AREA	_	_	_____	_____	_____
2	NUM-OF-ENTRIES	N	_	3		_____
2	DEP-ON-TABLE	_	_	_____		100 DEP ON NUM-OF-ENTRIES
3	DEP-ON-FIELD1	X	_	10		_____
3	DEP-ON-FIELD2	X	_	5		_____
_____	_____	_	_	_____	_____	_____
_____	_____	_	_	_____	_____	_____
1	DEP-ON-TBL-AREA	_	_	_____	_____	_____
2	DEP-ON-TABLE	_	_	_____		100 DEP ON NUM-OF-ENTRIES
3	DEP-ON-FIELD1	X	_	10		_____
3	DEP-ON-FIELD2	X	_	5		_____
2	NUM-OF-ENTRIES	N	_	3		_____
_____	_____	_	_	_____	_____	_____
_____	_____	_	_	_____	_____	_____

Figure 4-9   Incorrect Table Definitions.

blank. Because of this feature, it is possible to override certain occurrences of a table, and leave a default definition intact for the others.
The full value of the table in Figure 4-12 is

'XXX012035XXX048XXXXXXXXXXXX***'

LEVEL	FIELD NAME	T	I	CH/DG	OCCUR	VALUE/COMMENT/DEP ON/COPY
1	FIXED-LEN-AREA	_	_	_____	_____	_____
2	FIXED-LEN-TABLE	X	_	20	100	_____
2	FIXED-LEN-SUBSR	N	_	3		_____
2	FIXED-LEN-LIMIT	N	_	3		100
_____	_____	_	_	_____	_____	_____
1	ELE-FIXED-TABLE	X	_	20	100	_____
_____	_____	_	_	_____	_____	_____
1	DEP-ON-TBL-AREA	_	_	_____	_____	_____
2	FIXED-LEN-TABLE	_	_	_____	100	_____
3	FIXED-FIELD1	X	_	15		_____
3	FIXED-FIELD2	X	_	5		_____
_____	_____	_	_	_____	_____	_____

Figure 4-10   Fixed Length Table Area.

LEVEL	FIELD NAME	T	I	CH/DG	OCCUR	VALUE/COMMENT/DEP ON/COPY
1	TAXABLE-ST-TBL	_	_	_____	_____	_____
2	TAXABLE-TBL	_	_	_____	10	_____
3	TAXABLE-ST-CD	X	_	3		_____
3	TAXABLE-ST-FL	X	_	1		_____
3	TAXABLE-ST-NM	X	_	15		_____
_____	(1)	_	_	_____	_____	'011 INDIANA '
_____	(2)	_	_	_____	_____	'012 IOWA '
_____	(3)	_	_	_____	_____	'035 PENNSYLVANIA '
_____	(4)	_	_	_____	_____	'045 TEXAS '
_____	(5)	_	_	_____	_____	'048 VERMONT '
_____	(6)	_	_	_____	_____	'050 HAWAII '
1	TAXABLE-ST-TBL	X	_	19	10	_____
_____	(1)	_	_	_____	_____	'011 INDIANA '
_____	(2)	_	_	_____	_____	'012 IOWA '
_____	(3)	_	_	_____	_____	'035 PENNSYLVANIA '
_____	(4)	_	_	_____	_____	'045 TEXAS '
_____	(5)	_	_	_____	_____	'048 VERMONT '
_____	(6)	_	_	_____	_____	'050 HAWAII '
1	WKTAXABLE-ST-AR	_	_	_____	_____	_____
2	WKTAX-ST-CD	X	_	3		_____
2	WKTAX-ST-FL	X	_	1		_____
2	WKTAX-ST-NM	X	_	15		_____

Figure 4-11   Fixed Length Table with Predefined Values.

LEVEL	FIELD NAME	T	I	CH/DG	OCCUR	VALUE/COMMENT/DEP ON/COPY
1	TAXABLE-ST-TBL	X	_	3	10	'XXX'
_____	(2)	_	_	_____	_____	'012'
_____	(3)	_	_	_____	_____	'035'
_____	(5)	_	_	_____	_____	'048'
_____	(10)	_	_	_____	_____	'***'

Figure 4-12   Table with Predefined Values.

LEVEL	FIELD NAME	T	I	CH/DG	OCCUR	VALUE/COMMENT/DEP ON/COPY
1	MULTI-DIMEN-ARR	_	_	____	____	
2	LEVEL-ONE	_	_	____	3	
3	LEVEL-TWO	_	_	____	4	
4	LEVEL-THREE	X	_	3	5	

Figure 4-13   Multidimensional Arrays.

because only the second, third, fifth, and tenth occurrences of the table overrode the default value of 'XXX'.

It is also possible to set up multidimensional arrays, as shown in Figure 4-13.

In this array, we have three occurrences of level-one fields. These are each made up of four occurrences of level-two fields, which are in turn made up of 5 occurrences of level-three fields which are each three bytes long. Thus the entire length of the table is

```
(3 L1) * (4 L2) * ((5 L3) * 3 BYTES)) = TABLE SIZE
   3   *   4   *           15
   3   *   60
 180 BYTES
```

If we wished to access the first occurrence of level-one, the third occurrence of level-two, and the second occurrence of level-three, the syntax would be

```
MULTI-DINEN-ARR(1,3,2)
```

Procedure Section

All of the actual logic and commands that are executed by an IDEAL program are contained in the procedure section. The commands can be entered into this open FILL-IN screen in any format and position as long as they meet the required syntax and are in executable order.

Commands are grouped into executable units called procedures. These groupings are similar to paragraphs in COBOL; they can be called from another procedure, executed, and then have program control returned to the line of code following the call command. These

```
<<PROCEDURE-NAME>> PROCEDURE
   LINES OF EXECUTABLE CODE
ENDPROC
```

Figure 4-14   Basic Procedure.

subprocedures are delimited by a LABEL statement and an ENDPROC statement as shown in Figure 4-14.

As we see in Figure 4-14, the procedure name itself is enclosed by the symbols << and >>. The 15-character procedure name must meet the naming requirements already mentioned. The word PROCE-DURE identifies this grouping of code as an executable unit to the compiler, and thus is also required.

Let's take a look at how this is used. (See Figure 4-15.)

In this example, we are setting the value of the working storage field WK-FIELD to 'A'. We then pass control to the procedure named CALLED-PROC with the command DO and the procedure name. This area sets the value of WK-FIELD to 'B'. Control then returns to the MAIN-DRIVE procedure which sets the value of WK-FIELD to 'C'.

Another form of execution control is the LOOP statement. This reiterative statement is used to control the number of times a command or group of commands is executed during processsing.

This command can be used by executing the enclosed commands until a certain condition is reached. This condition can be a value that is read or accumulated by the commands, or an index that the LOOP statement is controlling reaching a specified limit.

Figure 4-16 is using the table we defined earlier in Figure 4-11. In this figure we see two examples of how a LOOP statement can be

```
<<MAIN-DRIVE>> PROCEDURE
   MOVE 'A' TO WK-FIELD
   DO CALLED-PROC
   MOVE 'C' TO WK-FIELD
ENDPROC

<<CALLED-PROC>> PROCEDURE
   MOVE 'B' TO WK-FIELD
ENDPROC
```

Figure 4-15   Procedure Control Example.

```
MOVE 0 TO WK-SUBSR
LOOP UNTIL WK-SUBSR EQ WK-SEARCH
      ADD 1 TO WK-SUBSR
      MOVE TAXABLE-ST-NM(WK-SUBSR) TO WKTAX-ST-NM
ENDLOOP


LOOP VARYING WK-SUBSR FROM 1 BY 1
      UNTIL WK-SUBSR GT WK-SEARCH
      MOVE TAXABLE-ST-NM(WK-SUBSR) TO WKTAX-ST-NM
ENDLOOP
```

Figure 4-16   LOOP Statement Example.

built. Notice that, unlike COBOL, the commands are not required to be placed in a separate paragraph, but can be placed inside the actual LOOP command. Let's assume that WK-SEARCH was set to the value of 4 by a previous piece of code. Each LOOP statement in Figure 4-16 would place 'TEXAS' into the field WKTAX-ST-NM, but would get there in a slightly different manner.

The first figure would add 1 to WK-SUBSR and move 'INDIANA' to WKTAX-ST-NM. It would then check to see if WK-SUBSR was equal to WK-SEARCH. Since WK-SUBSR (1) is less than WK-SEARCH (3), the test would fail and the code would be executed again. This would continue until WK-SUBSR was equal to WK-SEARCH. At that time the value of WKTAX-ST-NM would be 'TEXAS'.

However, we need to amend our logic slightly if IDEAL is controlling our subscript. In the second statement IDEAL sets WK-SUBSR to 1 and and executes the command. It then increments WK-SUBSR to the value of 2 and checks the test. WKTAX-ST-NM is still 'INDIANA' and WK-SUBSR is still less than WK-SEARCH, but WK-SUBSR is equal to 2. Thus, for WKTAX-ST-NM to be equal to 'TEXAS' we must end the loop the first time that WK-SUBSR is greater that WK-SEARCH.

Because of this increment-then-check policy, we need to be very careful when we are using an IDEAL-controlled subscript to search a table for a certain value.

For example, suppose that we want to search our table for the state name that corresponds to a certain code. Our logic would look something like Figure 4-17.

In this code, we are moving our table entry to a working storage area for use in both the loop testing and the result test. By doing this we avoid the problem of having to decrement the index before

```
LOOP VARYING WK-SUBSR FROM 1 BY 1
        UNTIL WK-SUBSR GT WK-LIMIT
           OR WKTAX-ST-CD EQ WKTAXCD-SRCH
              MOVE TAXABLE-ST-TBL(WK-SUBSR) TO WK-TAXABLE-ST-AR
ENDLOOP


IF WKTAX-ST-CD EQ WKTAXCD-SRCH
   MOVE WKTAX-ST-CD TO PANELNM.TAXST-NAME
ELSE
   MOVE 'UNKNOWN'    TO PANELNM.TAXST-NAME
ENDIF
```

Figure 4-17   Table Search Example.

we can use it outside the loop. Thus, if WKTAXCD-SRCH was set to '045' the result would be 'TEXAS'. Without this precaution, or the complicated decrementation of the index, our search result would be 'VERMONT'. And everybody knows that Vermont is a long way from Texas.

Another version of the LOOP statement allows us to place the UNTIL statements after the execution statements:

```
LOOP VARYING WK-SUBSR FROM 1 BY 1
              MOVE TAXABLE-ST-TBL(WK-SUBSR) TO WK-TAXABLE-ST-AR
        UNTIL WK-SUBSR GT WK-LIMIT
           OR WKTAX-ST-CD EQ WKTAXCD-SRCH
ENDLOOP


IF WKTAX-ST-CD EQ WKTAXCD-SRCH
   MOVE WKTAX-ST-CD TO PANELNM.TAXST-NAME
ELSE
   MOVE 'UNKNOWN'    TO PANELNM.TAXST-NAME
ENDIF
```

Here, because the test is executed after the MOVE statement, the code will always be executed once. The advantage of this type of processing is that it eliminates any need to initialize the comparison fields. For example, if we changed the search code to

```
LOOP VARYING WK-SUBSR FROM 1 BY 1
        UNTIL WK-SUBSR GT WK-LIMIT
           OR WKTAX-ST-CD GT WKTAXCD-SRCH
              MOVE TAXABLE-ST-TBL(WK-SUBSR) TO WK-TAXABLE-ST-AR
```

```
ENDLOOP
IF WKTAX-ST-CD EQ WKTAXCD-SRCH
    MOVE WKTAX-ST-CD TO PANELNM.TAXST-NAME
ELSE
    MOVE 'UNKNOWN'   TO PANELNM.TAXST-NAME
ENDIF
```

we would always have to reinitialize the value of WKTAX-ST-CD. But by executing the move first and then making the test, the initialization is done for us.

It is also possible to specify the number of times that a LOOP statement is executed:

```
MOVE 0 TO WK-SUBSR
MOVE 'UNKNOWN'   TO PANELNM.TAXST-NAME
LOOP 10 TIMES
        ADD 1 TO WK-SUBSR
        MOVE TAXABLE-ST-TBL(WK-SUBSR) TO WK-TAXABLE-ST-AR
        IF WKTAX-ST-CD EQ WKTAXCD-SRCH
            MOVE WKTAX-ST-CD TO PANELNM.TAXST-NAME
        ENDIF
ENDLOOP
```

Here the program will always read each entry in the table. If the correct entry is not found, then the initial value of "UNKNOWN' will be the search result. This is the least efficient method, and should only be used if the program really has to read every entry in the table as opposed to ending when it finds the requested entry.

MOVE and SET Statements

MOVE and SET statements are used to copy the data from a source field into a target field. When the statement is executed the value is copied from one to another, and the value in the source field is retained.

The MOVE and SET statements can be grouped into one of five basic formats. These are

1. Population of an elementary numeric field
2. Population of an elementary alphanumeric field
3. Movement of one group to another
4. Setting of a predefined flag value
5. Setting of a condition name

To discuss these different MOVE statements, let us take a few moments to define some working storage fields so that we can have some examples to work with.

LEVEL	FIELD NAME ON/COPY	T	I	CH/DG	OCCUR	VALUE/COMMENT/DEP
1	SOURCE-FIELDS					
2	SRC-ALPHA-1	X	_	6		"ABCDEF"
2	SRC-ALPHA-2	X		3		"XYZ"
2	SRC-ALPHA-3	X		4		"1234"
2	SRC-ALPHA-4	X		3		"123"
2	SRC-ALPHA-5	X		3		"12"
2	SRC-ALPHA-6	X		4		"12.4"
2	SRC-NUMER-1	N		7		1234567
2	SRC-NUMER-2	N		7.2		12345.12
2	SRC-NUMER-3	N		3.4		123.1234
1	TARGET-FIELDS					
2	TAR-ALPHA-1	X		6		
2	TAR-ALPHA-2	X		3		
2	TAR-ALPHA-3	X		7		
2	TAR-ALPHA-4	X		8		
2	TAR-ALPHA-5	X		9		
2	TAR-NUMER-1	N		7		
2	TAR-NUMER-2	N		5.2		
2	TAR-NUMER-3	N		3.4		

FORMAT 1 — Move to Numeric Field

In the first format, the population of an elementary numeric field, we have the simple format:

```
SET NUMERIC-FIELD = [ NUMERIC-EXPRESSION      ]
                    [ ALPHANUMERIC-EXPRESSION ]

MOVE [ ALPHANUMERIC-EXPRESSION ] TO NUMERIC-FIELD
     [ NUMERIC-EXPRESSION       ]
```

Here we are attempting to populate a numeric field with either a numeric or an alphanumeric expression:

NUM	SOURCE FIELD	TARGET FIELD	RESULTING VALUE OF TARGET FIELD
1	SRC-NUMER-1	TAR-NUMER-1	1234567
2	SRC-NUMER-1	TAR-NUMER-2	1234567.00
3	SRC-NUMER-1	TAR-NUMER-3	TRUNCATION ABEND
4	SRC-NUMER-2	TAR-NUMER-1	12345
5	SRC-NUMER-2	TAR-NUMER-2	12345.12
6	SRC-NUMER-2	TAR-NUMER-3	TRUNCATION ABEND
7	SRC-NUMER-3	TAR-NUMER-1	123
8	SRC-NUMER-3	TAR-NUMER-2	123.1200
9	SRC-NUMER-3	TAR-NUMER-3	123.1234

Figure 4-18   Numeric Elementary Field to Numeric Elementary Field.

1. Numeric expression

   a. Elementary numeric field
   b. Mathematical equation
   c. Numeric literal

2. Alphanumeric expression

   a. Alphanumeric field with numeric data
   b. Alpha literal with numeric data

Both the MOVE statement and the SET statement work under the same processing rules.

1. If the source is a numeric-expression

   a. data is moved, and decimal places are aligned
   b. low order digits are truncated if required
   c. high order digit truncation causes an abend

2. If the source is an alphanumeric-expression

   a. data is converted to a number
   b. if field contains non numeric characters, an abend occurs.

From these rules, we can build a table showing the results of moving one field to another. (See Figure 4-18.)

NUM	SOURCE FIELD	TARGET FIELD	RESULTING VALUE OF TARGET FIELD
1	SRC-ALPHA-3	TAR-NUMER-1	1234
2	SRC-ALPHA-3	TAR-NUMER-2	1234.00
3	SRC-ALPHA-3	TAR-NUMER-3	TRUNCATION ABEND
1	SRC-ALPHA-4	TAR-NUMER-1	123
2	SRC-ALPHA-4	TAR-NUMER-2	123.00
3	SRC-ALPHA-4	TAR-NUMER-3	123.0000
1	SRC-ALPHA-5	TAR-NUMER-1	12
2	SRC-ALPHA-5	TAR-NUMER-2	12.00
3	SRC-ALPHA-5	TAR-NUMER-3	12.0000
1	SRC-ALPHA-6	TAR-NUMER-1	12
2	SRC-ALPHA-6	TAR-NUMER-2	12.40
3	SRC-ALPHA-6	TAR-NUMER-3	12.4000

Figure 4-19   Alpha Elementary Field to Numeric Elementary Field.

In reading this table, we can see that (in line 1) by moving the 7.2 digit numeric field SRC-NUMER-1 to the 7 digit field TAR-NUMER-1 the decimal points are dropped off, but moving it to the 7.2 digit numeric field aligns the data on the decimal point (line 2). Moving it to the 3.4 digit field TAR-NUMER-3 causes truncation of the higher order digits, and in turn an abend occurs. The rest of the examples are processed in a similar manner. (See Figure 4-19.)

This processing is very similar to the table in Figure 4-18 because, although we are handling alphanumeric fields, they are first translated to numeric values. Then the same rules that apply to numeric moves are applied. However, since the fields SRC-ALPHA-1 and SRC-ALPHA-2 both contain character values, they would cause a DATA EXCEPTION (OC-7) abend.

FORMAT 2 — Move to Alphanumeric Field

A move to an alphanumeric field is a great deal less complex. In this format, the system simply starts laying the data from the source field into the target field from left to right. Because of this we can state the following rules:

1. If the value of the source is greater than the length of the target field, then truncation occurs to the right side.

```
NUM SOURCE FIELD     TARGET FIELD    RESULTING VALUE OF TARGET FIELD

  1  SRC-ALPHA-1      TAR-ALPHA-2       ABC

  2  SRC-ALPHA-2      TAR-ALPHA-2       XYZ

  3  SRC-ALPHA-4      TAR-ALPHA-2       123

  4  SRC-ALPHA-5      TAR-ALPHA-2       12
```

Figure 4-20   Elementary Field to Alpha Elementary Field.

2. If the value of the source is less than the target field, then the remaining right side of the target is padded with spaces.
3. If they are the same, an exact duplicate is made.

Line 1 of Figure 4-20 shows this truncation. Line 2 shows exact fit with alpha data. Line 3 shows exact fit with alpha-numeric data. Line 4 shows right side padding with spaces.

FORMAT 3 — Move by Name or Position

This format is used to move large groups of data from one area to another. This can be used to load items into a table or to populate a dataview from a working storage area.

There are some problems with both of these commands, which are the same as the COBOL MOVE CORRESPONDING command. MOVE BY POSITION requires exact alignment to function. Thus any change to the database requires a change to the working storage areas, so that they line up. One of the advantages of a relational database is that only the programs that use a particular field have to be changed when the database definition is changed. By using this command we eliminate one of our relational database advantages. MOVE BY NAME only works on elementary level items. It is also difficult to detect a misspelled name, which would prevent a match and consequently cause the field not to be populated.

To discourage the use of this bad coding habit, we will forgo furthur discussion of this command.

FORMAT 4 — Setting a Predefined Flag

```
SET  FLAG-NAME  EQ   TRUE     (ONLY THE SET COMMAND IS AVAILABLE)
                =    FALSE
```

We simply reference the flag field by name and set it to either TRUE or FALSE with the reserved words.

FORMAT 5 — Setting a Condition Name

```
SET CONDITION-NAME = TRUE     (ONLY THE SET COMMAND IS AVAILABLE)
```

Here we again reference the name of the condition, and set it to the desired value. If we defined the field *color* as

```
LEVEL FIELD NAME            T I CH/DG OCCUR VALUE/COMMENT/DEP ON

_____ _____  _ _ _____  _____ _____

1     FORM-5-EXAMPLE
2       COLOR               X     1
        RED                 C                "R"
        BLUE                C                "B"
        YELLOW              C                "Y"
        GREEN               C                "G"
```

and we executed the command:

```
SET RED = TRUE
```

IDEAL would move the value of 'R' to the field COLOR. Then, if the condition "IF RED" was encountered, it would pass.

Arithmetic Functions

IDEAL also has the standard arithmetic expressions of ADD, SUBTRACT, MULTIPLY, and DIVIDE. These commands are very straightforward; we simply add to and subtract from two fields.

```
ADD      INCREMENTING-VALUE TO    BASE-FIELD
SUBTRACT DECREMENTING-VALUE FROM BASE-FIELD
```

With these commands we can increase or decrease a *base field* by a given value. The *base field* serves as both the original value and the target field. The operating value can be either a number or a numeric expression. It is also important to note that

1. Both fields must begin with numeric values.

2. Both fields do not have to have the same decimal precision; alignment is based on the smaller value.
3. An error will occur if the first operand is longer than the second operand.
4. An overflow error will occur if the result is longer that the second operand.

Besides the two explicit ADD and SUBTRACT commands, arithmetic commands can be executed through use of the FORMAT 1 SET statements.

```
SET TARGET-FIELD = FIELD-1 FUNCTION FIELD-2
```

where FUNCTION is one of the standard arithmetic commands:

1. + ADDITION
2. - SUBTRACTION
3. * MULTIPLICATION
4. / DIVISION

We can also do exponentiation by placing "**EXPONENT" in the function area, where "EXPONENT" is an integer field containing the value of the exponent.

These expressions follow the standard order of evaluation, which is

1. Parenthesis
2. Exponentiation
3. Multiplication
4. Division
5. Addition
6. Subtraction
7. Left to right

IDEAL Internal Functions

IDEAL has a number of internal functions that can be used to accomplish different tasks. The names of these functions are reserved words and each starts with a $ symbol.

These functions can be grouped into one of four classifications:

1. Informational
2. Data movement or manipulation

3. Numeric
4. Boolean

Informational Functions

The *informational* functions provide information to the program by being the source field in a MOVE or SET statement. Thus we would have the command:

```
MOVE $FUNCTION TO TARGET-FIELD.
```

These functions include the following pieces of information:

1. $SPACES — moves spaces (HEX 40) to the target field.
2. $HIGH — moves high values (HEX FF) to the target field.
3. $LOW — Moves low values (HEX 00) to the target field.
4. $TERMINAL-ID — four character terminal identification, which relates to the terminal at which the program is currently running.
5. $TRANSACTION-ID — four character transaction identification used to access IDEAL.
6. $USER-ID — returns the three-character IDEAL user identification code for the user under whose ID the program is running.
7. $USER-NAME — returns the 15-character user name.
8. $LENGTH — returns the physical length of an alphanumeric string.
9. $DATE — returns the current date in the specified format.
10. $TIME — returns the current time in the specified format

The $TIME and $DATE functions have multiple formats which can be manipulated by adjusting a literal, which takes the form:

```
$DATE('LITERAL')     $TIME('LITERAL')
```

The $DATE literal is created by arranging certain codes. If we assume that today's date is the 16th of August, 1986, we could build the following table:

```
CODE          MEANING                  RESULT


YEAR      - YEAR IN FULL               1986
YY        - YEAR WITHOUT CENTURY         86
```

```
Y          - YEAR WITHOUT DECADE        6

MONTH      - MONTH SPELLED OUT      AUGUST
LCMONTH    - MONTH SPELLED OUT      August (FIRST LETTER IS UPPERCASE
                                           OTHERS ARE LOWERCASE)
MON        - MONTH ABBREVIATION      AUG
LCMON      - MONTH ABBREVIATION      Aug   (FIRST LETTER IS UPPERCASE
                                           OTHERS ARE LOWERCASE)
MM         - 2 DIGIT MONTH
             WITH LEADING ZERO        08
M          - 2 DIGTH MONTH
             WITHOUT LEADING ZERO     8

DD         - 2 DIGIT DAY
             WITH LEADING ZERO        16
D          - 2 DIGIT DAY
             WITHOUT LEADING ZERO     16
DDD        - 3 DIGIT DAY, NUMERIC,
             JULIAN DAY OF YEAR
WEEKDAY    - UPPERCASE DAY, SPELLED
             SPELLED OUT            SUNDAY
LCWEEKDAY  DAY SPELLED OUT          Sunday
DAY        - DAY ABBREVIATION       SUN
LCDAY      - DAY ABBREVIATION       Sun
```

We can then place any symbols or punctuation that we wish to use inside the literal. Thus the command LIST $DATE('YY/MM/DD') on our example date would yield the result 86/08/16.

We can also use this command to apply an *edit pattern* on, or to execute a *conversion* of, a supplied date other than the current date. To do this, we would code the command:

```
LIST $DATE('YY/MM/DD',DATE='YYMMDD')
```

where the YYMMDD is the literal date that we wish to process. It is required to be in the year — month — day format, or an error will occur. We can also code the command with the name of a field that contains the date in the proper format.

```
LIST $DATE('YY/MM/DD',DATE=WK-DATE-FIELD)
```

Other date manipulation functions include

1. $INTERNAL-DATE — returns the numeric internal date for the date requested. Value will be the number of days since 31 Dec., 1900.
2. $DAY — returns the numeric value of the day of the month requested.
3. $WEEKDAY — returns the numeric day of the week for the requested date. (Sunday=1,Monday=2,Tuesday=3)
4. $TODAY — returns the numeric internal date for the current date. Value will be the number of days since 31 Dec., 1900.
5. $MONTH — returns the numeric value of the requested month.
6. $YEAR — returns the four-digit year for the requested date.
7. $VERIFY-DATE — Boolean test to see if the requested date is a valid date.

The $TIME function works in a similar manner. If the current time is 12:30:10 PM, we could build the following table:

CODE	MEANING		RESULT
HH	HOUR WITH LEADING ZERO		12
H	HOUR WITHOUT LEADING ZERO		12
PP	HOUR WITH AM/PM DESIGNATION WITH LEADING ZERO		12 PM
P	HOUR WITH AM/PM DESIGNATION WITHOUT LEADING ZERO		12 PM
MM	MINUTE	30	30
SS	SECOND	10	10

Again any non-alphabetic character will be displayed as it appears in the literal. The command:

```
LIST $TIME('HH:MM:SS')
```

would yield the result 12:30:10.

Data Movement and Manipulation

It is also possible to do simple data manipulation with these IDEAL functions. These commands take the format:

```
MOVE $FUNCTION(SOURCE-FIELD,'PARAMETERS') TO TARGET FIELD
```

and include the following commands:

1. $EDIT — formats the field based on an edit pattern.
2. $ABS — sets a numeric field to its absolute value.
3. $NUMBER — translates an alphanumeric field to a numeric value using the same rules as the translation in a FORMAT 1 MOVE statement (move to a numeric field).
4. $ROUND — rounds a numeric field or expression based on the designated level.
5. $STRING — combines a group of elementary fields into a single field.
6. $SUBSTR — moves a portion of a large field into a smaller field
7. $TRANSLATE — translates the positions in a field from one value to another.
8. $HEX-TO-CHAR — moves the hexadecimal value of a field to a display field. The receiving field should be twice the length of the sending field.
9. $CHAR-TO-HEX — translates a string of display characters to hex format. There should always be an even number of display characters so that the conversion will work correctly.
10. $PAD — returns the value of a string that results from padding another string with certain characters.
11. $TRIM — returns the value of a string that results from trimming leading or trailing characters.

The $EDIT function takes data from a source field and places it in a target field with a new format. This feature can be used to display or suppress signs on numeric fields, add commas or punctuation to fields, or suppress the printing of zeroes on a numeric field. The command is

```
$EDIT(FIELD OR LITERAL,PIC='EDIT-PATTERN')
```

where the EDIT-PATTERN contains the definition of the pattern to be applied to the field or literal. Appendix A contains a table showing the valid characters that can be used in an edit pattern and the results of their usage. By referring to this table, we can see that the command

```
MOVE $EDIT(TOTAL-AMT,PIC=ZZ,ZZZ,ZZ9.99-)
      TO REPORT-FIELD.TOTAL-AMT
```

when applied to a field whose value is -2300.00 would print the result

```
2,300.00-
```

Another use for this command can be seen in the following example. If we have a line number which we need to increment and then display an alpha version with the leading zeroes in place, we could code it as

```
ADD 1 TO NUMERIC-LINE-NO
MOVE $EDIT(NUMERIC-LINE-NO,PIC='999') TO ALPHA-LINE-NO
LIST ALPHA-LINE-NO
```

which would place the leading zeroes as characters in the alpha field.

The $ROUND function rounds a numeric value based on either a supplied factor or on the attributes of a defined field. The command looks like this:

$$\text{\$ROUND}(X, \left\{ \begin{array}{l} \text{FACTOR=F} \\ \text{ATTR=id} \end{array} \right\})$$

The factor points to the level the number would be rounded to. If we have a factor that is greater than zero, say 5, the number would be rounded to the nearest multiple of 5. The value 233 would come out as 235.

If the factor is zero, then no rounding occurs.

If the rounding factor is less than zero, the number would be rounded up to that point. To round to the nearest tenth, the factor would be .1. To round to the nearest hundredth, the factor would be .01, and so forth.

The following examples show how this works:

```
MOVE $ROUND(257.6,FACTOR=1)     258   ROUNDS TO THE NEAREST INTEGER
MOVE $ROUND(257.6,FACTOR=5)     260   ROUNDS TO THE NEAREST MULTIPLE
                                      OF FIVE
MOVE $ROUND(2.5786,FACTOR=.1)   2.6   ROUNDS TO THE NEAREST TENTH
```

```
MOVE $ROUND(2.4786,FACTOR=.1)   2.5     "     "   "       "       "
MOVE $ROUND(2.4444,FACTOR=.1)   2.4     "     "   "       "       "
MOVE $ROUND(2.5786,FACTOR=.01) 2.58   ROUNDS  TO  THE  NEAREST
HUNDREDTH
MOVE $ROUND(2.4786,FACTOR=.01) 2.48     "     "   "       "       "
MOVE $ROUND(2.4444,FACTOR=.01) 2.44     "     "   "       "       "


SET WK-RESULT = $ROUND(21.22 / 7, FACTOR=.1)
                         3.3   ROUNDS  TO  THE  NEAREST  TENTH
```

The attribute (ATTR) clause causes the result to be rounded so that it will fit in the defined field. If we selected a field that had two decimal points, it would be the same as using a factor of .01.

The $STRING command is used to put multiple fields together in a single expression. We could write the command:

```
MOVE $STRING('SHIP-POINT ' , WK-PREV-SHPPNT , ' CONVERTED TO ' ,
            WK-NEW-SHPPNT)
  TO REPORT-FIELD.RESULT
```

which would result in the display:

```
SHIP-POINT AA CONVERTED TO AB.
```

With this command we are able to save working storage space. If we were to code this message in working storage, we would see the definition:

```
1   WK-CONV-MSG
 2     WK-CNV-MSG-F1    X    11        'SHIP-POINT'
 2     WK-PREV-SHPPNT   X    2
 2     WK-CNV-MSG-F2    X    14        ' CONVERTED TO
 2     WK-NEW-SHPPNT    X    2
```

In this example the use of the $STRING command has saved us 25 bytes of working storage.

The $SUBSTR command is the opposite of the $STRING function, in that it returns part of a larger string. We could take a longer field, like *customer-name*, and make an abreviated name without redefining a new working-storage field. Thus we could have the command:

```
SET CUSTOMER-DVW.ABREV-NAME = $SUBSR(CUST-NAME,START=1,LENGTH=20)
```

Without this command, we would have to define an additional working storage field and move the CUST-NAME from the database to the new field. By using this command, we again save ourselves working-storage space.

The $TRANSLATE command changes the value of single bytes in a longer field. We could move a numeric field to an alpha field, and replace the resulting spaces with zeroes.

```
ADD 1 TO NUMERIC-LINE-NO
MOVE NUMERIC-LINE-NO TO ALPHA-LINE-NO
SET ALPHA-LINE-NO = $TRANSLATE(ALPHA-LINE-NO,FROM=' ',TO='0')
```

The $PAD command takes a string, and while moving it to another field places padding values on either end of the string. The command is

```
$PAD(ALPHA-EXPRESSION,LENGTH=NUM-EXP,(RIGHT= )    ('A')
                                     (LEFT=  )    (ALPHA-FIELD)
                                     (CENTER=)
```

where

> ALPHA-EXPRESSION — is the string that we wish to manipulate.
> NUM-EXP — is the length of the resulting string.
> RIGHT/LEFT/CENTER — is the justification of the base string in the receiving field.
> 'A'/ALPHA-FIELD — is what the resulting string is to be padded with, either the character in the quotes, or value contained in ALPHA-FIELD.

As an example, lets say that we have the string 'POMONA' that we wish to center in the 10-byte field CITY, and surround with '*'. Our command would be:

```
MOVE $PAD('POMONA',LENGTH=10,(CENTER='*')) TO CITY
```

with the result '**POMONA**'.

The $TRIM is the opposite of the $PAD.

```
$TRIM(ALPHA-EXPRESSION,(RIGHT= )    ('A')              )
                      (LEFT=  )    (ALPHA-FIELD)  )

MOVE $TRIM(CITY,(RIGHT='*')) to CITY2
```

The result of this command would be '**POMONA '.

Numeric Functions

These functions include operations that manipulate values within a program in an arithmetic manner. These include

1. $COUNT — counts the number of times that a certain label in a procedure is executed.

   ```
   $COUNT(LABEL)
   ```

2. $INDEX — reads a large string, and finds the starting position of a smaller substring.

   ```
   $INDEX(SEARCH-STRING,SEARCH='SEARCH-FOR')
   ```

3. $REMAINDER — finds the remainder after a division is processed; for example:

   ```
   SET R = $REMAINDER(M,DIV=N)
   ```

   would set the field R to be the value of the remainder of M divided by N.
4. $SQRT — finds the square root of the given number.

   ```
   $SQRT(NUMERIC-EXPRESSION)
   ```

Boolean Functions

IDEAL Boolean functions are placed in an IF statement, and return a value of true or false. These commands include

1. $NUMERIC — determines if a field has only numeric characters, and thus can be converted to a numeric field.

2. $ALPHABETIC — determines if a field contains only standard characters, or spaces.
3. $VERIFY — determines if a field contains only specific values.

If the $NUMERIC test is applied to an alphanumeric field, the function will return true if the field has spaces in it. Thus the code

```
MOVE $STRING('    ','123') TO WK-FIELD
IF $NUMERIC(WK-FIELD)
   MOVE $NUMBER(WK-FIELD) TO WK-NUMERIC-FIELD
ENDIF
```

will abend because we tried to move spaces to a numeric field. To avoid this abend, we would have to write the following:

```
MOVE $STRING('    ', '123') TO WK-FIELD
IF $NUMERIC(WK-FIELD)
   SET WK-FIELD = $TRANSLATE(WK-FIELD,FROM=' ',TO='0')
   MOVE $NUMBER(WK-FIELD) TO WK-NUMERIC-FIELD
ENDIF
```

The $VERIFY can help eliminate some of this problem. The command is

```
$VERIFY((ALPHA-EXPRESSION),AGAINST=(NUMERIC,UCALPHA,LCALPHA))
```

which causes IDEAL to compare the characters against a selected, predefined character set (NUMERIC,UCALPHA,LCALPHA). Any combination of the three character sets can be selected. In addition, any other characters can be placed in quotes inside the AGAINST clause. The contents of the three character sets are

NUMERIC — only the digits 0–9; the $NUMERIC check recognizes the digits, leading spaces, trailing spaces, decimal points, and leading or trailing + or - signs.
UCALPHA — uppercase letters A–Z and spaces.
CALPHA — lowercase letters a–z and spaces.

From the preceding example, the command

```
MOVE $STRING('    ','123') TO WK-FIELD
IF $VERIFY(WK-FIELD,AGAINST=(NUMERIC))
   MOVE $NUMBER(WK-FIELD) TO WK-NUMERIC-FIELD
ENDIF
```

would have been false, thus avoiding the possible numeric abend. In addition, the commands

```
MOVE $STRING('12','.','3') TO WK-FIELD
IF $VERIFY(WK-FIELD,AGAINST=(NUMERIC,'.'))
    MOVE $NUMBER(WK-FIELD) TO WK-NUMERIC-FIELD
ENDIF
```

would have returned a true from the $VERIFY test, moving 12.3 to the field WK-NUMERIC-FIELD.

Conditional Statements

The conditional, or IF, statement is also used for program execution control. This statement takes the following form:

```
IF CONDITION
THEN
    STATEMENTS-T
ELSE
    STATEMENTS-F
ENDIF
```

where IF is the required reserve word, CONDITION is a logical comparison which can be either true or false, THEN is an optional keyword, STATEMENTS-T are statements that are executed if the condition is found to be true, STATEMENTS-F are optional statements that are executed if the condition is false, and ELSE is a keyword that is required when STATEMENTS-F are present.

The ENDIF statement is required whenever an IF statement is present, and is used to delimit the statement. When an ENDIF statement is encountered, all processing on the corresponding IF statement is ended.

For example:

```
IF WK-FIELD EQ '045'
    IF WK-SUBSR LT WK-LIMIT
       MOVE WK-NAME TO PANELNM.STATE-NM
    ELSE
       IF WK-SUBSR EQ WK-SUBLIMIT
          MOVE WK-ELSE-NAME TO PANELNM.STATENM
       ELSE
```

```
            MOVE 'UNKNOWN'     TO PANELNM.STATENM
        ENDIF
        IF WK-STATE-NM GT 'ALA'
            ADD 1 TO WK-COUNTER
        ENDIF
    ENDIF
ENDIF
```

The statement IF WK-STATE-NM GT 'ALA' would be queried regardless of the outcome of the comparision of WK-SUBSR to WK-SUBLIMIT (the third IF statement).

If we were to build this same statement in COBOL

```
IF WK-FIELD EQ '045'
    IF WK-SUBSR LT WK-LIMIT
        MOVE WK-NAME TO PANELNM.STATE-NM
    ELSE
        IF WK-SUBSR EQ WK-SUBLIMIT
            MOVE WK-ELSE-NAME TO PANELNM.STATENM
        ELSE
            MOVE 'UNKNOWN'     TO PANELNM.STATENM.

IF WK-FIELD EQ '045'
    IF WK-SUBSR LT WK-LIMIT
        MOVE WK-NAME TO PANELNM.STATE-NM
    ELSE
        IF WK-STATE-NM GT 'ALA'
            ADD 1 TO WK-COUNTER.
```

we would have to build the lower part of the structure into a small fragmented paragraph. Thus we can easily see the power of the IF-ENDIF structure in IDEAL.

SELECT

IDEAL also has a very powerful case structure available called the SELECT statement. This statement is used when we can have multiple values for the same field, all of which trigger selected responses from the program. This statement can respond on either the first true condition or on every true condition.

The format of this statement is as follows:

```
SELECT SELECT-SUBJECT

               NUMERIC-EXPRESSION
       WHEN  [ ALPHANUMERIC-EXPRESSION ]


               STATEMENTS-W
       WHEN NONE STATEMENTS-N
       WHEN ANY   STATEMENTS-A
ENDSELECT
```

where SELECT is the keyword command, WHEN marks the conditional statement, and ENDSELECT marks the end of the SELECT statement.

As an example, suppose we wanted to search for our state names without using a table, but wanted to use a SELECT statement instead. We would set it up as follows.

```
SELECT FIRST WKTAX-ST-SRCH
       WHEN '011' MOVE 'INDIANA'      TO PANELNM.STATENM
       WHEN '012' MOVE 'IOWA'         TO PANELNM.STATENM
       WHEN '035' MOVE 'PENNSYLVANIA' TO PANELNM.STATENM
       WHEN '045' MOVE 'TEXAS'        TO PANELNM.STATENM
       WHEN '048' MOVE 'VERMONT'      TO PANELNM.STATENM
       WHEN '050' MOVE 'HAWAII'       TO PANELNM.STATENM
       WHEN NONE  MOVE 'UNKNOWN'      TO PANELNM.STATENM
       WHEN ANY   ADD 1 TO WK-CN-FOUND
ENDSELECT
```

Again, if WKTAX-ST-SRCH was equal to '045', the result of our search would be "TEXAS." If WKTAX-ST-SRCH was equal to '046' then PANELNM.STATENM would be set equal to UNKNOWN. The WHEN ANY statement is executed whenever any of the other statements (except the WHEN NONE) are executed. Thus when WKTAX-ST-SRCH was '045', WK-CNT-FOUND was incremented. When it was '046', WK-CNT-FOUND was not incremented.

The word FIRST in the preceding statement is the optional default and can be added for readability.

It is also possible to have a SELECT statement execute every time it finds a positive condition instead of just on the first positive condition. This is done by specifying SELECT EVERY on the command statement instead of SELECT or SELECT FIRST.

In addition to functioning against different values of the same field, it is possible to specify functions against different combinations of fields and values.

For example:

```
SELECT EVERY ACTION
         WHEN FG-SHIP-TO-ERR EQ 1 DO SHIP-TO-ERROR
         WHEN FG-SHIP-TO-ERR EQ 2 DO SHIP-TO-INVAL
         WHEN FG-SALES-T-ERR EQ 1 DO SALES-TER-ERR
         WHEN FG-CUST-NO-ERR EQ 1 DO SHIP-TO-ERROR
         WHEN OTHER               DO OTHER-ERRORS
ENDSELECT
```

Thus, if any of these error codes are valued, the program will execute the paragraphs which deal with each of these errors. The keyword OTHER can be used interchangeably with the keyword NONE.

With this command we have an excellent tool for writing very structured and readable procedure code.

Database Access Statements

As we saw in our discussions in Chapter 2, the database files are accessed by an application program through previously defined dataviews and a procedure statement which has the following format:

```
FOR OPERAND DATAVIEW-NAME (NO UPDATE)
     WHERE       SELECTION-CONDITION
     ORDERED-BY (UNIQUE) (ASCENDING/DESCENDING) IDENTIFIER
           STATEMENTS
     ERROR PROCEDURES
           (IE: WHEN  NONE
                WHEN DUPLICATE)
ENDFOR
```

where

FOR — is the keyword verb.
OPERAND — determines what type of processing will be done.

DATAVIEW-NAME — is the name of the predefined logical view of the needed data.

NO UPDATE — tells IDEAL that these records are not going to be updated, therefore there is no need to obtain exclusive control of the records. This will override the command UPDATE = Y on the dataview definition.

WHERE keyword — shows that a record selection is to be made.

SELECTION CONDITION — is the selection that is to be made, and contains the database field to be selected on, a relational operator, and a value, literal, expression, or another field.

ORDERED BY — is a keyword that invokes a sort of the records that are extracted from the database before presentation to the application. They can be in either ascending or descending order, by field value. The unique operand tells IDEAL to return only one record for each value encountered by the selection routine.

IDENTIFIER — is the field on which the records are sorted.

STATEMENTS — are the procedure statements that access or update the data on the database record.

ERROR PROCEDURES — is code that is invoked when a dataview error is encountered. (Note, the words *error procedures* do not actually appear in the code but are used to show the positioning of commands such as WHEN DUPLICATE and WHEN NONE.)

When a FOR statement is encountered by the IDEAL compiler, the proper native database commands are placed in the object code. The dataview definition is also placed in the working storage of the object code. This space then serves as the IO area for the database segment in the program.

The selection of the native commands is based on the operand which is coded in the FOR statement. These operands can be

1. FIRST — reads the index and obtains the first record which has a key equal to the required value.
2. EACH — reads the index and obtains each record where the requested search field has a value equal to the requested value.
3. NEXT — reads every succeeding record on a QSAM dataset.
4. NEW — inserts a new record to the database.

We also pointed out in Chapter 2 that there are two different logical access methods that can be employed, either the READ or the LOCATE. The selection between these two is also made by the IDEAL compiler; its decision is based on the type of dataview selected. If a KEY-ONLY dataview is selected, then the LOCATE commands will be used. Otherwise, the READ commands will be used.

Let us look at some examples of the FOR statement to see how all of this works. Again, we are still referring to our logical model.

FOR FIRST

With this statement, we wish to process a single occurrence of a record. We do that based on the dataview type that we select.

1. If we select a key-only dataview, we can locate the record's position in the index. The FOR statement would look like this:

```
FOR FIRST KEY-ONLY-DVW
     WHERE KEY-ONLY-DVW.MASTER-KEY EQ SEARCH-VALUE
          SET FOUND-FLAG EQ TRUE
     WHEN  NONE
          SET FOUND-FLAG EQ FALSE
ENDFOR
```

With this statement, the application determines if there is an index entry with a certain value, and then it sets an appropriate flag in the application. This statement would in turn be compiled to use the LOCKY command.

2. If we select a normal update dataview, we would READ, HOLD, UPDATE, and REPLACE the record with the following FOR statement.

```
FOR FIRST DATAVIEW-1
     WHERE DATAVIEW-1.MASTER-KEY EQ SEARCH-VALUE
          MOVE A-NEW-VALUE TO DATAVIEW-1.FLDB
          MOVE A-NEW-VALUE TO DATAVIEW-1.FLDD
          MOVE A-NEW-VALUE TO DATAVIEW-1.FLDG
          SET FOUND-FLAG EQ TRUE
     WHEN  NONE
          SET FOUND-FLAG EQ FALSE
ENDFOR
```

When the FOR statement with an update dataview is encountered, IDEAL will use the logical command READ AND HOLD and will move the found record to the IO-AREA of the program. The application then updates the values of the fields in the IO-AREA as shown, and sets the found flag to true.

When the ENDFOR is encountered by the program, an UP-DATE command is executed, which will of course overlay the data in the database with the values that are now in the working storage area.

3. There will be a large number of situations in our processing where we are not be updating the database, but are only getting data for informational processing. Thus we have an opportunity for further efficiency by creating another special type of dataview, called the "read only" dataview. As the name implies, this dataview can be read, but the database cannot be updated by the FOR statement. The FOR statement is the same, but at compile time, the compiler uses a READ command instead of the READ AND HOLD. By doing this, we can eliminate a number of functions that the program would have to do if we used an update dataview. These are

   a. Elimination of the writing of the before processing image
   b. Elimination of the establishment of exclusive control
   c. Elimination of the writing of the after processing image
   d. Elimination of the comparison of before and after images
   e. Elimination of the physical update of the database
   f. Elimination of dynamic log processing

Thus we can see a significant savings in IO and processing time on each transaction.

FOR EACH

The FOR EACH statement works with the same three separate dataview types that the FOR FIRST statement uses. The difference is again found in the compiler output as it creates the object module.

If we were to use a key-only dataview:

```
FOR EACH   KEY-ONLY-DVW
      WHERE KEY-ONLY-DVW.MASTER-KEY EQ SEARCH-VALUE
            SET FOUND-FLAG EQ TRUE
      WHEN  NONE
            SET FOUND-FLAG EQ FALSE
ENDFOR
```

IDEAL will create a logical LOCATE to find the first occurrence of this value in the index, and will then issue a series of LOCATE NEXT DUPLICATE or LOCATE SEQUENTIAL commands until the entire index has been searched. This choice will again depend on our selection of a secondary key or the master key for our search.

IDEAL has also provided a number of other operands:

1. EQ — equal to
2. GT — greater than
3. LT — less than
4. GE — greater than or equal to
5. LE — less than or equal to

Therefore, if we were to code our FOR statement as

```
FOR EACH   KEY-ONLY-DVW
    WHERE KEY-ONLY-DVW.MASTER-KEY GE SEARCH-VALUE
          SET FOUND-FLAG EQ TRUE
    WHEN   NONE
          SET FOUND-FLAG EQ FALSE
ENDFOR
```

the program would pull the KEY-ONLY-DVW record which had a value EQUAL TO SEARCH-VALUE, or the first one that it found which is GREATER THAN SEARCH-VALUE with the LOCATE command. The succeeding records would then be pulled in with successive LOCATE SEQUENTIAL commands until the search was exhausted.

The logic is the same for the update and the read only dataview processing. Again the compiler will create a logical LOCATE command to position us in the database, and then create a series of READ commands to complete the request.

While the dataview is only updateable within the FOR statement, the dataview area is accessible at anytime after the corresponding database has been successfully accessed. Thus, we could write the following program:

```
FOR FIRST DATAVIEW-1
    WHERE DATAVIEW-1.MASTER-KEY EQ SEARCH-VALUE
          MOVE DATAVIEW-1.FLDA TO PANEL1.FLDA
          SET FOUND-FLAG EQ TRUE
    WHEN   NONE
          SET FOUND-FLAG EQ FALSE
ENDFOR

MOVE DATAVIEW-1.FLDA TO PANEL2.FLDA
ADD  DATAVIEW-1.FLDC TO WK-COUNTER
```

which shows us an example of using a dataview's fields outside the FOR structure. In this case, the working area that contains the dataview is populated by the call. Then, like any other temporary storage area, the fields remain populated after the ENDFOR. However, the programmer must be careful to avoid two potential problems:

1. If a successful call to the database has not yet been made with this dataview, any attempt to use the fields that belong to it will result in an abend called INVALID REFERENCE OF FIELD.
2. If a successful call has been made earlier in the run, then the dataview area will be populated with the data from that last call. Then, if the program failed to find the proper record, any references to the dataview would pick up the values of the last occurrence instead of the record that the program asked for.

The WHEN NONE clause is supplied to avoid these kinds of problems. This part of the statement is executed when the database search request cannot be fulfilled. We can populate our working storage fields with an initial value whenever we do not get the expected record. This can be done by setting a FLAG to tell the rest of the program that the expected record was not received, or by doing the actual moves under the WHEN NONE clause. It is also important to note that updates to the database are not possible within the WHEN NONE clause. This is because the application is unable to establish a position in the database. The WHEN NONE clause does not have any effect on the data that is resident in the dataview area. The dataview will still be unaccessable if there has not yet been a successful call made to the database. Similarly, if a previous call was successful, then the data from that call will still be resident in the dataview area.

DELETE

As we have seen, a FOR statement with an update dataview has exclusive control on a record when it executes its READ AND HOLD. Because of this ability, we do not need a specific call to the database just to delete a record.

```
FOR FIRST DATAVIEW-1
    WHERE DATAVIEW-1.MASTER-KEY EQ SEARCH-VALUE
        MOVE DATAVIEW-1.FLDA TO PANEL1.FLDA
```

```
          DELETE DATAVIEW-1
          SET FOUND-FLAG EQ TRUE
     WHEN NONE
          SET FOUND-FLAG EQ FALSE
ENDFOR
```

Just as a FOR statement does a logical update when a field on the dataview in working storage is changed, a logical delete is issued when the DELETE command is encountered. After a DELETE command is executed, the program cannot access the dataview area until another successful READ command is issued, because "logically" the record no longer exists. The record is physically deleted when the ENDFOR is reached.

FOR NEW

The FOR NEW statement, which is used to invoke the logical insert call, is perhaps the simplest of the database access statements, in that it primarily consists of the command, the name of the dataview being used, the statements that load the record, and an ENDFOR.

```
FOR NEW DATAVIEW-1
          MOVE PANEL1.MASTER-KEY TO  DATAVIEW-1.MASTER-KEY
          MOVE PANEL1.FLDA       TO  DATAVIEW-1.FLDA
          MOVE PANEL1.FLDB       TO  DATAVIEW-1.FLDB
          MOVE PANEL1.FLDC       TO  DATAVIEW-1.FLDC
          MOVE PANEL1.FLDD       TO  DATAVIEW-1.FLDD
ENDFOR
```

In this example, we have the situation where a database record is being created from data passed to it by an on-line screen. The application opens the dataview area to allow the fields to be loaded. Any field that is not physically loaded by the application will be populated by a default value of spaces for an alphanumeric field, and zeroes for a numeric field. However, from our own experience, we would recommend that any dataview that is used for inserting records into the database be the full record dataview, and that all of the fields on the record should be physically populated by the program. We say this because it

1. Ensures the correct population of the fields, rather than relying on the IDEAL language defaults.

2. Ensures exclusive control of the record that we are trying to create.
3. Enhances program documentation and readability.
4. Forces the programmer to consider the proper initial value of each field, so that data integrity can be maintained.

As with all of the other FOR statements, the physical update to the database occurs when the ENDFOR statement is reached. At this point the program performs all of the insert functions of index structuring and duplicate searching that we discussed in Chapter 2. It is at this point that the most common error processing occurs, called the DUPLICATE MASTER KEY error. Here, as the name implies, the master key of the the record that we are trying to add to the database already exists. This event causes the program to abend.

This abend can be avoided through the use of the WHEN DUPLI-CATE clause. Like the WHEN NONE clause, this clause traps the problem and allows processing to continue normally.

```
FOR NEW DATAVIEW-1
          MOVE PANEL1.MASTER-KEY TO   DATAVIEW-1.MASTER-KEY
          MOVE PANEL1.FLDA       TO   DATAVIEW-1.FLDA
          MOVE PANEL1.FLDB       TO   DATAVIEW-1.FLDB
          MOVE PANEL1.FLDC       TO   DATAVIEW-1.FLDC
          MOVE PANEL1.FLDD       TO   DATAVIEW-1.FLDD
          MOVE "RECORD ADDED"    TO   PANEL1.MESSAGE
      WHEN DUPLICATE
          MOVE "RECORD ALREADY EXISTS" TO PANEL1.MESSAGE
  ENDFOR
```

This code will then inform the operator that the record that he is trying to enter already exists. Without the clause, the program would abend, leaving the operator with only confusion.

In early versions of IDEAL, we could not place a FOR NEW statement under the WHEN NONE clause of another FOR statement. This was because when the WHEN NONE clause is executed, all positioning in, and logical updates to, the database were backed out at the ENDFOR statement. Thus, if we wished the program to make sure that a record did not exist with a FOR FIRST before trying to insert it, we would want to write it as

```
FOR FIRST DATAVIEW-1
    WHERE DATAVIEW-1.MASTER-KEY EQ PANEL1.MASTER-KEY
```

```
WHEN NONE
        FOR NEW DATAVIEW-1
            MOVE PANEL1.MASTER-KEY TO  DATAVIEW-1.MASTER-KEY
            MOVE PANEL1.FLDA       TO  DATAVIEW-1.FLDA
            MOVE PANEL1.FLDB       TO  DATAVIEW-1.FLDB
            MOVE PANEL1.FLDC       TO  DATAVIEW-1.FLDC
            MOVE PANEL1.FLDD       TO  DATAVIEW-1.FLDD
            MOVE "RECORD ADDED"    TO  PANEL1.MESSAGE
        ENDFOR
ENDFOR
```

But we must write it as

```
FOR FIRST DATAVIEW-1
    WHERE DATAVIEW-1.MASTER-KEY EQ PANEL1.MASTER-KEY
          SET FOUND-FLAG EQ TRUE
    WHEN  NONE
          SET FOUND-FLAG EQ FALSE
ENDFOR


IF NOT-FOUND
    FOR NEW DATAVIEW-1
            MOVE PANEL1.MASTER-KEY TO  DATAVIEW-1.MASTER-KEY
            MOVE PANEL1.FLDA       TO  DATAVIEW-1.FLDA
            MOVE PANEL1.FLDB       TO  DATAVIEW-1.FLDB
            MOVE PANEL1.FLDC       TO  DATAVIEW-1.FLDC
            MOVE PANEL1.FLDD       TO  DATAVIEW-1.FLDD
            MOVE "RECORD ADDED"    TO  PANEL1.MESSAGE
    ENDFOR
ENDIF
```

and use the value of the flag to determine the execution of the FOR
NEW statement. However, in the newer versions (IDEAL 1.1A and
on) we can place the FOR NEW command under the WHEN NONE
clause.

CHECKPOINT/BACKOUT

IDEAL has the same CHECKPOINT and BACKOUT statements
that native DATACOM processing has, and they function in the
same way. They are simply coded as CHECKPOINT or BACKOUT
anywhere in the program.

QSAM Processing

Another facility that IDEAL has is the ability to read sequential files into the environment for processing against the database. For example, we have a situation where one of our vendors sends us a tape containing invoices to us for material which he shipped directly to our customers at our request. We, in turn, load the information from that tape onto the database, compute the appropriate price and taxes, and create an invoice to send to our customers.

The reading of this sequential file is done by defining the record layout to the DATADICTIONARY as a QSAM dataview. The IDEAL application can then be written as

```
FOR EACH QSAM-DATAVIEW
        FOR NEW DATAVIEW1
            MOVE QSAM-DATAVIEW.MASTER-KEY TO DATAVIEW1.MASTER-KEY
            MOVE QSAM-DATAVIEW.FLDA        TO DATAVIEW1.FLDA
            MOVE QSAM-DATAVIEW.FLDB        TO DATAVIEW1.FLDB
            MOVE QSAM-DATAVIEW.FLDC        TO DATAVIEW1.FLDC
            MOVE QSAM-DATAVIEW.FLDD        TO DATAVIEW1.FLDD
        ENDFOR
ENDFOR
```

This code will read the entire QSAM file, in sequential order, and will create a DATAVIEW1 record on the database for each record that it reads in.

It is also possible for us to read the first record of the QSAM file independently of the rest of the file. For example, if we had a file with a header record on it, we could handle it in the following manner:

```
FOR FIRST QSAM-DATAVIEW
        DO PROC-HEADER
ENDFOR

FOR EACH QSAM-DATAVIEW
    IF FG-FIRST-TIME
        SET FG-FIRST-TIME TO FALSE
    ELSE
        FOR NEW DATAVIEW1
            MOVE QSAM-DATAVIEW.MASTER-KEY TO DATAVIEW1.MASTER-KEY
            MOVE QSAM-DATAVIEW.FLDA        TO DATAVIEW1.FLDA
            MOVE QSAM-DATAVIEW.FLDB        TO DATAVIEW1.FLDB
```

Here we get the first record and process the header data that it contains. We then read the entire file, skipping the first record, and begin loading the database.

We also have the option of coding it as

```
FOR EACH QSAM-DATAVIEW
    IF FG-FIRST-TIME
        DO PROC-HEADER
        SET FG-FIRST-TIME TO FALSE
    ELSE
        FOR NEW DATAVIEW1
            MOVE QSAM-DATAVIEW.MASTER-KEY TO DATAVIEW1.MASTER-KEY
            MOVE QSAM-DATAVIEW.FLDA        TO DATAVIEW1.FLDA
            MOVE QSAM-DATAVIEW.FLDB        TO DATAVIEW1.FLDB
            MOVE QSAM-DATAVIEW.FLDC        TO DATAVIEW1.FLDC
            MOVE QSAM-DATAVIEW.FLDD        TO DATAVIEW1.FLDD
        ENDFOR
    ENDFOR
ENDFOR
```

which allows us to eliminate the first read. This saves us some IO processing time.

Another option that is open to us is to use the FOR NEXT statement which we can control through an application LOOP statement. The FOR NEXT statement would read each of the records in the sequential file individually, after position had been established. For example, if we were to search through a sequential file for a certain record, we could write the following:

```
FOR FIRST QSAM-DATAVIEW
        DO PROC-HEADER
ENDFOR


LOOP UNTIL FG-RECD-FOUND
    FOR NEXT QSAM-DATAVIEW
        IF QSAM-DATAVIEW.MASTER-KEY EQ SEARCH-VALUE
            SET FG-RECD-FOUND TO TRUE
            FOR NEW DATAVIEW1
                MOVE QSAM-DATAVIEW.MSTR-KEY TO DATAVIEW1.MSTR-KEY
                MOVE QSAM-DATAVIEW.FLDA      TO DATAVIEW1.FLDA
                MOVE QSAM-DATAVIEW.FLDB      TO DATAVIEW1.FLDB
                MOVE QSAM-DATAVIEW.FLDC      TO DATAVIEW1.FLDC
                MOVE QSAM-DATAVIEW.FLDD      TO DATAVIEW1.FLDD
            ENDFOR
```

```
        ENDIF
      ENDFOR
  ENDLOOP
```

Here we will process the first header record. We will then read through each record, one at a time, until the record that we want to update the database with is found. When it is found, the update is made and the process is ended.

When working with QSAM files, it is important to remember that IDEAL only has the ability to read the records in the order that they appear. There is no update capability, although a new sequential file can be created with a FOR NEW statement and a different QSAM dataview name. Any manipulation of the actual file, such as resorting prior to input, must be handled outside the IDEAL environment. We will discuss the JCL requirements to handle a QSAM file in a later chapter.

It is also important to remember that, unlike a GSAM file in IMS/DLI coding, a QSAM file in IDEAL is not included in a CHECKPOINT. In IMS/DLI, it is possible to position a tape through a position counter on the log file during an IMS RESTART. IDEAL does not have this facility. Thus an IDEAL restart will position the input file at the begining.

FOR Statement Control

It is important to remember that the FOR statement is not only the access to the database, but it can, and often is, a control point in the processing. Thus it has the power to control the order of processing within an application, and often is the main drive routine of the program.

If we wished to report on every record of a database file, we would code it as follows:

```
                                                    LINE NUMBER
<<MAIN-DRIVE>> PROCEDURE                                 1
    FOR EACH  DATAVIEW-1                                 2
        WHERE DATAVIEW-1.FIELDA EQ SEARCH-VALUE          3
             DO REPORT-LOGIC                             4
             DO UPDATE-DVW                               5
    ENDFOR                                               6
    DO WRAP-UP-RPT                                       7
ENDPROC                                                  8
```

```
THIS PROGRAM WOULD IN TURN EXECUTE IN THE FOLLOWING SEQUENCE
    LINE
    1    OPEN ALL OF THE DATABASES AS DEFINED IN THE PROGRAMS
         FILE TABLE
    2,3  READ AND HOLD ON THE FIRST QUALIFYING RECORD
    4    EXECUTE THE PARAGRAPH REPORT-LOGIC (WHICH IN TURN
         PRODUCES OUR REPORT
    5    EXECUTES THE PARAGRAPH UPDATE-DVW (WHICH IN TURN UPDATES
         SOME OF THE FIELDS IN THE IO AREA OF OUR DATAVIEW
    6    REWRITES THE IO AREA TO THE DATABASE
    6    SEES IF THIS WAS THE LAST AVAILABLE RECORD
    6    IF IT WAS THE LAST AVAILABLE RECORD , BRANCHES TO LINE 7
    7    EXECUTES THE PARAGRAPH WRAP-UP-RPT
    8    ENDS THE PROGRAM
    6    IF IT IS NOT THE LAST RECORD , RETURNS CONTROL TO LINE 2
    2,3  EXECUTES A READ NEXT DUPLICATE AND HOLD
    2,3  REPEATS PROCESSING OF LINES 4 , 5 , AND 6.
```

When we are doing this type of processing, along a secondary key, we should observe that changing the value of a key during an update will not change the order in which the records come into the program. For example, if we are using the program above, and we were on the record where FIELDA had a value of 'CCC', changing its value to 'DDD' would not cause us to read the record again. This is because IDEAL locates all of the records that it will present to the FOR EACH at the begining of the request. Likewise, if a program with a FOR EACH is executed at the same time that a second program is creating new records in the database, the records that are created after the FOR EACH starts will not be picked up by the first program.

Another way that we can control the processing of FOR statements is through the commands QUIT and PROCESS NEXT. These two commands override the normal processing flow.

The QUIT command will end the processing of whatever has control at that time (RUN, FOR statement, LOOP, PROGRAM, PROCE-DURE). Processing will then go to the next logical statement. For example, the program

```
<<MAIN-DRIVE>> PROCEDURE                                  1
  <<MAIN-FOR>>                                            2
    FOR EACH  DATAVIEW-1                                  3
        WHERE DATAVIEW-1.FIELDA EQ SEARCH-VALUE           4
            IF DATAVIEW-1.FIELDB EQ 'QUIT'               5
                QUIT MAIN-FOR                            6
```

```
           ELSE                                      7
               DO REPORT-LOGIC                       8
               DO UPDATE-DVW                         9
           ENDIF                                    10
       ENDFOR                                       11
       DO WRAP-UP-RPT                               12
   ENDPROC                                          13
```

will function in the same manner that it did before, except that if the value of FIELDB is 'QUIT', the program will stop processing the FOR statement that the label MAIN-FOR refers to. Control will then go to line 12, which will produce the wrap-up report.

We could have written line 6 as QUIT PROGRAM. In this case, the entire program would have terminated, and the wrap-up report would not have been written.

If our FOR statement had been alone in its own procedure:

```
                                                LINE NUMBER
   <<MAIN-DRIVE>> PROCEDURE                          1
       DO MAIN-FOR                                   2
       DO WRAP-UP-RPT                                3
   ENDPROC                                           4

   <<MAIN-FOR>> PROCEDURE                            5
       FOR EACH   DATAVIEW-1                         6
           WHERE DATAVIEW-1.FIELDA EQ SEARCH-VALUE   7
               IF DATAVIEW-1.FIELDB EQ 'QUIT'        8
               QUIT MAIN-FOR                         9
           ELSE                                     10
               DO REPORT-LOGIC                       11
               DO UPDATE-DVW                        12
           ENDIF                                    13
       ENDFOR                                       14
   ENDPROC                                          15
```

The QUIT MAIN-FOR statement would have terminated the procedure, and processing would have continued with the next logical statement, DO WRAP-UP-RPT (line 3). We could have coded line 9 to read, QUIT MAIN-DRIVE since that paragraph is in control of the paragraph we are in. This command would have ended processing of both procedures and, in our case, terminated the program.

The PROCESS NEXT statement is similar to the QUIT statement in that it interrupts processing. However, it works on the individual occurrence of the data controlling the loop, rather than on the controlling code. For example, the program

```
                                                    LINE NUMBER
<<MAIN-DRIVE>> PROCEDURE                                  1
    <<MAIN-FOR>>                                          2
    FOR EACH   DATAVIEW-1                                 3
        WHERE DATAVIEW-1.FIELDA EQ SEARCH-VALUE           4
            IF DATAVIEW-1.FIELDB EQ 'SKIP'                5
                PROCESS NEXT MAIN-FOR                      6
            ELSE                                           7
                DO REPORT-LOGIC                            8
                DO UPDATE-DVW                              9
            ENDIF                                         10
    ENDFOR                                                11
    DO WRAP-UP-RPT                                        12
ENDPROC                                                  13
```

will stop processing on a record where the value of FIELDB is equal to SKIP and will get the next record.

Any updates that were to be applied to a dataview record that was interrupted with a QUIT or PROCESS NEXT command will be ignored.

The reader should note that excessive use of these two commands can have a detrimental effect on the structure of the program code and its readability. For example, the PROCESS NEXT could have been written to use an IF statement to bypass processing instead of interrupting the FOR statement. Thus these commands violate the rule of having only one exit per paragraph and should be used sparingly, if at all. We would recommend that the QUIT be used mainly to limit processing of database input to the program, and the PROCESS NEXT be used in an ERROR PROCEDURE (Chapter 10) to recover from an abend.

PDL Templates

As an additional help to the program developer, the IDEAL editor has a set of templates which can be called up when a program is being written.

These templates can be accessed by placing the appropriate two-character code in the command column of the procedure area at the line on which you wish the template to appear. The available templates are

```
FE                      FOR EACH
FF                      FOR FIRST
FN                      FOR NEW
IF                      IF
LO                      LOOP
PR                      PROCEDURE
ER                      ERROR PROCEDURE
SL                      SELECT
SF                      SELECT FIRST ACTION
SE                      SELECT EVERY ACTION
TR                      TRANSMIT
CL                      CALL USING
SA                      SET ATTRIBUTE
```

These commands then produce the following templates:

```
<<LABEL>>
FOR EACH DATAVIEW
    WHERE WHERE-CONDITION
    ORDERED BY IDENTIFIER ...
    :STATEMENTS
WHEN NONE
    :STATEMENTS
ENDFOR


<<LABEL>>
FOR THE FIRST NUMBER DATAVIEW
    WHERE WHERE-CONDITION
    ORDERED BY IDENTIFIER ...
    :STATEMENTS
WHEN NONE
    :STATEMENTS
ENDFOR


<<LABEL>>
FOR NEW DATAVIEW
    :STATEMENTS
WHEN DUPLICATE
    :STATEMENTS
ENDFOR


IF CONDITION
THEN
    :STATEMENTS
```

```
ELSE
    :STATEMENTS
ENDIF


<<LABEL>>
LOOP
    VARYING IDENTIFIER FROM 1 BY 1 UP THRU NUMBER
    :N TIMES
    :STATEMENTS
WHILE CONDITION
UNTIL CONDITION
    :STATEMENTS
ENDLOOP


<<LABEL>> PROCEDURE
    :STATEMENTS
ENDPROC


<<ERROR>> PROCEDURE
    :STATEMENTS
    LIST ERROR
    QUIT RUN
ENDPROC


SELECT IDENTIFIER
WHEN LITERAL,ARITH-EXPR,STRING-EXPR
    :STATEMENTS
WHEN LITERAL,ARITH-EXPR,STRING-EXPR
    :STATEMENTS
WHEN OTHER
    :STATEMENTS
WHEN ANY
    :STATEMENTS
ENDSEL

SELECT FIRST ACTION
WHEN CONDITION
    :STATEMENTS
WHEN CONDITION
    :STATEMENTS
WHEN OTHER
    :STATEMENTS
WHEN ANY
    :STATEMENTS
```

```
ENDSEL

SELECT EVERY ACTION
WHEN CONDITION
     :STATEMENTS
WHEN CONDITION
     :STATEMENTS
WHEN OTHER
     :STATEMENTS
WHEN ALL
     :STATEMENTS
WHEN ANY
     :STATEMENTS
ENDSEL


TRANSMIT PANEL
   REINPUT
   CLEAR
   CURSOR AT FIELDNAME/HOME

CALL PROGRAM USING
     INPUT  PARM-1,........PARM-N
     UPDATE PARM-1,........PARM-N

SET ATTRIBUTE 'HLIPUSENA' TEMP ON FIELDNAME
```

This facility can be very productive for both the beginning and the experienced programmer as it can be used to avoid a great deal of basic compile-time syntax errors, which can slow down development of a new application.

It is also possible to increase the number of statement lines that are generated by placing the desired number in front of the code in the command area.

Conclusions

In this chapter we have seen all of the basics of how to write an IDEAL program. We have identified it to the DATADICTIONARY. We have defined the internal working storage fields and the parameters that we wish to pass to other programs. We have learned how all of the basic PDL commands function, and how to access the database through the FOR statement. We have even discovered a way to make the editor save us some keying time by using the supplied code templates.

In the rest of this book we will see how the advanced features work, such as panel and report processing. But first, Chapter 5 contains a more in-depth look at how to access the database in the most efficient and logical manner.

Exercises

1. How can we make each of two fields with the same name unique? What other advantage can you see to making a habit of this practice?
2. Define *alpha* and *non-alpha* groups. What restrictions does IDEAL place on the movement of these two data structures?
3. What are the seven types of data that can be defined in an IDEAL working-storage area?
4. Translate the following working-storage definition into COBOL.

LEVEL	FIELD NAME	T	I	CH/DG	OCCUR	VALUE/COMMENT/DEP ON/COPY
1	WK-ALPHA-1	X	_	6	_____	'ALPHA1'
1	WK-ALPHA-GRP	_	_	_____	_____	_____
2	WK-ALPHA-GP1	X	_	3	_____	_____
2	WK-ALPHA-GP2	X	_	4	_____	_____
1	NUM-FIELD-1	N	_	5	_____	0
1	NUM-FIELD-1	U	_	5	_____	0
_____	_____	_	_	_____	_____	_____

5. Fill in the following working-storage area with this COBOL definition:

```
01  WK-NUM-ERR-MSG.
    05   WK-NUM-ERRORS   PIC 9(06) VALUE ZEROES.
    05   FILLER          PIC X(01) VALUE SPACES.
    05   FILLER          PIC X(16) VALUE 'WERE ENCOUNTERED'.
01  END-OF-FILE-FLAG     PIC X(01) VALUE 'FALSE'.
    88   END-OF-FILE               VALUE 'TRUE'.
01  COLOR-TYPE           PIC X(10) VALUE SPACES.
    88   TYPE-RED                  VALUE 'RED'.
    88   TYPE-YELLOW               VALUE 'YELLOW'.
    88   TYPE-GREEN                VALUE 'GREEN'.
    88   TYPE-BLUE                 VALUE 'BLUE'.
    88   TYPE-ORANGE               VALUE 'ORANGE'.
```

LEVEL FIELD NAME   T I CH/DG OCCUR VALUE/COMMENT/DEP ON/COPY
_____ _____ _ _ _____ _____ _____
_____ _____ _ _ _____ _____ _____
_____ _____ _ _ _____ _____ _____
_____ _____ _ _ _____ _____ _____
_____ _____ _ _ _____ _____ _____
_____ _____ _ _ _____ _____ _____
_____ _____ _ _ _____ _____ _____
_____ _____ _ _ _____ _____ _____
_____ _____ _ _ _____ _____ _____
_____ _____ _ _ _____ _____ _____
_____ _____ _ _ _____ _____ _____

6. Create a table definition that is initialized with the months of
    the year.

LEVEL FIELD NAME   T I CH/DG OCCUR VALUE/COMMENT/DEP ON/COPY
_____ _____ _ _ _____ _____ _____
_____ _____ _ _ _____ _____ _____
_____ _____ _ _ _____ _____ _____
_____ _____ _ _ _____ _____ _____
_____ _____ _ _ _____ _____ _____
_____ _____ _ _ _____ _____ _____
_____ _____ _ _ _____ _____ _____
_____ _____ _ _ _____ _____ _____
_____ _____ _ _ _____ _____ _____
_____ _____ _ _ _____ _____ _____
_____ _____ _ _ _____ _____ _____
_____ _____ _ _ _____ _____ _____
_____ _____ _ _ _____ _____ _____
_____ _____ _ _ _____ _____ _____

7. When we create a table without initial values, or only desig-
    nate some of the values, what will initially be placed in the
    rest of the table occurrences?
8. Build a three-dimensional array in the space provided.

LEVEL FIELD NAME   T I CH/DG OCCUR VALUE/COMMENT/DEP ON/COPY
_____ _____ _ _ _____ _____ _____
_____ _____ _ _ _____ _____ _____
_____ _____ _ _ _____ _____ _____
_____ _____ _ _ _____ _____ _____

------   ----------------------   -- -- -----   -----   ----------------------------
------   ----------------------   -- -- -----   -----   ----------------------------
------   ----------------------   -- -- -----   -----   ----------------------------
------   ----------------------   -- -- -----   -----   ----------------------------

9. Build a LOOP statement to read the table that we built in question 6, and find the number of the month that matches an input field WK-SRCH-MONTH.
10. How could we have obtained the same results without using a table?
11. What are the five major types of MOVE/SET statements?
12. Using the definition of these fields in the chapter, what will be the results of the following MOVE commands?

   a. SRC-NUMER-2   TO TAR-NUMER-2

   b. SRC-ALPHA-3   TO TAR-NUMER-2

   c. SRC-ALPHA-2   TO TAR-NUMER-3

   d. SRC-ALPHA-3   TO TAR-ALPHA-2

   e. SRC-ALPHA-3   TO TAR-ALPHA-4

13. What are the problems with MOVE BY NAME and MOVE BY POSITION?
14. What are the four types of IDEAL internal functions listed in the chapter, and the functions that belong to each?
15. What are the two types of SELECT statements?
16. What are the built-in conditions that we can use in SELECT statements?
17. What is the advantage of using a SELECT statement over

   a. compound IF
   b. hard-coded table

18. What are the different types of FOR statements and their uses?
19. What are the advantages of using read-only dataviews over update dataviews in an inquiry situation?
20. Can we access data in a dataview area outside the FOR construct? Can we move data to it?
21. What are the two FOR construct exception conditions and the purpose of each?
22. How can we change the order in which records in a QSAM file come into an IDEAL program?

23. How do we delete a database record?
24. Can we delete incoming records on a QSAM file?
25. Why can't we do CHECKPOINT/RESTART on an IDEAL QSAM file in the same way that we do with an IMS/DLI GSAM file?
26. If another program adds a record to a database that we are reading with a FOR EACH on a read-only dataview, will the new record be included in our processing?
27. What are the main uses for the QUIT and PROCESS NEXT statements?
28. What are the main problems with using QUIT and PROCESS NEXT commands?
29. List the PDL template commands and their meanings.

Exercises — Answers

1. How can we make each of two fields with the same name unique? What other advantage can you see to making a habit of this practice?

   a. Prefix the name with a higher-level name, such as the name of the panel or the dataview that it resides in.
   b. The practice adds to the readability of the IDEAL code by allowing the reader to more easily identify the field. This is particularly important when we consider the shortness of IDEAL field names.

2. Define *alpha* and *non-alpha* groups. What restrictions does IDEAL place on the movement of these two data structures?

   a. ALPHA-GROUP — A group of fields that is made up entirely of alpha data.
      NON-ALPHA GROUP — A group of fields that is a mixture of numeric and alpha data.
   b. IDEAL does not allow the movement of alpha groups to non-alpha groups to reduce the possibilities of OC-7 type abends, and because of the way that it stores numeric data.

3. What are the seven types of data that can be defined in an IDEAL working-storage area?

   X — Alpha data
   N — Signed numeric

U — Unsigned numeric
C — Condition
F — Flag
D — Date
V — Variable-length alphanumeric field

4. Translate the following working-storage definition into COBOL.

LEVEL	FIELD NAME	T	I	CH/DG	OCCUR	VALUE/COMMENT/DEP ON/COPY
1	WK-ALPHA-1	X		6	_____	'ALPHA1'
1	WK-ALPHA-GRP	_	_	_____	_____	_____
2	WK-ALPHA-GP1	X		3	_____	_____
2	WK-ALPHA-GP2	X		4	_____	_____
1	NUM-FIELD-1	N		5	_____	0
1	NUM-FIELD-1	U		5	_____	0
_____	_____	_	_	_____	_____	_____

```
01  WK-ALPHA-1      PIC  X(06) VALUE 'ALPHA1'.
01  WK-ALPHA-GRP.
    05  WK-ALPHA-GP1 PIC  X(03) VALUE SPACES.
    05  WK-ALPHA-GP2 PIC  X(04) VALUE SPACES.
01  NUM-FIELD-1     PIC  S9(05) VALUE +0.
01  NUM-FIELD-2     PIC  9(05) VALUE 0.
```

5. Fill in the following working-storage area with this COBOL definition:

```
01  WK-NUM-ERR-MSG.
    05  WK-NUM-ERRORS PIC 9(06) VALUE ZEROES.
    05  FILLER        PIC X(01) VALUE SPACES.
    05  FILLER        PIC X(16) VALUE 'WERE ENCOUNTERED'.
01  END-OF-FILE-FLAG  PIC X(01) VALUE 'FALSE'.
    88  END-OF-FILE             VALUE 'TRUE'.
01  COLOR-TYPE        PIC X(10) VALUE SPACES.
    88  TYPE-RED               VALUE 'RED'.
    88  TYPE-YELLOW            VALUE 'YELLOW'.
    88  TYPE-GREEN             VALUE 'GREEN'.
    88  TYPE-BLUE              VALUE 'BLUE'.
    88  TYPE-ORANGE            VALUE 'ORANGE'.
```

LEVEL	FIELD NAME	T	I	CH/DG	OCCUR	VALUE/COMMENT/DEP ON/COPY
1	WK-NUM-ERR-MSG	X		6	_____	'ALPHA1'
2	WK-NUM-ERROR	N		6	_____	0

2	WK-FILLER-1	X	1	_____	' '
2	WK-FILLER-2	X	16	_____	'WERE ENCOUNTERED'
1	END-OF-FILE	F	1	_____	TRUE
1	NUM-FIELD-1	X	10	_____	
	TYPE-RED	C			'RED'
	TYPE-YELLOW	C			'YELLOW'
	TYPE-GREEN	C			'GREEN'
	TYPE-BLUE	C			'BLUE'
	TYPE-ORANGE	C			'ORANGE'

6. Create a table definition that is initialized with the months of the year.

LEVEL	FIELD NAME	T	I	CH/DG	OCCUR	VALUE/COMMENT/DEP ON/COPY
1	MONTHS-OF-YEAR	X		10	12	
	(1)					'JANUARY'
	(2)					'FEBUARY'
	(3)					'MARCH'
	(4)					'APRIL'
	(5)					'MAY'
	(6)					'JUNE'
	(7)					'JULY'
	(8)					'AUGUST'
	(9)					'SEPTEMBER'
	(10)					'OCTOBER'
	(11)					'NOVEMBER'
	(12)					'DECEMBER'

7. When we create a table without specific values, or only designate some of the values, what will be placed in the rest of the table occurences?

Whatever is in the VALUE area of the line with the OCCURS area filled in.

8. Build a three-dimensional array in the space provided.

LEVEL	FIELD NAME	T	I	CH/DG	OCCUR	VALUE/COMMENT/DEP ON/COPY
1	MULTI-DIMENSION	_	_	_____	_____	_____
2	LEVEL-1	_	_	_____	3	_____

3	LEVEL-2	_ _ _____	4	_____
4	LEVEL-3	X 3	5	_____
_____	_____	_ _ _____ _____		_____
_____	_____	_ _ _____ _____		_____

9. Build a LOOP statement to read the table that we built in question 6, and find the number of the month that matches an input field WK-SRCH-MONTH.

```
LOOP VARYING WK-SUBSR FROM 1 BY 1
        UNTIL WK-SUBSR GT WK-LIMIT
          OR WK-SRCH-MONTH EQUAL TO WK-WORK-MONTH
            MOVE MONTHS-OF-YEAR(WK-SUBSR) TO WK-WORK-MONTH
ENDLOOP


IF MONTHS-OF-YEAR(WK-SUBSR) = WK-WORK-MONTH
   MOVE WK-SUBSR TO WK-SUBSR-RESULT
ELSE
   MOVE 13      TO WK-RESULT.
```

10. How could we have gotten the same results without using a table?

```
SELECT FIRST
        WHEN WK-SRCH-MONTH = 'JANUARY  '   MOVE  1 TO WK-RESULT
        WHEN WK-SRCH-MONTH = 'FEBUARY  '   MOVE  2 TO WK-RESULT
        WHEN WK-SRCH-MONTH = 'MARCH    '   MOVE  3 TO WK-RESULT
        WHEN WK-SRCH-MONTH = 'APRIL    '   MOVE  4 TO WK-RESULT
        WHEN WK-SRCH-MONTH = 'MAY      '   MOVE  5 TO WK-RESULT
        WHEN WK-SRCH-MONTH = 'JUNE     '   MOVE  6 TO WK-RESULT
        WHEN WK-SRCH-MONTH = 'JULY     '   MOVE  7 TO WK-RESULT
        WHEN WK-SRCH-MONTH = 'AUGUST   '   MOVE  8 TO WK-RESULT
        WHEN WK-SRCH-MONTH = 'SEPTEMBER'   MOVE  9 TO WK-RESULT
        WHEN WK-SRCH-MONTH = 'OCTOBER  '   MOVE 10 TO WK-RESULT
        WHEN WK-SRCH-MONTH = 'NOVEMBER '   MOVE 11 TO WK-RESULT
        WHEN WK-SRCH-MONTH = 'DECEMBER '   MOVE 12 TO WK-RESULT
        WHEN NONE                          MOVE 13 TO WK-RESULT
ENDSELECT
```

11. What are the five major types of MOVE/SET statements?

1. Population of an elementary numeric field
2. Population of an elementary alphanumeric field
3. Movement of one group to another

4. Setting of a predefined flag
5. Setting of a condition name

12. Using the definition of these fields in the chapter, what will be the results of the following MOVE commands?

a. SRC-NUMER-2   TO TAR-NUMER-2

b. SRC-ALPHA-3   TO TAR-NUMER-2

c. SRC-ALPHA-2   TO TAR-NUMER-3

d. SRC-ALPHA-3   TO TAR-ALPHA-2

e. SRC-ALPHA-3   TO TAR-ALPHA-4

a. TRUNCATION ERROR

b. TAR-NUMER-2 = 1234.00

c. INVALID NUMERIC ABEND

d. TAR-ALPHA-2 = "123"

e. TAR-ALPHA-4 = "1234   "

13. What are the problems with MOVE BY NAME and MOVE BY POSITION?

a. MOVE BY NAME works only on the elementary field level, with any group-level fields being ignored.

b. MOVE BY POSITION requires exact alignment to function. Any DB change requires redefinition of any other group that uses this command. It may also have unpredictable results when we try to process numeric data.

14. What are the four types of IDEAL internal functions listed in the chapter, and the functions that belong to each?

a. Informational

$SPACES
$HIGH
$LOW
$TERMINAL-ID
$TRANSACTION-ID
$USER-ID
$USER-NAME
$LENGTH
$DATE
$TIME

b. Data Movement or Manipulation

```
$EDIT
$ABS
$NUMBER
$ROUND
$STRING
$SUBSTR
$TRANSLATE
$HEX-TO-CHAR
$CHAR-TO-HEX
```

c. Numeric Functions

```
$COUNT
$INDEX
$REMAINDER
$SQRT
```

d. Boolean Functions

```
$NUMERIC
$ALPHABETIC
$VERIFY
```

15. What are the two types of SELECT statements?

```
SELECT FIRST, SELECT EVERY
```

16. What are the built-in conditions that we can use in SELECT statements?

```
WHEN ANY
WHEN OTHER
WHEN NONE
```

17. What is the advantage of using a SELECT statement over

a. compound IF
b. hard-coded table

a. Adds to readability, and ease of modification
b. Simpler to write and maintain, faster in execution

18. What are the different types of FOR statements and their uses?

    a. FOR NEW — inserts a new record into the database or QSAM file.
    b. FOR FIRST — obtains a specific record.
    c. FOR EACH — obtains a group of specific records.
    d. FOR NEXT — reads every succeeding record in a QSAM file.

19. What are the advantages of using read-only dataviews over update dataviews in an inquiry situation?

Elimination of the following functions:

    a. Writing of before-processing image to the log
    b. Establishment of exclusive control
    c. Writing of after-processing image to the log
    d. Comparison of before-and-after log images
    e. Physical overlay of the database
    f. Dynamic log processing

20. Can we access data in a dataview area outside the FOR construct? Can we move data to it?

We can access the data in the dataview area after any successful READ of that database record, not neccessarily the last READ that we tried to make. We can only move to the dataview area when inside a FOR construct.

21. What are the two FOR construct "exception conditions" and the purpose of each?

WHEN NONE — allows processing when a certain record is not found. Without this facility we increase the chances of having an INVALID REFERENCE OF FIELD error.
WHEN DUPLICATE — Controls processing when a program tries to insert a record into the database that already exists. If this clause is not present, the program will abend.

22. How can we change the order in which records in a QSAM file come into an IDEAL program?

They must be sorted by another facility (EASYTRIEVE, JCL SORT, etc.) before they come into the program.

23. How do we delete a database record?

We must write the command DELETE DATAVIEW-NAME inside a FOR FIRST or FOR EACH statement for that dataview.

24. Can we delete incoming records on a QSAM file?

No. But we can write logic to bypass them.

25. Why can't we do CHECKPOINT/RESTART on an IDEAL QSAM file in the same way that we do with an IMS/DLI GSAM file?

IDEAL does not keep the position of the QSAM FILE in its LOG when it does a CHECKPOINT, and IMS does.

26. If another program adds a record to a database that we are reading with a FOR EACH on a read-only dataview, will the new record be included in our processing?

No.

27. What are the main uses for the QUIT and PROCESS NEXT statements?

a. Early termination of a FOR EACH statement
b. Error processing recovery

28. What are the main problems with using the QUIT and PROCESS NEXT commands?

a. All database updates on the current record are backed out.
b. Reduces the structure and readability of the code by violating the one-entrance/one-exit rule.

29. List the PDL template commands and their meanings.

```
FE    FOR EACH
FF    FOR FIRST
FN    FOR NEW
IF    IF
```

```
LO    LOOP
PR    PROCEDURE
ER    ERROR PROCEDURE
SL    SELECT
SF    SELECT FIRST ACTION
SE    SELECT EVERY ACTION
TR    TRANSMIT
CL    CALL USING
SA    SET ATTRIBUTE
```

5

Relational Algebra and Database Efficiencies

Introduction

In this chapter we will discuss how to use the FOR statement to relate different databases together in order to manipulate the data they contain. We will also discuss some of the rules that should be followed to efficiently access the databases.

The study of how relational databases can be manipulated together is called relational algebra. There are eight different functions within this study. These are

1. SELECT
2. UNION
3. INTERSECTION
4. DIFFERENCE
5. PRODUCT
6. PROJECT
7. JOIN
8. DIVIDE

In this chapter we will define each of these relations in turn and provide examples of how to code them in IDEAL. But first, let us create an example database to use in our discussion.

Example Database

Let us take for our example the *invoicing system* of a small distribution company. We will find three databases within it, one contains the *customer* list, another has the *equipment* list, and the third shows the *history of customer purchases.*

```
CUSTOMER DATABASE
DATAVIEW NAME = CUSTOMER-RCD
MASTER KEY    = CUST-NO
```

CUST-NO	CUST-NAME	TELEPHONE	TYPE	CITY
C1	SMITH	224-3601	20	TAMPA
C2	JONES	554-3904	10	IRVING
C3	BLAKE	632-0422	10	IRVING
C4	CLARK	961-0731	20	TAMPA
C5	ADAMS	491-6203	30	DURHAM

```
EQUIPMENT DATABASE
DATAVIEW NAME = EQUIPMENT-RCD
MASTER-KEY    = EQUIP-NO
```

EQUIP-NO	EQUIP-NAME	COLOR	WEIGHT	WAREHOUSE
E1	MM	RED	12	TAMPA
E2	SLIM	WHITE	7	IRVING
E3	WALL	BROWN	7	ST PETE
E4	DESK	TAN	9	TAMPA
E5	WALL	WHITE	5	IRVING
E6	PAC	YELLOW	10	TAMPA

```
CUSTOMER EQUIPMENT HISTORY
DATAVIEW NAME = CUST-EQUIP-RCD
MASTER KEY    = CUST-NO THRU EQUIP-NO
SECONDARY KEY = CUST-NO
SECONDARY KEY = EQUIP-NO
```

CUST-NO	EQUIP-NO	QUANTITY
C1	E1	3
C1	E2	2

C1	E3	4
C1	E4	2
C1	E5	1
C1	E6	1
C2	E1	3
C2	E2	4
C3	E2	2
C4	E2	2
C4	E4	3
C4	E5	4

Now that we have our databases, let us see how we can use them.

Relational Algebra

Relational algebra deals with the manipulation of sets of data. A *set* can be defined as a group of data items that have some attribute in common. Thus we can have the set of our current customers. This set would be populated with all of the customer numbers in our database. We can also define another set as all of the customers in our database that are located in the city of Tampa. This set is made up of customers C1 (Smith) and C4 (Clark). It is also possible to define a set which does not have any members, such as the set of customers in our database who are in Philadelphia. This would be an empty, or null set.

Relational algebra deals with the manipulation of these sets and subsets to produce other sets. We could create a query which said: Create a set which is made up of those customers who are in Tampa.

To answer this query, we would

1. Find those customers who are in Tampa:

   a. C1 - SMITH
   b. C4 - CLARK

This operation is called the SELECT.

SELECT — creates a table from rows of an existing table to satisify some condition.

The SELECT algorithm is the one that serves as the basis for all the other algorithms. It consists of a single FOR statement.

```
<<SELECT>> PROCEDURE
   FOR EACH   CUSTOMER-RCD
       WHERE  CUSTOMER-RCD.CITY EQ 'TAMPA'
              LIST CUSTOMER-RCD.CUST-NO
                   CUSTOMER-RCD.CUST-NAME
                   CUSTOMER-RCD.TELEPHONE
                   CUSTOMER-RCD.TYPE
                   CUSTOMER-RCD.CITY
   ENDFOR
ENDPROC


C1   SMITH   224-3601   20   TAMPA
C4   CLARK   961-0731   20   TAMPA
```

Here we will search every record on the customer database and will display a report line when those records with a CITY field equal to TAMPA are found.

If we expand on this simple query we could create another that said

Create a set which is made up of

1. Those customers whose city is Tampa
2. Those customers who own equipment number E1.

To answer this query, we would

1. Find those customers who are in Tampa:

   a. C1 - SMITH
   b. C4 - CLARK

2. We would then read through the customer-equipment database and find those customers who own equipment numbered E1:

   a. C1
   b. C2

3. Combine these two sets to create a resultant set, which would contain:

   a. C1 - SMITH
   b. C4 - CLARK

   c. C1

   d. C2

4. We would then remove the duplicate result (C1) and create the final set:

   a. C1

   b. C2

   c. C4

This operation is called a *union*.

UNION — records where the data meets either one of two conditions:

```
<<UNION>> PROCEDURE
  FOR EACH CUSTOMER-RCD
          IF CUSTOMER-RCD.CITY EQ 'TAMPA'
             LIST 'CUS'
                    CUSTOMER-RCD.CUST-NO
                    CUSTOMER-RCD.CUST-NAME
                    CUSTOMER-RCD.CITY
          ELSE
             FOR FIRST CUST-EQUIP-RCD
                WHERE CUST-EQUIP-RCD.CUST-NO EQ CUSTOMER-RCD.CUST-NO
                  AND CUST-EQUIP-RCD.EQUIP-NO EQ 'E1'
                     LIST 'CER'
                            CUSTOMER-RCD.CUST-NO
                            CUSTOMER-RCD.CUST-NAME
                            CUSTOMER-RCD.CITY
                ENDFOR
             ENDIF
     ENDFOR
  ENDPROC
```

With this code, we are looking for every customer who is either located in Tampa or has purchased equipment number E1. To do this, we will conduct a search through the customer database. We can do this because we know through normalization that every customer we service is listed on the database, and that each of these customers is listed only once. We will read each customer record and see if their city is Tampa. If it is, we will write out the record. If they are not in Tampa, we will go to the customer-equipment database and try to find a record which has the same customer number and equipment number E1. If a record is found we will write it out, otherwise we will get the next customer record.

Our resulting output will be

```
CUS C1 SMITH TAMPA
CER C2 JONES IRVING
CUS C4 CLARK TAMPA
```

Smith and Clark live in Tampa, and Jones bought equipment E1. Smith also purchased equipment E1, but that will not be shown by this algorithm. This is because the search criterion was completed when we discovered that Smith was in Tampa, and we did not have to go to the customer-equipment database.

INTERSECTION — records whose values meet both requirements.

The *intersection* algorithm is the direct opposite of the union algorithm. Here we are trying to find those customers who are in Tampa and bought equipment E1. To do this, we need only make a slight modification to our union algorithm.

```
<<INTERSECTION>> PROCEDURE
   FOR EACH CUSTOMER-RCD
           IF CUSTOMER-RCD.CITY EQ 'TAMPA'
               FOR FIRST CUST-EQUIP-RCD
                   WHERE CUST-EQUIP-RCD.CUST-NO
                       EQ CUSTOMER-RCD.CUST-NO
                     AND CUST-EQUIP-RCD.EQUIP-NO EQ 'E1'
                       LIST CUSTOMER-RCD.CUST-NO
                           CUSTOMER-RCD.CUST-NAME
                           CUSTOMER-RCD.CITY
                           CUST-EQUIP-RCD.EQUIP-NO
                           CUST-EQUIP-RCD.QTY
               ENDFOR
           ENDIF
   ENDFOR
```

By removing the ELSE statement, we will check the customer-equipment database when we have a Tampa customer instead of when we do not. Thus when customers C1 and C4 are encountered, we try to find a CUST-EQUIP-RCD with an equal CUST-NO and EQUIP-NO value of E1. The customer C1 record will be successful in this second search, while customer C4 will not. Our resulting report would then only have one entry on it.

```
C1 SMITH TAMPA E1 3
```

DIFFERENCE — one condition is true and one is false.

Let's suppose that our sales force wants to sell more of equipment number E1 in the Tampa area. To do this, they will want to start with all of the customers in Tampa who have not yet purchased product E1. The algorithm to find them would be

```
<<DIFFERENCE>> PROCEDURE
   FOR EACH  CUSTOMER-RCD
       WHERE CUSTOMER-RCD.CITY EQ 'TAMPA'
              FOR EACH  CUST-EQUIP-RCD
                  WHERE CUST-EQUIP-RCD.CUST-NO
                        EQ CUSTOMER-RCD.CUST-NO
                    AND CUST-EQUIP-RCD.EQUIP-NO EQ 'E1'
                  WHEN  NONE
                        LIST 'CUST NO'
                             CUSTOMER-RCD.CUST-NO
                             '-'
                             CUSTOMER-RCD.CUST-NAME
                             'HAS NO E1 EQUIPMENT'
              ENDFOR
   ENDFOR
ENDPROC
```

Here, instead of writing out our report line under the positive condition, we will write it out under the negative condition, by using the WHEN NONE statement. Thus customers C1 and C4 will again be selected from the customer database, but when the search of the CUST-EQUIP-RCD is made, the WHEN NONE statement will be executed for customer C4. The resulting report line will be

```
CUST NO C4 - CLARK HAS NO E1 EQUIPMENT
```

We can, of course, combine the intersection and difference algorithms to produce a combined report.

```
<<INTER-DIFF>> PROCEDURE
   FOR EACH  CUSTOMER-RCD
       WHERE CUSTOMER-RCD.CITY EQ 'TAMPA'
              FOR EACH  CUST-EQUIP-RCD
                  WHERE CUST-EQUIP-RCD.CUST-NO
                        EQ CUSTOMER-RCD.CUST-NO
```

```
                  AND CUST-EQUIP-RCD.EQUIP-NO EQ 'E1'
                      LIST CUSTOMER-RCD.CUST-NO
                           '-'
                           CUSTOMER-RCD.CUST-NAME
                           CUSTOMER-RCD.CITY
                           CUST-EQUIP-RCD.EQUIP-NO
                           CUST-EQUIP-RCD.QTY
                  WHEN  NONE
                      LIST CUSTOMER-RCD.CUST-NO
                           '-'
                           CUSTOMER-RCD.CUST-NAME
                           CUSTOMER-RCD.CITY
                           'HAS NO E1 EQUIPMENT'
            ENDFOR
      ENDFOR
   ENDPROC
```

Here, the search of the CUST-EQUIP-RCD with customer C1 is successful, while customer C4 is found to have not purchased any E1 equipment. Our resulting output is

```
C1 - SMITH TAMPA E1    3
C4 - CLARK TAMPA HAS NO E1 EQUIPMENT


PRODUCT : SET OF ALL POSSIBLE COMBINATIONS
```

The PRODUCT algorithm is simply the matching of each member of one set against each occurrence of a second set. We do this by placing the FOR EACH statement for the second set inside the FOR EACH statement of the driving set. This will cause us to search through the entire second set for every record available in the first set.

```
FOR EACH CUSTOMER-RCD
        FOR EACH EQUIPMENT-RCD
            LIST CUSTOMER-RCD.CUST-NO
                 EQUIPMENT-RCD.EQUIP-NO
        ENDFOR
ENDFOR
```

This algorithm will produce the following report:

```
C1 E1
C1 E2
```

```
C1  E3
C1  E4
C1  E5
C1  E6
C2  E1
C2  E2
C2  E3
C2  E4
C2  E5
C2  E6
C3  E1
C3  E2
C3  E3
C3  E4
C3  E5
C3  E6
C4  E1
C4  E2
C4  E3
C4  E4
C4  E5
C4  E6
C5  E1
C5  E2
C5  E3
C5  E4
C5  E5
C5  E6
```

PROJECT — creates a table from columns of an existing table that satisifies some condition (yields a vertical subset of a given relation).

Here we wish to have a list of all of the cities in which we have customers. Since city values are not unique on the database as customer numbers are, we will have to find a way to eliminate the duplicates. This task can be accomplished with a work database, where we would write a record each time we found a unique city, an internal table that would be a substitution for the work DB, an ORDERED BY clause and an IF statement (as we have done), or with the UNIQUE clause on the WHERE statement.

```
<<PROJECT>> PROCEDURE
  FOR EACH  CUSTOMER-RCD
```

```
              ORDERED BY CUSTOMER-RCD.CITY
                 IF  CUSTOMER-RCD.CITY NOT EQ WK-PREV-CITY
                    LIST CUSTOMER-RCD.CUST-NO
                         CUSTOMER-RCD.CITY
                    MOVE CUSTOMER-RCD.CITY TO WK-PREV-CITY
                 ENDIF
           ENDFOR
      ENDPROC
```

Here, we will read each CUSTOMER-RCD on the database, but instead of having the records come into the program in their normal CUST-NO order, they will come in as if they were stored in the following order:

```
--------------------------------------------------
  CUST-NO   CUST-NAME   TELEPHONE   TYPE   CITY
    C5        ADAMS      491-6203     30    DURHAM
    C2        JONES      554-3904     10    IRVING
    C3        BLAKE      632-0422     10    IRVING
    C1        SMITH      224-3601     20    TAMPA
    C4        CLARK      961-0731     20    TAMPA
--------------------------------------------------
```

They are ordered first by city, and then by customer number within that city. The first, second, and fourth records will be selected, as they are the first occurrence of each city value.

```
   C5   DURHAM
   C2   IRVING
   C1   TAMPA
```

JOIN — If two relations each have an attribute drawing their values from a common domain, then these two relations may be joined when the value of their attributes are equal.

A *domain* is a listing of all of the possible values that a field can have, whether they are actually used or not. In our case, the domain of the EQUIP-NO field includes any combination of a letter and a number. Thus we have the values E1, E2, E3, E4, E5, E6, which are already defined, or allocated, on our database. We also have other values, such as F1, D7, G2, etc., which have not been used yet. In the JOIN algorithm, we are trying to find those records where the value of a certain field is the same on both the searching and the searched record. The code

```
FOR EACH EQUIPMENT-RCD
            FOR EACH   CUST-EQUIP-RCD
                WHERE CUST-EQUIP-RCD.EQUIP-NO
                      EQ EQUIPMENT-RCD.EQUIP-NO
                      LIST CUST-EQUIP-RCD.EQUIP-NO
                           CUST-EQUIP-RCD.CUST-NO
                           CUST-EQUIP-RCD.QTY
                WHEN   NONE
                      LIST 'NO SALES FOUND FOR THIS PART'
            ENDFOR
    ENDFOR
```

will read each equipment record (which again has all of the "allocated" values of the domain, each being listed only once) and tries to find those records on the CUST-EQUIP-RCD which have the same value. The results of such a search against our database would be

```
E1   C1   3
E1   C2   3
E2   C1   2
E2   C2   4
E2   C3   2
E2   C4   2
E3   C1   4
E4   C1   2
E4   C4   3
E5   C1   1
E5   C4   4
E6   C1   1
```

DIVIDE — divides a relation with a degree of R and S by another relation with a degree of S, producing another relation with a degree of R.

In the *divide* function, we wish to create a set where a single entity has two characteristics. This could be a selection where the two attributes are in the same field on two different records, or two different fields on the same record. We might want to find those pilots who can fly both the 707 and the 747. We could also wish to find those direct parts where the product family is 'AAA'.

The simplest of these two possibilities is where we wish to search for multiple characteristics on the same record. This can be done by placing an AND clause on the WHERE statement.

For example, we could wish to find the equipment numbers of wall segments that are sold at the Irving warehouse. To do this, the FOR statement would be

```
FOR EACH  EQUIPMENT-RCD
    WHERE EQUIPMENT-RCD.EQUIP-NAME = 'WALL'
      AND EQUIPMENT-RCD.WAREHOUSE  = 'IRVING'
          LIST EQUIPMENT-RCD.EQUIP-NO
               EQUIPMENT-RCD.EQUIP-NAME
               EQUIPMENT-RCD.WAREHOUSE
ENDFOR
```

The resulting report would show only EQUIP-NO E5, because only E5 is called a 'WALL' and is stocked at Irving. EQUIP-NO E3 is also a WALL, but it is stocked in 'ST PETE'.

In a more complex example of the divide function, we wish to find those entities which have both required values in the same field. For this example, we will first define a new database which shows the parts that are included in a *kit*, and thus should be sold together.

```
E#  KIT#

E1  KIT1
E2  KIT1
```

In this example, Kit number 1 (KIT1) is made up of EQUIP-NO E1 and E2.

We will then write a program that will find each customer who owns a complete kit.

```
<<DIVIDE>> PROCEDURE
   FOR EACH CUSTOMER-RCD
           MOVE $SPACES TO WK-PREV-KIT
           MOVE 'Y'     TO FG-KIT-FOUND
           FOR EACH KIT-RCD
               IF WK-PREV-KIT EQ $SPACES
                  MOVE KIT-RCD.KIT-NO TO WK-PREV-KIT
               ELSE
                  IF KIT-RCD.KIT-NO NOT EQ WK-PREV-KIT
                     DO CHECK-N-WRITE
                     MOVE KIT-RCD.KIT-NO TO WK-PREV-KIT
                  ENDIF
```

```
                ENDIF
                DO SRCH-CUST-EQUIP
            ENDFOR
            DO CHECK-N-WRITE
    ENDFOR
ENDPROC


<<CHECK-N-WRITE>> PROCEDURE
    IF FG-KIT-FOUND EQ 'Y'
        LIST CUSTOMER-RCD.CUST-NO
            WK-PREV-KIT
    ELSE
        MOVE 'Y' TO FG-KIT-FOUND
    ENDIF
ENDPROC


<<SRCH-CUST-EQUIP>> PROCEDURE
    FOR FIRST CUST-EQUIP-RCD
        WHERE CUST-EQUIP-RCD.CUST-NO  EQ CUSTOMER-RCD.CUST-NO
          AND CUST-EQUIP-RCD.EQUIP-NO EQ KIT-RCD.EQUIP-NO
        WHEN  NONE
            MOVE 'N' TO FG-KIT-FOUND
    ENDFOR
ENDPROC
```

For every customer on the customer database, we will try to find which ones own a complete set of the defined KIT1, which means that they own EQUIP-NO E1 and E2. We will therefore try to find a CUST-EQUIP-RCD for each record in each kit type, with each CUST-NO.

When this is run, we will find that customers C1 and C2 both own KIT1. We can say this because both customers C1 and C2 own EQUIP-NO E1 and E2.

```
C1   E1   E2
C2   E1   E2
```

This is equivalent to saying CUSTOMERS C1 and C2 own KIT1, because KIT1 consists of EQUIPMENT E1 and E2.

```
C1   KIT1
C2   KIT1
```

Non-Key Access to the Database

So far in our discussions, we have seen applications with FOR statements that accessed the database either by the master key or by a predefined secondary key. A relational database, unlike other types of database structures, has the ability to access on either parts of the key, combinations of the key fields, or a non-keyed field. This is possible through the liberal use of the WHERE clause in the FOR statement.

Let us recall the SELECT algorithm that we discussed earlier.

```
<<SELECT>> PROCEDURE
   FOR EACH  CUSTOMER-RCD
        WHERE CUSTOMER-RCD.CITY EQ 'TAMPA'
              LIST CUSTOMER-RCD.CUST-NO
                   CUSTOMER-RCD.CUST-NAME
                   CUSTOMER-RCD.TELEPHONE
                   CUSTOMER-RCD.TYPE
                   CUSTOMER-RCD.CITY
   ENDFOR
ENDPROC
```

We should also recall that we did not define the city field as a secondary index on the customer file. Since the native calls can only function on an index, this command forces DATACOM to build what is called a *temporary index*. This index will serve as a secondary index to the file for the duration of the call to the database. To create this index, DATACOM will

1. Do a physical read on each customer database record.
2. Create a secondary index record, pointing back to the master key record.
3. Sort this secondary key index into its native order.

Then, after the system has done all of this overhead work, it will begin returning records that fulfill the request of the application. This is done by reading each of the new secondary index records, finding those whose value is Tampa, reading the corresponding data record, and returning it to the application.

When the ENDFOR is reached, DATACOM is forced through the final indignity of having to delete the index and reclaim the space. We can easily see the disadvantage of this kind of processing, especially in an on-line environment. The operator could start the application and go to lunch while waiting for it to respond.

There are two solutions to this problem; the choice depends on the number of times and the way that this access is required to be made. These solutions are

1. Create a permanent secondary index on the database. This solution is best when there are a large number of applications that will need a specific city selection. This is particularly true in the on-line environment when we wish to reduce the number of records accessed so that we can keep response time at a minimum.

    The disadvantage of this solution is that there is a certain amount of overhead that is associated with the maintenance of a secondary index. If we recall the discussion of update processing that we had in Chapter 2, we can see the number of tasks that we must undergo to change, add, or delete a record with a secondary key. Four is the recommended maximum number of secondary keys that should be allowed on a database.

2. We can recode the selection process of our application to use an IF statement instead of the WHERE statement.

```
<<SELECT>> PROCEDURE
    FOR EACH CUSTOMER-RCD
            IF CUSTOMER-RCD.CITY EQ 'TAMPA'
               LIST CUSTOMER-RCD.CUST-NO
                    CUSTOMER-RCD.CUST-NAME
                    CUSTOMER-RCD.TELEPHONE
                    CUSTOMER-RCD.TYPE
                    CUSTOMER-RCD.CITY
            ENDIF
    ENDFOR
ENDPROC
```

Here we will read each customer record into our application in master-key (CUST-NO) order. While we will still have a great deal of IO, we will avoid the creation, sorting, and selection processing of the temporary index. This solution is best when our selection is to be the main drive of a batch program, or if we have a very small database table that we are trying to access.

Temporary indexes are also built under a number of other circumstances:

1. When an ORDERED BY clause is used for a field that is not part of a key access
2. When a signed numeric field is used, even if it is a secondary index key
3. When the descending order clause is used
4. When the creation of an index will reduce the number of records that are searched
5. When it will cause the elimination of duplicate records during the search

Another database efficiency problem that often occurs, and that is related to temporary index building, is called *population counting*. This situation occurs when we have a FOR statement with WHERE clauses that contain two different keys.

Let's recall part of our INTERSECTION algorithm:

```
<<INTERSECTION>> PROCEDURE
    FOR EACH   CUST-EQUIP-RCD
        WHERE CUST-EQUIP-RCD.CUST-NO   EQ CUSTOMER-RCD.CUST-NO
          AND CUST-EQUIP-RCD.EQUIP-NO EQ 'E1'
              LIST CUST-EQUIP-RCD.CUST-NO
    ENDFOR
ENDPROC
```

Here, DATACOM will count the number of records in the CUST-NO index that have the requested CUST-NO value, and then count the number of EQUIP-NO secondary keys on this database that have a value of E1. It does this to find that index with the smallest number of records that fulfill the search criterion. In our example, if we assume that the required CUST-NO is C1, DATACOM will execute its count and find that the CUST-NO key has six entries and the EQUIP-NO has two. Therefore, DATACOM will access the file along the EQUIP-NO key. If the required CUST-NO was C3, the population count would be 1 to 2, and the CUST-NO index would be the main drive.

To avoid this type of overhead, it is important that the programmer make the decision about which index should be used, instead of allowing the machine do it. This is done by replacing the AND statement in the WHERE clause with an IF statement:

```
<<POPULATION-CNT>> PROCEDURE
    FOR EACH   CUST-EQUIP-RCD
        WHERE CUST-EQUIP-RCD.CUST-NO   EQ CUSTOMER-RCD.CUST-NO
```

```
        IF CUST-EQUIP-RCD.EQUIP-NO EQ 'E1'
           LIST CUST-EQUIP-RCD.CUST-NO
        ENDIF
    ENDFOR
ENDPROC
```

This CUST-EQUIP-RCD database also demonstrates another situation which causes population counting called *redundant keys*. As you will recall, we defined this database as having a master key of CUST-NO through EQUIP-NO, and individual secondary keys of CUST-NO and EQUIP-NO. Whenever any of these fields are accessed, DATACOM must again go through its population counting routines to determine if the master or the secondary keys should be used. In addition, this situation will cause extra database key maintenance, and extra storage will have to be allocated.

A second inefficient key usage that occurs is found when a request requires multiple *traversals*, or reads, of the entire index to be fulfilled. This can occur in a number of situations.

The first is when an OR statement is used to relate two keys together that have, nominally, nothing in common. If we changed our example:

```
<<POPULATION-CNT>> PROCEDURE
    FOR EACH  CUST-EQUIP-RCD
        WHERE CUST-EQUIP-RCD.CUST-NO  EQ CUSTOMER-RCD.CUST-NO
           OR CUST-EQUIP-RCD.EQUIP-NO EQ 'E1'
              LIST CUST-EQUIP-RCD.CUST-NO
    ENDFOR
ENDPROC
```

We would see the same population counting that we previously encountered. In addition, DATACOM would have to build a temporary index of the selected records to avoid accessing the same record twice. If CUST-NO were equal to C2 we would select the first and the seventh records based on EQUIP-NO, and the seventh and eighth records based on CUST-NO. Our index would then consist of the first, seventh, and eighth records.

A second occurrence of this traversal problem occurs when a NOT EQUAL or 'NE' relational operator is used on a single key.

```
<<POPULATION-CNT>> PROCEDURE
    FOR EACH  CUST-EQUIP-RCD
        WHERE CUST-EQUIP-RCD.CUST-NO NE CUSTOMER-RCD.CUST-NO
```

```
              LIST CUST-EQUIP-RCD.CUST-NO
   ENDFOR
ENDPROC
```

This would again require that the entire index file be searched. To avoid this, we would simply recode it as

```
<<TRAVERSALS>> PROCEDURE
   FOR EACH   CUST-EQUIP-RCD
       WHERE CUST-EQUIP-RCD.CUST-NO LT CUSTOMER-RCD.CUST-NO
          OR CUST-EQUIP-RCD.CUST-NO GT CUSTOMER-RCD.CUST-NO
             LIST CUST-EQUIP-RCD.CUST-NO
   ENDFOR
ENDPROC
```

This would skip that part of the index which is equal to our CUST-NO value, and just give us the beginning and end of the file.

Multiple traversals of an index also occur when excessive OR statements are used. For example, if we added the following values to our customer database:

```
-------------------------------------------------
  CUST-NO   CUST-NAME   TELEPHONE   TYPE   CITY
    D1        BRANT                   20    MEMPHIS
    D2        BRANT                   20    MEMPHIS
    D3        BRANT                   20    MEMPHIS
    D4        BRANT                   20    MEMPHIS
    D5        BRANT                   20    MEMPHIS
    D6        BRANT                   20    MEMPHIS
-------------------------------------------------
```

and we created the following program:

```
<<TRAVERSALS>> PROCEDURE
   FOR EACH   CUSTOMER-RCD
       WHERE CUSTOMER-RCD.CUST-NO EQ 'C1' OR 'C4' OR 'D1' OR 'D2'
                                OR 'D3' OR 'D4' OR 'D5' OR 'D6'
             LIST CUSTOMER-RCD.CUST-NO
   ENDFOR
ENDPROC
```

We would find the application making eight full passes at the index, one for each OR statement. To reduce this, we could recode the algorithm:

```
<<TRAVERSALS>> PROCEDURE
   FOR EACH   CUSTOMER-RCD
        WHERE CUSTOMER-RCD.CUST-NO EQ 'C1' or 'C4'
           OR CUSTOMER-RCD.CUST-NO GT 'D1'
               LIST CUSTOMER-RCD.CUST-NO
   ENDFOR
ENDPROC
```

This would only require three passes of the index. This also would not build a temporary index. Since our selection is on a single field, there is no possibility of duplicate records which would have to be eliminated.

At this point we need to ask the question, is CUST-NO the best access field for this application, or is there another field that could link all of these records together? Let us remember all the work that was done in the first chapter to normalize our database. This was done so that every field on the record related only to the key record in the hope that the values in the informational fields that follow it could be grouped to meet certain requests. In our example, we should notice that all of the customer numbers that we selected have a type code of 20. Thus we should consider making our record selection based on the type field, either as another secondary key, or as a single reading pass of the datafile with an IF statement.

```
<<TRAVERSALS-1>> PROCEDURE
   FOR EACH   CUSTOMER-RCD
        WHERE CUSTOMER-RCD.TYPE EQ '20'
               LIST CUSTOMER-RCD.CUST-NO
   ENDFOR
ENDPROC
```

```
<<TRAVERSALS-2>> PROCEDURE
   FOR EACH   CUSTOMER-RCD
               IF CUSTOMER-RCD.TYPE EQ '20'
                   LIST CUSTOMER-RCD.CUST-NO
               ENDIF
   ENDFOR
ENDPROC
```

This will solve the traversal problems, but may create other problems. The choice will have to be based on the balance of needs between the specific application and the overall system.

Yet another problem that occurs is when a secondary key is set up for a field that can have a value of *spaces* or *low values*. If the database is set up in such a way that keys with a blank value are not created, code which tries to find blank records will cause the entire master key file to be searched. Every record on the master key file that does not have a secondary key entry will then fulfill the search criterion.

All of this processing is handled in DATACOM by a facility called *compound Boolean selection*, or CBS. In fact, the only time that CBS overhead is not invoked is when a call to the database

1. Is a simple condition.
2. Uses the EQ operator.
3. The first operand of the WHERE clause is the full key.
4. There is not an ORDERED BY clause.

Anything beyond this causes CBS overhead. Thus we need to

1. Define secondary keys.
2. Eliminate redundant keys.
3. Develop dataviews that consist only of keyed fields.
4. Take advantage of index retrieval.
5. Avoid excessive population counting.
6. Avoid multiple traversals that cause temporary indexes to be built.
7. Avoid use of the NE operator.
8. Avoid selection on blank fields.
9. Replace excessive 'OR's.
10. Use native key for sequential retrieval when possible.
11. Consider sorting in a program instead of using an ORDERED BY clause in batch processing.

Conclusions

In this chapter we have seen how to use the FOR statement in all basic relational algorithms. We have also reviewed the different principles that affect how efficiently we access the database. These rules and principles are important because an application that is written in IDEAL (or any relational language), will be highly dependent on the values, cleanliness, and structure of the data. In relational database programming, nearly all of the programs are driven by a FOR EACH statement, or a panel processing statement, which does a FOR FIRST as soon as it comes into the program. Therefore the success of any system will be based on how quickly and easily it can access the database.

Exercises

Author's Note

When the IDEAL product is installed at a site, two test databases are installed with the appropriate dataviews. These two dataviews are

```
ID-EMPLOYEE
     NUMBER              U     5        K
     NAME                X     24
     STREET-ADDRESS      X     24
     CITY-ADDRESS        X     15
     STATE-ADDRESS       X     2        P
     ZIP-CODE-LOC        X     5
     SOCIAL-SECURITY     N     9

ID-PAYROLL
     NUMBER              U     5        K
     ACTIVITY-CODE       X     1
     ACTIVITY-STATUS     X     1
     CURRENT-RATE        U     6.2
     YTD-WAGES           U     6.2
     YTD-COMMISSION      U     6.2
     YTD-TAX             U     6.2
```

We will be using these databases in the exercises for this chapter and in many of the subsequent chapters so that you may begin coding the answers into the system to see the actual results.

1. What is *relational algebra*?
2. Write a program which will produce a union of the employee and the payroll file. Find those employees who live in Utah (UT) or make a salary in excess of 1000.00 per pay period. List out the employee number, state and city address, and current wage rate.
3. Change the above program to be an intersection between the two values.
4. Difference. Change the above program to find those employees who live in Utah and do not have a wage rate greater than 1000.00.
5. Write a product algorithm between ADDRESS-STATE and the ACTIVITY-CODE on the payroll file.

6. Select each employee record with a number between 10000 and 20000. Print number, name, address, and current rate.
7. In the product solution, why was the ID-EMPLOYEE dataview selected as the second record to be searched?
8. What is a temporary index?
9. Why should they be avoided?
10. Under what circumstances will IDEAL not build temporary indexes?
11. What can we do to avoid or reduce temporary indexing?
12. What is the recommended maximum number of secondary keys that a database should have?
13. What efficiency problem will be encountered in the following code?

```
FOR EACH   ID-EMPLOYEE
     WHERE ID-EMPLOYEE.NUMBER         LT '11000'
       AND ID-EMPLOYEE.STATE-ADDRESS EQ 'UT'
           LIST ID-EMPLOYEE.NUMBER
                ID-EMPLOYEE.STATE-ADDRESS
                ID-EMPLOYEE.SOCIAL-SECURITY
ENDFOR
```

14. Rewrite the code to eliminate the problem.
15. What is the problem demonstrated by this example?

```
FOR EACH   ID-PAYROLL
     WHERE ID-PAYROLL.NUMBER EQ 11000 OR 12000
        OR ID-PAYROLL.NUMBER GT 13000
           LIST ID-PAYROLL.NUMBER
                ID-PAYROLL.CURRENT-RATE
ENDFOR
```

16. In the product solution, what could we have done differently to make the solution more efficient?

Exercises — Answers

1. What is *relational algebra*?

The study of how relational databases can be manipulated. It includes the study of the functions:

```
UNION
INTERSECTION
DIFFERENCE
PRODUCT
SELECT
PROJECT
JOIN
DIVIDE
```

2. Write a program which will produce a union of the employee and the payroll file. Find those employees who live in Utah (UT) or make a salary in excess of 1000.00 per pay period. List out the employee number, state and city address, and current wage rate.

```
<<UNION>> PROCEDURE
   FOR EACH ID-EMPLOYEE
            FOR FIRST ID-PAYROLL
               WHERE ID-PAYROLL.NUMBER = ID-EMPLOYEE.NUMBER
                     IF ID-EMPLOYEE.ADDRESS-STATE = 'UT'
                        DO LIST-OUTPUT
                     ELSE
                        IF ID-PAYROLL GT 1000.00
                           DO LIST-OUTPUT
                        ENDIF
                     ENDIF
            ENDFOR
   ENDFOR
ENDPROC

<<LIST-OUTPUT>> PROCEDURE
   LIST ID-EMPLOYEE.NUMBER
        ID-EMPLOYEE.ADDRESS-CITY
        ID-EMPLOYEE.ADDRESS-STATE
        ID-PAYROLL.CURRENT-RATE
ENDPROC
```

3. Change the above program to be an intersection between the two values.

```
<<INTERSECTION>> PROCEDURE
   FOR EACH ID-EMPLOYEE
            FOR FIRST ID-PAYROLL
               WHERE ID-PAYROLL.NUMBER = ID-EMPLOYEE.NUMBER
```

```
                              IF  ID-EMPLOYEE.ADDRESS-STATE = 'UT'
                                 IF  ID-PAYROLL  GT  1000.00
                                    DO  LIST-OUTPUT
                                 ENDIF
                              ENDIF
                  ENDFOR
      ENDFOR
ENDPROC


<<LIST-OUTPUT>>  PROCEDURE
   LIST  ID-EMPLOYEE.NUMBER
         ID-EMPLOYEE.ADDRESS-CITY
         ID-EMPLOYEE.ADDRESS-STATE
         ID-PAYROLL.CURRENT-RATE
ENDPROC
```

4. Difference. Change the above program to find those employees who live in Utah and do not have a wage rate greater than 1000.00.

```
<<DIFFERENCE>>  PROCEDURE
   FOR EACH  ID-EMPLOYEE
                  FOR FIRST  ID-PAYROLL
                     WHERE  ID-PAYROLL.NUMBER = ID-EMPLOYEE.NUMBER
                        IF  ID-EMPLOYEE.ADDRESS-STATE = 'UT'
                           IF  ID-PAYROLL  LE  1000.00
                              DO  LIST-OUTPUT
                           ENDIF
                        ENDIF
                  ENDFOR
      ENDFOR
ENDPROC


<<LIST-OUTPUT>>  PROCEDURE
   LIST  ID-EMPLOYEE.NUMBER
         ID-EMPLOYEE.ADDRESS-CITY
         ID-EMPLOYEE.ADDRESS-STATE
         ID-PAYROLL.CURRENT-RATE
ENDPROC
```

5. Write a product algorithm between ADDRESS-STATE and the ACTIVITY-CODE on the payroll file.

```
<<PRODUCT>> PROCEDURE
   MOVE $SPACES   TO WK-ACTIVITY-CD
   MOVE $SPACES   TO WK-STATE
   FOR EACH   ID-PAYOLL
        ORDERED BY ID-PAYROLL.ACTIVITY-CODE
        IF ID-PAYROLL.ACTIVITY-CODE NOT EQUAL WK-ACTIVITY-CD
            MOVE ID-PAYROLL.ACTIVITY-CODE   TO WK-ACTIVITY-CD
            MOVE $SPACES                 TO WK-STATE
            FOR EACH   ID-EMPLOYEE
                ORDERED BY ID-EMPLOYEE.STATE-ADDRESS
                IF ID-EMPLOYEE.STATE-ADDRESS NOT EQUAL WK-STATE
                    MOVE ID-EMPLOYEE.STATE-ADDRESS   TO WK-STATE
                    LIST ID-PAYROLL.ACTIVITY-CODE
                            ID-EMPLOYEE.STATE-ADDRESS
                ENDIF
            ENDFOR
        ENDIF
   ENDFOR
ENDFOR
```

6. Select each employee record with a number between 10000 and 20000. Print number, name, address, and current rate.

```
<<SELECT>> PROCEDURE
   FOR EACH ID-EMPLOYEE
        IF ID-EMPLOYEE.NUMBER    GT 10000
           AND ID-EMPLOYEE.NUMBER LT 20000
           FOR FIRST ID-PAYROLL
               WHERE ID-PAYROLL.NUMBER = ID-EMPLOYEE.NUMBER
                    LIST ID-EMPLOYEE.NUMBER
                         ID-EMPLOYEE.NAME
                         ID-EMPLOYEE.STREET-ADDRESS
                         ID-EMPLOYEE.CITY-ADDRESS
                         ID-EMPLOYEE.STATE-ADDRESS
                         ID-PAYROLL.CURRENT-RATE
           ENDFOR
        ENDIF
   ENDFOR
ENDPROC
```

7. In the product solution, why was the ID-EMPLOYEE dataview selected as the record to be searched?

Of the two search fields, ID-PAYROLL.ACTIVITY-STATUS and ID-EMPLOYEE.STATE-ADDRESS, only the second field was already defined as a key. When we placed the ORDERED BY clause on the ID-PAYROLL FOR statement, we caused a secondary index to be built for that database. However, the ORDERED BY clause was redundant for the ID-EMPLOYEE database. Thus we choose this order so that we would only have to build a temporary index once for the run, instead of for each change in the value of STATE-ADDRESS.

8. What is a temporary index?

It is a secondary index that is built by the compound Boolean selection facility on a temporary basis. It lasts for the duration of the FOR statement that created it.

9. Why should they be avoided?

Temporary index building consumes both CPU time and real time, and it is gone as soon as the search request is fulfilled.

10. Under what circumstances will IDEAL not build temporary indexes?

When a call to the database
   1. Is a simple condition.
   2. Uses the EQ operator.
   3. The first operand of the WHERE clause is the full key.
   4. There is not an ORDERED BY clause.

11. What can we do to avoid or reduce temporary indexing?

   1. Define secondary keys.
   2. Eliminate redundant keys.
   3. Develop dataviews that consist only of keyed fields.
   4. Take advantage of index retrieval.
   5. Avoid excessive population counting.
   6. Avoid multiple traversals that cause temporary indexes to be built.
   7. Avoid use of the NE operator.
   8. Avoid selection on blank fields.
   9. Replace excessive 'OR's.
   10. Use native key for sequential retrieval when possible.

11. Consider sorting in a program instead of using an OR-DERED BY clause in batch processing.

12. What is the recommended maximum number of secondary keys that a database should have?

Four

13. What efficiency problem will be encountered by the following code?

```
FOR EACH   ID-EMPLOYEE
      WHERE ID-EMPLOYEE.NUMBER           LT '11000'
         AND ID-EMPLOYEE.STATE-ADDRESS EQ 'UT'
            LIST ID-EMPLOYEE.NUMBER
                  ID-EMPLOYEE.STATE-ADDRESS
                  ID-EMPLOYEE.SOCIAL-SECURITY
ENDFOR
```

The code will cause population counting because CBS will first read both of the key fields to establish which one has the smallest record set that will fulfill the request. When this has been determined, it will build a temporary index of those records that qualify.

14. Rewrite the code to eliminate the problem.

```
FOR EACH   ID-EMPLOYEE
      WHERE ID-EMPLOYEE.NUMBER           LT '11000'
            IF ID-EMPLOYEE.STATE-ADDRESS EQ 'UT'
               LIST ID-EMPLOYEE.NUMBER
                     ID-EMPLOYEE.STATE-ADDRESS
                     ID-EMPLOYEE.SOCIAL-SECURITY
            ENDIF
ENDFOR
```

15. What is the problem demonstrated by this example?

```
FOR EACH   ID-PAYROLL
      WHERE ID-PAYROLL.NUMBER EQ 11000 OR 12000
         OR ID-PAYROLL.NUMBER GT 13000
            LIST ID-PAYROLL.NUMBER
                  ID-PAYROLL.CURRENT-RATE
ENDFOR
```

Program will cause multiple traversals of the index to fulfill the request.

16. In the product solution, what could we have done differently to make the solution more efficient?

There are two possible better solutions:

1. Since the field STATE-ADDRESS is a secondary key through the concept of data integrity, there should logically be another DB table that contains the valid state codes for the system. Thus we should have been able to use that table for our second search file instead of the ID-EMPLOYEE file.

2. Since this file doesn't exist, and we can assume that there are a finite number of values for the STATE-ADDRESS field, we could have done a single pass on the ID-EMPLOYEE database to build an internal program table that we could have looped through instead. This would have saved IO and time by allowing us to process the second search through a finite number of table records, instead of the larger group of database records.

6

Calls and Subroutines

Many times during the design and development of an application, it is necessary (or expedient) to build and call a subroutine. This module would then be called and executed whenever any application in the system needs to execute a certain function.

This can be done for any number of reasons, such as isolating a difficult piece of logic so that it can be developed and tested on its own. We can also build important logic into a subroutine so that we can guarantee ourselves the same results whenever we execute it from different programs. The building of subroutines to handle common functions also saves coding time by reducing the number of times that the function has to be written and tested.

For example, in our system we have an algorithm that determines the tax rates that should be applied to each shipment that leaves our warehouse. This is done by taking the basic codes from the shipping address file, and then applying different overrides to them. These overrides include code dealing with variables like this:

1. Material is for internal usage or resale.
2. Material is for use within the receiving state or another state.
3. Local rapid transit tax is to be applied.
4. Material is shipped from the Everett warehouse and used in Everett, somewhere else in Washington state, or another state.
5. Receiving state has the customer pay his sales tax directly to the state or collects it in another way.

6. It's a Tuesday following a full moon in August.
7. etc.

This six-page routine is called by many different programs within our billing system, which makes it a perfect candidate for coding as a subroutine because

1. The same algorithm is used by multiple programs.
2. Only one program needs to be changed if one of the tax rules is changed (or they add a new one, like an override for a solar eclipse).
3. It can be coded by itself, and then all of the unit testing can be done by setting up a "test stand" which only passes the parameters to the subroutine and displays the returned results.

In this chapter we will explore the different types of subroutines and how they can be executed, including calls to programs which are outside of the IDEAL environment. We will also explore some of the efficiency concerns in the proper design, selection, and coding of sub-routines.

There are basically two types of subroutines, those from which we wish to return (such as the one above, where we call it and expect certain information returned) and ones that are independent of the calling program, such as a program called from a menu program, or one that displays information in an error situation and terminates the calling program.

In either case, it is neccessary to pass information between the programs. These pieces of information, called *parameters*, are stored in the working storage area of the calling program, and are then shared by the called program. We can either protect these fields or allow the called program to update them.

To understand how all this works, let's go through the steps of the development and execution of the subroutine. To do this, let's set up an order entry system for our sample distribution company. Each order in the system will have a distinct order control number. The next available order control number (ORDER-CNTL-NO) will be stored in a small database, and our subroutine will be the program that gets the next number from the database, increments the database record, writes a record out to an audit file, and returns the number to the calling program. We will call this program ORDCNTL, and it will have the following format.

The resource table will include references to two databases:

1. ORD-CNTL-UPD — which is the update dataview of the order control number file.
2. OCN-AUDIT-UPD — which is where we will write out our audit record.

The working-storage area will not be used in this particular algorithm, but can contain any needed data in the standard formats.

The parameter section will contain a receiving area for the parameters that are sent down from the drive routine:

```
----------------------------------------------------------------------

IDEAL:PARAMETER DEFINITION   PGM ORDCNTL (001) TEST        SYS: DEV

LEVEL FIELD NAME       T I CH/DG OCCUR U M COMMENTS/DEP ON
1      P-PROGRAM-NAME   X      8        I I : NAME OF THE CALLING PGM
1      P-ORD-CNTL-NO    X      6        U I : ORD-CNTL-NO RETURNED

_____ _____ _ _ _____ _____ _ _ _____
======================B O T T O M===================================
```

Here we have two fields defined, or rather accessible, to the called program from the program storage of the calling program. The character "I" in the update column of the definition (column marked "U") means that the field P-PROGRAM-NAME is only an input field, and as such is protected. The U means that the subroutine can update the field P-ORD-CNTL-NO. The characters P- on the front of the field names are not required by IDEAL, but are put there for readability in the procedure section of this example. The column marked "M" refers to the type of parameter matching that is to be used. The selection is placed on level 1 fields, and applies only to that field or group. It can be either Identical matching (I) or Dynamic matching (D).

Identical parameter matching requires that all of the attributes of the receiving parameter must be completely defined, and that they must match the attributes of the data item in the calling program. Dynamic parameter matching uses the definition of the data item in the calling program as the definition in the called program. The new calling program attributes will override the defined attributes in the called program. This allows IDEAL to avoid parameter matching abends, and is the default selection. However, Identical parameter matching is more efficient because all of the attributes are known at compile time. For this reason we will use Identical matching in our examples.

The procedure area would then look like this:

```
----------------------------------------------------------------------
IDEAL: PROCEDURE DEFINITION  PGM ORDCNTL (001) TEST      SYS: DEV
....+....1....+....2....+....3....+....4....+....5.....+....6....+.
======================================================================
<<ORDCNTL>> PROCEDURE
  FOR FIRST ORD-CNTL-UPD
      WHERE ORD-CNTL-UPD.REC-TYPE = 'BIL'
            MOVE $EDIT(ORD-CNTL-UPD.ORD-CNTL-NO,PIC='999999')
              TO P-ORD-CNTL-NO
            ADD 1 TO ORD-CNTL-UPD.ORD-CNTL-NO
            DO WRITE-AUDIT-RCD
      WHEN  NONE
            MOVE 'XXXXXX' TO P-ORD-CNTL-NO
  ENDFOR
ENDPROC


<<WRITE-AUDIT-RCD>> PROCEDURE
  FOR NEW OCN-AUDIT-UPD
      MOVE P-PROGRAM-NAME    TO OCN-AUDIT-UPD.PROGRAM-NAME
      MOVE P-ORD-CNTL-NO     TO OCN-AUDIT-UPD.ORDER-CNTL-NO
      MOVE $USER-NAME        TO OCN-AUDIT-UPD.LAST-OPER-ID
      MOVE $DATE('YYMMDD')   TO OCN-AUDIT-UPD.DAT-LST-MOD
      MOVE $TIME('HHMMSS')   TO OCN-AUDIT-UPD.TIM-LST-MOD
  ENDFOR
ENDPROC
========================B O T T O M============================
```

We then have to write the calling program, which we will name
program ORDENTRY.

The resource table will contain the name, version, and location of
the subroutine. The subroutine can exist in any of the subsystems of
the CICS region, and can be any TEST or PROD version of the
program. It is, however, most efficient if all the programs are in the
same subsystem.

```
----------------------------------------------------------------------
IDEAL: RESOURCE TABLE        PGM ORDENTRY (001) TEST     SYS: DEV
======================================================================
DATAVIEW       VERS   PANEL   VERS   REPORT   VERS   PROGRAM  VERS SYS
                                                     ORDCNTL  0001 DEV
_____  ____   _____ ____   _____ ____
========================B O T T O M============================
```

Thus our table points to program version 1, which resides in the DEV subsystem of this CICS region. It is not possible to call a program that resides in a different CICS region.

We would then code our working-storage section to define the two passed parameters:

```
-----------------------------------------------------------------
IDEAL: WORKING DATA DEFN.   PGM ORDENTRY (001) TEST       SYS: DEV

LEVEL FIELD NAME          T I CH/DG OCCUR VALUE/COMMENTS/DEP
ON/COPY
1     W-PROGRAM-NAME        X      8
1     W-ORD-CNTL-NO         X      6

_____ _____ _ _ _____ _____ _____
========================B O T T O M===============================
```

and our procedure definition to call the subroutine. (A great deal of program has been removed to show only the subroutine call).

```
-----------------------------------------------------------------
IDEAL: PROCEDURE DEFINITION  PGM ORDENTRY (001) TEST     SYS: DEV
....+....1....+....2....+....3....+....4....+....5.....+....6....+.
=================================================================
<<ORDENTRY>> PROCEDURE
   :
   MOVE "ORDENTRY" TO W-PROGRAM-NAME
   CALL ORDCNTL USING INPUT  W-PROGRAM-NAME
                      UPDATE W-ORD-CNTL-NO
   :
ENDPROC
===========================B O T T O M===========================
```

The reader should note at this time that we have not done any special coding for this process other than the CALL statement and the population of the PARAMETER screen of the ORDCNTL program. When these two areas are coded, it is important that the parameters in the CALL statement are in the same order, and correspond with, level 1 fields in the parameter fill-in screen, and that their data types match.

In addition, the following rules apply to the population of the CH/DG and the internal representation attributes.

For *dynamic* matching:

```
TYPE FIELD UPDATE INTENT RULE

____ _____ _____ _____
X    CH/DG    EITHER       REQUIRED
V    CH/DG    UPDATE       REQUIRED - MUST MATCH EXACTLY
V    CH/DG    INPUT        REQUIRED - LENGTH OF FIELD IN CALLED PGM
                                    - GE LENGTH IN CALLING PGM
N    CH/DG    EITHER       OPTIONAL - MUST MATCH IF SPECIFIED
U    CH/DG    EITHER       OPTIONAL - MUST MATCH IF SPECIFIED
D    CH/DG    EITHER       OPTIONAL - MUST MATCH IF SPECIFIED
ALL   I       EITHER       MUST BE BLANK
```

For *identical* matching:

```
TYPE FIELD UPDATE INTENT RULE

____ _____ _____ _____
ALL  CH/DG    EITHER       REQUIRED - MUST MATCH
N     I       EITHER       REQUIRED - MUST MATCH
U     I       EITHER       REQUIRED - MUST MATCH
D     I       EITHER       REQUIRED - MUST MATCH
X     I       EITHER       MUST BE BLANK
V     I       EITHER       MUST BE BLANK
F     I       EITHER       MUST BE BLANK
C     I       EITHER       MUST BE BLANK
```

Any violation of these rules will cause a *run-time parameter* error which will abend the program.

Now let's examine what happens when we run program OR-DENTER.

IDEAL programs function in what is known as *psuedo-conversational* mode. This means that whenever the processing hits a logical end, called a *transaction boundary*, but not the actual end of the program, all of the information that is needed by the program to resume processing is written out to *temporary storage*, and the program is removed from the CPU. Examples of a boundary include the transmission of a panel to an operator, or the calling of a subroutine from which we are going to return. This type of processing allows the main memory to be used by another program while the first program waits for control to be returned.

By comparison, a *fully conversational* language leaves all of the program resources in core while the program is waiting. This is what happens in many personal computers, where there is no other demand for the central processor during the wait state. An example of a *non-conversational* language is IBM's IMS/DLI, where all of the resources are purged when the screen is sent to the user.

To do this, an IDEAL load module is broken into two parts, a *reentrant*, and a *non-reentrant* part. The reentrant part consists of the actual program instructions, which can be shared by many users who are executing the same transaction. The non-reentrant area is distinct to each transaction, and consists of the data stores and values that each user is working with (working storage, dataviews, panel definitions, etc.)

When a transaction is started, a new copy of the non-reentrant area is created in main storage. If no other user is running the same transaction, then a copy of the reentrant part is also brought in. Otherwise, the existing copy is shared by both users. This is much like reading a book over someone's shoulder, with the book being the reentrant, or shared, resource, and the mind of each reader the non-reentrant area. Both readers see the same words, and read the same passages, but they each get something different out of it. What each reader gets out of it depends on their attention and their understanding of the material. In the same way, our two users can execute the same program, and get different values from it, depending on the input that they give to it.

When program ORDENTRY is started, both sections (reentrant and non-reentrant) are copied into main storage. When the instruction to call program ORDCNTL is encountered, the non-reentrant part of ORDENTRY would have to be copied into temporary storage, and ORDCNTL would be started. When ORDCNTL finishes, it is purged from the system, and ORDENTRY would be brought out of temporary storage and reloaded into main storage.

If we expand our program, we can see a potential efficiency problem and hopefully avoid it in our designs. Let us say that we had a program and some subroutines that had the structure chart shown in Figure 6-1.

Here we see a main program with seven subprograms that it can call. We will also state that each of these subprograms has a panel associated with it. Each time one of these programs is executed, the program in the chain above it has to be copied to temporary storage. Thus while we are running program D, all of the non-reentrant areas of programs MAIN, A, B, and C are waiting in the tempoary storage area. Thus in this design massive amounts of temporary storage must be kept active during the MAIN program's execution of the subroutines.

Then, because of IDEAL's requirement that a called module must return to the program that called it, each program in the chain must

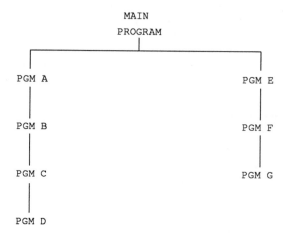

Figure 6-1   Subroutines in Vertical Stacking Design.

be copied out of temporary storage, restarted, and ended as the program above it is restarted.

This problem can be aggravated further if we fail to observe the rules of a concept called *locality of reference*.

Locality of reference can be thought of as a measure of how closely all of the data items that are required by a program are stored in physical memory. This is important because a passed parameter is really stored within the data area of the calling program, and is only pointed to by the called program. Thus if program A passed a field from the MAIN program, which in turn passed it to A, which in turn passed it to B, and so on to program D, and D transmitted its panel, causing a transaction boundary, the non-reentrant parts of all of the programs in the chain above it would have to be copied into temporary storage, simply because they each referenced the same field.

Thus, to avoid all of this IO to and from temporary storage, and the massive usage of this facility, it is recommended that IDEAL subroutines be designed on a horizontal basis, as in Figure 6-2, as opposed to the stacking shown in Figure 6-1. This will create a program structure that is at the most two levels deep, which reduces the need for temporary storage usage and IO processing overhead.

Another way to reduce the usage of temporary storage is to limit the size of the non-reentrant part of the load module. This is done by keeping the size and number of fields in working storage to a minimum. For example, it is recommended that messages from the program to the operator be coded as literals in the procedure section,

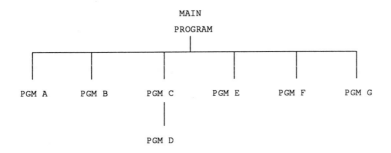

Figure 6-2   Subroutines in Horizontal Design.

rather than as data items in working storage. We could then use the $STRING command to combine pieces of information into a single message.

Another way to affect the amount of temporary storage usage and IO processing is through the way the *run-status* of the program is set. There are three statuses that can be selected; *resident, shared,* or *non-resident.* This status affects only the reentrant part of the program.

When a program is resident, its reentrant part is loaded when the first user runs the program, and is held in memory until the last user is done. By not having to constantly load and unload the program from storage, we save ourselves the IO cost. However, we must pay for it by having it permanently take up main memory, thus reducing the available resources for other programs. Therefore resident status should only be set on heavily used transactions, such as driver menus, which are in a state of constant use.

A shared program is also loaded when the first user requests it, as is the resident program. However, a shared program is deleted when the use counter is zero, rather than waiting for the last user to leave the system. While this requires the system to get another copy of the program whenever the user calls it up, it saves the permanent allocation of main memory.

A non-shared program has a separate copy of its reentrant data for each user running the program. This type of status is employed for very small and infrequently used programs like error or initialization routines. Here the program is only brought in when it is needed and is immediately released when it is finished. This saves storage space because the program is not called in until needed, but it can also take up extra space by having multiple copies of the same reentrant code in memory.

Another tool that can affect temporary storage utilization is the IDEAL RELEASE command. This command can be executed after the program has successfully returned from the CALL command, and it is used to release the called program from the temporary storage chain. However, when the program is needed again, another copy must be brought in from the libraries. If this is done too often, the overhead from this IO could offset the efficiency we gained through our RELEASE command.

Another point to consider in our design of subroutines is the number and size of the parameters being passed. Because of the processing in and out of temporary storage, it is neccessary to limit the size of these parameters as far as possible. One technique that can be used is to write the data out to a temporary database in one program and read it back in the next. For example, let's recall the program structure in Figure 6-1 which could be the design of a program that created on-line shipsets. The MAIN program can complete and select the shipset for printing, and the left leg of the structure can be the actual print structure. Program A extracts the basic print data, program B adds some additional information to it, program C is the IDEAL/COBOL interface entry, and program D is the CICS/COBOL program that formats the print. With this structure we have a choice between passing all of this data between the programs or having program A write it out to a temporary database, which programs B and D would read in and process. If we wrote the data out to a temporary database, all that we would have to pass between the programs is the key to the datafile.

When IDEAL passes parameters to another IDEAL program, it actually passes the physical memory address to the called program. So, when the called program refers to the parameter name, it is referring to the actual piece of data in the calling program. Then, when the call statement is executed, each field referenced is lined up with a level 1 field in the parameter fill-in of the called program. This line- up is done on a one-for-one basis. If more data items are passed than are listed, a compile-time error occurs.

If one of the passed parameters is a group field, then the individual fields of the group are aligned using the rules for MOVE BY POSITION.

Thus if we had two programs with the following definitions:

```
---------------------------------------------------------------------
IDEAL:PARAMETER DEFINITION   PGM CALLED   (001) TEST        SYS: DEV

LEVEL FIELD NAME      T I CH/DG OCCUR U M COMMENTS/DEP ON/COPY
```

```
1       P-PASSED-PARM   X       3               U I : RUN COMMAND PASSED PARM
_____  _____ _ _ _____ _____ _ _ _____
=====================B O T T O M================================
```

```
----------------------------------------------------------------
IDEAL: WORKING DATA DEFN.   PGM CALLING  (001) TEST      SYS: DEV

LEVEL FIELD NAME          T I CH/DG OCCUR VALUE/COMMENTS/DEP ON/COPY
1     W-PASSED-PARM
2       W-CUST-NO         X    2
2       W-SUMMARY-ONLY    X    1
1     W-SALES-AMT         N    5.2

_____  _____ _ _ _____ _____ _____
=====================B O T T O M================================
```

the statement

```
CALL CALLED USING W-PASSED-PARM
```

would be successful, because the level 1 fields lined up. On the other hand, the statement

```
CALL CALLED USING W-CUST-NO
                  W-SUMMARY-ONLY
```

would fail because it would try to line up the field W-CUST-NO with the field P-PASSED-PARM, which have different lengths.

It is also possible to pass a parameter to a program at the beginning of its execution. This is done by using the PARM clause of the RUN command:

```
RUN PGMNAME PARM 'PARAMETER DATA'
```

This data area is received through the parameter area of the program. The fill-in screen must be completed with a single level 1 field, which has the same length as the literal string that we are passing. If we have more that one field in the string, then we need to move the parameter to a working-storage area, which will have the multiple field definitions. The parameter field must also be set to input only.

```
-------------------------------------------------------------------
IDEAL:PARAMETER DEFINITION  PGM PASSPARM(001) TEST      SYS: DEV


LEVEL FIELD NAME         T I CH/DG OCCUR U M COMMENTS/DEP ON
1     P-PASSED-PARM      X    3           I I : RUN COMMAND PASSED PARM
_____ _____ _ _ _____ _____ _ _ _____
======================B O T T O M=================================
```

```
-------------------------------------------------------------------
IDEAL: WORKING DATA DEFN.   PGM PASSPARM (001) TEST      SYS: DEV


LEVEL FIELD NAME         T I CH/DG OCCUR VALUE/COMMENTS/DEP ON/COPY
1     W-PASSED-PARM
2       W-CUST-NO        X    2
2       W-SUMMARY-ONLY   X    1
1     W-SALES-AMT        N   5.2
_____ _____ _ _ _____ _____ _____
======================B O T T O M=================================
```

```
-------------------------------------------------------------------
IDEAL: PROCEDURE DEFINITION  PGM PASSPARM (001) TEST     SYS: DEV
....+....1....+....2....+....3....+....4....+....5.....+....6....+.
=================================================================
<<PASSPARM>> PROCEDURE
  MOVE P-PASSED-PARM TO W-PASSED-PARM
  FOR EACH   CUST-EQUIP-DVW
      WHERE CUST-EQUIP-DVW.CUST-NO  = W-CUST-NO
            IF W-SUMMARY-ONLY = 'N'
               LIST W-CUST-NO W-EQUIP-NO CUST-EQUIP-DVW.SALES
            ENDIF
            SET W-SALES-AMT = CUST-EQUIP-DVW.SALES + W-SALES-AMT
    ENDFOR
    LIST W-CUST-NO ' TOTAL ' W-SALES-AMT
  ENDPROC
======================B O T T O M=================================
```

In our example (PASSPARM), we read the parameter in with the command

```
RUN PASSPARM PARM 'C1Y'
```

The program will then move the parm to working storage, where we will find the customer number on which we wish to report. We will also see if this is a summary or a detail request from the second field.

Calling Non-IDEAL Programs

We also have the ability in IDEAL to call non-IDEAL programs to take advantage of some of the facilities that IDEAL does not have.

For example, the early versions of IDEAL did not have the ability to communicate the fact that an abend had occurred during in batch job. When this happened, all of the job system and users codes would show as zero. (We will discuss how to run batch jobs in Chapter 9.)

Thus, when we had an abend, we needed to pass a code to the system. We did this by calling a COBOL program, which in turn passed a value to the RETURN-CODE register.

We will call our COBOL program RETURNCD.

```
IDENTIFICATION DIVISION.
PROGRAM-ID. RETURNCD.
ENVIRONMENT DIVISION.
INPUT-OUTPUT SECTION.
FILE-CONTROL.
DATA DIVISION.
FILE SECTION.
WORKING-STORAGE SECTION.

LINKAGE SECTION.
01  PASSED-RETURN-CD      PIC XXX.

PROCEDURE DIVISION.
MAIN-LINE.
      MOVE PASSED-RETURN-CD TO RETURN-CODE.
      GOBACK.
```

This program will simply accept the parameter, pass it through the special RETURN-CODE register to the operating system, and return to the calling IDEAL program.

We would then set up an entry in IDEAL which will allow the program to be recognized by the DATADICTIONARY. We will create the program RETURNCD in IDEAL (it must have the same name as the COBOL program) and fill in the IDE section as follows:

```
------------------------------------------------------------------------
IDEAL: PGM IDENTIFICATION  PGM RETURNCD (001) TEST SYS: DEV FILL-IN
PROGRAM RETURNCD
DATE CREATED XX/XX/XX     DATE LAST MODIFIED XX/XX/XX
                         TIME LAST MODIFIED XX/XX

NEW COPY ON CALL? N
SHORT DESCRIPTION  POPULATE COBOL 'RETURN-CODE'
LANGUAGE: COBOL
DESCRIPTION:
    PROGRAM MASK TO ALLOW CALLING OF THE CORRESPONDING COBOL
    PROGRAM.

        ----------------------------------------------------
========================B O T T O M==================================
```

Note that we have designated the language as COBOL. The NEW
COPY ON CALL functions the same way that the RUN STATUS
command does, in that the system will retain or refresh the program
storage in memory when the IDEAL program calls this subroutine.
We will then go in and define the parameter section so that it
matches the LINKAGE SECTION of the COBOL program.

```
------------------------------------------------------------------------
IDEAL:PARAMETER DEFINITION  PGM PASSPARM(001) TEST      SYS: DEV

LEVEL FIELD NAME      T I CH/DG OCCUR U M COMMENTS/DEP ON/COPY
1      P-RETURN-CODE   X     3         U I : ERROR CODE PASSED PARM

_____  _____ _ _ _____ _____ _ _ _____
========================B O T T O M==================================
```

Since this "program" is marked as COBOL, it is not possible to
compile it with the IDEAL compiler. Its main purpose is to serve as
an entry in the DATADICTIONARY, so that when we compile the
calling program it will have an address with which to refer to this
module.

We will then change our PASSPARM program to call this
RETURNCD program.

```
------------------------------------------------------------------------
IDEAL: PROGRAM RESOURCES  PGM PASSPARM(001) TEST      SYS:DEV FILL-IN

  DATAVIEW   VER  PANEL     VER   REPORT    VER   PROGRAM  VER  SYS
                                                  RETURNCD 0001 DEV
_____ ____ _____ ____  _____ ____
```

```
_____ ____   _____ ____     _____ ____   _____ ____ ___
_____ ____   _____ ____     _____ ____   _____ ____ ___

-----------------------------------------------------------------------
IDEAL: WORKING DATA DEFN.   PGM PASSPARM (001) TEST        SYS: DEV

LEVEL FIELD NAME        T I CH/DG OCCUR VALUE/COMMENTS/DEP ON/COPY
1     W-RETURN-CD       X    3
_____ _____ _ _ _____ _____ _____
=======================B O T T O M===============================


-----------------------------------------------------------------------
IDEAL: PROCEDURE DEFINITION  PGM PASSPARM (001) TEST       SYS: DEV
....+....1....+....2....+....3....+....4....+....5.....+....6....+.
=======================================================================
<<PASSPARM>> PROCEDURE
  .

  .

ENDPROC

<<ERROR>> PROCEDURE
  MOVE $ERROR-DVW-STATUS TO W-RETURN-CD
  CALL RETURNCD USING W-RETURN-CD
  QUIT RUN.
ENDPROC
=======================B O T T O M===============================
```

Here we have placed a call to the RETURNCD program in the special ERROR PROCEDURE. This paragraph is automatically executed when a fatal error is encountered. (This procedure is the main subject of Chapter 10.) This program will in turn access the DATADICTIONARY for the location of RETURNCD, with which it will begin the COBOL program. The register will be populated, and control will return to the PASSPARM program, which will be terminated.

It should be noted here that when we call a program in another language, some of the parameter rules change. Instead of passing the actual address of the parameters, as it does with an IDEAL subroutine, it moves the parameter data to a temporary storage area and passes the new addresses. It then moves only those parameters that are marked as update back to the original data stores. Also, all calls to a non-IDEAL subroutine must use dynamic parameter passing, and both the CH/DG and the internal representation attributes are required.

We also cannot pass conditions, flags, or dates to another language because they are not standard data constructs, and therefore cannot be defined by the called non-IDEAL program.

While we lose the availability of these IDEAL data structures when calling a non-IDEAL program, we can still use the different types of numeric data, which we identify in the internal representation field:

Z — Zoned decimal
P — Packed decimal
B — Binary

These three data types are defined in COBOL with the USAGE IS clause.

Zoned decimal — Usage is DISPLAY
Packed decimal — Usage is COMP-3
Binary — Usage is COMP.

Even though the data type is defined in the parameter fill-in, it is neccessary to use the standard-length notations in the CH/DG column. Thus we need to convert the actual COBOL lengths to IDEAL lengths. This can be done as follows.

Zoned Decimal

The length value for the zoned decimal will be equal to the number of decimal (base 10) digits. Thus the following fill-in results:

```
-------------------------------------------------------------------
IDEAL:PARAMETER DEFINITION  PGM ZONEDEC (001) TEST        SYS: DEV


LEVEL FIELD NAME        T I CH/DG OCCUR U M COMMENTS/DEP ON/COPY
1     P-ZONED-3         N Z  3            U  : PIC S9(03) DISPLAY.
1     P-ZONED-4         N Z  4            U  : PIC S9(04) DISPLAY.
1     P-ZONED-5         N Z  5            U  : PIC S9(05) DISPLAY.
1     P-ZONED-5-2       N Z  5.2          U  : PIC S9(05)V99 DISPLAY.
                                                     .
_____ _____ _ _ _____ _____ _ _ _____
========================B O T T O M=================================
```

Packed Decimal

The packed decimal requires a half byte for every decimal (base 10) digit, plus a half byte for the sign. Thus the following results:

```
------------------------------------------------------------------
IDEAL:PARAMETER DEFINITION  PGM PACKDEC (001) TEST      SYS: DEV

LEVEL FIELD NAME      T I CH/DG OCCUR U M COMMENTS/DEP ON/COPY
1     P-PACKED-3      N P   3          U  : PIC S9(03) COMP-3.
1     P-PACKED-4      N P   4          U  : PIC S9(04) COMP-3.
1     P-PACKED-5      N P   5          U  : PIC S9(05) COMP-3.
1     P-PACKED-5-2    N P   5.2        U  : PIC S9(05)V99 COMP-3.
========================B O T T O M=================================
```

Binary

The size requirement for binary data is based on the fact that IDEAL will only allocate on a half- or a full-word boundary. Therefore allocation will be one half-word of space for every four bytes, with an additional half-word for any remaining bytes.

```
------------------------------------------------------------------
IDEAL:PARAMETER DEFINITION  PGM BINARY  (001) TEST      SYS: DEV

LEVEL FIELD NAME      T I CH/DG OCCUR U M COMMENTS/DEP ON/COPY
1     P-PACKED-3      N B   3          U  : PIC S9(03) COMP.
1     P-PACKED-4      N B   4          U  : PIC S9(04) COMP.
1     P-PACKED-5      N B   5          U  : PIC S9(05) COMP.
1     P-PACKED-5-2    N B   5.2        U  : PIC S9(05)V99 COMP.
========================B O T T O M=================================
```

However, the actual lengths only matter to an assembler application. As can be seen, the actual COBOL allocation corresponds to the CH/DG representation on the screen.

When we wish to call a COBOL program from an on-line IDEAL program, it is neccessary to set the program up as a CICS program. We would begin by creating the same IDEAL entry that we set up for the COBOL batch program. In this case, we will define three level 1 parameters, which will be passed to the COBOL program.

```
----------------------------------------------------------------
IDEAL:PARAMETER DEFINITION  PGM CALLCICS(001) TEST      SYS: DEV

LEVEL FIELD NAME       T I CH/DG OCCUR U M COMMENTS/DEP ON/COPY
1     P-PARAMETER-1     X    3          U  : FIRST PARAMETER
1     P-PARAMETER-2     X    4          U  : SECOND PARAMETER
1     P-PARAMETER-3     X    5          U  : THIRD PARAMETER
=======================B O T T O M================================
```

We would then have the systems programmers set up an entry with our program name in the CICS 'PROGRAM PROPERTIES TABLE' (PPT).

We would then write the following COBOL program:

```
IDENTIFICATION DIVISION.
PROGRAM-ID. CALLCICS.
ENVIRONMENT DIVISION.
INPUT-OUTPUT SECTION.
FILE-CONTROL.
DATA DIVISION.
FILE SECTION.
WORKING-STORAGE SECTION.

LINKAGE SECTION.
01  POINTERS.
    05  FILLER           PIC S9(08) COMP.
    05  POINTER-TWA      PIC S9(08) COMP.
    05  POINTER-ID-1     PIC S9(08) COMP.
    05  POINTER-ID-2     PIC S9(08) COMP.
    05  POINTER-ID-3     PIC S9(08) COMP.

01  TWA-AREA.
    05  TWA-PARM-1       PIC S9(08) COMP.
    05  TWA-PARM-2       PIC S9(08) COMP.
    05  TWA-PARM-3       PIC S9(08) COMP.

01  P-PARAMETER-1        PIC  X(03).
01  P-PARAMETER-2        PIC  X(04).
01  P-PARAMETER-3        PIC  X(05).

PROCEDURE DIVISION.
MAIN-LINE.
    EXEC CICS
```

```
      ADDRESS TWA (POINTER-TWA)
END-EXEC.

MOVE TWA-PARM-1       TO POINTER-ID-1.
MOVE TWA-PARM-2       TO POINTER-ID-2.
MOVE TWA-PARM-3       TO POINTER-ID-3.

PERFORM MAIN-PROCESS.
EXEC CICS
     RETURN
END-EXEC.
GOBACK.
```

Here we begin the processing by calling CICS to get the address of the TWA (transaction work area). This in turn contains the address in main memory of the parameters that we passed to the program. By moving the TWA data to the corresponding pointers, we gain access to the data that we passed to the COBOL program. With that access established we can execute the algorithm that uses the data (paragraph MAIN-PROCESS). When this is completed, we execute another CICS command that ends this module and transfers control back to the calling IDEAL program.

The pointers group must be the first entry in the LINKAGE SECTION. The first field is used by COBOL to provide addressability to the other fields in the list.

As we mentioned above, it is possible to call a subroutine that is not located in the same system in which we are running.

When an IDEAL/CICS region is established, it is possible to set it up with multiple systems available to it. Each system will contain its own program, panel, and report directories. This allows us to keep all of our production source code in one system (PRD), to do program development in another (DEV), and make emergency production fixes in a third (WOR). We do this by specifying the system where the module that we want resides in the system column (SYS) of the resource table.

For example, if we were making major changes to our ORDENTRY program in DEV, and wanted to use the production version of ORDCNTL we would change the resource table to be

```
-----------------------------------------------------------------------
IDEAL: PROGRAM RESOURCES   PGM ORDENTRY(001) TEST     SYS:DEV FILL-IN

DATAVIEW      VER  PANEL    VER   REPORT    VER   PROGRAM  VER  SYS
```

```
_____ ____   _____ ____    _____ ____    ORDCNTL  0001 PRD
_____ ____   _____ ____    _____ ____    _____ ____ ___
_____ ____   _____ ____    _____ ____    _____ ____ ___

---------------------------------------------------------------------
```

Now when ORDENTRY is run, we will pick up the version 1 of ORDCNTL that resides in the PRD system. It should be noted that if the subroutine uses a panel or a report resource, that resource must reside in the system where the calling program resides. This is because IDEAL uses the calling program's system library.

All systems within a region point to the same databases. This allows us to do parallel testing of a production program and its replacement to make sure they have the same results.

Conclusions

In this chapter we have seen how to efficiently call and design both IDEAL and non-IDEAL subroutines. However, the debate still rages as to when to use a subroutine, or keep the logic within the main program. To help with this we will list the advantages and the disadvantages of each choice:

Calling a Subroutine

1. Provides a single, common piece of code that can be used by multiple programs.
2. Increases the level of program modularity.

   a. Program can be developed and tested independently of drive program.
   b. Only a single program needs to be changed and recompiled when a design change is made to the algorithm.

3. Increases readability by isolating data with parameters.
4. Called module and its resources can be released.
5. Increases the overhead in the DATADICTIONARY.
6. Less efficient at run time.

Internal DO Statement

1. Common algorithm must be coded in each program that uses it.
2. All data in the program is available.
3. Entire program is involved in development and subsequent changes to the algorithm.
4. Resources cannot be released at run time.
5. Overall performance is more efficient because we limit the use of temporary storage.

With these arguments in mind, we need to see how often the algorithm is used. If it is called often and easily isolated, we should consider using a subroutine.

Exercises

1. List the main advantages to the use of a subroutine.
2. List the two different types of IDEAL parameters, and the purpose of each.
3. Create the parameter section of the receiving subroutine of the the following calls.

```
     a.  CALL CALLED USING INPUT  W-PASSED-PARM
                           UPDATE W-SALES-AMT
                                  W-COST-AMT
```

```
------------------------------------------------------------------
IDEAL: WORKING DATA DEFN.   PGM CALLING  (001) TEST      SYS: DEV

LEVEL FIELD NAME            T I CH/DG OCCUR VALUE/COMMENTS/DEP ON/COPY
1     W-PASSED-PARM
  2     W-PARM-1A           X    2
  2     W-PARM-1B           X    1
1     W-SALES-AMT           N    5.2
1     W-COST-AMT            N    5.2

_____ _____ _ _ _____ _____ _____
========================B O T T O M=============================


------------------------------------------------------------------
IDEAL:PARAMETER DEFINITION  PGM CALLED  (001) TEST      SYS: DEV
```

```
LEVEL FIELD NAME      T I CH/DG OCCUR U M COMMENTS/DEP ON/COPY
_____ _____ _ _ _____ _____ _ _ _____
_____ _____ _ _ _____ _____ _ _ _____
_____ _____ _ _ _____ _____ _ _ _____
_____ _____ _ _ _____ _____ _ _ _____
========================B O T T O M=================================
```

b. CALL CALLED USING INPUT W-PARA-AREA

```
--------------------------------------------------------------------
IDEAL: WORKING DATA DEFN.   PGM CALLING  (001) TEST       SYS: DEV

LEVEL FIELD NAME           T I CH/DG OCCUR VALUE/COMMENTS/DEP ON/COPY
1     W-PARA-AREA
 2      W-PASSED-PARM
  3       W-PARM-1A        X     2
  3       W-PARM-1B        X     1
 2      W-SALES-AMT        N     5.2
 2      W-COST-AMT         N     5.2
_____ _____ _ _____ _____ _____
========================B O T T O M=================================
```

```
--------------------------------------------------------------------
IDEAL:PARAMETER DEFINITION  PGM CALLED  (001) TEST       SYS: DEV

LEVEL FIELD NAME      T I CH/DG OCCUR U M COMMENTS/DEP ON/COPY
_____ _____ _ _ _____ _____ _ _ _____
_____ _____ _ _ _____ _____ _ _ _____
_____ _____ _ _ _____ _____ _ _ _____
_____ _____ _ _ _____ _____ _ _ _____
_____ _____ _ _ _____ _____ _ _ _____
========================B O T T O M=================================
```

4. Write the CALL statement between the following working-storage and parameter area.

```
--------------------------------------------------------------------
IDEAL: WORKING DATA DEFN.   PGM CALLING  (001) TEST       SYS: DEV

LEVEL FIELD NAME           T I CH/DG OCCUR VALUE/COMMENTS/DEP
ON/COPY
1     W-PARA-AREA
 2      W-PASSED-PARM
```

```
   3      W-PARM-1A          X     2
   3      W-PARM-1B          X     1
   1      W-SALES-AMT        N P   5.2
   1      W-COST-AMT         N P   5.2

  _____  _____  _ _  _____  _____  _____
  ======================B O T T O M=================================
```

```
  ----------------------------------------------------------------------

IDEAL:PARAMETER DEFINITION   PGM CALLED   (001) TEST      SYS: DEV

LEVEL FIELD NAME        T I CH/DG OCCUR U M COMMENTS/DEP ON/COPY
  1     W-PARA-AREA
  2     W-PASSED-PARM
   3      W-PARM-1A          X     2        I I
   3      W-PARM-1B          X     1        I I
  1     W-SALES-AMT        N P   5.2        U I
  1     W-COST-AMT         N P   5.2        U I

  _____  _____  _ _  _____  _____  _  _____
  ======================B O T T O M=================================
```

5. How many fields can be in the parameter fill-in for a program receiving a batch parm?
6. What is the purpose of the IDEAL skeleton program that is created when calling a COBOL program?
7. What is *locality of reference*? Why is it important?
8. What are the three IDEAL program run statuses? Which is the most common?
9. What is the purpose of the RELEASE command?
10. What is the name of the CICS table that we must update to run a CICS COBOL subroutine from IDEAL?
11. What are the three types of numeric fields that we can pass to a non-IDEAL subroutine?
12. What would be the corresponding COBOL definition of a numeric parameter with a length of 6.3? What are the three assembler lengths?
13. What is the main concern about calling a program in another system in the CICS region?

Exercises — Answers

1. List the main advantages to the use of a subroutine.

1. Provides a single, common piece of code that can be used by multiple programs.
2. Increases the level of program modularity.

   a. Program can be developed and tested independently of drive program.
   b. Only a single program needs to be changed and recompiled when a design change is made to the algorithm.

3. Increases readability by isolating data as parameters.
4. Called module and its resources can be released.

2. List the two different types of IDEAL parameters and the purpose of each.

```
I - INPUT  , U - UPDATE
```

Protect from or allow the subroutine to update the field in the calling program.

3. Create the parameter section of the receiving subroutine of the the following calls.

```
a.  CALL CALLED USING INPUT  W-PASSED-PARM
                     UPDATE  W-SALES-AMT
                             W-COST-AMT
```

```
------------------------------------------------------------------
IDEAL: WORKING DATA DEFN.   PGM CALLING  (001) TEST       SYS: DEV

LEVEL FIELD NAME          T I CH/DG OCCUR VALUE/COMMENTS/DEP ON/COPY
1     W-PASSED-PARM
 2      W-PARM-1A         X      2
 2      W-PARM-1B         X      1
1     W-SALES-AMT         N P  5.2
1     W-COST-AMT          N P  5.2

_____ _____ _ _ _____ _____ _____
========================B O T T O M===============================


------------------------------------------------------------------
IDEAL:PARAMETER DEFINITION  PGM CALLED  (001) TEST       SYS: DEV

LEVEL FIELD NAME       T I CH/DG OCCUR U M COMMENTS/DEP ON/COPY
```

```
1       P-PASSED-PARM   X       3           I I : RUN COMMAND PASSED PARM
1       P-SALES-AMT     N P     5.2         U I : RUN COMMAND PASSED PARM
1       P-COST-AMT      N P     5.2         U I : RUN COMMAND PASSED PARM

_____  _____  _ _  _____  _____  _  _____
=====================B O T T O M==================================
```

```
--------------------------------------------------------------------
IDEAL:PARAMETER DEFINITION  PGM CALLED  (001) TEST       SYS: DEV

LEVEL FIELD NAME        T I CH/DG OCCUR U M COMMENTS/DEP ON/COPY
1       P-PASSED-PARM
2         W-PARM-1A     X       2           I I
2         W-PARM-1B     X       1           I I
1       P-SALES-AMT     N P     5.2         U I
1       P-COST-AMT      N P     5.2         U I

_____  _____  _ _  _____  _____  _ _  _____
=====================B O T T O M==================================
```

    b. CALL CALLED USING INPUT W-PARA-AREA

```
--------------------------------------------------------------------
IDEAL: WORKING DATA DEFN.   PGM CALLING  (001) TEST      SYS: DEV

LEVEL FIELD NAME            T I CH/DG OCCUR VALUE/COMMENTS/DEP ON
1       W-PARA-AREA
2         W-PASSED-PARM
3           W-PARM-1A   X       2
3           W-PARM-1B   X       1
2         W-SALES-AMT   N P     5.2
2         W-COST-AMT    N P     5.2

_____  _____  _ _  _____  _____  _____
=====================B O T T O M==================================
```

```
--------------------------------------------------------------------
IDEAL:PARAMETER DEFINITION  PGM CALLED  (001) TEST       SYS: DEV

LEVEL FIELD NAME        T I CH/DG OCCUR U M COMMENTS/DEP ON/COPY
1       P-PARA-AREA
2         P-PASSED-PARM X       3           I I
2         P-SALES-AMT   N P     5.2         I I
2         P-COST-AMT    N P     5.2         I I

_____  _____  _ _  _____  _____  _ _  _____
=====================B O T T O M==================================
```

```
------------------------------------------------------------------------
IDEAL:PARAMETER DEFINITION  PGM CALLED  (001) TEST      SYS: DEV


LEVEL FIELD NAME       T I CH/DG OCCUR U M COMMENTS/DEP ON/COPY
1     P-PARA-AREA
2     P-PASSED-PARM
3       P-PARA-1A       X     2          I I
3       P-PARA-1B       X     1          I I
2     P-SALES-AMT      N P   5.2         I I
2     P-COST-AMT       N P   5.2         I I


_____  _____ _ _ _____  _____ _ _ _____
========================B O T T O M===================================
```

4. Write the CALL statement between the following working-
   storage and parameter areas.

```
------------------------------------------------------------------------
IDEAL: WORKING DATA DEFN.   PGM CALLING  (001) TEST      SYS: DEV


LEVEL FIELD NAME       T I CH/DG OCCUR VALUE/COMMENTS/DEP ON/COPY
1     W-PARA-AREA
2     W-PASSED-PARM
3       W-PARM-1A       X     2
3       W-PARM-1B       X     1
1     W-SALES-AMT      N P   5.2
1     W-COST-AMT       N P   5.2


_____  _____ _ _ _____  _____ _____
========================B O T T O M===================================
```

```
------------------------------------------------------------------------
IDEAL:PARAMETER DEFINITION  PGM CALLED  (001) TEST      SYS: DEV
LEVEL FIELD NAME       T I CH/DG  OCCUR U M COMMENTS/DEP ON/COPY
1     W-PARA-AREA
2     W-PASSED-PARM
3       W-PARM-1A       X     2          I I
3       W-PARM-1B       X     1          I I
1     W-SALES-AMT      N P   5.2         U I
1     W-COST-AMT       N P   5.2         U I


_____  _____ _ _ _____  _____ _ _ _____
========================B O T T O M===================================
```

```
CALL CALLED USING INPUT  W-PARA-AREA
                 UPDATE  W-SALES-AMT
                         W-COST-AMT
```

5. How many fields can be in the parameter fill-in for a program receiving a batch parm?

One level 1 field, which has the same length as the passed literal.

6. What is the purpose of the IDEAL skeleton program that is created when calling a COBOL program?

Creates a reference in the DATADICTIONARY for the called program to find at run time, and for the compiler to reference at compile time.

7. What is *locality of reference*? Why is it important?

Measures how close fields are in physical memory. Determines how much data must be held in temporary storage when a subroutine is called.

8. What are the three IDEAL program run statuses? Which is the most common?

a. resident
b. shared
c. non-shared

Shared is the most common and the most efficient choice.

9. What is the purpose of the RELEASE command?

Reduces the amount of temporary storage used by releasing resources such as panels and programs when they are no longer needed.

10. What is the name of the CICS table that we must update to run a CICS COBOL subroutine from IDEAL?

PPT — Program Properties Table

11. What are the three types of numeric fields that we can pass to a non-IDEAL subroutine?

a. Zoned decimal
b. Packed decimal

    c.   Binary

12. What would be the corresponding COBOL definition of a numeric parameter with a length of 6.3? What are the three assembler lengths?

```
a.  ZONED DECIMAL    PIC S9(06)V999    9 BYTES
b.  PACKED DECIMAL   PIC S9(06)V999    5 BYTES
c.  BINARY           PIC S9(06)V999    6 BYTES
```

13. What is the main concern about calling a program in another system in the same CICS region?

The resources (panels and reports) listed in the called program's resource table must be available in the calling program's system.

7

IDEAL Panels and Panel Processing

Panels are a series of screens that allow the user to have on-line access to the database. They are, in reality, a series of programs that

1. Display a formatted screen on a CRT
2. Extract information from the screen and format it for input to an application program
3. Begin the application program
4. Receive information from the application program by serving as the working storage area for the panel
5. Place the received information into the formatted screen fields
6. Display the screen on the CRT

In this chapter, we will discuss how these panel programs interface with our application programs, and how they can be used effectively. We will then discuss the fill-in screens that are used to define and maintain a panel definition, along with some application examples.

Panel Interfaces

We can best begin our discussion with a simple diagram. (See Figure 7-1.)

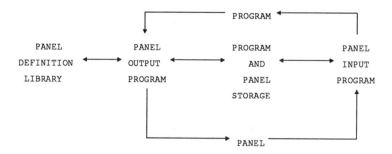

Figure 7-1   Initial Panel/program Interface.

The process begins when an IDEAL application program is run. The application program is used to control the timing of the transmission of the screen to the user. This is done with the PDL command:

```
TRANSMIT PANEL-NAME
        (REINPUT)
        (CLEAR)
        (CURSOR AT FIELD POSITION)
        (          HOME          )
        (ALARM)
```

When this command is executed, the application program is disabled. Because IDEAL is a psuedo-conversational language, all of the working storage is saved. This allows processing to resume where it left off. The panel's OUTPUT program then begins. If this is the first use of the panel by the program during this session, then a copy of the screen layout definition is brought in from the panel library. This definition contains the following information for each field that will appear on the screen:

1. Length of the field
2. Initial value

   a. Literal string
   b. Output fill character (spaces, underlines, low values)

3. Protected from Input/Unprotected
4. SKIP/AUTO STOP
5. Intensity of display (highlight, lowlight, invisible, color)
6. Numeric only/Alphanumeric

```
IDEAL:                                                    DISPLAY

              C L A R I F Y   E D I T   V I O L A T I O N S

    COUNT 0000000000      20
                          1**


    1 - 1 IDSCCEVM05E - NUMBER MUST BE FROM 0 THRU 10


    TYPE RETURN OR PRESS PF2 TO RETURN TO MAIN PANEL
```

Figure 7-2   CLARIFY Screen Example.

7. Input fill character
8. Edit pattern

A copy of this information is written to a temporary storage area for future reference and update by the application. The panel is then "painted" on the CRT screen by the PANEL-OUTPUT program, which also applies all of the output fill characters to the fields.

The user then keys in any required information and hits either the ENTER key or an appropriate PF key. When this happens, the PANEL-INPUT program takes control. This program begins by applying any edit criterion designated in the panel definition. This can include

1. Minimum value.
2. Maximum value.
3. Numeric data only.
4. Field is required as input.
5. Number of decimal values that must be input (precision).
6. Field is required to be completely filled in.

If any of these edits fail, the screen is returned to the user, with the offending field marked and a display that suggests the use of the CLARIFY screen. This screen is controlled by the INPUT program and shows the detail of the error (see Figure 7-2).

This screen is usually reached by having the operator hit the PF3 key, and returned from by hitting the PF2 key.

Another panel controlled by the PANEL-INPUT program is the HELP panel. This is created to help the operator better understand the function of the main panel by supplying instructions in an on-line mode. This panel is a screen full of previously formatted literals, and is reached by hitting PF key 1 and returned from with PF key 2.

When the PANEL-INPUT program is satisfied with the data that has been provided, it separates the data from the screen literals, and passes it on to the application program. The program then executes the next sequential instruction following the TRANSMIT, and continues processing from there. We can think of the TRANSMIT statement as a *book mark* in the program.

When the next TRANSMIT is encountered, the same procedure is followed except that the panel definition is taken from the program storage area instead of the panel library. The output fill characters are then applied to any field that the program has not updated, and any required edit patterns are also applied to the screen data.

Now that we understand the basic processing logic of IDEAL panels, let's discuss how we define and control it.

IDEAL Panel Definitions

Like most IDEAL entities, the panel definition facility consists of a series of fill-in screens that the programmer uses to supply information to the compiler. It then takes the information and converts it into machine instructions, creating the PANEL-INPUT and OUTPUT programs. The fill-in screens for the panel definition are

1. IDENTIFICATION (IDE) — contains the panel name and description.
2. PARAMETER (PAR) — specifies the panel global parameters.
3. LAYOUT (LAY) — is used by the programmer to specify the position and length of each field on the screen.
4. SUMMARY (SUM) — is generated by the panel facility from the layout screen, and is used to specify the name of the field, and the high-level attributes.
5. EXTENDED FIELD (FIE) — is generated from the entry on the summary screen, and is used to further define the attributes of the field.
6. IRULES (IRU) — summary screen, shows the input rules of all of the fields that make up the panel.
7. ORULES (ORU) — summary screen, shows the output rules of all of the fields that make up the panel.
8. FACSIMILE (FAC) — shows the panel as it will appear to the user when transmitted.

```
IDEAL: PANEL PARAMETERS     PNL XXXXXXXX (XXX) XXXX     SYS: XXX FILL-IN


START      FIELD SYMBOL _ NEW     FIELD SYMBOL _
END        FIELD SYMBOL _ DELETE FIELD SYMBOL _
REPEATING GROUP SYMBOL _


INPUT  FILL CHARACTER   _ (S=SPACE, L=LOWVAL, Z=ZEROES, U=_,OTHER=ITSELF
OUTPUT FILL CHARACTER   _ (S=SPACE, L=LOWVAL, Z=ZERORS, U=_,OTHER=ITSELF
NON-DISPLAY CHARACTER   _ (S=SPACE, OTHER=AS SPECIFIED)
ERROR FILL CHARACTER    _ (AS SPECIFIED)
CASE TRANSLATION        _ (U=UPPER, M=MIXED)


REQUIRED                _ (Y=YES, N=NO)
ERROR HANDLING          _ (N=NONE, *=FILL W/ERRORFILL, H=HIGH INTENSITY,
                          (B=BOTH: H IF ILLEGAL VALUE & * IF REQ MISSING


PANEL WIDTH          ___ (A VALUE BETWEEN 80 and 236)
PF1=HELP, PF3=CLARIFY _ (Y=YES, N=NO)
PF7=SCR -, PF8=SCR+   _ (N=NO, Y=OPT Y, Z=OPT Z)
  PF10=SCR TOP, PF11=SCR BOT   (OPTION Y)
  PF10=SCR LEFT,PF11=SCR RIGHT (OPTION Z)
EDIT-RULE ERROR PROC   _ (C=CLARIFY COMMAND, A=APPLICATION)
PROCESS APPL ON SCROLL _ (Y=YES,N=NO)
HELP PANEL NAME    _____ VERSION ___
PREFIX PANEL NAME  _____ VERSION ___
SUFFIX PANEL NAME  _____ VERSION ___
------------------------- B O T T O M -------------------------------
```

Figure 7-3 Parameter Screen Fill-In.

The parameter screen specifies those options that affect the processing of the entire panel. These include the control characters for the layout panel, the default editing and fill characteristics, the definition of PF key functions, and the names of the help and other associated panels. (See Figure 7-3.)

The first group of fields are used on the layout panel, and will be discussed in a moment. the second group are the default field attributes:

INPUT FILL CHARACTER — the value that will be assigned to any alphanumeric byte that is not keyed in. Numeric fields are always filled with zeroes.

OUTPUT FILL CHARACTER — the value that will appear on the screen when the application moves low values to the field.

NON-DISPLAY CHARACTER — the value that will appear when a non-displayable character is encountered by the PANEL-OUT-PUT program.

ERROR FILL CHARACTER — the character that is shown when the panel-input program encounters an error, and reshows the panel to the user.

CASE TRANSLATION — determines if the case of the data is to be translated before it goes to the application. (NOTE: we recommend that all panel data be used as uppercase only. This makes application coding easier, and keeps the data in the database cleaner. DATACOM will see uppercase A and lowercase a as not equal to each other.)

REQUIRED — specifies if a field is required by the PANEL-INPUT program, or can be omitted.

ERROR HANDLING — specifies how a field that the PANEL-INPUT program rejects is to be highlighted to the user.

PANEL WIDTH — allows the developer to create a screen that is wider than the standard 80-byte screen.

EDIT-RULE ERROR PROC — tells the PANEL-INPUT program how to handle any edit errors that it encounters. If the value is "C," the default value, then the CLARIFY screen will be displayed. If the value is set to "A," then the application will deal with the error. The function $PANEL-ERROR will be set to true, to tell the application program that an error has been encountered and passed on.

PROCESS APPL ON SCROLL — tells IDEAL whether to pass control back to the application program when a scroll key is pressed.

The third area of the panel allows for the handling of PF-key processing by the panel-input program. If the value is set to "N", then the application program must substitute for this process.

The fourth area of the screen allows us to enable the PF keys that we will use for scrolling. PF keys 7 and 8 allow us to move up or down one screen respectively. This feature is implemented with either a Y or a Z value. These values designate the usage of PF keys 10 and 11. If option Y is selected, then these keys will be used to go to the top or the bottom of the screen. If option Z is selected, then the keys will be used to move left and right on an extra-wide panel.

The fifth area identifies the HELP, PREFIX, and SUFFIX PANELS. The HELP panel again contains literal display information that tells the user more about the panel they are using. PREFIX and

SUFFIX panels are also made up of literal fields, and can be used to display such common pieces of information such as copyrights, company logos, etc. They come up at the top and the bottom, respectively, of the main panel.

The next screen that we encounter in our development work is the LAYOUT screen, which comes to us initially as a large open area, upon which we "paint" the layout of our panel.

To see how this is done, let us develop a panel that can be used to do on-line maintenance to the equipment database that we developed in Chapter 5. We would first create the panel and fill in the required fields on the IDENTIFICATION screen. We would then set up the parameter fill-in as follows:

```
---------------------------------------------------------------------------
IDEAL: PANEL PARAMETERS     PNL EQUIPMNT (001) TEST     SYS: DEV FILL-IN


START      FIELD SYMBOL ^ NEW     FIELD SYMBOL +

END        FIELD SYMBOL ; DELETE FIELD SYMBOL *

REPEATING GROUP SYMBOL @


INPUT  FILL CHARACTER  S (S=SPACE, L=LOWVAL, Z=ZEROES, U=_,OTHER=ITSELF

OUTPUT FILL CHARACTER  U (S=SPACE, L=LOWVAL, Z=ZERORS, U=_,OTHER=ITSELF

NON-DISPLAY CHARACTER  S (S=SPACE, OTHER=AS SPECIFIED)

ERROR FILL CHARACTER   * (AS SPECIFIED)

CASE TRANSLATION       U (U=UPPER, M=MIXED)


REQUIRED               N (Y=YES, N=NO)

ERROR HANDLING         * (N=NONE, *=FILL W/ERRORFILL, H=HIGH INTENSITY,
                         (B=BOTH: H IF ILLEGAL VALUE & * IF REQ MISSING


PANEL WIDTH            (A VALUE BETWEEN 80 AND 236)

PF1=HELP, PF3=CLARIFY  Y (Y=YES, N=NO)

PF7=SCR -, PF8=SCR+    N (N=NO, Y=OPT Y, Z=OPT Z)

  PF10=SCR TOP, PF11=SCR BOT    (OPTION Y)

  PF10=SCR LEFT,PF11=SCR RIGHT (OPTION Z)

EDIT-RULE ERROR PROC   C (C=CLARIFY COMMAND, A=APPLICATION)

PROCESS APPL ON SCROLL N (Y=YES,N=NO)


HELP PANEL NAME   _____  VERSION ___

PREFIX PANEL NAME _____  VERSION ___

SUFFIX PANEL NAME _____  VERSION ___


--------------------------- B O T T O M ---------------------------------
```

For our layout work symbols, we used a group of special characters that we were sure would not appear on the panel. Otherwise, the panel translator would try to use our literals as field position commands. Further, we told the input program to pad any unkeyed bytes with spaces, and to make sure that all of the data comes in as uppercase. We also told the output program to fill in any unused fields with underscores, so that they will appear on the screen and the operator can fill them in. We will use the standard PF-1, PF-2, and PF-3 conventions, but will handle our own scrolling.

We will then call up the LAYOUT screen and proceed to be artistic.

```
IDEAL: PANEL LAYOUT        PNL EQUIPMNT (001) TEST    SYS: DEV FILL-IN
START: ^    END: ;      NEW: +       DELETE: *      REPEAT: @
....+....1....+....2....+....3....+....4....+....5....+....6....+...7..
    +_____;     +EQUIPMENT DATABASE MAINTENANCE PROGRAM;

    +OPTION; +_; +(A=ADD V=VIEW U=UPDATE D=DELETE);

    +EQUIPMENT-NO; +__;
    +EQUIPMENT-NAME+_____;
    +COLOR;        +_____;
    +WEIGHT;       +_____; +IN POUNDS;
    +WAREHOUSE;    +_____;

    +MESSAGE;      +_____;
============================B O T T O M===============================
```

We would then hit the ENTER key; the translator would review the layout for syntax errors and, if satisfied, make the following conversion:

```
IDEAL: PANEL LAYOUT        PNL EQUIPMNT (001) TEST    SYS: DEV FILL-IN
START: ^    END: ;      NEW: +       DELETE: *      REPEAT: @
....+....1....+....2....+....3....+....4....+....5....+....6....+...7..
    ^_____;     ^EQUIPMENT DATABASE MAINTENANCE PROGRAM;

    ^OPTION; ^_; ^(A=ADD V=VIEW U=UPDATE D=DELETE);

    ^EQUIPMENT-NO; ^__;
    ^EQUIPMENT-NAME^_____;
    ^COLOR;        ^_____;
```

```
^WEIGHT;              ^_____; ^IN POUNDS;

^WAREHOUSE;     ^_____;


^MESSAGE;       ^_____;
----------------------- B O T T O M ------------------------------
```

Here all of the *new* symbols have been converted to *field start* symbols. Also, the unused lines below the message line have been dropped from the screen definition.

We can continue to manipulate the layout of this screen with the field commands and the insert and delete keys on the keyboard. For example, we can move the option field over to line up with the other input fields by using the insert key. The user doesn't want the 'IN POUNDS' message, so we will place an asterisk (*) on its start field indicator. These changes would result in the following screen:

```
_____
IDEAL: PANEL LAYOUT       PNL EQUIPMNT (001) TEST     SYS: DEV FILL-IN
START: ^    END: ;     NEW: +      DELETE: *     REPEAT: @
....+....1....+....2....+....3....+....4....+....5....+....6....+...7..
      ^_____;      ^EQUIPMENT DATABASE MAINTENANCE PROGRAM;

   ^OPTION;        ^_; ^(A=ADD V=VIEW U=UPDATE D=DELETE);

   ^EQUIPMENT-NO; ^__;
   ^EQUIPMENT-NAME^_____;
   ^COLOR;         ^_____;
   ^WEIGHT;              ^_____;
   ^WAREHOUSE;     ^_____;


   ^MESSAGE;       ^_____;
----------------------- B O T T O M ------------------------------
```

We could have also pressed the ERASE EOF key to eliminate the IN POUNDS literal. The use of this key deletes everything from the cursor position to the end of the line.

To add lines to the screen, we would simply place the cursor where we wish the additional lines to be placed, and either press PF12 or type the word "input" into the command line, and press the ENTER key.

We should also note that the literal 'EQUIPMENT NAME' does not have an END OF FIELD mark. This is possible because the translator can take the next START FIELD mark on the same line as the END FIELD mark of the previous field. This allows us to keep the number of bytes between fields to a minimum.

Our next step is to call up the summary screen. This screen is built from the information on the layout screen and the parameter screen, and in our example would appear as:

```
-------------------------------------------------------------------------
IDEAL: FIELD SUMMARY TABLE    PNL EQUIPMNT (001) TEST  SYS: DEV FILL-IN
=========================================================================
      ^_____;      ^EQUIPMENT DATABASE MAINTENANCE PROGRAM;
      1               2
      ^OPTION;        ^_;  ^(A=ADD V=VIEW U=UPDATE D=DELETE);
      3               4    5

..........................................................................
SEQ LV FIELD NAME        ATTR   T LEN   IN.DP OCC COMMENTS
--- -- ---------------   ------ - ----  ----- --- ------------------------
 1   2                   PSL    X    8
 2   2                   PSL    X   38             EQUIPMENT DATABASE MAINT
 3   2                   PSL    X    6             OPTION
 4   2                   PSL    X    1
 5   2                   PSL    X   30             (A=ADD V=VIEW U=UPDATE D
 6   2                   PSL    X   12             EQUIPMENT-NO
 7   2                   PSL    X    2
 8   2                   PSL    X   14             EQUIPMENT-NAME
 9   2                   PSL    X   10
10   2                   PSL    X    5             COLOR
11   2                   PSL    X   10
12   2                   PSL    X    6             WEIGHT
13   2                   PSL    X    5
14   2                   PSL    X    9             WAREHOUSE
15   2                   PSL    X   10
16   2                   PSL    X    7             MESSAGE
17   2                   PSL    X   41
```

The top of the screen is taken up by an area that shows the numbering of the fields in the panel. Other fields in this area can be accessed by simply scrolling through the area.

The sequence number (SEQ), attribute (ATTR), type (T), length (LEN), and comments columns were automatically populated. The sequence column is the number of the field on the screen. This numbering begins in the upper left-hand column, and goes left to right, top to bottom. The level number refers to the grouping of fields, which is similar to the levels in a working-storage screen. The whole panel is level 1, and the individual elementary fields are level 2. This is done because the summary table functions like a working-storage area for the panel fields when it is compiled into the program. The default attributes are set to PSL (protected, skip, lowlight), the type is set to X for alphanumeric, and the length is taken from the LAYOUT screen. The COMMENTS column is populated with the literal value of the field on the screen.

All of these columns can be updated here, except for the SEQUENCE and the LENGTH fields, which must be changed on the layout screen.

The first thing that we need to supply is the field name. This will be the name that the application program will use when it needs to reference the field. Next we need to review the assigned attributes. These attributes can take a combination of the following values:

P — Protected field that can only be displayed; field value cannot be changed.

U — Unprotected field that can be entered, modified, or deleted.

S — SKIP — Protected field that does not allow entry by the cursor into the field.

H — High-intensity character display.

L — Low-intensity character display.

I — The field is invisible to the user.

E — ENSURE RECEIVE — Value is assumed to always have been entered by the user; if not, the input fill characters are placed in the entire field.

A — Field can accept any member of the standard character set.

N — Field will only accept numeric characters (this feature only works on terminals with a corresponding numeric lock capability).

C — Field contains the cursor. On transmission of the screen only one field can contain this marking, or a compile time error will occur.

The suggested attribute combinations are:

```
PROTECTED FIELD     - PSHCE
                        L
                        I


UNPROTECTED FIELD - UAHCE
                      NL
                       I
```

The type field can be either X for an alphanumeric field, or N for a numeric field. It is also important that the attribute (A/N) agree with the type field. When the type is set to N we can open the IN.DP field, which stands for INTEGER-DECIMAL. We can then specify the combination of decimal and integer values to be used by the field. The total number of bytes (integer + decimal) cannot exceed 15 characters, although the total length of the field can exceed 15 characters.

We are postponing the discussion of the OCC column until later in this chapter.

The comments field is populated with the value placed in the field on the layout screen until something else is typed onto it. The field will then retain the new value, until something else is typed over it.

With all of this in mind, we would populate our summary screen as follows:

```
------------------------------------------------------------------------
IDEAL: FIELD SUMMARY TABLE    PNL EQUIPMNT (001) TEST  SYS: DEV FILL-IN
========================================================================
       ^_____;      ^EQUIPMENT DATABASE MAINTENANCE PROGRAM;
       1                2

       ^OPTION;           ^_; ^(A=ADD V=VIEW U=UPDATE D=DELETE);
       3                 4   5

.........................................................................
SEQ LV FIELD NAME        ATTR   T LEN  IN.DP OCC COMMENTS
--- -- ---------------   ------ - ---- ----- --- ------------------------
  1  2 CURR-DATE         PSL    X    8
  2  2                   PSL    X   38              EQUIPMENT DATABASE MAINT
  3  2                   PSL    X    6              OPTION
  4  2 OPTION            UALCE  X    1
  5  2                   PSL    X   30              (A=ADD V=VIEW U=UPDATE D
  6  2                   PSL    X   12              EQUIPMENT-NO
  7  2 EQUIP-NO          UALE   X    2
  8  2                   PSL    X   14              EQUIPMENT-NAME
  9  2 EQUIP-NAME        UALE   X   10
 10  2                   PSL    X    5              COLOR
 11  2 COLOR             UALE   X   10
 12  2                   PSL    X    6              WEIGHT
 13  2 WEIGHT            UNLE   X    5  3.1
 14  2                   PSL    X    9              WAREHOUSE
 15  2 WAREHOUSE         UALE   X   10
 16  2                   PSL    X    7              MESSAGE
 17  2 MESSAGE           PSL    X   41
```

Here we have used the corresponding database field names for the screen field names. We have left the PSL attributes on all of the literal fields, and on each of the fields (CURR-DATE and MESSAGE) which are populated and maintained by the program. We also made the weight field a numeric field, and defined it as having three integers and one decimal place. All the other fields are set to 'UALE', which allows alphanumeric data to be placed in each field. If nothing is entered, then the input fill character will be used. The cursor will always appear on the option field.

We can continue our description of the panel with the extended field definition screen. Each field has one, and it is created from the combination of data on the three previous screens. It is accessed by typing "FIE" and the sequence number of the field. Thus if we wanted to work on the weight field, we would enter

```
FIE 13
```

and would obtain the following screen.

```
--------------------------------------------------------------------
FIELD NAME       WEIGHT


COMMENTS         _____

TYPE             N   (X=ALPHANUMERIC, N=NUMERIC, G=GROUP)

OCCURRENCES      __  (FOR GROUPS ONLY)

ATTRIBUTE        UNLE (U=UNPROT   H=HIGHLIGHT    A=327X ALPHA     )

                      (P=PROT     I=INVISIBLE    N=327X NUMERIC   )

                      (S=SKIP     L=LOWLIGHT     E=ENSURE RECIEVED)

                      (C=CURSOR                                   )

COLOR            N   (N=NEUTRAL, B=BLUE, R=RED, P=PINK, G=GREEN,)

                      (T=TURQUOISE, Y=YELLOW, W=WHITE/BLACK      )

EX HIGHLIGHTING  N   (N=NONE, B=BLINK, R=REVERSE VIDEO, U=UNDERSCORE)

OUTPUT FILL CHAR U   (S=SPACES, L=LOWVAL, U=_, OTHER=ITSELF)

ERROR HANDLING   *   (N=NONE, *=FILL *, H=HIGHLIGHT)

                      (B=BOTH: H IF ILLEGAL VALUE & * IF REQD IS MISSING

REQUIRED         N   (Y=YES, N=NO)

MUST-FILL        N   (Y=YES, N=NO)

MINIMUM VALUE    _____ MAXIMUM VALUE _____

JUSTIFY INPUT    N   (N=NO, L=LEFT, R=RIGHT, A=ALIGN BY DECIMAL)


INPUT FILL CHAR  Z   (S=SPACES, L=LOWVAL, Z=ZEROES, U=_, OTHER=ITSELF)

VARIABLE DELIM   _

CASE             U   (U=UPPER, M=MIXED)

EDIT PATTERN     _____

IN.DP            3.1 (INTEGERS.DECIMALS)
```

```
MIN REQ DECIMALS _    (VALID ONLY FOR TYPE=N AND JUSTIFY=A)
ALLOW DIGIT SEP   _    (Y=YES, N=NO)
ALLOW MINUS SIGN _     (Y=YES, N=NO)
ALLOW CURRENCY    _    (Y=YES, N=NO)
CHECK DIGIT         _    (N=NONE, T=MODULO 10, E=MODULO 11)
```

To which we would make the following changes:

```
-----------------------------------------------------------------------
IDEAL: EXTENDED FIELD DEFN.   PNL EQUIPMNT (001) TEST  SYS:DEV  FILL-IN


        ^WEIGHT;    ^#####;
      12          13
....+....1....+....2....+....3....+....4....+....5....+....6....+....7.
FIELD NAME    WEIGHT


COMMENTS            _____
TYPE          N    (X=ALPHANUMERIC, N=NUMERIC, G=GROUP)
OCCURRENCES   __    (FOR GROUPS ONLY)
ATTRIBUTE     UNLE (U=UNPROT  H=HIGHLIGHT    A=327X ALPHA     )
                   (P=PROT    I=INVISIBLE    N=327X NUMERIC    )
                   (S=SKIP    L=LOWLIGHT     E=ENSURE RECIEVED)
                   (C=CURSOR                                   )
COLOR         N    (N=NEUTRAL, B=BLUE, R=RED, P=PINK, G=GREEN,)
                   (T=TURQUOISE, Y=YELLOW, W=WHITE/BLACK      )
EX HIGHLIGHTING N  (N=NONE, B=BLINK, R=REVERSE VIDEO, U=UNDERSCORE)
OUTPUT FILL CHAR U (S=SPACES, L=LOWVAL, U=_, OTHER=ITSELF)
ERROR HANDLING *   (N=NONE, *=FILL *, H=HIGHLIGHT)
                   (B=BOTH: H IF ILLEGAL VALUE & * IF REQD IS MISSING
REQUIRED      N    (Y=YES, N=NO)
MUST-FILL     N    (Y=YES, N=NO)
MINIMUM VALUE _____ MAXIMUM VALUE _____
JUSTIFY INPUT A    (N=NO, L=LEFT, R=RIGHT, A=ALIGN BY DECIMAL)


INPUT FILL CHAR Z  (S=SPACES, L=LOWVAL, Z=ZEROES, U=_, OTHER=ITSELF)
VARIABLE DELIM  _
CASE          U    (U=UPPER, M=MIXED)
EDIT PATTERN  ZZZ.9
IN.DP         3.1 (INTEGERS.DECIMALS)
MIN REQ DECIMALS 1 (VALID ONLY FOR TYPE=N AND JUSTIFY=A)
ALLOW DIGIT SEP  N (Y=YES, N=NO)
ALLOW MINUS SIGN N (Y=YES, N=NO)
ALLOW CURRENCY   N (Y=YES, N=NO)
CHECK DIGIT      N (N=NONE, T=MODULO 10, E=MODULO 11)
```

This will cause the input program to make sure that the value entered contains at least one field after the decimal point. It will also cause the input program to remove the entered decimal point before placing the rest of the digits into the application program field. We will also force the output program to apply the edit pattern ZZZ.9 to the field before it is displayed.

We will discuss the other fields on this screen in further detail later in this chapter.

The next step in the development process is the review and testing of the finished panel definition through the facsimile screen.

```
----------------------------------------------------------------
   _____      EQUIPMENT DATABASE MAINTENANCE PROGRAM


   OPTION            _    (A=ADD V=VIEW U=UPDATE D=DELETE)


   EQUIPMENT-NO    __
   EQUIPMENT-NAME  _____
   COLOR           _____
   WEIGHT          _____         .
   WAREHOUSE       _____


   MESSAGE          _____
```

Here we see the panel as the user will see it when he runs the corresponding program. We can also test our input routines. If we were to hit the enter button, we would have the following return:

```
1-IDSCDISP06E - ONE OR MORE FIELDS IN ERROR. USE "CLARIFY" FOR DETAILS.

----------------------------------------------------------------
   _____      EQUIPMENT DATABASE MAINTENANCE PROGRAM


   OPTION               (A=ADD V=VIEW U=UPDATE D=DELETE)


   EQUIPMENT-NO
   EQUIPMENT-NAME
   COLOR
   WEIGHT              *****
   WAREHOUSE


   MESSAGE          _____
```

We could then hit PF-3 and see the corresponding CLARIFY screen and/or hit PF-1 to see any HELP panel that we have defined.

```
---------------------------------------------------------------------------
IDEAL:                                                              DISPLAY

                    C L A R I F Y   E D I T   V I O L A T I O N S

    WEIGHT                      _____
                              1*****

    1 - NUMBER MUST HAVE ONE DECIMAL PLACE

    TYPE RETURN OR PRESS PF2 TO RETURN TO MAIN PANEL
```

Programming Samples

Now that we have completed our panel definitions, we can build the application code that will use it. The main paragraph of that code is as follows:

```
<<EQUIPMNT>> PROCEDURE
   REFRESH EQUIPMNT
   MOVE $DATE('YY/MM/DD') TO EQUIPMNT.CURR-DATE
   MOVE 'ENTER FIRST EQUIPMENT RECORD TO PROCESS'
        TO EQUIPMNT.MESSAGE
   TRANSMIT EQUIPMNT
   LOOP UNTIL $PF2 OR $PF14
        SELECT EQUIPMNT.OPTION
                WHEN 'V'  DO VIEW-RECORD
                WHEN 'A'  DO EDIT-INPUT
                          DO ADD-RECORD
                WHEN 'D'  DO DELETE-RECORD
                WHEN 'U'  DO EDIT-INPUT
                          DO UPDATE-RECORD
                WHEN 'R'  DO RESET-PANEL
                WHEN NONE DO INVALID-OPTION
        ENDSELECT
        TRANSMIT EQUIPMNT
   ENDLOOP
ENDPROC
```

Here we begin by forcing the program to obtain a fresh copy of the panel by doing a REFRESH command. This command is redundant if this is a stand-alone program because the first TRANSMIT will do the same thing. However, if this is being run as a subordinate program to some kind of processing menu that does not use the RELEASE command, then the program will continue to use the last version of the screen that it had in storage. We then move an initial message literal to the message field on the screen, load the date, and TRANSMIT the panel.

When the operator returns the panel to the program, it picks up at the next sequential instruction, which in this case is the beginning of the LOOP statement.

This loop is what we will use to control the processing of the requests and the timing of the transmissions of the panel. Processing will proceed until the operator hits the PF-2 key (or the PF-14 key on a terminal with 24 keys). This can happen after the first TRANSMIT, which will cancel all processing (as in the case of choosing the wrong program to run), or after the second TRANSMIT, which will drop us out of the loop.

Until that time, the processing will be controlled by the SELECT statement, which will make its choice based on the supplied option.

Because of this "book mark" type of processing, which is available through IDEAL's psuedo-conversational design, we can see a real benefit to structuring our program in this manner.

We can now explore the individual processing paragraphs.

```
<<VIEW-RECORD>> PROCEDURE
   FOR FIRST EQUIPMENT-DVW
      WHERE EQUIPMENT-DVW.EQUIP-NO EQ EQUIPMNT.EQUIP-NO
               MOVE EQUIPMENT-DVW.EQUIP-NAME TO EQUIPMNT.EQUIP-NAME
               MOVE EQUIPMENT-DVW.COLOR       TO EQUIPMNT.COLOR
               MOVE EQUIPMENT-DVW.WEIGHT      TO EQUIPMNT.WEIGHT
               MOVE EQUIPMENT-DVW.WAREHOUSE   TO EQUIPMNT.WAREHOUSE
               MOVE 'RECORD FOUND '           TO EQUIPMNT.MESSAGE
         WHEN NONE
               MOVE $LOW                      TO EQUIPMNT.EQUIP-NAME
               MOVE $LOW                      TO EQUIPMNT.COLOR
               MOVE $LOW                      TO EQUIPMNT.WEIGHT
               MOVE $LOW                      TO EQUIPMNT.WAREHOUSE
               MOVE 'RECORD NOT FOUND '       TO EQUIPMNT.MESSAGE
      ENDFOR
   ENDPROC
```

Here we are obtaining the actual record on the database, and displaying it on the screen. Moving the $LOW function into the fields on the WHEN NONE condition causes the PANEL-OUTPUT program to recognize them as null fields and substitute the output fill character. These fields would appear on the screen with underscore characters in them. If this was not done, they would contain the last value that was placed in them. This is either a value placed there by the application or by the PANEL-INPUT program through the input fill character.

```
<<EDIT-INPUT>> PROCEDURE
   MOVE 'Y' TO FG-INPUT-CORR
   IF EQUIPMNT.WAREHOUSE = $SPACES
       MOVE 'N'                         TO FG-INPUT-CORR
       MOVE $LOW                        TO EQUIPMNT.WAREHOUSE
       SET ATTR 'UAHE'                  ON EQUIPMNT.WAREHOUSE
       MOVE 'ENTER WAREHOUSE NUMBER' TO EQUIPMNT.MESSAGE
   ELSE
       FOR FIRST WAREHOUSE-DVW
           WHERE WAREHOUSE-DVW.WAREHOUSE   EQ EQUIPMNT.WAREHOUSE
                 SET ATTR 'UALE'           ON EQUIPMNT.WAREHOUSE
           WHEN NONE
                 MOVE 'N'                  TO FG-INPUT-CORR
                 SET ATTR 'UAHE'           ON EQUIPMNT.WAREHOUSE
                 MOVE 'INVALID WAREHOUSE' TO EQUIPMNT.MESSAGE
       ENDFOR
   ENDIF
ENDPROC
```

Checking of the EQUIPMNT.WAREHOUSE field is an example of the usage of the ensure receive characteristic of the panel. As you will recall, we set the attribute string on the field to be UALE, (unprotected, alphanumeric, lowlight, ensure receive), and the input fill character to spaces. Then, if the operator does not update the warehouse field, the PANEL-INPUT program will detect it and change the value to spaces (the input fill character). If this is not done, the field would contain the output fill character which it last had. In our case this would be '_____'.

This would of course be captured when the edit is executed. But when the database is updated in this manner by a field that is not edited, there is no way to make sure that the operator entered data into the field. Unless the field has the ensure receive option, it is possible to place the underscore marks on the database instead of the spaces that we desire. Therefore it is recommended that each input field on the panel be set to ensure receive.

We can also see in this example the use of dynamic changes to the panel attributes. When this command is executed, the update is made to the version of the panel in the program storage area. The syntax of this command is

```
SET ATTRIBUTE 'HLIPUSENAC' (TEMP) ON FIELD-IDENTIFIER
   ATTR
```

Here 'HLIPUSENAC' are the different attributes that can be combined, just as they were on the summary fill-in screen.

We can make the change to the field on either a permanent basis, which will be retained until it is changed again or the panel is refreshed, or on a temporary basis, where the changes will be retained until the panel is transmitted again. (Early releases of IDEAL had problems with the use of temporary attributes, in that the attributes would occasionally overrun the end of a field, and they would go away on return from a CLARIFY or a HELP panel. These two problems were fixed under the 1.2 release of the product.)

This change command can also be used to change the color and extended highlight attributes in facilities where these options are available.

Below we see another method that we can use to clear a panel, or the fields of a panel. The RESET command sets the field to its input fill character, and returns its attribute string to its original status.

```
<<RESET-PANEL>> PROCEDURE
   RESET EQUIPMNT.EQUIP-NO
   RESET EQUIPMNT.EQUIP-NAME
   RESET EQUIPMNT.COLOR
   RESET EQUIPMNT.WEIGHT
   RESET EQUIPMNT.WAREHOUSE
   RESET EQUIPMNT.MESSAGE
ENDPROC
```

This is much more efficient than the REFRESH command, as the changes are made to the version in the program memory instead of getting a fresh copy from the panel library. We could have also written the paragraph as

```
<<RESET-PANEL>> PROCEDURE
   RESET EQUIPMNT
ENDPROC
```

which, of course, would reset all of the fields on the panel. If the field is not updated by the program between this command and the next TRANSMIT, the field will appear on the screen with its output fill character.

We will discuss the other paragraphs of this program as part of the exercises at the end of this chapter.

Repeating Groups

Many times in IDEAL processing, it is necessary or desirable to view certain similar pieces of data from a large number of records. We can do this by assigning an individual name to each occurrence of a field, or we can create a repeating group in the panel.

This repeating group is very similar in processing to the table setup in a working-storage area, in that it is referenced by a subscript. This is because of the way that the panel functions as the working storage and IO area for the panel during processing.

To see how all this works, let's recall the KIT database that we developed in Chapter 5. As you will recall, it contained one record for every part of a kit (which is in turn defined as a specific combination of equipment records). Thus the layout:

EQUIP-NO	KIT-NO	NUM-OF-PARTS
E1	KIT1	5
E2	KIT1	6
E3	KIT1	4
E4	KIT1	5
E5	KIT1	6
E6	KIT1	4
EZ	KIT1	4
E3	KIT2	3
E4	KIT2	2
E1	KIT3	1
E5	KIT3	1
E6	KIT4	3

We will then need an application to read and display this database on a kit basis. We will call the panel and the program KITVIEW. (See Figure 7-4.)

We will set up the extended field definition for weight, as we did on the last screen. We will set up the number field in the same way.

As we can see from the facsimile screen in Figure 7-4, we have room on the screen for all of the data from one kit and one equipment record. However because of the columnar nature of the data, we can set this panel up with a repeating group. To do this, we edit the summary screen and change the level numbers of those fields

```
IDEAL: PANEL PARAMETERS    PNL KITVIEW (001) TEST    SYS: DEV FILL-IN


START    FIELD SYMBOL ^ NEW    FIELD SYMBOL +
END      FIELD SYMBOL ; DELETE FIELD SYMBOL *
REPEATING GROUP SYMBOL @


INPUT  FILL CHARACTER  S (S=SPACE, L=LOWVAL, Z=ZEROES, U=_,OTHER=ITSELF
OUTPUT FILL CHARACTER  U (S=SPACE, L=LOWVAL, Z=ZERORS, U=_,OTHER=ITSELF
NON-DISPLAY CHARACTER  U (S=SPACE, OTHER=AS SPECIFIED)
ERROR FILL CHARACTER   * (AS SPECIFIED)
CASE TRANSLATION       U (U=UPPER, M=MIXED)


REQUIRED               Y (Y=YES, N=NO)
ERROR HANDLING         * (N=NONE, *=FILL W/ERRORFILL, H=HIGH INTENSITY,)
                         (B=BOTH: H IF ILLEGAL VALUE & * IF RQD MISSING)


PANEL WIDTH           80 (A VALUE BETWEEN 80 AND 236)
PF1=HELP, PF3=CLARIFY  Y (Y=YES, N=NO)
PF7=SCR -, PF8=SCR+    N (N=NO, Y=OPT Y, Z=OPT Z)
  PF10=SCR TOP, PF11=SCR BOT    (OPTION Y)
  PF10=SCR LEFT,PF11=SCR RIGHT  (OPTION Z)
EDIT-RULE ERROR PROC   C  (C=CLARIFY COMMAND, A=APPLICATION)
PROCESS APPL ON SCROLL N  (Y=YES, N=NO)
HELP PANEL NAME   _____   VERSION ___
PREFIX PANEL NAME _____   VERSION ___
SUFFIX PANEL NAME _____   VERSION ___


-------------------------- B O T T O M --------------------------------



_____
IDEAL: PANEL LAYOUT        PNL EQUIPMNT (001) TEST    SYS: DEV FILL-IN
START: ^    END: ;    NEW: +    DELETE: *    REPEAT: @
....+....1....+....2....+....3....+....4....+....5....+....6....+...7..
      ^_____;    ^KIT ASSEMBLY AND MAKEUP REVIEW PROGRAM;

  ^KIT NUMBER; ^_____;

  ^EQUIP-NO    NAME           COLOR      WEIGHT      NUMBER;
    ^__;    ^_____;    ^_____;    ^_____;    ^___;

  ^MESSAGE;    ^_____;
---------------------------- BOTTOM -----------------------------------
```

Figure 7-4   Panel Kitview Definition

```
---------------------------------------------------------------------------
IDEAL: FIELD SUMMARY TABLE    PNL EQUIPMNT (001) TEST  SYS: DEV FILL-IN
===========================================================================
   ^_____;    ^KIT ASSEMBLY AND MAKEUP REVIEW PROGRAM;
   1             2
   ^KIT NUMBER;    ^_____;
   3              4
...........................................................................
SEQ LV FIELD NAME       ATTR    T LEN  IN.DP OCC COMMENTS
--- -- --------------- ------ - ---- ----- --- ------------------------
  1  2 CURR-DATE        PSL    X    8
  2  2                  PSL    X   38            KIT ASSEMBLY AND MAKEUP
  3  2                  PSL    X   10            KIT NUMBER
  4  2 KIT-NUMBER       UALEC  X    5
  5  2                  PSL    X   60            EQUIP-NO      NAME
  6  2 EQUIP-NO         PSL    X    2            EQUIPMENT-NO
  7  2 EQUIP-NAME       PSL    X   10
  8  2 COLOR            PSL    X   10            EQUIPMENT-NAME
  9  2 WEIGHT           PSL    N    5  3.1
 10  2 NUMBER           PSL    N    3  3         COLOR
 11  2                  PSL    X    7            MESSAGE
 12  2                  PSL    X   41


---------------------------------------------------------------------------
   _____        KIT ASSEMBLY AND MAKEUP REVIEW PROGRAM


   KIT NUMBER     _____


   EQUIP-NO    NAME              COLOR      WEIGHT    NUMBER
    ___     _____     _____   _____    ____


   MESSAGE         _____
--------------------------- BOTTOM --------------------------------
```

Figure 7-4   (continued) Panel Kitview Definition

that we want to be in the group from 2 to 3. When we do this and hit the ENTER button, we obtain the following screen:

```
---------------------------------------------------------------------------
IDEAL: FIELD SUMMARY TABLE    PNL EQUIPMNT (001) TEST  SYS: DEV FILL-IN
===========================================================================
   ^_____;    ^KIT ASSEMBLY AND MAKEUP REVIEW PROGRAM;
```

```
  1                2
 ^KIT NUMBER;      ^_____;
  3                4
 ..........................................................................
 SEQ LV FIELD NAME      ATTR    T LEN  IN.DP OCC COMMENTS
 --- -- ---------------  ------  - ---- ----- --- -----------------------
   1  2 CURR-DATE        PSL     X    8
   2  2                  PSL     X   38            KIT ASSEMBLY AND MAKEUP
   3  2                  PSL     X   10            KIT NUMBER
   4  2 KIT-NUMBER       UALEC   X    5
   5  2                  PSL     X   60            EQUIP-NO       NAME
   6  2                                       *
   7  3 EQUIP-NO         PSL     X    2            EQUIPMENT-NO
   8  3 EQUIP-NAME       PSL     X   10
   9  3 COLOR            PSL     X   10            EQUIPMENT-NAME
  10  3 WEIGHT           PSL     N    5   3.1
  11  3 NUMBER           PSL     N    3   3        COLOR
  12  2                  PSL     X    7            MESSAGE
  13  2                  PSL     X   41
```

We then overtype the * in the OCC column with the number of occurrences that we want to have in our repeating group. For our purposes, we will use a value of 10. (The removal of a repeating group is done by simply reversing the processing, changing the level 3 to level 2. This can also be done to remove a certain field from the group. We can also remove the repeating group definition from the panel by placing a "D" in the OCC column.)

It should be noted at this point that we are limited to having only one repeating group per panel definition.

Our layout and facsimile screens would then look like this:

```
 ------------------------------------------------------------------------
 IDEAL: PANEL LAYOUT        PNL EQUIPMNT (001) TEST     SYS: DEV FILL-IN
 START: `    END: ;    NEW: +      DELETE: *     REPEAT: @
 ....+....1....+....2....+....3....+....4....+....5....+....6....+...7..
     ^_____;     ^KIT ASSEMBLY AND MAKEUP REVIEW PROGRAM;

   ^KIT NUMBER; ^_____;

   ^EQUIP-NO      NAME              COLOR        WEIGHT      NUMBER;
      @__;     @_____;      @_____;    @_____;     @___;

   ^MESSAGE;          ^_____;
 ----------------------------- BOTTOM ----------------------------------
```

```
------------------------------------------------------------------------
    _____        KIT ASSEMBLY AND MAKEUP REVIEW PROGRAM


    KIT NUMBER      _____


    EQUIP-NO      NAME            COLOR        WEIGHT      NUMBER

       __     _____    _____    _____      ____
       __     _____    _____    _____      ____
       __     _____    _____    _____      ____
       __     _____    _____    _____      ____
       __     _____    _____    _____      ____
       __     _____    _____    _____      ____
       __     _____    _____    _____      ____
       __     _____    _____    _____      ____
       __     _____    _____    _____      ____
       __     _____    _____    _____      ____


    MESSAGE         _____
---------------------------- BOTTOM -------------------------------
```

We would then write the following application code to process this
program.

```
<<KITVIEW>> PROCEDURE
  REFRESH  KITWIEW
  MOVE $DATE('YY/MM/DD')  TO KITVIEW.CURR-DATE
  MOVE 'ENTER KIT NUMBER' TO KITVIEW.MESSAGE
  TRANSMIT KITVIEW
  LOOP UNTIL $PF2 OR $PF14
       DO PROC-REQUEST
       TRANSMIT KITVIEW
  ENDLOOP
ENDPROC


<<PROC-REQUEST>> PROCEDURE
  MOVE 0                 TO WK-SUBSR
  MOVE KITVIEW.KIT-NO    TO WK-KIT-NO
  RESET KITVIEW
  MOVE WK-KIT-NO         TO KITVIEW.KIT-NO
  FOR EACH  KIT-DTL-DVW
      WHERE KIT-DTL-DVW.KIT-NO EQ KITVIEW.KIT-NO
            ADD 1 TO WK-SUBSR
            MOVE KIT-DTL-DVW.EQUIP-NO   TO KITVIEW.EQUIP-NO(WK-SUBSR)
            MOVE KIT-DTL-DVW.NUMBER     TO KITVIEW.NUMBER  (WK-SUBSR)
```

```
                  DO GET-EQUIP-DVW
        WHEN  NONE
                  MOVE 'KIT NOT FOUND ON THE DATABASE' TO KITVIEW.MESSAGE
     ENDFOR
   ENDPROC


<<GET-EQUIP-DVW>> PROCEDURE
  FOR FIRST EQUIP-DVW
        WHERE EQUIP-DVW.EQUIP-NO EQ KIT-DTL-DVW.EQUIP-NO
                  MOVE EQUIP-DVW.EQUIP-NAME TO KITVIEW.EQUIP-NAME(WK-SUBSR)
                  MOVE EQUIP-DVW.WEIGHT     TO KITVIEW.WEIGHT    (WK-SUBSR)
                  MOVE EQUIP-DVW.COLOR      TO KITVIEW.COLOR     (WK-SUBSR)
        WHEN  NONE
                  MOVE 'NOT FOUND '         TO KITVIEW.EQUIP-NAME(WK-SUBSR)
                  MOVE 0                    TO KITVIEW.WEIGHT    (WK-SUBSR)
                  MOVE $LOW                 TO KITVIEW.COLOR     (WK-SUBSR)
     ENDFOR
   ENDPROC
```

WK-SUBSR is a numeric working-storage field that we are using as the subscript for the panel's repeating group. As the reader can see, we cleared the panel by using the RESET command. We then read each kit record with the requested number and reload the panel by incrementing the subscript.

Thus, the results of our first request would be

```
------------------------------------------------------------------------
   YY/MM/DD      KIT ASSEMBLY AND MAKEUP REVIEW PROGRAM


   KIT NUMBER    KIT1


   EQUIP-NO      NAME           COLOR        WEIGHT      NUMBER
      E1         MM             RED           12.0         5
      E2         SLIM           WHITE          7.0         6
      E3         WALL           BROWN          7.0         4
      E4         DESK           TAN            9.0         5
      E5         WALL           WHITE          5.0         6
      E6         PAC            YELLOW        10.0         4
      EZ         NOT FOUND      _____      .0         0




   MESSAGE          _____
```

This is all well and good, until we run into the problem of having more records than entries in the table. When this happens, the IDEAL program abends with an INVALID SUBSCRIPT abend.

To avoid this problem, we must make allowances for it in our program by limiting the number of records that are extracted and loaded out to the panel. In our simple example, we can limit the number of records read in the FOR statement:

```
FOR FIRST 10 KIT-DTL-DVW
    WHERE    KIT-DTL-DVW.KIT-NO EQ KITVIEW.KIT-NO
        ADD 1 TO WK-SUBSR
        MOVE KIT-DTL-DVW.EQUIP-NO    TO KITVIEW.EQUIP-NO(WK-SUBSR)
        MOVE KIT-DTL-DVW.NUMBER      TO KITVIEW.NUMBER   (WK-SUBSR)
        DO GET-EQUIP-DVW
    WHEN   NONE
        MOVE 'KIT NOT FOUND ON THE DATABASE' TO KITVIEW.MESSAGE
ENDFOR
```

However, this is not always practical, from either a design or a program maintenance point of view. (Hard coding of values tends to be frowned upon.) To remedy this situation, IDEAL provides us with a function called $PANEL-GROUP-OCCURS, which will return the value of the number of records in a panel group.

Thus we could make the following change:

```
MOVE $PANEL-GROUP-OCCURS TO WK-LIMIT
<<PANEL-LOAD>>
FOR EACH   KIT-DTL-DVW
    WHERE KIT-DTL-DVW.KIT-NO EQ KITVIEW.KIT-NO
        ADD 1 TO WK-SUBSR
        IF WK-SUBSR GT WK-LIMIT
           QUIT PANEL-LOAD
        ELSE
           MOVE KIT-DTL-DVW.EQUIP-NO TO KITVIEW.EQUIP-NO(WK-SUBSR)
           MOVE KIT-DTL-DVW.NUMBER   TO KITVIEW.NUMBER   (WK-SUBSR)
           DO GET-EQUIP-DVW
        ENDIF
    WHEN   NONE
        MOVE 'KIT NOT FOUND ON THE DATABASE' TO KITVIEW.MESSAGE
ENDFOR
```

Sometimes it is also neccessary to have more entries in a panel's table size than will fit on a single screen. IDEAL allows this to happen through the use of its scrolling facility.

This facility is controlled by the PANEL INPUT program, and is implemented by turning on the scrolling flag on the panel parameter screen. This facility allows the use of

```
KEY         OPTION Y              OPTION Z

            STANDARD WIDTH        EXTENDED WIDTH


PF 7        DOWN                  DOWN

PF 8        UP                    UP

PF 10       TOP                   LEFT

PF 11       BOTTOM                RIGHT
```

To see this, we will make the following changes to our KITVIEW panel:

1. Set the scroll flag to 'Y'.
2. Change the number of occurrences to 25.
3. Move the message line to a position above the data table.

We will also assume that KIT6 is made up of 15 different parts and that our user has a 15-line screen. Then, when we run a request for KIT6, we would obtain the following logical screen:

```
XX/XX/XX            KIT ASSEMBLY AND REVIEW PROGRAM


KIT NUMBER KIT6     MESSAGE    KIT FOUND


EQUIP-NO       NAME          COLOR         WEIGHT       NUMBER
   E1          MM            RED            12.0          5
   E2          SLIM          WHITE          12.0          5
   E3          WALL          BROWN          12.0          5
   E4          DESK          TAN            12.0          5
   E5          WALL          WHITE          12.0          5
   E6          PAC           YELLOW         12.0          5
   E7          NOT FOUND     _____       .0          0
   E8          NOT FOUND     _____       .0          0
   E9          MMA           RED             1.0          5
   A1          MMS           RED             2.0          6
   A2          MMD           RED             3.0          5
   A3          MMF           RED             4.0          4
   A4          MMG           RED             5.0          1
   A5          MMH           RED             6.0          2
```

A6	MMN	RED	7.0	3
——	————————	————————	—————	———
——	————————	————————	—————	———
——	————————	————————	—————	———
——	————————	————————	—————	———
——	————————	————————	—————	———
——	————————	————————	—————	———
——	————————	————————	—————	———
——	————————	————————	—————	———
——	————————	————————	—————	———
——	————————	————————	—————	———

of which the user would see

```
XX/XX/XX              KIT ASSEMBLY AND REVIEW PROGRAM


KIT NUMBER KIT6    MESSAGE    KIT FOUND


EQUIP-NO     NAME        COLOR      WEIGHT   NUMBER
  E1        MM          RED         12.0      5
  E2        SLIM        WHITE       12.0      5
  E3        WALL        BROWN       12.0      5
  E4        DESK        TAN         12.0      5
  E5        WALL        WHITE       12.0      5
  E6        PAC         YELLOW      12.0      5
  E7        NOT FOUND   _____    .0      0
  E8        NOT FOUND   _____    .0      0
  E9        MMA         RED          1.0      5
```

and hitting PF-8 would show

```
  A1        MMS         RED          2.0      6
  A2        MMD         RED          3.0      5
  A3        MMF         RED          4.0      4
  A4        MMG         RED          5.0      1
  A5        MMH         RED          6.0      2
  A6        MMN         RED          7.0      3
 ---       ----------  ----------  ------   ----
 ---       ----------  ----------  ------   ----
 ---       ----------  ----------  ------   ----
 ---       ----------  ----------  ------   ----
```

—	————	————	———	——
—	————	————	———	——
—	————	————	———	——
—	————	————	———	——
—	————	————	———	——

Hitting PF-11 at this point will place the last physical panel-table element on the bottom of the screen:

A2	MMD	RED	3.0	5
A3	MMF	RED	4.0	4
A4	MMG	RED	5.0	1
A5	MMH	RED	6.0	2
A6	MMN	RED	7.0	3
––	————	————	———	——
––	————	————	———	——
––	————	————	———	——
––	————	————	———	——
––	————	————	———	——
––	————	————	———	——
––	————	————	———	——
––	————	————	———	——
––	————	————	———	——
––	————	————	———	——

Note that here we lost the A1 entry, because the last table line, (which in our case is blank) is now displayed, whereas last time it was the 16th record.

Likewise, hitting PF-7 at this point would cause the next 15 lines to be displayed:

```
XX/XX/XX              KIT ASSEMBLY AND REVIEW PROGRAM


KIT NUMBER KIT6    MESSAGE    KIT FOUND


EQUIP-NO      NAME        COLOR       WEIGHT      NUMBER
    E1        MM          RED          12.0          5
    E2        SLIM        WHITE        12.0          5
    E3        WALL        BROWN        12.0          5
    E4        DESK        TAN          12.0          5
    E5        WALL        WHITE        12.0          5
```

E6	PAC	YELLOW	12.0	5
E7	NOT FOUND	_____	.0	0
E8	NOT FOUND	_____	.0	0
E9	MMA	RED	1.0	5
A1	MMS	RED	2.0	6

And, of course, PF-10 will put the first physical line on the top of the screen.

```
XX/XX/XX          KIT ASSEMBLY AND REVIEW PROGRAM


KIT NUMBER KIT6    MESSAGE    KIT FOUND


EQUIP-NO      NAME        COLOR      WEIGHT    NUMBER
   E1         MM          RED         12.0       5
   E2         SLIM        WHITE       12.0       5
   E3         WALL        BROWN       12.0       5
   E4         DESK        TAN         12.0       5
   E5         WALL        WHITE       12.0       5
   E6         PAC         YELLOW      12.0       5
   E7         NOT FOUND   _____    .0        0
   E8         NOT FOUND   _____    .0        0
   E9         MMA         RED          1.0        5
```

There are a number of disadvantages to IDEAL's scrolling techniques which we should discuss here. As the reader will recall from our efficiency discussions in Chapter 4, whenever a program sends a screen to the user, the program is disabled, and all of its non-shared resources are copied out to temporary storage. One of these copied resources is the panel. Thus if we have a large panel, say one that had the maximumn of 99 occurrences, we would use a lot of disk space in temporary storage.

To reduce this inefficiency, we need to reduce the size of the non-shared part of the program. To do this, we can reduce the number of occurrences of the panel to a single screen size and substitute something else for this storage.

For example, we could read the data into a working-storage table and populate the screen from there. This is more efficient because working storage takes up less temporary storage space than the same data on a panel. To see this we can build the following program:

```
<<KITVIEW>> PROCEDURE
   REFRESH  KITVIEW
```

```
      TRANSMIT KITVIEW
      LOOP UNTIL $PF2 OR $PF14
              DO LOAD-WORK-STOR
              DO LOAD-OUT-SCR
              TRANSMIT KITVIEW
              LOOP UNTIL $PF2 OR $PF14
                      OR KITVIEW.KIT-NO = WK-KIT-NO
                      DO SET-SCR-INDEX
                  SELECT FIRST
                      WHEN $PF7  DO SCROLL-UP
                      WHEN $PF8  DO SCROLL-DOWN
                      WHEN $PF10 DO SCROLL-TOP
                      WHEN $PF11 DO SCROLL-BOTTOM
                  ENDSELECT
              ENDLOOP
        ENDLOOP
      ENDPROC


    <<SET-SCR-INDEX>> PROCEDURE
      IF $PF7
        IF WK-BEGIN-POINT = 1
          MOVE 'TOP OF DATA ALREADY REACHED' TO KITVIEW.MESSAGE
        ELSE
          SET WK-BEGIN-POINT = WK-BEGIN-POINT + WK-SCR-LENGTH
          LOOP VARYING WK-PANEL-SUBSR FROM 1 BY 1
                  UNTIL WK-PANEL-SUBSR GT WK-PANEL-LIMIT
                      DO LOAD-SCREEN
                      ADD 1 TO WK-BEGIN-POINT
          ENDLOOP
        ENDIF
      ENDIF
    ENDPROC
```

Here we start by initializing the panel, and transmitting it for the first time. When we receive the request back, we will read the database and load it into our working storage table (paragraph named LOAD-WORK-STOR, not shown), and load the first screen. We then see if the operator has either changed the request, or wishes to see more of this one. If they wish to scroll, we simply compute the starting position in the table, and reload the screen.

This solution also overcomes another disadvantage in that it allows the screen header to always be visible to the operator. Otherwise, as different parts of the physical screen are shown, the header will or will not be seen, depending on positioning.

This solution, however, does not completely eliminate the temporary storage problem. We can further reduce the storage usage by reading only those records which will fill the screen. Thus, we have the program

```
<<KITVIEW>> PROCEDURE
  REFRESH  KITVIEW
  TRANSMIT KITVIEW
  MOVE $PANEL-GROUP-OCCURS TO WK-PANEL-LIMIT
  LOOP UNTIL $PF2 OR $PF14
          MOVE $SPACES TO WK-BEGIN-POINT
          DO LOAD-OUT-SCR
          TRANSMIT KITVIEW
          LOOP UNTIL $PF2 OR $PF14
                OR KITVIEW.KIT-NO = WK-KIT-NO
              MOVE KITVIEW.EQUIP-NO(WK-PANEL-LIMIT) TO WK-BEGIN-POINT
              DO LOAD-OUT-SCR
              TRANSMIT KITVIEW
          ENDLOOP
  ENDLOOP
ENDPROC


<<LOAD-OUT-SCR>> PROCEDURE
  <<LOAD-OUT-FOR>>
  MOVE 0 TO WK-SUBSR
  FOR EACH   KIT-DTL-DVW
      WHERE KIT-DTL-DVW.KIT-NO   EQ KITVIEW.KIT-NO
          IF KIT-DTL-DVW.EQUIP-NO GT WK-BEGIN-POINT
            ADD 1 TO WK-SUBSR
            IF WK-SUBSR LT WK-PANEL-LIMIT
              MOVE KIT-DTL-DVW.EQUIP-NO TO KITVIEW.EQUIP-NO(WK-SUBSR)
                 "
                 "
                 "
            ELSE
              QUIT LOAD-OUT-FOR
            ENDIF
          ENDIF
  ENDFOR
ENDPROC
```

Here, by stopping our read loop as soon as we have enough records, we avoid reading, or writing to temporary storage, those records that are not yet ready be to seen. The main drawback of this approach under IDEAL 1.3 is that it only has the ability to scroll through the database in one direction.

Under IDEAL 1.4 we have the ORDERED BY DESCENDING command available. We would then change the program to

```
<<KITVIEW>> PROCEDURE
  REFRESH  KITVIEW
  TRANSMIT KITVIEW
  MOVE $PANEL-GROUP-OCCURS TO WK-PANEL-LIMIT
  LOOP UNTIL $PF2 OR $PF14
        MOVE $SPACES TO WK-BEGIN-POINT
        DO LOAD-OUT-SCR
        TRANSMIT KITVIEW
        LOOP UNTIL $PF2 OR $PF14
              OR KITVIEW.KIT-NO = WK-KIT-NO
            IF $PF7
              MOVE KITVIEW.EQUIP-NO(1) TO WK-BEGIN-POINT
              DO LOAD-OUT-PF7
            ELSE
              MOVE KITVIEW.EQUIP-NO(WK-PANEL-LIMIT)
                TO WK-BEGIN-POINT
              DO LOAD-OUT-PF7
            ENDIF
            TRANSMIT KITVIEW
        ENDLOOP
  ENDLOOP
ENDPROC


<<LOAD-OUT-PF7>> PROCEDURE
  <<LOAD-FOR-PF7>>
  MOVE $PANEL-GROUP-OCCURS TO WK-SUBSR
  FOR EACH  KIT-DTL-DVW
      WHERE KIT-DTL-DVW.KIT-NO   EQ KITVIEW.KIT-NO
      ORDERED BY KIT-DTL-DVW.KIT-NO DESCENDING
        IF KIT-DTL-DVW.EQUIP-NO LT WK-BEGIN-POINT
          SUBTRACT 1 FROM WK-SUBSR
          IF WK-SUBSR GT 0
            MOVE KIT-DTL-DVW.EQUIP-NO TO KITVIEW.EQUIP-NO(WK-SUBSR)
              "
              "
          ELSE
            QUIT LOAD-FOR-PF7
          ENDIF
        ENDIF
```

```
    ENDFOR

  ENDPROC


  <<LOAD-OUT-PF8>> PROCEDURE

    <<LOAD-FOR-PF8>>

    MOVE 0 TO WK-SUBSR

    FOR EACH   KIT-DTL-DVW

        WHERE KIT-DTL-DVW.KIT-NO    EQ KITVIEW.KIT-NO

          IF KIT-DTL-DVW.EQUIP-NO GT WK-BEGIN-POINT

              ADD 1 TO WK-SUBSR

              IF WK-SUBSR LT WK-PANEL-LIMIT

                 MOVE KIT-DTL-DVW.EQUIP-NO TO KITVIEW.EQUIP-NO(WK-SUBSR)
                        "

                        "

              ELSE

                  QUIT LOAD-FOR-PF8

              ENDIF

          ENDIF

    ENDFOR

  ENDPROC
```

The new code will start loading records into the last position in the screen table, and continue until it reaches the first occurrence. These techniques are quite useful when the number of records is greater than the 99-occurrence screen table limit.

We can use a combination of these three methods:

1. IDEAL native scrolling
2. Working storage scrolling
3. Database reading limit

to solve any scrolling need that we might encounter. The selection should be based on:

1. Program design needs
2. Data complexity
3. Panel header view requirements
4. Temporary storage limitations
5. System IO loading
6. Time available to write the application

Another potential pitfall that we face with a scrolling panel is the fact that the ENSURE RECEIVE option only functions with that part of the physical panel that is being seen by the operator. Thus, if we were to use our KITVIEW program for creating or adding to kits, we would need to make sure that our updating logic was not allowed to go past the bottom of the physical screen. If this was not done, the program would abend when it looked in the numeric weight field and found underscores. Thus we recommend that any update panels only be allowed to be the size of the available screen. We should consider a *unit of work* to be the updating or addition of a single record.

This unit-of-work requirement is also important when we consider the timing on the database interface. Whenever a TRANSMIT occurs, a database CHECKPOINT is issued at the beginning of the procedure. Thus if we were updating a series of records in a database with input from the screen, and we tried to code it like this:

```
FOR EACH EQUIPMENT-DVW
        TRANSMIT EQUIPUPD
        MOVE EQUIPUPD.WEIGHT TO EQUIPMENT-DVW.WEIGHT
ENDFOR
```

we would get an abend, because the CHECKPOINT took away the control that we had on the record and would not allow the replace to occur at the ENDFOR.

Efficiencies

In discussing efficiencies in panel processing, there are two important areas to check. The first is the processing of data in and out of temporary storage. the other is the IO requirements to the panel source storage library.

In the first area, the most important thing to do is to limit the size and number of panels that are attached to the program. We have already talked about some ways to limit the use of scrolling resources. Another is to limit the number of panels that are attached. When we remember that HELP panels, PREFIX panels, and SUFFIX panels are all copied in and out of temporary storage at every TRANSMIT, our desire to use them should diminish accordingly.

Another path that we can take to limit temporary storage usage is through the use of the RELEASE command. When this command is issued, the temporary storage space that was taken up by the panel is released. This does not detach the panel from the program, but merely releases the temporary storage.

Whenever the panel is needed again by the program, it will go out and get a fresh copy from the panel library. This, of course, affects our second area of efficiency, IO from the panel library.

To limit IO to this library, it is neccessary to limit the number of times that we need to have a fresh copy of the panel. There are only two times in the life of a transaction that we should do this: at the beginning of the program, and after a RELEASE command. All of the other times we should use another tool. This can include the RESET command, which sets the attributes to their original status and values non-protected fields with input fill characters. Another tool that we can use is the CLEAR operand on the TRANSMIT command. This clear command causes the all non-protected fields to be filled with their output fill characters and sent to the operator. With these two commands, we should be able to reset any panel without getting a fresh copy from the program library.

An additional efficiency tool that we have is the REINPUT clause of the TRANSMIT command. This causes all of the fields on a panel to retain their input value through subsequent transmits until they are changed by the operator. This is good for panels that go through multiple transmits trying to pass all of the edits in the application program.

Extended Field Definitions

As promised, we will now discuss in detail the fields of the EXTENDED FIELD DEFINITION screen.

Actually, there are two different screens that can appear when the FIE screen is accessed, one for numeric fields, and the other for alphanumeric fields. We will begin our discussion with the alphanumeric field. Let's say that we wished to view the FIE screen for the field KIT-NO of our KITVIEW screen. We would edit the panel, and enter the command:

```
FIE 4
```

which would give us the display:

```
        KIT NUMBER      _____

        3               *****


....+....1....+....2....+....3....+....4....+....5....+....6....+..
FIELD NAME      KIT-NUMBER          FIELD NUMBER  4  FIELD LENGTH 5

COMMENTS        _____

TYPE            X    (X=ALPHANUMERIC, N=NUMERIC, G=GROUP)

OCCURANCES      __   (FOR GROUPS ONLY)
```

```
ATTRIBUTE         UALE (U=UNPROT   H=HIGHLIGHT   A=327X ALPHA      )
                       (P=PROT     I=INVISIBLE   N=327X NUMERIC    )
                       (S=SKIP     L=LOWLIGHT    E=ENSURE RECIEVED )
                       (C=CURSOR                                   )
COLOR             N    (N=NEUTRAL, B=BLUE, R=RED, P=PINK, G=GREEN, )
                       (T=TURQUOISE, Y=YELLOW, W=WHITE/BLACK       )
EX HIGHLIGHTING   N    (N=NONE, B=BLINK, R=REVERSE VIDEO, U=UNDERSCORE)
OUTPUT FILL CHAR  U    (S=SPACES, L=LOWVAL, U=_, OTHER=ITSELF)
ERROR HANDLING    *    (N=NONE, *=FILL *, H=HIGHLIGHT)
                       (B=BOTH: H IF ILLEGAL VALUE & * IF REQD IS MISSING
REQUIRED          N    (Y=YES, N=NO)
MUST-FILL         N    (Y=YES, N=NO)
MINIMUM VALUE     _____ MAXIMUM VALUE _____
JUSTIFY INPUT     N    (N=NO, L=LEFT, R=RIGHT, A=ALIGN BY DECIMAL)

INPUT FILL CHAR   S    (S=SPACES, L=LOWVAL, Z=ZEROES, U=_, OTHER=ITSELF)
VARIABLE DELIM    _
```

The top portion of the screen shows the entire screen line from the layout screen that contains the field in question, and marks the field with ****. The next five entry lines are obtained from the summary screen. These include the name of the field, its relative position on the screen, and its length. We can also see the documenting comments that were entered into the field on the far right-hand side of the summary screen. We then see the field type and its attributes. The occurrences field is populated if this is the level 2 field of a group definition.

After we have seen these informational fields, we can enter the data that is unique to this fill-in screen.

If the user's terminal has a multicolor capacity, we might wish to use different colors as a form of highlighting. A selection of any of the listed colors can be made, but only one can be used at a time. This attribute can also be overriden through the use of temporary attributes in the program. This attribute will of course be ignored if the panel is used on a monochrome screen.

The extended highlighting attribute is another form of highlighting. We can of course ignore the feature, cause the field to blink (flash highlight/lowlight), to reverse video (the field area is light and the letters are dark), or to appear with underscores along with the data.

The output fill character (and the input fill character) are initially populated here from the parameter fill-in screen. The entries on this screen can be used to override the defaults set on the parameter screen.

The error-handling attribute is used by the PANEL-INPUT program to mark an offending field whenever it encounters an input edit error. We can, of course, ignore this option (which will cause the operator to have to guess where the error is), or we can have the field filled with asterisks, or we can have it highlighted. The default attribute is to have the field filled with asterisks and highlighted.

The REQUIRED option is a PANEL-INPUT program edit, which when used requires the operator to enter a value before the panel is passed to the program. This can be used alone or in conjunction with the minimum and maximum fields, which require the entered value to be within a certain range.

The MUST-FILL option requires the operator to fill in the entire input field with data.

The INPUT JUSTIFICATION field is used to align data input within the field for proper presentation to the program. We can again ignore the option, which causes the default alignments to be used. We can also use left (default for alphanumeric data) or right (default for numeric data) justification. This causes the first (or last) byte of the data to begin in the left- (or right-) most byte of the field.

Another option we have is used for numeric data that contains a decimal point. This option is called ALIGN BY DECIMAL.

ALIGN BY DECIMAL option causes the PANEL-INPUT program to recognize a period that is imbedded in the input field as a decimal point. Without this option, the period would be recognized as non-numeric data, which would cause an ERROR to be returned. If the ALIGN BY DECIMAL option is used, and no decimal point is provided, then all of the data will be placed to the left of an implied decimal point.

The variable delimiter field is used to end data that is too long that is placed in a panel field. Through the use of this option, the panel-input program will only recognize those characters as input that are to the left of the delimiter.

The case parameter is the same as the one on the parameter screen and is here to be an override for this specific field. Again, for reasons of data integrity, we would recommend that all data be entered as uppercase.

The extended-field-definition screen for a numeric field has the following additional options for the field KITVIEW.WEIGHT.

```
EDIT PATTERN      ZZZ.9

IN.DP             3.1 (INTEGERS.DECIMALS)

MIN REQ DECIMALS 1    (VALID ONLY FOR TYPE=N AND JUSTIFY=A)

ALLOW DIGIT SEP  N    (Y=YES, N=NO)

ALLOW MINUS SIGN N    (Y=YES, N=NO)
```

```
ALLOW CURRENCY   N   (Y=YES, N=NO)
CHECK DIGIT      N   (N=NONE, T=MODULO 10, E=MODULO 11)
```

The edit-pattern field causes the panel-output program to apply the stated edit pattern to the field before it is displayed to the user.

The IN.DP field describes the length and distribution of the integer and decimal places in the field. This information is populated from the IN.DP field on the summary screen. Our weight field consists of two integers and one decimal place.

The minimum required decimals field defines the decimal precision that the operator must enter. This is only available with the ALIGN BY DECIMAL option (since this is the only one that allows a decimal point to be physically entered). It must also be less than or equal to the number of decimal places from the IN.DP field.

The next three fields again help with the readability of the input by the operator. They allow the operator to enter commas, minus signs, and currency symbols, which are in turn removed from the data by the PANEL-INPUT program. When the minus sign is used, the data will be sent to the program as a negative number.

The last option is for check digit processing. A *check digit* is a field that is equal to the result of some algorithm that is applied to the other numbers in a field. This is done to aid in data integrity by limiting the number of possible combinations of data that can be entered into the system.

For example, we could say that we had a four-position field, with the first three being the data and the fourth being the check digit. We could then assign the check digit to be the last digit of the sum of the first three. Thus the value 456 would have a check digit of 5.

```
  4
  5
 +6
 ___
 15
$ CHECK DIGIT
```

The IDEAL language provides two very complicated algorithmns called MODULO-10 and MODULO-11. However, due to their complexity we do not feel that they will be of general use, and so we will not discuss them here.

Instead of viewing each field on a separate screen, IDEAL now provides summary screens for the input and the output processing rules. The input rules table (IRULES) appears as follows:

```
------------------------------------------------------------------------
IDEAL:INPUT RULES TABLE      PNL KITVIEW  (001)      SYS:DEV
========================================================================
       KIT NUMBER        _____
       3                 4


....+....1....+....2....+....3....+....4....+....5....+....6....+....7.
SEQ FIELD NAME       E R MINIMUM         MAXIMUM         J I C MN D M A C M
                     H Q VALUE           VALUE           S F S DP S S C D F
--- -------------- - - -------------- --------------- - - - -- - - - - -
  3                  * N                                 N S U
  4 KIT-NUMBER       * N                                 N S U
  5                  * N                                 N S U
  6                  * N                                 N S U
  7 EQUIP-NO         * N                                 N S U
  8 EQUIP-NAME       * N                                 N S U
  9 COLOR            * N                                 N S U
 10 WEIGHT           * N                                 N Z U  1 N N N N N
 11 NUMBER           * N                                 N Z U    N N N N N
 12                  * N                                 N S U
 13                  * N                                 N S U
```

The screen is similar to the summary screen in that it shows part
of the layout screen on the top of its display. The field abbreviations
are as follows:

```
EH — ERROR HANDLING
RQ — REQUIRED
JS — JUSTIFICATION
IF — INPUT FILL CHARACTER
CS — CASE
MN/DP — MINIMUM REQUIRED DECIMALS
DS — ALLOW DIGIT SEPARATOR
MS — ALLOW MINUS SIGN
AC — ALLOW CURRENCY
CD — CHECK DIGIT
MF — MUST-FILL
```

The output rules table (ORULES) appears as follows:

```
------------------------------------------------------------------------
IDEAL:OUTPUT RULES TABLE     PNL KITVIEW  (001)      SYS:DEV
========================================================================
```

```
     KIT NUMBER     _____
        3              4
....+....1....+....2....+....3....+....4....+....5....+....6....+....7.
SEQ FIELD NAME      EDIT PATTERN                        O   E
                                                        F C H

--- -------------- -------------------------------- - - -
  3                                                   U N N
  4 KIT-NUMBER                                        U N N
  5                                                   U N N
  6                                                   U N N
  7 EQUIP-NO                                          U N N
  8 EQUIP-NAME                                        U N N
  9 COLOR                                             U N N
 10 WEIGHT         ZZZ.9                              U N N
 11 NUMBER         ZZ9                                U N N
 12                                                   U N N
 13                                                   U N N
```

The field abbreviations are as follows:

```
OF — OUTPUT FILL CHARACTER
 C — COLOR
EH — EXTENDED HIGHLIGHT
```

These screens can be used to update the extended field definitions and are particularly useful when building a new panel definition.

Other Facilities

In addition to the many topics and panel-processing tools that we have discussed, IDEAL has a number of built-in functions that can prove useful.

These functions have the following syntax:

```
$FUNCTION(PANEL-NAME) (FIELD-NAME)
```

and are listed as

```
$ENTER
$PFN
$RECEIVED
$EMPTY
$CURSOR
```

```
$PANEL-GROUP-OCCURS.

$KEY
```

The $ENTER and $PFN tell the program if the return from the TRANSMIT was started with the operator hitting the ENTER key or a particular program function (PF) key.

The $EMPTY and $RECEIVED functions are used to determine if the operator, the program, or the ENSURE RECEIVE command placed a value in a particular field.

$EMPTY will be true if the panel was just refreshed, reset, transmitted with a CLEAR command, or the field was cleared with the ERASE EOF key. The $RECEIVED command will test true if the user put data into the field on this TRANSMIT, on the previous TRANSMIT with the REINPUT option, or the field or the panel were set to ENSURE RECEIVED.

The $CURSOR tells if a particular field contained the cursor at the time of the TRANSMIT return.

The $PANEL-GROUP-OCCURS function returns the number of times that a table occurs in the panel definition.

The $KEY function returns the last key pressed on the last panel transmitted.

Screen Design Considerations

Not only must the screen work in an efficient manner, but its layout must be such that it can be used effectively. If the screen display is cluttered, difficult to understand, or filled with jargon that the user is not familiar with, they will not accept the new system. This is particularly true when we remember that people are resistant to change, and so the new screen must be significantly better and easier to use than what they already have.

We can use several criteria to judge the effectiveness and design of a screen. These include

1. The format and the content of the screen:

   a. Is the screen as uncluttered as possible, or does it carry extraneous information, separators, redundant headers, etc.? The screen should appear as neat and uncluttered as possible. Field and group separation should be done with open or white space. Fields and captions should be aligned in columns, and their left margins justified.

b. Is the data easy to find, or is it scattered around the screen? The human eye will begin scanning a screen in the upper left-hand corner of the screen, and will then move through the display in a clockwise direction. Related data should be grouped together, with the most important data placed near the beginning of this path.

c. Are the captions and literals easy to understand? The user will not always understand computer jargon, nor always recognize a field by the same name that the DATADIC-TIONARY will recognize. The field captions must always be in the user's language.

d. Are the captions and literals placed in a consistent manner?

   1) When there is a single piece of data it should be placed to the right of the caption, separated by a colon and a space, and differentiated from the literal by color or display intensity.

   2) When multiple occurrences of data are available, they should be placed in a column, with the caption at the top of the column.

e. Is the required cursor movement minimized? Control fields, and fields that are changed often should be placed near the top of the screen.

f. Is the purpose and function of the screen easy to understand? Instructional help messages should be clear and consistent, not only on the screen but throughout the system.

g. Many data entry screens are used in conjunction with a "source document" which contains the information to be entered into the system. The screen layout should be as similar to the layout of the source document as possible.

h. Is the input field length and position easy to recognize? The empty field should be filled with underscores. If the highlight attribute is used it should be applied to the data field and not to the caption.

2. The structure and content of data on the screen:

   a. Is the data on the screen arranged in a logical manner? Is it obvious what pieces of information are related? Is the organization consistent with the real world? For example, if we are displaying an address record, you would expect it to appear in the same format it would if you were going to use it on a letter. You would also expect to see it separated from other data on the screen.

b.   Can the screen elements be identified without reading captions? Similar items should be placed in consistent places from screen to screen, and the proper amount of white space should be used.

c.   Is the most important data at the top of the screen, or is it scattered around? Scanning on an inquiry screen should be done from the top of the screen down, left to right.

3.   Organization of groups of screens:

a.   Is all of the data necessary to a given task displayed on the same screen? The program should use as few screens as possible, to save machine resources and the user's time. However only data necessary to accomplish the task should appear. The data should be separated at logical and natural points, (one screen for order header data and another for order line data).

b.   Is there a clear indication of when an action updates the database? There should always be a clear feedback to the user of what the program is doing, and there should be a specific action to initiate a database update after the edits have been cleared.

c.   Is the menu processing selection clear and flexible? The selections on the menu screen should be ordered as follows:

1)   Sequence of their logical processing occurrence.
2)   Frequency of their usage.
3)   Alphabetic order if it is a long list or if the list is without a logical order.

The menu should be able to process not only the logical relationships, but all of their logical alternatives. The user should also have the ability to skip the menu and go straight to any critical or often-used screens. PF key usage should be consistent throughout the system, and can be used to provide an easy "panic mode" escape route.

4.   Screen keying procedures:

a.   Are there any special keying rules? The error rate increases when the operator must remember special rules, such as character replacement, special data relationships that must be entered, or the frequent use of the shift key. Editing rules should be consistent, and only the data in error should be rekeyed.

b. Is there a lot of cursor movement required during data input? Cursor movement should be top to bottom, left to right. The initial cursor position should be on the first character of the first field to be entered.

We can see some of these techniques in the following example. Let's say that we wished to design a screen that will display sales by customer. We could create the following screen:

```
DISPLAY OF EQUIPMENT SALES BY CUSTOMER          CUST-NO    __

CUSTOMER NAME:    _____
TELEPHONE    :    _____
CUSTOMER TYPE:    __
CITY ADDRESS :    _____


EQUIPMENT NO/NAME        WAREHOUSE        QUANTITY SOLD
       __ _____       _____         _____
       __ _____       _____         _____
       __ _____       _____         _____
       __ _____       _____         _____
       __ _____       _____         _____
       __ _____       _____         _____
       __ _____       _____         _____
       __ _____       _____         _____
       __ _____       _____         _____
       __ _____       _____         _____
       __ _____       _____         _____


   ENTER FIRST CUSTOMER NUMBER
```

If we were to request the sales for customer C1, we would see the following results:

```
DISPLAY OF EQUIPMENT SALES BY CUSTOMER          CUST-NO    C1

CUSTOMER NAME:   SMITH
TELEPHONE    :   224-3601
```

```
CUSTOMER TYPE:   20
CITY ADDRESS :   TAMPA


EQUIPMENT NO/NAME        WAREHOUSE        QUANTITY SOLD
        E1 MM            TAMPA                3
        E2 SLIM          IRVING               2
        E3 WALL          ST PETE              3
        E4 DESK          TAMPA                2
        E5 WALL          IRVING               1
        E6 PAC           TAMPA                1



ENTER NEW CUSTOMER WHEN READY
```

The following design techniques can be observed in this example:

1. The screen is uncluttered, and the separation between the customer and the sales data is accomplished with space and the display table header instead of markings.
2. The required data is easy to find. The input field is in the upper right-hand corner, being the third item the user will see following the name of the screen and the caption. Thus the user should know immediately what data the screen is requesting.
3. The field captions are spelled out for the user to understand, not shortened to the database field names.
4. The single-field captions are placed to the left of the data fields, which are all vertically aligned. The columnar data is also aligned and centered under the captions. (The EQUIP-MENT-NO and NAME are placed under the appropriate part of the literal, which in turn groups the two related pieces of data together.)
5. The screen title tells the users exactly what information they can get from the screen.
6. The help message tells exactly what needs to be done.
7. All fields are filled with underscores during the initial display so that the user can better understand the definition of each field, and in turn the purpose of the screen.
8. The data is logically arranged, with the equipment name immediately following the equipment number. The customer and the equipment/sales data are internally grouped, but are separated from each other.
9. All of the data that is neccessary to examine what this customer has bought, and to give some clue as to why they bought

it, are displayed on the screen. Unimportant data, like color and weight, have been left off.

10. The screen shows the sales for a single customer.

11. The user needs to key in only the predefined customer number.

Conclusions

We have now completed our discussion of one of IDEAL's most powerful coding tools, panel definition and panel processing. Anyone who has tried to align MIDS, MODS, DIFS, DOFS, and working storage through a basic mapping support facility, and then had to "regen" it for a simple change will really appreciate this facility. Here, all five of those elements are combined into one fill-in facility, with all of the alignment taken care of. And to test the changes, all we have to do is recompile the program. Not a GEN or a TEST MFS function in sight.

The other great advantage is the bookmark-like transmit facility. This facility adds greatly to the structure of our code. In other languages, when we do our INSERT through the PCB to the operator, we lose our position, and have to return each time to the top of the program. Through this facility, we come back to the place where we left off when we did the transmit, as if we simply said, "Move screen to user."

We hope that you will find this panel processing facility as useful as we do.

The exercises at the end of this chapter are designed to help you better understand how the facility works.

We learn by doing.

Exercises

1. The PANEL-INPUT and PANEL-OUTPUT programs that we discussed in the chapter are generated by the compiler to process the screens. List the basic functions of these two programs.

2. What are the standard IDEAL program function key assignments?

3. Name and list the purpose of the eight panel definition fill-in screens.

4. What are the advantages of prefix and suffix panels? What are the disadvantages?

5. Design and create a panel that will be able to do maintenance on the customer database. (CUSTMANT)
6. Name and list the purpose of each of the standard panel field attributes.
7. Describe the purpose and function of the ENSURE RECEIVED facility.
8. What is the difference between the numeric and the alphanumeric EXTENDED FIELD DEFINITION screens?
9. Since the alphanumeric extended field definition screen does not contain an edit field, how could we send an edited version of an alphanumeric field to the panel? (For instance, the database field INVOICE.DATE-SHIPPED.)
10. What are the advantages to IDEAL's psuedo-conversational type of on-line processing. What are the disadvantages?
11. Complete the remaining paragraphs for the EQUIPMNT program that we started in this chapter.
12. What are the commands that can be used to reinitialize a panel during processing?
13. What is the command to set the attributes of the field KIT-VIEW.EQUIP-NO to unprotected, alphanumeric, highlight, and ensure receive on a temporary basis?
14. Besides changing the level numbers on the summary screen, how else can we designate the members of a panel group?
15. How many repeating groups can be on a panel?
16. What are the three types of panel scrolling and the advantages and disadvantages of each?
17. When using the function $PANEL-GROUP-OCCURS, why is it necessary to move it to a working-storage field? Why can't it serve as the limiter?
18. If we had two panels attached to the same program, how could we designate on which panel a PF KEY was used in our code?
19. What are the two areas of efficiency that we wish to concentrate on the most when designing an on-line application?
20. What is the purpose of putting some fields on both the parameter screen and the extended field definition?
21. Our KITVIEW.WEIGHT field is defined as numeric, with a 3.1 length. Complete the following table with the entered results against the alignment types.

INPUT

12.1_   12___   _120_   __120

------- ---------- ------------ ----------- -----------

```
J   RIGHT
U
S   _____   _____   _____   _____   _____
T
I   LEFT
F
I   _____   _____   _____   _____   _____
C
A   NONE
T
I   _____   _____   _____   _____   _____
O
N   ALIGN
    DCMAL
    _____   _____   _____   _____   _____
```

22. List the cases where $RECIEVED and $EMPTY are true.
23. What are the four areas of screen design that we can use to judge the effectiveness of a new screen?
24. What can happen if these techniques are not observed?
25. Using the techniques above, design a screen to display CUSTOMER SALES by EQUIPMENT-NO, using the example databases from Chapter 5.

Exercises — Answers

1. The PANEL-INPUT and PANEL-OUTPUT programs that we discussed in the chapter are generated by the compiler to process the screens. List the basic functions of these two programs.

```
A) PANEL INPUT:
    1) RECIEVE THE PANEL FROM THE CRT
    2) AUTOMATIC PANEL SCROLLING
    3) APPLICATION OF EDITS
        1) REQUIRED
        2) MUST FILL
        3) MINIMUM VALUE
        4) MAXIMUM VALUE
        5) MINIMUM REQUIRED DECIMALS
    4) CASE TRANSLATION
    5) APPLICATION OF INPUT FILL CHARACTERS
```

```
    6) DISPLAY OF CLARIFY SCREEN
    7) DISPLAY OF HELP PANELS
    8) INPUT FIELD JUSTIFICATION
    9) REMOVAL OF SPECIAL CHARACTERS
   10) CHECK DIGIT PROCESSING


B) PANEL OUTPUT
    1) PASSING OF PANEL TO CRT
    2) PROCESSING OF EDIT PATTERNS
    3) OUTPUT FILL CHARACTER
    4) RETRIEVAL OF PANEL SOURCE LIBRARY
```

2. What are the standard IDEAL program function key assignments?

	OPTION Y	OPTION Z
PF KEY 1	HELP	HELP
PF KEY 2	END	END
PF KEY 3	CLARIFY	CLARIFY
PF KEY 7	SCROLL UP	SCROLL UP
PF KEY 8	SCROLL DOWN	SCROLL DOWN
PF KEY 10	TOP OF PHYSICAL SCREEN	SCROLL LEFT
PF KEY 11	BOTTOM OF PHYSICAL SCREEN	SCROLL RIGHT

3. Name and list the purpose of the eight panel definition fill-in screens.

   a. IDENTIFICATION (IDE) — contains the panel name and identification.
   b. PARAMETER (PARM) — specifies panel global parameters.
   c. LAYOUT (LAY) — specifies position and length of each field on the screen.
   d. SUMMARY (SUM) — used to specify field level, name, basic description.
   e. EXTENDED FIELD (FIE) — further specifies field attributes.
   f. INPUT RULES (IRU) — summarizes input processing rules.
   g. OUTPUT RULES (ORU) — summarizes of output processing rules.
   h. FACSIMILE (FAC) — displays finished product and allows testing of panel-input and panel-output functions

4. What are the advantages of prefix and suffix panels? What are
    the disadvantages?

    Advantages: reduction of duplicate code and maintenance
    Disadvantage: temporary storage processing

5. Design and create a panel that will be able to do maintenance
    on the customer database. (CUSTMANT)

```
IDEAL: PANEL PARAMETERS    PNL CUSTMANT (001) TEST    SYS: DEV FILL-IN


START     FIELD SYMBOL ^ NEW     FIELD SYMBOL +

END       FIELD SYMBOL ; DELETE FIELD SYMBOL *

REPEATING GROUP SYMBOL @


INPUT  FILL CHARACTER  S (S=SPACE, L=LOWVAL, Z=ZEROES, U=_,OTHER=ITSELF

OUTPUT FILL CHARACTER  U (S=SPACE, L=LOWVAL, Z=ZERORS, U=_,OTHER=ITSELF

NON-DISPLAY CHARACTER  S (S=SPACE, OTHER=AS SPECIFIED)

ERROR FILL CHARACTER   * (AS SPECIFIED)

CASE TRANSLATION       U (U=UPPER, M=MIXED)

REQUIRED               N (Y=YES, N=NO)

ERROR HANDLING         B (N=NONE, *=FILL W/ERRORFILL, H=HIGH INTENSITY,
                          (B=BOTH: H IF ILLEGAL VALUE & * IF REQ MISSING


PANEL WIDTH           80 (A VALUE BETWEEN 80 AND 236)

PF1=HELP, PF3=CLARIFY  Y (Y=YES, N=NO)

PF7=SCR -, PF8=SCR+    N (N=NO, Y=OPT Y, N=OPT N)

  PF10=SCR TOP, PF11=SCR BOT     (OPTION Y)

  PF10=SCR LEFT,PF11=SCR RIGHT   (OPTION Z)

EDIT-RULE ERROR PROC   C  (C=CLARIFY COMMAND, A=APPLICATION)

PROCESS APPL ON SCROLL N  (Y=YES, N=NO)

HELP PANEL NAME   _____     VERSION ___

PREFIX PANEL NAME _____     VERSION ___

SUFFIX PANEL NAME _____     VERSION ___


-------------------------- B O T T O M --------------------------------
```

```
IDEAL: PANEL LAYOUT       PNL CUSTMANT (001) TEST      SYS: DEV FILL-IN
START: ^    END: ;    NEW: +    DELETE: *    REPEAT: @
....+....1....+....2....+....3....+....4....+....5....+....6....+...7..
```

```
+_____;    +CUSTOMER DATABASE MAINTENANCE PROGRAM;


+OPTION; +_; +(A=ADD V=VIEW U=UPDATE D=DELETE);


+CUSTOMER-NO    +__;
+CUSTOMER-NAME;+_____;
+TELEPHONE;     +_____;
+TYPE;          +__;
+CITY;          +_____;


+MESSAGE;       +_____;
```

```
-------------------------- B O T T O M -----------------------------


-------------------------------------------------------------------------
IDEAL: FIELD SUMMARY TABLE    PNL CUSTMANT (001) TEST  SYS: DEV FILL-IN
=========================================================================
    ^_____;    ^CUSTOMER DATABASE MAINTENANCE PROGRAM;
    1              2
    ^OPTION;       ^_; ^(A=ADD V=VIEW U=UPDATE D=DELETE);
    3              4   5
.........................................................................
SEQ LV FIELD NAME     ATTR   T LEN  IN.DP OCC COMMENTS
--- -- --------------- ------ - ---- ----- --- -------------------------
  1  2 CURR-DATE       PSL    X   8
  2  2                 PSL    X  38              CUSTOMER DATABASE MAINTE
  3  2                 PSL    X   6              OPTION
  4  2 OPTION          UALE   X   1
  5  2                 PSL    X  30              (A=ADD V=VIEW U=UPDATE D
  6  2                 PSL    X  12              CUSTOMER-NO
  7  2 CUST-NO         UALE   X   2
  8  2                 PSL    X  14              CUSTOMER-NAME
  9  2 CUST-NAME       UALE   X  10
 10  2                 PSL    X   5              TELEPHONE
 11  2 TELEPHONE       UALE   X   7
 12  2                 PSL    X   6              TYPE
 13  2 TYPE            UALE   X   2
 14  2                 PSL    X   9              CITY
 15  2 CITY            UALE   X  10
 16  2                 PSL    X   7              MESSAGE
```

```
17   2 MESSAGE          PSH     X    41


--------------------------------------------------------------------
IDEAL: EXTENDED FIELD DEFN.   PNL CUSTMANT (001) TEST  SYS:DEV  FILL-IN


        ^TYPE;      ^##;
        12          13
....+....1....+....2....+....3....+....4....+....5....+....6....+....7.
FIELD NAME       TYPE


COMMENTS              _____
TYPE             X   (X=ALPHANUMERIC, N=NUMERIC, G=GROUP)
OCCURANCES       __  (FOR GROUPS ONLY)
ATTRIBUTE       UALE (U=UNPROT  H=HIGHLIGHT    A=327X ALPHA     )
                     (P=PROT    I=INVISIBLE    N=327X NUMERIC   )
                     (S=SKIP    L=LOWLIGHT     E=ENSURE RECIEVED)
                     (C=CURSOR                                  )
COLOR            N   (N=NEUTRAL, B=BLUE, R=RED, P=PINK, G=GREEN,)
                     (T=TURQUOISE, Y=YELLOW, W=WHITE/BLACK      )
EX HIGHLIGHTING  N   (N=NONE, B=BLINK, R=REVERSE VIDEO, U=UNDERSCORE)
OUTPUT FILL CHAR U   (S=SPACES, L=LOWVAL, U=_, OTHER=ITSELF)
ERROR HANDLING   *   (N=NONE, *=FILL *, H=HIGHLIGHT)
                     (B=BOTH: H IF ILLEGAL VALUE & * IF REQD IS MISSING
REQUIRED         N   (Y=YES, N=NO)
MUST-FILL        N   (Y=YES, N=NO)
MINIMUM VALUE    10                      MAXIMUM VALUE 40
JUSTIFY INPUT    N   (N=NO, L=LEFT, R=RIGHT, A=ALIGN BY DECIMAL)


INPUT FILL CHAR  S   (S=SPACES, L=LOWVAL, Z=ZEROES, U=_, OTHER=ITSELF)
VARIABLE DELIM   _
CASE             U   (U=UPPER, M=MIXED)


_____         CUSTOMER DATABASE MAINTENANCE PROGRAM


OPTION    _    (A=ADD V=VIEW U=UPDATE D=DELETE)


CUSTOMER-NO     __
CUSTOMER-NAME   _____
TELEPHONE       _____
TYPE            __
CITY            _____


MESSAGE                 _____
```

6. Name and list the purpose of each of the standard panel field attributes.

P — Protected field that can only be displayed
U — Unprotected field
S — Automatic skip, cursor cannot enter this area with tab keys
H — High-intensity character display
L — Low-intensity character display
I — Field is invisible on the screen
E — Ensure receive
A — Field can accept any alphanumeric data
N — Field can only accept numeric data
C — Cursor position at this field on transmission

7. Describe the purpose and function of the ENSURE RECEIVED facility.

The purpose of this attribute is to ensure that a field is populated with either a user input value or a default input fill character. This allows for data integrity by making sure that the null values of the output fill character do not end up on the database.

8. What is the difference between the numeric and the alphanumeric extended field definition screens?

The numeric extended field definition screen contains the fields:

1. Edit pattern
2. IN.DP
3. Minimum required decimals
4. Allow digit separator
5. Allow minus sign
6. Allow currency
7. Check digit routine selection

9. Since the alphanumeric extended field definition screen does not contain an edit clause, how could we send an edited version of an alphanumeric field to the panel? (For instance, the database field INVOICE.DATE-SHIPPED.)

```
MOVE $EDIT(INVOICE.DATE-SHIPPED,PIC='XX/XX/XX')
```

```
MOVE $STRING(INVOICE.DATE-SHIP-YY, '/',
             INVOICE.DATE-SHIP-MM, '/',
             INVOICE.DATE-SHIP-DD)
```

10. What are the advantages to IDEAL's psuedo-conversational type of on-line processing? What are the disadvantages?

Psuedo-conversational programming of this type is easier to code and is inherently more reliable because the non-shared resources are retained while the program is waiting for the users response.

However, the price for this is increased IO as the non-shared resources are written in and out of temporary storage. We must also allocate the resources and space for the handling and the availability of this temporary storage.

11. Complete the remaining paragraphs for the EQUIPMNT program that we started in this chapter.

```
<<ADD-RECORD>> PROCEDURE
  IF FG-INPUT-CORR = 'Y'
    FOR NEW   EQUIPMENT-DVW
            MOVE EQUIPMNT.EQUIP-NAME TO EQUIPMENT-DVW.EQUIP-NAME
            MOVE EQUIPMNT.COLOR      TO EQUIPMENT-DVW.COLOR
            MOVE EQUIPMNT.WEIGHT     TO EQUIPMENT-DVW.WEIGHT
            MOVE EQUIPMNT.WAREHOUSE  TO EQUIPMENT-DVW.WAREHOUSE
            MOVE 'RECORD ADDED '            TO EQUIPMNT.MESSAGE
        WHEN DUPLICATE
            MOVE 'RECORD ALREADY EXISTS' TO EQUIPMNT.MESSAGE
    ENDFOR
  ENDIF
ENDPROC


<<UPDATE-RECORD>> PROCEDURE
  IF FG-INPUT-CORR = 'Y'
    FOR FIRST EQUIPMENT-DVW
      WHERE EQUIPMENT-DVW.EQUIP-NO EQ EQUIPMNT.EQUIP-NO
            MOVE EQUIPMNT.EQUIP-NAME TO EQUIPMENT-DVW.EQUIP-NAME
            MOVE EQUIPMNT.COLOR      TO EQUIPMENT-DVW.COLOR
            MOVE EQUIPMNT.WEIGHT     TO EQUIPMENT-DVW.WEIGHT
            MOVE EQUIPMNT.WAREHOUSE  TO EQUIPMENT-DVW.WAREHOUSE
            MOVE 'RECORD UPDATED'           TO EQUIPMNT.MESSAGE
        WHEN NONE
            MOVE 'RECORD NOT FOUND '        TO EQUIPMNT.MESSAGE
```

```
    ENDFOR
  ENDIF
ENDPROC


<<DELETE-RECORD>> PROCEDURE
  FOR FIRST EQUIPMENT-DVW
      WHERE EQUIPMENT-DVW.EQUIP-NO EQ EQUIPMNT.EQUIP-NO
            DELETE EQUIPMENT-DVW
            MOVE 'RECORD DELETED'       TO EQUIPMNT.MESSAGE
      WHEN  NONE
            MOVE 'RECORD NOT FOUND '    TO EQUIPMNT.MESSAGE
  ENDFOR
ENDPROC
```

12. What are the commands that can be used to reinitialize a panel during processing?

    a. REFRESH — obtains a new copy of the panel from the source library.

    b. RESET — fills an unprotected field with its input fill character and resets the attributes to their original values.

    c. TRANSMIT CLEAR — fills unprotected fields with their output fill characters.

    d. $LOW — moving $LOW to a field causes it to be seen on the screen with its output fill character.

13. What is the command to set the attributes of the field KITVIEW.EQUIP-NO to unprotected, alphanumeric, highlight, and ensure receive on a temporary basis?

```
SET ATTRIBUTE 'UAHE' TEMP ON KITVIEW.EQUIP-NO
```

14. Besides changing the level numbers on the summary screen, how else can we designate the members of a panel group?

Place the repeating group symbol on the starting position marker on each field that we wish to be in the group.

15. How many repeating groups can be on a panel?

One group per panel definition.

16. What are the three types of panel scrolling that we discussed and the advantages and disadvantages of each?

```
1.  PANEL-INPUT PROGRAM CONTROLLED
    ADV - EASY OF CODING
        - RELIABILITY
    DIS - SIZE OF DATASET TO BE COPIED IN AND OUT OF TEMPORARY
          STORAGE
        - CAN LOSE SIGHT OF PANEL HEADER PART OF SCREEN
2.  WORKING STORAGE TABLE
    ADV - REDUCES SIZE OF NON-SHARED RESOURCES
        - CAN STILL SCROLL IN BOTH DIRECTIONS
        - ALLOWS RETENTION OF VIEW OF HEADER PORTION OF SCREEN
    DIS - COMPLICATED PIECE OF CODING
        - STILL HAS LARGE SIZE NON-SHARED RESOURCE AREA
3.  ENDING FOR STATEMENT
    ADV - LIMITS SIZE OF NON-SHARED RESOURCES
        - NOT EFFECTED BY 99 LINE GROUP LIMIT
    DIS - MULTIPLE IO REQUESTS TO THE DATABASE
```

17. When using the function $PANEL-GROUP-OCCURS, why is it necessary to move it to a working-storage field? Why can't it serve as the limiter?

    This is not a query function, but the execution of a small macro that goes to the panel definition and returns the length of the panel's repeating group.

18. If we had two panels attached to the same program, how could we designate on which panel a PF key was used in our code?

    ```
    IF $PF2(PANELNM)
    ```

19. What are the two areas of efficiency that we wish to concentrate on the most when designing an on-line application?

    a. Size of non-shared resources that must be written in and out of temporary storage
    b. IO to the panel source library

20. What is the purpose of putting some fields on both the parameter screen and the extended field definition.

    The attributes and options selected on the parameter screen apply to all of the fields on the screen, unless they are overridden on the extended field definition screen.

21. Our KITVIEW.WEIGHT field is defined as numeric, with a 3.1 length. Complete the following table with the entered results against the alignment types.

INPUT

		12.1_	12___	_120_	__120
J	RIGHT	ERROR	001.2	012.0	012.0
U					
S					
T					
I	LEFT	ERROR	120.0	120.0	120.0
F					
I					
C					
A	NONE	ERROR	120.0	120.0	012.0
T					
I					
O					
N	ALIGN DCMAL	012.1	012.0	120.0	120.0

22. List the cases where $RECEIVED and $EMPTY are true.

$RECEIVED

1. User updated the field on the screen on the last TRANSMIT cycle.
2. User updated the field on the screen on a previous TRANSMIT, and the REINPUT clause was used.
3. Field had the ENSURE RECEIVED attribute set on.

$EMPTY

1. Field was not modified by the program or the operator.
2. Field was erased with the ERASE EOF key.
3. Field was emptied with a TRANSMIT CLEAR command.
4. RESET statement was used on the field or the entire panel.
5. Panel was cleared with a REFRESH command.

23. What are the four areas of screen design that we can use to judge the effectiveness of a new screen?

    a. The format and content of the screen
    b. The structure and content of data on the screen
    c. Organization of groups of screens
    d. Screen keying procedures

24. What can happen if these techniques are not observed?

    The users will resist and reject the implementation of the new system. They will find ways to undermine its effectiveness, or to go around it. At worst they will ignore it and continue to do their work in the old manner. The new feature must not be as good as the old — it must be significantly better.

25. Using the techniques above, design a screen to display customer sales by EQUIPMENT-NO, using the example databases from Chapter 5.

```
DISPLAY OF CUSTOMER SALES BY EQUIPMENT-NO    EQUIP-NO    __

EQUIPMENT-NAME:  _____
COLOR        :  _____
WEIGHT       :  _____
WARE HOUSE   :  _____


CUSTOMER NO/NAME          WAREHOUSE        QUANTITY SOLD

  __ _____        _____        _____
  __ _____        _____        _____
  __ _____        _____        _____
  __ _____        _____        _____
  __ _____        _____        _____
  __ _____        _____        _____
  __ _____        _____        _____
  __ _____        _____        _____
  __ _____        _____        _____
  __ _____        _____        _____
  __ _____        _____        _____
  _____
```

8

Report Definition and Usage

Introduction

Although IDEAL is primarily designed to give the user on-line access to specific pieces of data, there is also a REPORT facility available that will generate reports on large volumes of data. These reports can then be used to send information to people outside of the system, to do trend analysis, to create and document audit trails, to create archives, etc.

The reports are defined and developed through the report definition facility (RDF). The definitions are created through the use of five different menu screens:

IDENTIFICATION — identifies the report to the DATADICTION-ARY.
PARAMETER — maintains those parameters that effect the processing of the entire report.
HEADING — defines the report heading that appears on each page.
DETAIL — defines the layout of the individual report lines.
COLUMN — defines the heading of each column on the report.

The parameters on each of these screens are used by IDEAL to create the logic that is required to produce the required report. When the program that uses the report is compiled, the parameters are read in, and the program is compiled with this code in it, much like a statically linked subroutine.

In fact, the report definition functions much like an output procedure of a COBOL report-generating program with an internal SORT. In that type of environment, the program would read in the records that it wants to report on, extract the data, release it to a sort, sort it, return from the sort, manipulate control breaks, accumulate headers, print lines, etc.

In an IDEAL program, we still read in the data and extract the information that we want. Then we issue the command:

```
PRODUCE RPTNAME
```

where RPTNAME is the name of the report defintion, and all of the rest is handled automatically. This includes

1. Current date printing
2. Page-number accumulation
3. Vertical tabbing
4. Horizontal tabbing
5. Sorting
6. Column totaling and averaging
7. Control breaks
8. Control heading and footing

Thus the production of a report requires very little coding beyond the selection of data from the input.

In this chapter we will discuss each of these screens in detail, and then review some examples to see how they work together.

Identification

The identification screen contains data that identifies the report to the DATADICTIONARY, and contains the same information that is to be found in the IDE screen of the program and panel definitions.

Parameter

The parameter fill-in screen contains the global parameters of the report. These include report SIZE, types of processing, page number and date processing. The basic screen is pictured in Figure 8-1.

```
------------------------------------------------------------------------
IDEAL: RPT PARAMETERS          RPT XXXXXXXX (XXX) XXXX        SYS: XXX


LINES PER PAGE ON PRINTOUT       .. XX  ( 1 THRU 250)
REPORT WIDTH                     XXX (40 THRU 230)
SPACING BETWEEN LINES            X   ( 1 THRU 3)
SPACING BETWEEN COLUMNS          XX  ( 0 THRU 66 OR A=AUTOMATIC)
SUMMARIES ONLY                   X   (Y=YES,N=NO)
COLUMN HEADINGS DESIRED          X   (Y=YES,N=NO)
COLUMN HEADINGS INDICATION       X   (U=UNDERSCORE,N=NONE,D=DASHES)
CONTROL BREAK HEADING            X   (Y=YES,N=NO)
CONTROL BREAK FOOTING            X   (Y=YES,N=NO)
GROUP CONTINUATION AT TOP OF PAGE  X   (Y=YES,N=NO)
ANNOTATED COUNT IN CONTROL FOOTINGS X  (Y=YES,N=NO)
REPORT FINAL SUMMARY TITLE       X   (Y=YES,N=NO)
  SPACING BEFORE SUMMARY         X   (1 THRU 9 = LINES,P=NEW PAGE)
  TITLE         _____


DATE
  POSITION       XX    (NO=NONE,BR=BOT.RIGHT,BL=BOT.LEFT,BC=BOT.CTR
                        TR=TOP RIGHT,TL=TOP LEFT,TC=TOP CENTER)
  FORMAT         XXXXXXXXXXXX


PAGE NUMBERS
  POSITION       XX
  FORMAT         H     (D=DIGITS ONLY, H=WITH HYPHENS, P=PAGE    NNN)


PAGE HEADING
  HEADING        XXXXXXXXXXXXXXXXXXXXXXXXXXXXXXXXXXXXXXXXXXXX
  POSITION       X     (C=CENTER, L=LEFT JUSTIFY, R=RIGHT JUSTIFY)


LINES PER PAGE NO PRINTOUT       XX  ( 1 THRU 250)
REPORT WIDTH                     XXX (40 THRU 230)
-------------------------------------------------------------
```

Figure 8-1   Basic Parameter Screen Example.

These two parameters define the *logical size* of each report page. It should be noted that each of these parameters have acceptable values which are outside the range of most printers. If the report width is greater than the printer carriage, then the right-hand side of the report will be truncated. If the lines per page is greater than the physical length of the paper, then the report will keep right on going over the paper folds until it comes to a logical page break. Thus, if you were printing 6 lines per inch on standard 11 x 15 paper and had the PARM set to 80, you would be well into your second piece of paper before the page break occurred.

SPACING BETWEEN LINES   X (1 THRU 3)

This parameter defines how many lines will be advanced before the print line is written. When the parameter is

   1 — Each line immediatly follows the previous line.
   2 — A line is skipped between each detail line.
   3 — Two lines are skipped between each detail line.

This is very similar to the AFTER ADVANCING clause of the COBOL WRITE command, which would be coded as

```
1 — WRITE REPORT-LINE AFTER ADVANCING 1 LINES.
2 — WRITE REPORT-LINE AFTER ADVANCING 2 LINES.
3 — WRITE REPORT-LINE AFTER ADVANCING 3 LINES.
```

SPACING BETWEEN COLUMNS   XX (0 THRU 66 OR A=AUTOMATIC)

This command handles the horizontal tabbing between the report columns. The number represents the number of positions that will be skipped before each column is placed on the report. The A, or AUTOMATIC, command computes the total length of the data columns on the line, subtracts that value from the report width parameter, and evenly distributes the remainder between the columns and the left and right margins.

SUMMARIES ONLY   X (Y=YES,N=NO)

This parameter suppresses the printing of the detail records and only prints the summary and total lines. The default is NO, which allows printing of all of the records.

COLUMN HEADINGS DESIRED   X (Y=YES,N=NO)

This command tells IDEAL to print or suppress the printing of the column heading line. By not printing the column headings, it is possible to print a report which just shows the detail records. When we do this, we will be able to capture the report in a standard dataset and pass it to another program for furthur processing. Thus we have an easy way to download data from IDEAL to other types of processing.

**COLUMN HEADINGS INDICATION   X (U=UNDERSCORE,N=NONE,
                                   D=DASHES)**

After the column heading line is written, IDEAL will automatically write out a line which will separate the headings from the detail records. This line can contain either spaces, dashes (----------), or underscores (_____). The positions of these marks are dependent on the positions of the detail columns, obeying the same tabbing rules, and covering the same width.

CONTROL BREAK HEADING   X (Y=YES,N=NO)
CONTROL BREAK FOOTING   X (Y=YES,N=NO)

Control-break headings are printed whenever the value of a control field changes. A control field is one which, when its value changes, requires the report to do something. This can include printing of a total line, causing a page break, displaying running totals, supression of printing of a field, etc. Whenever one of these breaks occurs, a header or footer line can be printed. These lines include a set of asterisks which show the level of the break, the name of the field, and its old value (before the break occurred). The asterisks are displayed as two for the first level, four for the second level, six for the third level, etc. If we had a report that had two break fields, our print lines would take the format:

```
**STATE UTAH
****CITY SALT LAKE CITY
```

GROUP CONTINUATION AT TOP OF PAGE   X (Y=YES,N=NO)

The group continuation is similar in format to the control-break heading line, although opposite in meaning. This message is printed when a page break occurs without a control break occurring. In this case, we would have the following results:

```
**STATE UTAH (CONT.)
****CITY SALT LAKE CITY (CONT.)
```

Again we have the asterisk, the field name, and the current field value. We also have the word (CONT.), which shows that this is a continuation of the group.

ANNOTATED COUNT IN CONTROL FOOTINGS   X (Y=YES,N=NO)

This parameter allows for the printing of a count of the number of detail lines that were printed before a break occurred, and is found in the heading or footing area.

```
REPORT FINAL SUMMARY TITLE          X    (Y=YES,N=NO)
  SPACING BEFORE SUMMARY            X    (1 THRU 9 = LINES,P=NEW PAGE)
  TITLE     XXXXXXXXXXXXXXXXXXXXXXXXXXXXXXXXXXXXXXXXX
```

These parameters control the printing of a grand total line on the bottom of the report. the first parameter turns on the function, the second causes print line advancement before writing (either a certain number of lines or to the top of the next page), and the third contains a title to be placed on the line.

In addition to the above parameters, IDEAL can also control the processing of a date stamp, a page counter, and a simple one-line page header.

The date and the page header can be placed in any one of six positions or turned off entirely. These positions are

NO — Function is not implemented.
BR — Last line on the logical page, right justified.
BL — Last line on the logical page, left justified.
BC — Last line on the logical page, centered.
TR — Top line on the logical page, right justified.
TL — Top line on the logical page, left justified.
TC — Top line on the logical page, centered.

Neither of the parameters can be placed in the same position, an edit at the time that the report is created or modified ensures that. However, both parameters can be placed on the same line. If either of the fields are centered, and there is a report header designated, it will be written on a separate line, along with the other parameter if they are both designated for the same line.

The DATE FORMAT parameter is a free-form area that can take any combination of the following specifications along with special characters or spaces:

YEAR — current 4-character year
YY — 2-character year without century
Y — 1-character year without century or decade
MONTH — current month spelled out
LMONTH — current month in lowercase, with an uppercase first character
MON — 3-character alpha abbreviation
MM — 2-character numeric month (01–12)
M — 2-character numeric month (1–12) no leading ZERO
DD — 2-character day (01–31)
D — 2-character day (1–31) no leading zero

The page format can take one of three different values:

D — only the absolute page numbers
H — the absolute page numbers, delimited with hyphens
P — The page number preceded by a 1- to 8-character string. The default value for this string is 'PAGE', but it can take any value.

The page heading parameter allows a simple one-line page header to be allocated to the report. It can take any literal value and can be placed either in the center of the page, or it can be placed between the date and page parameters. The heading line will then be placed as far right or left as it can go, using either the report margin, or the PAGE-NO/DATE PARM, if one is encountered.

Heading

The heading fill-in is used to define more complicated report headings than is possible with the single-line heading field on the parameter screen. This fill-in screen has the format shown in Figure 8-2.

```
--------------------------------------------------------------------
IDEAL: RPT PAGE HEADING     RPT XXXXXXXX (XXX) TEST    SYS: XXX FILL-IN

FIELD NAME, LITERAL, FUNCTION              COLUMN
OR ARITHMETIC EXPRESSION                   W
                                           ID TAB EDIT PATTERN  COMMAND
                                           TH
-------------------------------------------- -- --- ------------ ------
_____ __ ___ _____ 000010
_____ __ ___ _____ 000020
_____ __ ___ _____ 000030
_____ __ ___ _____ 000040
_____ __ ___ _____ 000050
_____ __ ___ _____ 000060
_____ __ ___ _____ 000070
_____ __ ___ _____ 000080
_____ __ ___ _____ 000090
_____ __ ___ _____ 000100
_____ __ ___ _____ 000110
```

Figure 8-2   Report Heading Fill-In Screen.

With this screen and the date and page parameters from the parameter screen, IDEAL is able to define the report page headers at program compile time.

The first column is used to define the value of the field. This can be either an alphanumeric literal, a field that is defined in the program (either in working storage or a field on a dataview that is accessed by the program), or an arithmetic expression or function that is made up of fields defined in the program. If the identifier is too long for the space provided, it can be continued on the next line by placing a semicolon (;) at the end of the name on the first line. The other columns will be populated on the first line.

The second column is used to define the length of the field if it is different from the defined length of the field. If we select a field that is defined in the program, or place a literal in the field, IDEAL can take that defined length, or the count of the characters in the literal, for the field length value. We can, of course, place the value in this field for purposes of documentation and readability.

The column field handles both the vertical and horizontal tabbing between fields. The field can take one of three formats. It can be either the horizontal position of the start of the field, it can be a

```
--------------------------------------------------------------------
IDEAL: RPT DETAIL DEFN.        RPT XXXXXXXX (XXX) XXXX        SYS:XXX

FIELD NAME, LITERAL        SORT  BREAK  FUNCTION COLUMN
FUNCTION, OR               L A   L S I  T M M A  H W
ARITHMETIC EXPRESSION      V /   V K N  O A I V  D ID TAB EDIT PATTERN
                          L D   L P D  T X N G  G TH
-------------------------  - -   - - -  - - - -  - -- --- -------------
========== TOP ==========  = =   = = =  = = = =  = == === =============
-------------------------        - -    - - - -  - -- --- -------------
-------------------------  - -   - - -  - - - -  - -- --- -------------
-------------------------  - -   - - -  - - - -  - -- --- -------------
-------------------------  - -   - - -  - - - -  - -- --- -------------
-------------------------  - -   - - -  - - - -  - -- --- -------------
-------------------------  - -   - - -  - - - -  - -- --- -------------
======== BOTTOM =========  = =   = = =  = = = =  = == === =============
```

Figure 8-3   Detail Fill-In Screen.

horizontal distance between fields (+NN), or it can be a number of vertical lines advanced before the next line is printed. It is also possible to tab to the next page, with the character P.

The edit pattern, if specified, is applied to the value of the field at the time the page header is written out. This edit pattern function follows the same rules, and uses the same symbols, as the $EDIT function that we saw in Chapter 4.

The fourth fill-in screen is used to determine the position, length, value, and operations on the various columns of the report. This screen, called the detail screen, has the format shown in Figure 8-3.

As can be seen, this fill-in screen can be divided into six functional areas. These are

1. Column Identification
2. SORT Function
3. Control Break Definition
4. Manipulation Functions
5. Column Definitions
6. Column Edit Patterns

The column identifications and edit patterns perform in the same way they did in the heading definition screen.

The SORT function allows us to sort the detail records as they are sent to the report with the PRODUCE statement, in the same way that we release and return records from a COBOL INTERNAL SORT. If nothing is coded in this space, then the report records will be written out in the same order that they were produced. Otherwise, we place the level number of the field in the sort sequence in the LVL column, and either an "A" or a "D" in the second column, for ascending order or descending order. This order selection can be independent for each field with, for example, ascending order for the first and third fields, and descending for the second field. The level numbers take the value of 1 through 9, with 1 being the primary sort field, 2 being the secondary, etc.

To avoid any confusion, it should be noted that all of the output records are sorted before the actual report writing commences.

The second area contains the control-break definitions. This is the most powerful part of the report fill-in, as it controls all of the page and line breaks, and the printing of the break fields. The first column again defines the break level, 1 through 9. The second column, the skip parameter, defines the vertical tabbing that occurs when the break is encountered. The character P means that a page break will occur. Otherwise, we can designate to skip from 1 to 9 lines, or, if the field is left blank, IDEAL will use the spacing between lines parameter from the PARM screen. The IND, or indication parameter, controls the printing of the break field. We can either print the field (R), or we can have a group break, which prints only when the value changes (G or BLANK), or we can never print the field on the detail line.

The fourth area causes the report writer to do arithmetic functions to the fields. These functions can be

1. Column totals
2. Maximum value encountered in the column
3. Minimum value encountered in the column
4. Average value encountered in the column

These fields can in turn take one of three values:

1. BLANK — no processing will be done.
2. A — value will print on its own line, with an annotating description.
3. S — value will print on a summary line, with the values of the other columns.

Each function has its own summary line. Thus, if we choose to, we could create four summary line entries under each column, one for each function. It should also be noted that when IDEAL encounteres a summary function, it tries to allocate a width that is four spaces longer than the defined field length. Thus we could get compiler warning messages about insufficient length if our spacing or our edit pattern designations do not compensate for this addition.

The fifth area defines the position and function of the column and its associated heading. Here we define the width of the column, its vertical and horizontal tabbing, and where IDEAL can get the value of the column heading literal from.

The column width can be designated here, or we can rely on IDEAL to generate it. This occurs in the following hierarchy:

1. Designated width on the fill-in screen.
2. Width of the sourcing field, as defined in the program that produces the report.
3. The width of the column header.
4. If a summary total is specified, then four positions are added to the value of the length of the source field.
5. The length of the edit pattern that is used.

The tabbing function is the same as the one that we described on the header screen. We can designate one of the following:

1. The use of the spacing-between-columns parameter
2. Relative spacing from the end of the last field
3. Absolute spacing, designing the actual location of the begining of the field
4. Vertical tabbing of a number of lines to 250
5. Page break

The column heading designator can also take one of three values. It can be SPACES, which will cause IDEAL to use the designation contained in the DATADICTIONARY, or the field name. A value of N will cause supression of the column heading. A value of U will cause IDEAL to use the value defined in the last fill-in screen, the COL, or column heading screen.

Figure 8-4 shows the basic layout of this screen.

When this screen is displayed, the first four columns will already be filled in from the values that were entered on the detail screen, with one line being shown for each detail screen line. These fields

```
-------------------------------------------------------------------------
IDEAL: RPT COLUMN HEADINGS    RPT XXXXXXXX (XXX) XXXX      SYS: DOC
FIELD NAME, LITERAL          COLUMN
FUNCTION OR                  H  W
ARITHMETIC EXPRESSION        D  ID TAB HEADINGS
                             G  TH
------------------------- - -- --- --------------------------------------
========== TOP ========== = == === =======================================
_____ _ __ ___ _____
_____ _ __ ___ _____
_____ _ __ ___ _____
_____ _ __ ___ _____
_____ _ __ ___ _____
_____ _ __ ___ _____
======== BOTTOM ========= = == === =======================================
```

Figure 8-4   Column Heading Layout Screen.

can in turn be modified on this screen, and the changes will be seen when the detail screen is again displayed.

The heading field is used to define the column heading literal. The literal can be continued on the next line by putting a +00 in the tab column. The literal will be centered over the top of the column and, as a default, placed on a single line. To place a column header on multiple lines, we place a special character at the beginning of the literal and anywhere we wish to have a line break. Thus the literal 'CUSTOMERS NAME' will appear on one line, while the literal '/CUSTOMERS/NAME' will appear as

```
CUSTOMERS
  NAME
```

Before we look at some coding examples, let's discuss how the IDEAL REPORT WRITER logically works.

The easiest way to understand the functioning of the IDEAL report is to think of it as a statically linked sub-routine in the reporting program. When a program is compiled, the compiler also reads in any associated report definitions, and using the values that were placed in the fill-in screens, creates the proper load modules. These load modules are then invoked whenever we use the PRODUCE command.

This PRODUCE command is very similar to a call to a subroutine, with the passed parameters being the data items that were identified in the report definition as being on, or operative in, the report.

Let's say now that we wish to create a report that will print the customer database that we created in Chapter 5. As you will recall, that file had the following layout:

LV C FIELD-NAME	PARENT-NAME	DISPL	LENGTH	T	J	S
01 S CUST-NO		0	2	C	L	N
01 S CUST-NAME		2	10	C	L	N
01 S TELEPHONE		12	7	C	L	N
01 S TYPE		19	2	C	L	N
01 S CITY		21	15	C	L	N

We would then fill in the report definition screens as follows:

```
------------------------------------------------------------------
IDEAL: RPT PARAMETERS        RPT EXAMPLE1 (001) TEST        SYS: DEV

LINES PER PAGE ON PRINTOUT        54   ( 1 THRU 250)
REPORT WIDTH                      80   (40 THRU 230)
SPACING BETWEEN LINES             1    ( 1 THRU 3)
SPACING BETWEEN COLUMNS           02   ( 0 THRU 66 OR A=AUTOMATIC)
SUMMARIES ONLY                    N    (Y=YES,N=NO)
COLUMN HEADINGS DESIRED           Y    (Y=YES,N=NO)
COLUMN HEADINGS INDICATION        U    (U=UNDERSCORE,N=NONE,D=DASHES)
CONTROL BREAK HEADING             N    (Y=YES,N=NO)
CONTROL BREAK FOOTING             N    (Y=YES,N=NO)
GROUP CONTINUATION AT TOP OF PAGE N    (Y=YES,N=NO)
ANNOTATED COUNT IN CONTROL FOOTINGS N  (Y=YES,N=NO)
REPORT FINAL SUMMARY TITLE        N    (Y=YES,N=NO)
   SPACING BEFORE SUMMARY               (1 THRU 9 = LINES,P=NEW PAGE)
   TITLE      _____

DATE
   POSITION          TL    (NO=NONE,BR=BOT.RIGHT,BL=BOT.LEFT,BC=BOT.CTR
                            TR=TOP RIGHT,TL=TOP LEFT,TC=TOP CENTER)
   FORMAT            YY/MM/DD

PAGE NUMBERS
   POSITION          TR
   FORMAT            D     (D=DIGITS ONLY, H=WITH HYPHENS, P=PAGE    NNN)
```

```
PAGE HEADING

    HEADING          CUSTOMER INFORMATION AUDIT REPORT

    POSITION         C    (C=CENTER, L=LEFT JUSTIFY, R=RIGHT JUSTIFY)


-------------------------------------------------------------------------
IDEAL: RPT DETAIL DEFN.     RPT EXAMPLE1 (001) TEST         SYS:DEV

FIELD NAME, LITERAL        SORT  BREAK  FUNCTION COLUMN

FUNCTION, OR               L  A  L  S  I   T  M  M  A   H  W

ARITHMETIC EXPRESSION      V  /  V  K  N   O  A  I  V   D  ID  TAB  EDIT PATTERN

                          L  D  L  P  D   T  X  N  G   G  TH

-------------------------  -  -  -  -  -   -  -  -  -   -  --  ---  --------------
========== TOP ==========  =  =  =  =  =   =  =  =  =   =  ==  ===  ==============
CUSTOMER.CUST-NO                                                   U   __  ____  _____
CUSTOMER.CUST-NAME         __    __  __ __   __ __  __ __   U   __  ____  _____
CUSTOMER.TELEPHONE         __    __  __ __   __ __  __ __   U   __  ____  _____
CUSTOMER.TYPE              __    __  __ __   __ __  __ __   U   __  ____  _____
CUSTOMER.CITY              __    __  __ __   __ __  __ __   U   __  ____  _____
======== BOTTOM ==========  = =   = = =    = = = =    =  ==  ===  ==============


-------------------------------------------------------------------------
IDEAL: RPT COLUMN HEADINGS    RPT EXAMPLE1 (001) TEST        SYS: DEV
FIELD NAME, LITERAL        COLUMN
FUNCTION OR                H  W
ARITHMETIC EXPRESSION      D  ID  TAB  HEADINGS
                          G  TH
-------------------------  -  --  ---  -------------------------------------
========== TOP ==========  =  ==  ===  =====================================
CUSTOMER.CUST-NO           _  __  ___  CUSTNO
CUSTOMER.CUST-NAME         _  __  ___  CUST  NAME
CUSTOMER.TELEPHONE         _  __  ___  TELEPHONE
CUSTOMER.TYPE             _  __  ___  TP
CUSTOMER.CITY             _  __  ___  CITY
======== BOTTOM ==========  =  ==  ===  ====================================
```

We should take note of a number of items from this example:

Parameter Screen

1. We will place 56 lines on each report page.
2. The maximumn width of our report will be 80 columns, (so that it will fit on this page).
3. We will tab two spaces between every column on the report.
4. We will not skip any lines between our detail lines.

5. We will place a series of underscore characters below each of the column headers, for the width of the column.
6. We will place the date in a year/month/day format in the top left corner of the report.
7. We will place the page number in the top right corner.
8. We will center the title, customer information audit report, on the top of each page.
9. We have not invoked the header definition screen.

Detail Screen

1. We are using the actual DATAVIEW fields as our report fields. This means that when the PRODUCE statement is accessed, the report line will contain the values from the current dataview work area.
2. We will use the column headers as defined on the COL screen.
3. We are depending on the default lengths for our column widths. This will result in the following definitions:

```
CUSTOMER.CUST-NO      2  length of COLUMN HEADER
CUSTOMER.CUST-NAME   10  length of DATA ITEM
CUSTOMER.TELEPHONE    9  length of COLUMN HEADER
CUSTOMER.TYPE         2  length of DATA ITEM
CUSTOMER.CITY         2  length of DATA ITEM
```

Then, using the SELECT algorithm that we saw in Chapter 5, we can write the following program:

```
FOR EACH CUSTOMER
        PRODUCE EXAMPLE1
ENDFOR
```

which would produce the following report:

```
85/03/20      CUSTOMER INFORMATION AUDIT REPORT              -1-


CUSTNO   CUST   NAME   TELEPHONE   TY       CITY
_____  ___  _____  _____   __   _____
  C1          SMITH     2243601     20       TAMPA
  C2          JONES     5543904     10       IRVING
  C3          BLAKE     6320422     10       IRVING
  C4          CLARK     9610731     20       TAMPA
  C5          ADAMS     4916203     30       DURHAM
```

At this point, we can note two things that should be changed on this report. First, we do not have a delimiter between the prefix and the suffix of the telephone number, and second, the report is all on the left side of the page. To correct this, we can make the following simple changes to the detail screen:

```
-------------------------------------------------------------------------
IDEAL: RPT DETAIL DEFN.      RPT EXAMPLE1 (001) TEST        SYS:DEV


FIELD NAME, LITERAL       SORT  BREAK  FUNCTION COLUMN

FUNCTION, OR              L A   L S I  T M M A  H W

ARITHMETIC EXPRESSION     V /   V K N  O A I V  D ID TAB EDIT PATTERN

                          L D   L P D  T X N G  G TH

-------------------------  - -  - - -  - - - -  - -- --- -------------
========== TOP ==========  = =  = = =  = = = =  = == === =============
CUSTOMER.CUST-NO           _ _  _ _ _  _ _ _ _  U __ 011 _____
CUSTOMER.CUST-NAME         _ _  _ _ _  _ _ _ _  U __ ___ _____
CUSTOMER.TELEPHONE         _ _  _ _ _  _ _ _ _  U __ ___ XXX-XXXX
CUSTOMER.TYPE             _ _  _ _ _  _ _ _ _  U __ ___ _____
CUSTOMER.CITY             _ _  _ _ _  _ _ _ _  U __ ___ _____
======== BOTTOM =========  = =  = = =  = = = =  = == === =============
```

With these changes, we will begin our first column in position 11, and place a dash between the portions of the telephone number. The edit pattern is still shorter than the column header, so the width default will not change. The resulting report will be

```
85/03/20      CUSTOMER INFORMATION AUDIT REPORT           -1-


        CUSTNO  CUST  NAME  TELEPHONE  TY      CITY

        ------  ----------  ---------  ---  -------------
          C1      SMITH     224-3601   20      TAMPA
          C2      JONES     554-3904   10      IRVING
          C3      BLAKE     632-0422   10      IRVING
          C4      CLARK     961-0731   20      TAMPA
          C5      ADAMS     491-6203   30      DURHAM
```

much better.

While it is very easy to code a report using the dataview names, this presents a problem whenever we encounter a condition where only a portion of our data is available. For example, if we ran the above report program, and a condition occurred where we did not find any customer records, we would not produce a report. This could cause a great deal of consternation when someone did not receive an expected report or an explanation.

To overcome this problem, we recommend that you always use working-storage fields as the report data fields and move the required data to them from the dataview before the PRODUCE statement.

Thus, we would define a working-storage area with

```
1   REPORT-AREA
    2   CUST-NO       X    2
    2   CUST-NAME     X    10
    2   TELEPHONE     X    8
    2   TYPE          X    2
    2   CITY          X    15
```

change our detail screen to read

```
------------------------------------------------------------------------
IDEAL: RPT DETAIL DEFN.      RPT EXAMPLE1 (001) TEST        SYS:DEV


FIELD NAME, LITERAL        SORT  BREAK  FUNCTION COLUMN

FUNCTION, OR               L A   L S I  T M M A  H W

ARITHMETIC EXPRESSION      V /   V K N  O A I V  D ID TAB EDIT PATTERN

                          L D   L P D  T X N G  G TH

-------------------------  - -   - - -  - - - -  - -- --- -------------
========== TOP ==========  = =   = = =  = = = =  = == === =============
REPORT-AREA.CUST-NO        _ _   _ _ _  _ _ _ _  U __ 011 _____
REPORT-AREA.CUST-NAME      _ _   _ _ _  _ _ _ _  U __ ____ _____
REPORT-AREA.TELEPHONE      _ _   _ _ _  _ _ _ _  U __ ____ _____
REPORT-AREA.TYPE           _ _   _ _ _  _ _ _ _  U __ ____ _____
REPORT-AREA.CITY           _ _   _ _ _  _ _ _ _  U __ ____ _____
======= BOTTOM =========  = =   = = =  = = = =  = == === =============
```

and our program to

```
FOR EACH CUSTOMER
        MOVE CUSTOMER.CUST-NO    TO REPORT-AREA.CUST-NO
        MOVE CUSTOMER.CUST-NAME TO REPORT-AREA.CUST-NAME
        MOVE CUSTOMER.TYPE       TO REPORT-AREA.CUST-TYPE
        MOVE CUSTOMER.CITY       TO REPORT-AREA.CUST-CITY
        MOVE $EDIT(CUSTOMER.TELEPHONE,PIC='XXX-XXXX')
             TO REPORT-AREA.TELEPHONE
        PRODUCE EXAMPLE1
    WHEN NONE
```

```
MOVE '**'                  TO REPORT-AREA.CUST-NO
MOVE '**********'          TO REPORT-AREA.CUST-NAME
MOVE '**********'          TO REPORT-AREA.TELEPHONE
MOVE '**'                  TO REPORT-AREA.CUST-TYPE
MOVE '***************'     TO REPORT-AREA.CUST-CITY
PRODUCE EXAMPLE1
PRODUCE EXAMPLE1
MOVE '******'             TO REPORT-AREA.CUST-NO
MOVE 'NO RECORDS'          TO REPORT-AREA.CUST-NAME
MOVE '  FOUND   '          TO REPORT-AREA.TELEPHONE
MOVE 'TO'                  TO REPORT-AREA.CUST-TYPE
MOVE 'REPORT   ******'     TO REPORT-AREA.CUST-CITY
PRODUCE EXAMPLE1
PRODUCE EXAMPLE1
MOVE '******'             TO REPORT-AREA.CUST-NO
MOVE '**********'          TO REPORT-AREA.CUST-NAME
MOVE '**********'          TO REPORT-AREA.TELEPHONE
MOVE '**'                  TO REPORT-AREA.CUST-TYPE
MOVE '***************'     TO REPORT-AREA.CUST-CITY
PRODUCE EXAMPLE1
PRODUCE EXAMPLE1
ENDFOR
```

Under normal processing this code would produce the same report that we saw before. We will also produce the following printout under the WHEN NONE condition.

```
85/03/20      CUSTOMER INFORMATION AUDIT REPORT          -1-


      CUSTNO  CUST  NAME  TELEPHONE  TY      CITY

      _____  _____  _____  ___  _____

      ******  **********  ********  **  ***************
      ******  **********  ********  **  ***************
      ******  NO RECORDS    FOUND    TO  REPORT   ******
      ******  NO RECORDS    FOUND    TO  REPORT   ******
      ******  **********  ********  **  ***************
      ******  **********  ********  **  ***************
```

The reader should also notice that we chose to use the $EDIT command on the telephone number field instead of using the edit function of the report screen. This was done to avoid having the report editor put a dash in the middle of our message, as if it was a telephone number. From this we can see that we have a great deal of flexibility available to us when we use the working-storage fields instead of the dataview fields.

In addition to doing straight dumps of the database, it is also possible to create reports that manipulate the data as it is being extracted.

Let's suppose that we wanted to see year-to-date sales by customer number. To do this, we would create the following report definition.

```
------------------------------------------------------------------------
IDEAL: RPT PARAMETERS          RPT EXAMPLE2 (001) TEST        SYS: DEV


LINES PER PAGE ON PRINTOUT      54  ( 1 THRU 250)

REPORT WIDTH                    072 (40 THRU 230)

SPACING BETWEEN LINES           1   ( 1 THRU 3)

SPACING BETWEEN COLUMNS         02  ( 0 THRU 66 OR A=AUTOMATIC)

SUMMARIES ONLY                  N   (Y=YES,N=NO)

COLUMN HEADINGS DESIRED         Y   (Y=YES,N=NO)

COLUMN HEADINGS INDICATION      U   (U=UNDERSCORE,N=NONE,D=DASHES)

CONTROL BREAK HEADING           N   (Y=YES,N=NO)

CONTROL BREAK FOOTING           N   (Y=YES,N=NO)

GROUP CONTINUATION AT TOP OF PAGE  X  (Y=YES,N=NO)

ANNOTATED COUNT IN CONTROL FOOTINGS X  (Y=YES,N=NO)

REPORT FINAL SUMMARY TITLE      X   (Y=YES,N=NO)

SPACING BEFORE SUMMARY          X   (1 THRU 9 = LINES,P=NEW PAGE)

TITLE      _____


DATE
   POSITION        TR    (NO=NONE,BR=BOT.RIGHT,BL=BOT.LEFT,BC=BOT.CTR
                          TR=TOP RIGHT,TL=TOP LEFT,TC=TOP CENTER)
   FORMAT      YY/MM/DD


PAGE NUMBERS
   POSITION        TL
   FORMAT          D     (D=DIGITS ONLY, H=WITH HYPHENS, P=PAGE    NNN)


PAGE HEADING
   HEADING         YEAR TO DATE SALES BY CUSTOMER
   POSITION        C     (C=CENTER, L=LEFT JUSTIFY, R=RIGHT JUSTIFY)


------------------------------------------------------------------------
IDEAL: RPT DETAIL DEFN.      RPT EXAMPLE2 (001) TEST      SYS:DEV


FIELD NAME, LITERAL        SORT  BREAK  FUNCTION COLUMN
FUNCTION, OR               L A   L S I  T M M A   H W
```

```
ARITHMETIC EXPRESSION        V /  V K N  O A I V  D ID TAB EDIT PATTERN
                             L D  L P D  T X N G  G TH

------------------------     - -  - - -  - - - -  - -- --- -------------
========= TOP =========      = =  = = =  = = = =  = == === =============
RPT-AREA.CUST-NO             _ _  1 _ G  _ _ _ _  U __ 011 _____
RPT-AREA.CUST-NAME           _ _  _ _ G  _ _ _ _  U __ ___ _____
RPT-AREA.EQUIP-NO            _ _  _ _ _  _ _ _ _  U __ ___ _____
RPT-AREA.EQUIP-NAME          _ _  _ _ _  _ _ _ _  U __ ___ _____
RPT-AREA.QUANTITY            _ _  _ _ _  _ _ _ _  U __ ___ _____
======= BOTTOM =========     = =  = = =  = = = =  = == === =============



---------------------------------------------------------------------------
IDEAL: RPT COLUMN HEADINGS    RPT EXAMPLE2 (001) TEST      SYS: DEV
FIELD NAME, LITERAL          COLUMN
FUNCTION OR                  H W
ARITHMETIC EXPRESSION        D ID TAB HEADINGS
                             G TH

------------------------     - -- --- ------------------------------------
========= TOP =========      = == === ====================================
RPT-AREA.CUST-NO             U __ 011 CUSTNO
RPT-AREA.CUST-NAME           U __ ___ CUST  NAME
RPT-AREA.EQUIP-NO            U __ ___ EQUIPNO
RPT-AREA.EQUIP-NAME          U __ ___ DESCRIPION
RPT-AREA.QUANTITY            U __ ___ QUANTITY
======= BOTTOM =========     = == === ====================================
```

We would then write the following program:

```
<EXAMPLE2> PROCEDURE
  FOR EACH CUST-EQUIP-RCD
          FOR FIRST CUSTOMER
              WHERE CUSTOMER.CUST-NO EQ CUST-EQUIP-RCD.CUST-NO
                  MOVE CUSTOMER.CUST-NAME   TO RPT-AREA.CUST-NAME
              WHEN  NONE
                  MOVE $SPACES              TO RPT-AREA.CUST-NAME
          ENDFOR
          FOR FIRST EQUIP-RCD
              WHERE EQUIP-RCD.EQUIP-NO EQ CUST-EQUIP-RCD.EQUIP-NO
                  MOVE EQUIP-RCD.EQUIP-NAME TO RPT-AREA.EQUIP-NAME
              WHEN  NONE
                  MOVE $SPACES              TO RPT-AREA.EQUIP-NAME
          ENDFOR
          MOVE CUST-EQUIP-RCD.CUST-NO  TO RPT-AREA.CUST-NO
          MOVE CUST-EQUIP-RCD.EQUIP-NO TO RPT-AREA.EQUIP-NO
```

```
          MOVE $EDIT(CUST-EQUIP-RCD.QUANTITY,PIC='ZZZZ9')
                                    TO RPT-AREA.QUANTITY
          PRODUCE EXAMPLE2
    WHEN NONE
          DO NULL-REPORT
  ENDFOR
```

This will produce the following report:

```
86/03/20        YEAR TO DATE SALES BY CUSTOMER              -1-


    CUSTNO  CUST NAME  EQUIPNO  DESCRIPTION  QUANTITY

    -------  ---------  -------  -----------  --------

     C1       SMITH      E1      MM               3
              SMITH      E2      SLIM             2
              SMITH      E3      WALL             4
              SMITH      E4      DESK             2
              SMITH      E5      WALL             1
              SMITH      E6      PAC              1
     C2       JONES      E1      MM               3
              JONES      E2      SLIM             4
     C3       BLAKE      E2      SLIM             2
     C4       CLARK      E2      SLIM             2
              CLARK      E4      DESK             3
              CLARK      E5      WALL             4
```

As you can see, we used the control break facility to suppress the printing of the repeating customer numbers, which simplifies the appearance of the report.

We can also use the report facility to create reports with lines that are in a different order than as extracted from the database. Let's say that we wish to have page breaks on customer number, and report breaks on the customer-type field. We will also add a unit-price field to the equipment record, so that we can compute total sales. The sort will be by customer-type and then by customer number. Our report screens will look like this:

```
-------------------------------------------------------------------------

IDEAL: RPT PARAMETERS         RPT EXAMPLE2 (001) TEST         SYS: DEV


LINES PER PAGE ON PRINTOUT       54  ( 1 THRU 250)
REPORT WIDTH                    072 (40 THRU 230)
SPACING BETWEEN LINES            1   ( 1 THRU 3)
SPACING BETWEEN COLUMNS         02  ( 0 THRU 66 OR A=AUTOMATIC)
```

```
SUMMARIES ONLY                        N   (Y=YES,N=NO)

COLUMN HEADINGS DESIRED               Y   (Y=YES,N=NO)

COLUMN HEADINGS INDICATION            U   (U=UNDERSCORE,N=NONE,D=DASHES)

CONTROL BREAK HEADING                 N   (Y=YES,N=NO)

CONTROL BREAK FOOTING                 Y   (Y=YES,N=NO)

GROUP CONTINUATION AT TOP OF PAGE  X  (Y=YES,N=NO)

ANNOTATED COUNT IN CONTROL FOOTINGS X  (Y=YES,N=NO)

REPORT FINAL SUMMARY TITLE            X   (Y=YES,N=NO)

   SPACING BEFORE SUMMARY             P   (1 THRU 9 = LINES,P=NEW PAGE)

   TITLE    TOTAL YEAR TO DATE SALES _____


DATE

   POSITION        TR    (NO=NONE,BR=BOT.RIGHT,BL=BOT.LEFT,BC=BOT.CTR

                         TR=TOP RIGHT,TL=TOP LEFT,TC=TOP CENTER)

   FORMAT          YY/MM/DD


PAGE NUMBERS

   POSITION        TL

   FORMAT          D     (D=DIGITS ONLY, H=WITH HYPHENS, P=PAGE    NNN)


PAGE HEADING

   HEADING         YEAR TO DATE SALES BY CUST TYPE AND CUSTOMER

   POSITION        C     (C=CENTER, L=LEFT JUSTIFY, R=RIGHT JUSTIFY)


------------------------------------------------------------------------

IDEAL: RPT DETAIL DEFN.     RPT EXAMPLE2 (001) TEST      SYS:DEV


FIELD NAME, LITERAL       SORT  BREAK  FUNCTION COLUMN

FUNCTION, OR              L A   L S I  T M M A  H W

ARITHMETIC EXPRESSION     V /   V K N  O A I V  D ID TAB EDIT PATTERN

                          L D   L P D  T X N G  G TH

------------------------  - -   - - -  - - - -  - -- --- --------------

========= TOP =========   = =   = = =  = = = =  = == === ==============

RPT-AREA.CUST-TYPE        1 A   1 _ N  _ _ _ _  N  __ ___ _____

RPT-AREA.CUST-NO          2 A   2 P G  _ _ _ _  U  __ 005 _____

RPT-AREA.CUST-NAME        _ _   _ _ _  _ _ _ _  U  __ ___ _____

RPT-AREA.EQUIP-NO         _ _   _ _ _  _ _ _ _  U  __ ___ _____

RPT-AREA.EQUIP-NAME       _ _   _ _ _  _ _ _ _  U  __ ___ _____

RPT-AREA.QUANTITY         _ _   _ _ _  _ _ _ _  U  __ ___ _____

RPT-AREA.EXTENDED-AMT     _ _   _ _ _  S _ _ _  U  __ ___ _____

======== BOTTOM =========  = =   = = =  = = = =  = == === ==============


------------------------------------------------------------------------

 IDEAL: RPT COLUMN HEADINGS    RPT EXAMPLE2 (001) TEST     SYS: DEV
```

```
FIELD NAME, LITERAL        COLUMN

FUNCTION OR                H W

ARITHMETIC EXPRESSION      D ID TAB HEADINGS

                           G TH

------------------------   - -- ---  ------------------------------------

========== TOP ========== = == === ====================================

RPT-AREA.CUST-TYPE         N  __ ___  _____

RPT-AREA.CUST-NO           U  __ 005 CUSTNO

RPT-AREA.CUST-NAME         U  __ ___ CUST  NAME

RPT-AREA.EQUIP-NO          U  __ ___ EQUIPNO

RPT-AREA.EQUIP-NAME        U  __ ___ DESCRIPION

RPT-AREA.QUANTITY          U  __ ___ QUANTITY

RPT-AREA.EXTENDED-AMT      U  __ ___ SALES AMT

======== BOTTOM ========== = == === ====================================
```

We should note a number of changes to the screens. First, we enabled the flag which puts out control footing lines. Second, we added the facility to print a total summary line on the last page. Third, we added a field called REPORT-AREA.CUST-TYPE. This field will not appear on any report lines, but will be used as a sort field and a control break field by IDEAL. Fourth, we added a second sort parameter on the customer number. Finally, we added another field for the EXTENDED-AMT, and enabled its total flag to produce a summary line at each customer number or customer type break.

The only change that has to happen to our program is the addition of two lines of code, one to populate the RPT-AREA.CUST-TYPE field, and the other to populate the edited value of RPT-AREA.EX-TENDED-AMT. All of the other changes are internal to the REPORT WRITER and were made by the compiler. We will then have the following report result:

```
86/03/20    YEAR TO DATE SALES BY CUST TYPE AND CUSTOMER    -1-


CUSTNO  CUST  NAME  EQUIPNO  DESCRIPTION  QUANTITY  SALES AMT

_____ _____ _____  _____ _____ _____

  C2      JONES      E1       MM              3        4.50

          JONES      E2       SLIM            4        6.50


CUSTOMER C2 ****                                      11.00


86/03/20    YEAR TO DATE SALES BY CUST TYPE AND CUSTOMER    -2-


CUSTNO  CUST  NAME  EQUIPNO  DESCRIPTION  QUANTITY  SALES AMT

_____ _____ _____  _____ _____ _____
```

```
   C3        BLAKE      E2      SLIM              2       3.00


CUSTOMER C3 ****                                         3.00
CUST-TYPE 10 **                                         14.00


86/03/20    YEAR TO DATE SALES BY CUST TYPE AND CUSTOMER    -3-


CUSTNO  CUST  NAME  EQUIPNO  DESCRIPTION  QUANTITY  SALES AMT

_____  _____  _____  _____  _____  _____

   C1        SMITH      E1      MM                3       4.50
             SMITH      E2      SLIM              2       3.00
             SMITH      E3      WALL              4       6.00
             SMITH      E4      DESK              2       3.00
             SMITH      E5      WALL              1       1.50
             SMITH      E6      PAC               1       1.50


CUSTOMER C1 ****                                        19.50


86/03/20    YEAR TO DATE SALES BY CUST TYPE AND CUSTOMER    -4-


CUSTNO  CUST  NAME  EQUIPNO  DESCRIPTION  QUANTITY  SALES AMT

_____  _____  _____  _____  _____  _____

   C4        CLARK      E2      SLIM              2       3.00
             CLARK      E4      DESK              3       4.50
             CLARK      E5      WALL              4       6.00


CUSTOMER C4 ****                                        13.50
CUST-TYPE 20 **                                         33.00


86/03/20    YEAR TO DATE SALES BY CUST TYPE AND CUSTOMER    -4-


CUSTNO  CUST  NAME  EQUIPNO  DESCRIPTION  QUANTITY  SALES AMT

_____  _____  _____  _____  _____  _____


TITLE    TOTAL YEAR TO DATE SALES                       47.00
```

Here we should note that the sort forced the report to show customers C2 and C3 first because they are customer type 10 instead of customer type 20. We had a page break on each of the customer numbers, with an annotated total at the bottom of each page. We also had another total when the type changed from 10 to 20.

We can observe that we are wasting a lot of our report line with repeating customer data. We can solve this problem by putting all of this data into the page header, on a separate line. We do this through the use of the header fill-in screen, as shown.

```
------------------------------------------------------------------------
IDEAL: RPT PAGE HEADING    RPT EXAMPLE2 (001) TEST    SYS: DEV FILL-IN

FIELD NAME, LITERAL, FUNCTION          COLUMN
OR ARITHMETIC EXPRESSION                W
                                       ID TAB EDIT PATTERN   COMMAND
                                       TH
----------------------------------------- -- --- ------------- ------
'YEAR TO DATE SALES BY CUST-TYPE'      31 015 _____   000010
'AND CUSTOMER'                         12 +01 _____   000020
_____ __ L01 _____   000030
'CUSTOMER '                            09 006 _____   000040
RPT-AREA.CUST-NO                       02 +02 _____   000050
RPT-AREA.CUST-NAME                     10 +02 _____   000060
RPT-AREA.CITY                          15 +01 _____   000070
RPT-AREA.TELEPHONE                     08 +01 _____   000080
========================================================================
```

On this screen we have defined our header and positioned it so that there is sufficient room for the date and page parms that we requested on the parm screen. We then define the customer data header line by tabbing a line with the L01 command and then defining the customer information fields. We then have to make a minor program change to tell the program to suppress printing of the CUST DATA on the detail line:

```
------------------------------------------------------------------------
IDEAL: RPT DETAIL DEFN.     RPT EXAMPLE2 (001) TEST        SYS:DEV

FIELD NAME, LITERAL     SORT  BREAK  FUNCTION COLUMN
FUNCTION, OR            L A   L S I  T M M A  H W
ARITHMETIC EXPRESSION   V /   V K N  O A I V  D ID TAB EDIT PATTERN
                       L D   L P D  T X N G  G TH
------------------------ - -   - - -  - - - -  - -- --- -------------
========== TOP ==========  = =   = = =  = = = =  = == === =============
RPT-AREA.CUST-TYPE     1 A   1 _ N   _ _ _ _  N  __ ____ _____
RPT-AREA.CUST-NO       2 A   2 P N   _ _ _ _  N  __ ____ _____
RPT-AREA.EQUIP-NO      _ _   _ _ _   _ _ _ _  U  __ 005 _____
RPT-AREA.EQUIP-NAME    _ _   _ _ _   _ _ _ _  U  __ ____ _____
RPT-AREA.EQUIP-COLOR   _ _   _ _ _   _ _ _ _  U  __ ____ _____
RPT-AREA.QUANTITY      _ _   _ _ _   _ _ _ _  U  __ ____ _____
```

```
RPT-AREA.EXTENDED-AMT         _ _  _ _ _   S  _ _ _    U   __  ___   _____
======= BOTTOM =========   = =  = = =   = = = =   = ==  ===  =============
```

This allows us to put more information on the detail line and in the header. The only program change is to add the code to again populate these additional fields. The resulting report looks like this:

```
86/03/20    YEAR TO DATE SALES BY CUST TYPE AND CUSTOMER    -1-


CUSTOMER C2 JONES      IRVING        554-3904


    EQUIPNO  DESCRIPTION   COLOR    QUANTITY  SALES AMT

    _____  _____   _____   _____  _____

      E1       MM          RED         3        4.50
      E2       SLIM        WHITE       4        6.50


  CUSTOMER C2 ****                              11.00
86/03/20    YEAR TO DATE SALES BY CUST TYPE AND CUSTOMER    -2-


CUSTOMER C3 BLAKE      IRVING        632-0422


    EQUIPNO  DESCRIPTION   COLOR    QUANTITY  SALES AMT

    _____  _____   _____   _____  _____

      E2       SLIM        WHITE       2        3.00


  CUSTOMER C3 ****                               3.00
  CUST-TYPE 10 **                               14.00


86/03/20    YEAR TO DATE SALES BY CUST TYPE AND CUSTOMER    -3-


CUSTOMER C1 SMITH      TAMPA         224-3601


    EQUIPNO  DESCRIPTION   COLOR    QUANTITY  SALES AMT

    _____  _____   _____   _____  _____

      E1       MM          RED         3        4.50
      E2       SLIM        WHITE       2        3.00
      E3       WALL        BROWN       4        6.00
      E4       DESK        TAN         2        3.00
      E5       WALL        WHITE       1        1.50
      E6       PAC         YELLOW      1        1.50


  CUSTOMER C1 ****                              19.50


86/03/20    YEAR TO DATE SALES BY CUST TYPE AND CUSTOMER    -4-
```

```
CUSTOMER C4 CLARK       TAMPA          961-0731


    EQUIPNO  DESCRIPTION    COLOR    QUANTITY  SALES AMT

    _____  _____  _____  _____  _____
       E2       SLIM        WHITE       2        3.00
       E4       DESK        TAN         3        4.50
       E5       WALL        WHITE       4        6.00


  CUSTOMER C4 ****                               13.50
  CUST-TYPE 20 **                                33.00


86/03/20    YEAR TO DATE SALES BY CUST TYPE AND CUSTOMER    -4-


CUSTOMER C4 CLARK       TAMPA          961-0731


    EQUIPNO  DESCRIPTION    COLOR    QUANTITY  SALES AMT

    _____  _____  _____  _____  _____


     TOTAL YEAR TO DATE SALES                   47.00
```

With a report with data groups as small as these, you can see that we can have a great deal of wasted paper. Thus we might like to see multiple customers per page. To do this, we would make the following changes to our fill-in screens:

```
-----------------------------------------------------------------------

IDEAL: RPT PARAMETERS          RPT EXAMPLE2 (002) TEST        SYS: DEV


LINES PER PAGE ON PRINTOUT         54  ( 1 THRU 250)
REPORT WIDTH                       072 (40 THRU 230)
SPACING BETWEEN LINES              1   ( 1 THRU 3)
SPACING BETWEEN COLUMNS            02  ( 0 THRU 66 OR A=AUTOMATIC)
SUMMARIES ONLY                     N   (Y=YES,N=NO)
COLUMN HEADINGS DESIRED            Y   (Y=YES,N=NO)
COLUMN HEADINGS INDICATION         U   (U=UNDERSCORE,N=NONE,D=DASHES)
CONTROL BREAK HEADING              Y   (Y=YES,N=NO)
CONTROL BREAK FOOTING              Y   (Y=YES,N=NO)
GROUP CONTINUATION AT TOP OF PAGE  Y   (Y=YES,N=NO)
ANNOTATED COUNT IN CONTROL FOOTINGS X  (Y=YES,N=NO)
REPORT FINAL SUMMARY TITLE         X   (Y=YES,N=NO)
   SPACING BEFORE SUMMARY          P   (1 THRU 9 = LINES,P=NEW PAGE)
   TITLE    TOTAL YEAR TO DATE SALES _____


DATE
```

```
POSITION          TR    (NO=NONE,BR=BOT.RIGHT,BL=BOT.LEFT,BC=BOT.CTR
                        TR=TOP RIGHT,TL=TOP LEFT,TC=TOP CENTER)
FORMAT            YY/MM/DD

PAGE NUMBERS
  POSITION        TL
  FORMAT          D     (D=DIGITS ONLY, H=WITH HYPHENS, P=PAGE     NNN)

PAGE HEADING
  HEADING         YEAR TO DATE SALES BY CUST TYPE AND CUSTOMER
  POSITION        C     (C=CENTER, L=LEFT JUSTIFY, R=RIGHT JUSTIFY)
```

```
------------------------------------------------------------------------
IDEAL: RPT PAGE HEADING    RPT EXAMPLE2 (001) TEST    SYS: DEV FILL-IN

FIELD NAME, LITERAL, FUNCTION            COLUMN
OR ARITHMETIC EXPRESSION                 W
                                         ID TAB EDIT PATTERN   COMMAND
                                         TH
-------------------------------------- -- --- ------------- ------
'YEAR TO DATE SALES BY CUST-TYPE'        31 015 _____ 000010
'AND CUSTOMER'                           12 +01 _____ 000020
========================================================================
------------------------------------------------------------------------
IDEAL: RPT DETAIL DEFN.     RPT EXAMPLE2 (002) TEST      SYS:DEV

FIELD NAME, LITERAL       SORT  BREAK  FUNCTION COLUMN
FUNCTION, OR             L A   L S I   T M M A  H W
ARITHMETIC EXPRESSION    V /   V K N   O A I V  D ID TAB EDIT PATTERN
                        L D   L P D   T X N G  G TH
------------------------ - -  - - -   - - - -  - -- --- -------------
========== TOP ========= = =  = = =   = = = =  = == === =============
RPT-AREA.CUST-TYPE       1 A   1 2 N  _ _ _ _  N __ ____ _____
RPT-AREA.CUST-NO         2 A   2 2 N  _ _ _ _  N __ ____ _____
RPT-AREA.EQUIP-NO        _ _  _ _ _   _ _ _ _  U __ 005  _____
RPT-AREA.EQUIP-NAME      _ _  _ _ _   _ _ _ _  U __ ____ _____
RPT-AREA.QUANTITY        _ _  _ _ _   _ _ _ _  U __ ____ _____
RPT-AREA.EXTENDED-AMT    _ _  _ _ _   S _ _ _  U __ ____ _____
======== BOTTOM ========= = =  = = =   = = = =  = == === =============
```

```
------------------------------------------------------------------------
IDEAL: RPT COLUMN HEADINGS    RPT EXAMPLE2 (001) TEST     SYS: DEV
FIELD NAME, LITERAL          COLUMN
FUNCTION OR                  H W
```

```
ARITHMETIC EXPRESSION     D  ID TAB HEADINGS
                          G  TH
------------------------- - -- --- ------------------------------------
========= TOP ========= = == === =====================================
RPT-AREA.CUST-TYPE        N  __ ___ _____
RPT-AREA.CUST-NO          N  __ ___ _____
RPT-AREA.EQUIP-NO         U  __ 005 EQUIPNO
RPT-AREA.EQUIP-NAME       U  __ ___ DESCRIPION
RPT-AREA.QUANTITY         U  __ ___ QUANTITY
RPT-AREA.EXTENDED-AMT     U  __ ___ SALES AMT
======== BOTTOM ========= = == === =====================================
```

Here we set the control break heading flag on. We also set the skip indicators on the two control fields to two lines, instead of a page break. Again, there are no changes required to be made to the application program. The report that would result from this run would look like:

```
86/03/20    YEAR TO DATE SALES BY CUST TYPE AND CUSTOMER    -1-

CUST-TYPE 10 **
CUSTOMER C2   ****

      EQUIPNO DESCRIPTION   COLOR   QUANTITY  SALES AMT

      _____ _____  _____ _____  _____
        E1      MM          RED         3        4.50
        E2      SLIM        WHITE       4        6.50

CUSTOMER C2 ****                                11.00


CUSTOMER C3 ****

      EQUIPNO DESCRIPTION   COLOR   QUANTITY  SALES AMT

      _____ _____  _____ _____  _____
        E2      SLIM        WHITE       2        3.00

CUSTOMER C3 ****                                 3.00
CUST-TYPE 10 **                                 14.00


CUST-TYPE 20 **
CUSTOMER C1 ****

      EQUIPNO DESCRIPTION   COLOR   QUANTITY  SALES AMT

      _____ _____  _____ _____  _____
```

E1	MM	RED	3	4.50
E2	SLIM	WHITE	2	3.00
E3	WALL	BROWN	4	6.00
E4	DESK	TAN	2	3.00
E5	WALL	WHITE	1	1.50
E6	PAC	YELLOW	1	1.50

CUSTOMER C1 ****   19.50

CUSTOMER C4 ****

EQUIPNO	DESCRIPTION	COLOR	QUANTITY	SALES AMT
E2	SLIM	WHITE	2	3.00
E4	DESK	TAN	3	4.50
E5	WALL	WHITE	4	6.00

CUSTOMER C4 ****   13.50
CUST-TYPE 20 **   33.00

86/03/20   YEAR TO DATE SALES BY CUST TYPE AND CUSTOMER   -2-

EQUIPNO	DESCRIPTION	COLOR	QUANTITY	SALES AMT

TOTAL YEAR TO DATE SALES   47.00

The only problem here is that we have to give up the descriptive data that we had on the header line in the earlier version. This information could easily be critical to anyone who didn't know who customer C1 is or where he is located. To restore this information, without reverting to the page-break method, we could change the program to handle all of the work. To do this, we would define our detail as a single line. We would then have to define our column headers, detail lines, break total lines in working storage, and, as the program progresses, move each working-storage area to the report line, and produce the report. The program would also have to take care of accumulating and reinitializing each of the break totals. In addition to the extra coding involved, we would have to use an ORDERED BY clause in our FOR statement, on a non-keyed field, in the place of the report generator sort parameter. We have already seen the cost of doing this, in Chapter 5, and this problem gets worse as our report program gets more and more complicated. In fact, as the degree of complexity increases, the advantages to using the IDEAL access methods become greatly overshadowed by the inefficiencies in coding time, working-storage size, paging of temporary storage, extra MOVE statements, temporary indexing, etc.

To solve this problem, we would recommend that we use IDEAL to extract the data, which could then be passed onto report programs which are written in more powerful languages, such as COBOL, EASYTRIEVE, or SAS. In this way, we have the best of both worlds; IDEAL's ability to access the DATACOM databases, and the report language's ability to produce reports.

```
-----------------------------------------------------------------------

IDEAL: RPT PARAMETERS          RPT EXAMPLE4 (001) TEST          SYS: DEV


LINES PER PAGE ON PRINTOUT         250 ( 1 THRU 250)
REPORT WIDTH                       140 (40 THRU 230)
SPACING BETWEEN LINES              1   ( 1 THRU 3)
SPACING BETWEEN COLUMNS            00  ( 0 THRU 66 OR A=AUTOMATIC)
SUMMARIES ONLY                     N   (Y=YES,N=NO)
COLUMN HEADINGS DESIRED            N   (Y=YES,N=NO)
COLUMN HEADINGS INDICATION         N   (U=UNDERSCORE,N=NONE,D=DASHES)
CONTROL BREAK HEADING              N   (Y=YES,N=NO)
CONTROL BREAK FOOTING              N   (Y=YES,N=NO)
GROUP CONTINUATION AT TOP OF PAGE  N   (Y=YES,N=NO)
ANNOTATED COUNT IN CONTROL FOOTINGS N  (Y=YES,N=NO)
REPORT FINAL SUMMARY TITLE         N   (Y=YES,N=NO)
   SPACING BEFORE SUMMARY          1   (1 THRU 9 = LINES,P=NEW PAGE)
   TITLE        _____


DATE
   POSITION        NO    (NO=NONE,BR=BOT.RIGHT,BL=BOT.LEFT,BC=BOT.CTR
                          TR=TOP RIGHT,TL=TOP LEFT,TC=TOP CENTER)
   FORMAT          YY/MM/DD


PAGE NUMBERS
   POSITION        NO
   FORMAT          H     (D=DIGITS ONLY, H=WITH HYPHENS, P=PAGE   NNN)


PAGE HEADING
   HEADING
   POSITION        C     (C=CENTER, L=LEFT JUSTIFY, R=RIGHT JUSTIFY)
```

```
------------------------------------------------------------------------
IDEAL: RPT DETAIL DEFN.       RPT EXAMPLE4 (001) TEST        SYS:DEV


FIELD NAME, LITERAL          SORT   BREAK   FUNCTION COLUMN
FUNCTION, OR                 L  A   L S I   T M M A  H W
ARITHMETIC EXPRESSION        V  /   V K N   O A I V  D ID TAB EDIT PATTERN
                             L  D   L P D   T X N G  G TH

-------------------------    -  -   - - -   - - - -  - --  ---  --------------
========== TOP ==========    =  =   = = =   = = = =  = ==  ===  ==============
RPT-AREA.CUST-TYPE           1  A   _ _ _   _ _ _ _  N  __  ___  _____
RPT-AREA.CUST-NO             2  A   _ _ _   _ _ _ _  N  __  ___  _____
RPT-AREA.CUST-NAME           _  _   _ _ _   _ _ _ _  N  __  ___  _____
RPT-AREA.CITY                _  _   _ _ _   _ _ _ _  N  __  ___  _____
RPT-AREA.TELEPHONE           _  _   _ _ _   _ _ _ _  N  __  ___  _____
RPT-AREA.EQUIP-NO            _  _   _ _ _   _ _ _ _  N  __  ___  _____
RPT-AREA.EQUIP-NAME          _  _   _ _ _   _ _ _ _  N  __  ___  _____
RPT-AREA.QUANTITY            _  _   _ _ _   _ _ _ _  N  __  ___  _____
RPT-AREA.EXTENDED-AMT        _  _   _ _ _   _ _ _ _  N  __  ___  _____
======== BOTTOM =========    =  =   = = =   = = = =  = ==  ===  ==============
```

As the reader will see, we have simply turned all of the options off. This will allow us to use IDEAL to extract the data from the database. The report can then sort the output, and send it to the dataset that it is pointed to in the JCL. (This JCL stream is dealt with in depth in Chapter 9). This has advantages over the use of a QSAM dataset in that we have the ability to sort the output before it is released. We also have the ability to create record counts and run totals for cross referencing of the output. We have the additional advantage of being able to easily set up the original extract layout and make subsequent changes to it. This is particularly helpful for the creation of ad-hoc or "quick and dirty" applications. The only problem that we encounter is that the IDEAL REPORT WRITER will keep trying to produce page headers, which in our case will be a blank line after every 250 lines of data. This can be easily dealt with by some form of preprocessing, which would keep these blank records out of the report routine.

With the release of the IDEAL 1.4 product, we now have the ability to produce a report facsimile. This is accessed through the last option of the PROCESS menu. The prompt screen for this process appears as:

```
PRODUCE RPT    _____
               (1)
FOR PROGRAM    _____  VERSION  ____
```

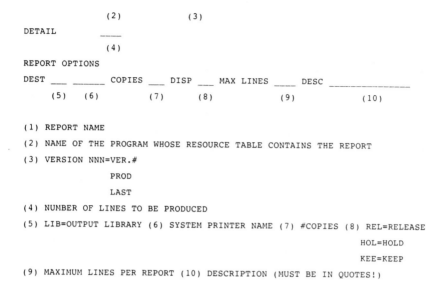

```
              (2)              (3)
DETAIL              ____
              (4)
REPORT OPTIONS
DEST ___ _____ COPIES ___ DISP ___ MAX LINES ____ DESC _____
     (5)   (6)          (7)      (8)           (9)              (10)


(1) REPORT NAME
(2) NAME OF THE PROGRAM WHOSE RESOURCE TABLE CONTAINS THE REPORT
(3) VERSION NNN=VER.#
              PROD
              LAST
(4) NUMBER OF LINES TO BE PRODUCED
(5) LIB=OUTPUT LIBRARY (6) SYSTEM PRINTER NAME (7) #COPIES (8) REL=RELEASE
                                                              HOL=HOLD
                                                              KEE=KEEP
(9) MAXIMUM LINES PER REPORT (10) DESCRIPTION (MUST BE IN QUOTES!)
```

As you can see, this feature will allow us to test the field definitions and functions that we have required, before we run any actual data through it. Thus we can have a fully functional report definition completed before we try to test the application, removing one more variable from our testing function.

Conclusions

In this chapter we have discussed the functioning of the IDEAL REPORT WRITER complex. In understanding this facility, it is important to remember to think of it as a statically linked subroutine, which when called will build the required report around our supplied detail lines. Thus, all that the application has to worry about is the population of the detail lines.

We also saw that, like all tools, IDEAL has limitations regarding complexity. However, if we recognize these limitations and live within their bounds, then we can use the REPORT WRITER as a data extractor, which in turn feeds programs written in more powerful reporting languages.

These other products can then do statistical processing, create charts and graphs, feed other systems, etc.

Granted, the IDEAL REPORT WRITER has limitations. But I also wouldn't want to cut down a tree with an "all purpose" Swiss army knife.

Exercises

1. What are the five parts of an IDEAL report definition?
2. What functions are available in the IDEAL REPORT WRITER?
3. Where are the two places that we can define a report header?
4. Why is a compiler warning message issued nearly every time we use the summary function on the detail screen?
5. What problem can be encountered if we use database names in the report fields?
6. Which is better to use, a report SORT statement or an ORDERED BY clause on the FOR statement?
7. How could we use the report facility to produce a download file from the database?
8. Define a report that can be used for a simple audit of data on the equipment database.

```
------------------------------------------------------------------------

IDEAL: RPT PARAMETERS          RPT XXXXXXXX (XXX) XXXX        SYS: XXX


LINES PER PAGE ON PRINTOUT        XX  ( 1 THRU 250)
REPORT WIDTH                      XXX (40 THRU 230)
SPACING BETWEEN LINES             X   ( 1 THRU 3)
SPACING BETWEEN COLUMNS           XX  ( 0 THRU 66 OR A=AUTOMATIC)
SUMMARIES ONLY                    X   (Y=YES,N=NO)
COLUMN HEADINGS DESIRED           X   (Y=YES,N=NO)
COLUMN HEADINGS INDICATION        X   (U=UNDERSCORE,N=NONE,D=DASHES)
CONTROL BREAK HEADING             X   (Y=YES,N=NO)
CONTROL BREAK FOOTING             X   (Y=YES,N=NO)
GROUP CONTINUATION AT TOP OF PAGE X   (Y=YES,N=NO)
ANNOTATED COUNT IN CONTROL FOOTINGS X (Y=YES,N=NO)
REPORT FINAL SUMMARY TITLE        X   (Y=YES,N=NO)
   SPACING BEFORE SUMMARY         X   (1 THRU 9 = LINES,P=NEW PAGE)
   TITLE    _____


DATE
   POSITION        XX   (NO=NONE,BR=BOT.RIGHT,BL=BOT.LEFT,BC=BOT.CTR
                         TR=TOP RIGHT,TL=TOP LEFT,TC=TOP CENTER)
   FORMAT          XXXXXXXXXXXX


PAGE NUMBERS
   POSITION        XX
   FORMAT          H    (D=DIGITS ONLY, H=WITH HYPHENS, P=PAGE    NNN)
```

```
PAGE HEADING
   HEADING          XXXXXXXXXXXXXXXXXXXXXXXXXXXXXXXXXXXXXXXXX
   POSITION         X    (C=CENTER, L=LEFT JUSTIFY, R=RIGHT JUSTIFY)


-----------------------------------------------------------------------
IDEAL: RPT PAGE HEADING    RPT XXXXXXXX (XXX) TEST    SYS: XXX FILL-IN


FIELD NAME, LITERAL, FUNCTION                COLUMN
OR ARITHMETIC EXPRESSION                     W
                                             ID TAB EDIT PATTERN  COMMAND
                                             TH
------------------------------------------- -- --- ------------- ------
_____ __ ___ _____ 000010
_____ __ ___ _____ 000020
_____ __ ___ _____ 000030
_____ __ ___ _____ 000040
_____ __ ___ _____ 000050
_____ __ ___ _____ 000060
_____ __ ___ _____ 000070
_____ __ ___ _____ 000080
_____ __ ___ _____ 000090
_____ __ ___ _____ 000100
_____ __ ___ _____ 000110


-----------------------------------------------------------------------
IDEAL: RPT DETAIL DEFN.     RPT XXXXXXXX (XXX) XXXX      SYS:XXX


FIELD NAME, LITERAL      SORT  BREAK  FUNCTION COLUMN
FUNCTION, OR            L A   L S I  T M M A  H W
ARITHMETIC EXPRESSION   V /   V K N  O A I V  D ID TAB EDIT PATTERN
                       L D   L P D  T X N G  G TH
----------------------- - - - - - - - - - - - - -- --- -------------
========== TOP ========== = =  = = =  = = = =  = == === =============
_____ _ _  _ _ _  _ _ _ _  _ __ ___ _____
_____ _ _  _ _ _  _ _ _ _  _ __ ___ _____
_____ _ _  _ _ _  _ _ _ _  _ __ ___ _____
_____ _ _  _ _ _  _ _ _ _  _ __ ___ _____
_____ _ _  _ _ _  _ _ _ _  _ __ ___ _____
_____ _ _  _ _ _  _ _ _ _  _ __ ___ _____
======== BOTTOM ========= = =  = = =  = = = =  = == === =============


-----------------------------------------------------------------------
IDEAL: RPT COLUMN HEADINGS    RPT XXXXXXXX (XXX) XXXX      SYS: XXX
FIELD NAME, LITERAL       COLUMN
```

```
FUNCTION OR              H W
ARITHMETIC EXPRESSION    D ID TAB HEADINGS
                         G TH
------------------------ - -- --- ------------------------------------
========== TOP ========= = == === ====================================
_____ _ __ ___ _____
_____ _ __ ___ _____
_____ _ __ ___ _____
_____ _ __ ___ _____
_____ _ __ ___ _____
_____ _ __ ___ _____
======== BOTTOM ========= = == === ====================================
```

9. Define a report that we could use when reporting against the CUST-EQUIP database. This report will be sorted by WAREHOUSE EQUIP-NO and by CUST-NO. EQUIP-NO, and warehouse information should appear on the report header.

```
------------------------------------------------------------------------
IDEAL: RPT PARAMETERS           RPT XXXXXXXX (XXX) XXXX        SYS: XXX


LINES PER PAGE ON PRINTOUT          XX  ( 1 THRU 250)
REPORT WIDTH                        XXX (40 THRU 230)
SPACING BETWEEN LINES               X   ( 1 THRU 3)
SPACING BETWEEN COLUMNS             XX  ( 0 THRU 66 OR A=AUTOMATIC)
SUMMARIES ONLY                      X   (Y=YES,N=NO)
COLUMN HEADINGS DESIRED             X   (Y=YES,N=NO)
COLUMN HEADINGS INDICATION          X   (U=UNDERSCORE,N=NONE,D=DASHES)
CONTROL BREAK HEADING               X   (Y=YES,N=NO)
CONTROL BREAK FOOTING               X   (Y=YES,N=NO)
GROUP CONTINUATION AT TOP OF PAGE   X   (Y=YES,N=NO)
ANNOTATED COUNT IN CONTROL FOOTINGS X   (Y=YES,N=NO)
REPORT FINAL SUMMARY TITLE          X   (Y=YES,N=NO)
  SPACING BEFORE SUMMARY            X   (1 THRU 9 = LINES,P=NEW PAGE)
  TITLE          _____


DATE
  POSITION       XX   (NO=NONE,BR=BOT.RIGHT,BL=BOT.LEFT,BC=BOT.CTR
                       TR=TOP RIGHT,TL=TOP LEFT,TC=TOP CENTER)
  FORMAT         XXXXXXXXXXXX


PAGE NUMBERS
  POSITION       XX
  FORMAT         H    (D=DIGITS ONLY, H=WITH HYPHENS, P=PAGE    NNN)
```

```
PAGE HEADING
    HEADING        XXXXXXXXXXXXXXXXXXXXXXXXXXXXXXXXXXXXXXXXXX
    POSITION       X    (C=CENTER, L=LEFT JUSTIFY, R=RIGHT JUSTIFY)


-------------------------------------------------------------------------
IDEAL: RPT PAGE HEADING    RPT XXXXXXXX (XXX) TEST    SYS: XXX FILL-IN

FIELD NAME, LITERAL, FUNCTION            COLUMN
OR ARITHMETIC EXPRESSION                 W
                                         ID TAB EDIT PATTERN   COMMAND
                                         TH
----------------------------------------- -- --- ------------- ------
_____ __ ___ _____ 000010
_____ __ ___ _____ 000020
_____ __ ___ _____ 000030
_____ __ ___ _____ 000040
_____ __ ___ _____ 000050
_____ __ ___ _____ 000060
_____ __ ___ _____ 000070
_____ __ ___ _____ 000080
_____ __ ___ _____ 000090
_____ __ ___ _____ 000100
_____ __ ___ _____ 000110


-------------------------------------------------------------------------
IDEAL: RPT DETAIL DEFN.      RPT XXXXXXXX (XXX) XXXX       SYS:XXX

FIELD NAME, LITERAL        SORT  BREAK  FUNCTION COLUMN
FUNCTION, OR              L A   L S I   T M M A  H W
ARITHMETIC EXPRESSION     V /   V K N   O A I V  D ID TAB EDIT PATTERN
                         L D   L P D   T X N G  G TH
------------------------- - -   - - -   - - - -  - -- --- -------------
========== TOP ========== = =   = = =   = = = =  = == === =============
_____ _ _   _ _ _   _ _ _ _  _ __ ___ _____
_____ _ _   _ _ _   _ _ _ _  _ __ ___ _____
_____ _ _   _ _ _   _ _ _ _  _ __ ___ _____
_____ _ _   _ _ _   _ _ _ _  _ __ ___ _____
_____ _ _   _ _ _   _ _ _ _  _ __ ___ _____
_____ _ _   _ _ _   _ _ _ _  _ __ ___ _____
======== BOTTOM ========= = =   = = =   = = = =  = == === =============


-------------------------------------------------------------------------
IDEAL: RPT COLUMN HEADINGS   RPT XXXXXXXX (XXX) XXXX      SYS: XXX
FIELD NAME, LITERAL        COLUMN
```

```
FUNCTION OR               H  W
ARITHMETIC EXPRESSION     D  ID  TAB  HEADINGS
                          G  TH
------------------------  -  --  ---  -------------------------------------
========== TOP ==========  =  ==  ===  =====================================
_____   _  __  ___  _____
_____   _  __  ___  _____
_____   _  __  ___  _____
_____   _  __  ___  _____
_____   _  __  ___  _____
_____   _  __  ___  _____
======== BOTTOM =========  =  ==  ===  =====================================
```

Exercises — Answers

1. What are the five parts of an IDEAL REPORT DEFINITION?

    IDENTIFICATION — identifies the report to the DATADIC-
    TIONARY.
    PARAMETER — defines global report parameters.
    HEADING — defines the report page headers.
    DETAIL — defines report detail lines.
    COLUMN — defines report column headers.

2. What functions are available in the IDEAL REPORT WRITER?

    Current Date Printing
    Page Number Accumulation
    Vertical Tabbing
    Horizontal Tabbing
    Sorting
    Column Totaling and Averaging
    Control Breaks
    Control Heading and Footing
    Page Breaking

3. Where are the two places that we can define a report header?

    Parameter Screen
    Header Screen

4. Why is a compiler warning message issued nearly every time
    we use the summary function on the detail screen?

The message 'INSUFFICIENT COLUMN WIDTH' is issued because IDEAL adds four bytes to the defined length of the field as a space allocation for its accumulator.

5. What problem can be encountered if we use database names in the report fields?

   If the database fields are used in the field definitions, then a report line can only be generated if a successful database access is made. Thus we are unable to produce a null, or "nothing to report" report. Also, we cannot move edited data, or put out information other than what is on the database, without updating the database.

6. Which is better to use, a report SORT statement or an ORDERED BY clause on the FOR statement?

   The report SORT feature is faster than the ORDERED BY, which would build a temporary key.

7. How could we use the report facility to produce a download file from the database?

   By turning off all of the header defaults, we could produce a report and send it to an OS dataset. The dataset can then be manipulated by a COBOL program to remove the blank lines that IDEAL produces after every 250 lines as a report header.

8. Define a report that can be used for a simple audit of data on the equipment database.

```
---------------------------------------------------------------------
IDEAL: RPT PARAMETERS           RPT EQUIPRPT (001) TEST        SYS: DEV

LINES PER PAGE ON PRINTOUT         55   ( 1 THRU 250)
REPORT WIDTH                      132   (40 THRU 230)
SPACING BETWEEN LINES               1   ( 1 THRU 3)
SPACING BETWEEN COLUMNS            02   ( 0 THRU 66 OR A=AUTOMATIC)
SUMMARIES ONLY                      N   (Y=YES,N=NO)
COLUMN HEADINGS DESIRED             Y   (Y=YES,N=NO)
COLUMN HEADINGS INDICATION          U   (U=UNDERSCORE,N=NONE,D=DASHES)
CONTROL BREAK HEADING               N   (Y=YES,N=NO)
CONTROL BREAK FOOTING               N   (Y=YES,N=NO)
GROUP CONTINUATION AT TOP OF PAGE   N   (Y=YES,N=NO)
```

```
ANNOTATED COUNT IN CONTROL FOOTINGS N   (Y=YES,N=NO)
REPORT FINAL SUMMARY TITLE           N   (Y=YES,N=NO)
  SPACING BEFORE SUMMARY             N   (1 THRU 9 = LINES,P=NEW PAGE)
  TITLE        _____


DATE
  POSITION        TL    (NO=NONE,BR=BOT.RIGHT,BL=BOT.LEFT,BC=BOT.CTR
                         TR=TOP RIGHT,TL=TOP LEFT,TC=TOP CENTER)
  FORMAT          YY/MM/DD


PAGE NUMBERS
  POSITION        TR
  FORMAT          P     (D=DIGITS ONLY, H=WITH HYPHENS, P=PAGE    NNN)


PAGE HEADING
  HEADING         EQUIPMENT DATABASE AUDIT REPORT
  POSITION        C     (C=CENTER, L=LEFT JUSTIFY, R=RIGHT JUSTIFY)


------------------------------------------------------------------------
IDEAL: RPT PAGE HEADING    RPT EQUIPRPT (001) TEST    SYS: DEV FILL-IN

FIELD NAME, LITERAL, FUNCTION          COLUMN
OR ARITHMETIC EXPRESSION               W
                                       ID TAB EDIT PATTERN   COMMAND
                                       TH
------------------------------------------ -- --- ------------- ------
_____ __ ___ _____  000010
_____ __ ___ _____  000020
_____ __ ___ _____  000030
_____ __ ___ _____  000040
_____ __ ___ _____  000050
_____ __ ___ _____  000060
_____ __ ___ _____  000070
_____ __ ___ _____  000080
_____ __ ___ _____  000090
_____ __ ___ _____  000100
_____ __ ___ _____  000110


------------------------------------------------------------------------
IDEAL: RPT DETAIL DEFN.    RPT EQUIPRPT (001) TEST      SYS:DEV

FIELD NAME, LITERAL        SORT  BREAK  FUNCTION COLUMN
FUNCTION, OR              L A   L S I  T M M A   H W
ARITHMETIC EXPRESSION     V /   V K N  O A I V   D ID TAB EDIT PATTERN
```

```
                                  L D   L P D   T X N G   G TH
-------------------------         - -   - - -   - - - -   - --  ---  -------------
========== TOP ==========         = =   = = =   = = = =   = ==  ===  =============
RPT-AREA.EQUIP-NO                 _ _   _ _ _   _ _ _ _   U __  +20  _____
RPT-AREA.EQUIP-NAME               _ _   _ _ _   _ _ _ _   U __  ___  _____
RPT-AREA.COLOR                    _ _   _ _ _   _ _ _ _   U __  ___  _____
RPT-AREA.WEIGHT                   _ _   _ _ _   _ _ _ _   U __  ___  _____
RPT-AREA.WAREHOUSE                _ _   _ _ _   _ _ _ _   U __  ___  _____

_____      - -   - - -   - - - -   - --  ---  _____
======== BOTTOM =========         = =   = = =   = = = =   = ==  ===  =============


--------------------------------------------------------------------------
IDEAL: RPT COLUMN HEADINGS     RPT XXXXXXXX (XXX) XXXX      SYS: DEV
FIELD NAME, LITERAL            COLUMN
FUNCTION OR                    H W
ARITHMETIC EXPRESSION          D ID TAB HEADINGS
                               G TH
-------------------------      - --  ---  -------------------------------------
========== TOP ==========      = ==  ===  ====================================
RPT-AREA.EQUIP-NO              U __  +20  NO
RPT-AREA.EQUIP-NAME            U __  ___  EQUIP NAME
RPT-AREA.COLOR                 U __  ___  COLOR
RPT-AREA.WEIGHT               U __  ___  WEIGHT
RPT-AREA.WAREHOUSE            U __  ___  WAREHOUSE

_____  - __  ___  _____
======== BOTTOM =========     = ==  ===  ====================================
```

9. Define a report that we could use when reporting against the
   CUST-EQUIP database. This report will be sorted by
   WAREHOUSE EQUIP-NO and by CUST-NO. EQUIP-NO, and
   warehouse information should appear on the report header.

```
--------------------------------------------------------------------------
IDEAL: RPT PARAMETERS          RPT SALESRPT (001) TEST        SYS: DEV

LINES PER PAGE ON PRINTOUT     55  ( 1 THRU 250)
REPORT WIDTH                   132 (40 THRU 230)
SPACING BETWEEN LINES          1   ( 1 THRU 3)
SPACING BETWEEN COLUMNS        02  ( 0 THRU 66 OR A=AUTOMATIC)
SUMMARIES ONLY                 N   (Y=YES,N=NO)
COLUMN HEADINGS DESIRED        Y   (Y=YES,N=NO)
COLUMN HEADINGS INDICATION     U   (U=UNDERSCORE,N=NONE,D=DASHES)
CONTROL BREAK HEADING          N   (Y=YES,N=NO)
CONTROL BREAK FOOTING          N   (Y=YES,N=NO)
```

```
GROUP CONTINUATION AT TOP OF PAGE    N    (Y=YES,N=NO)
ANNOTATED COUNT IN CONTROL FOOTINGS  N    (Y=YES,N=NO)
REPORT FINAL SUMMARY TITLE           N    (Y=YES,N=NO)
   SPACING BEFORE SUMMARY            N    (1 THRU 9 = LINES,P=NEW PAGE)
   TITLE          _____


DATE
   POSITION        NO    (NO=NONE,BR=BOT.RIGHT,BL=BOT.LEFT,BC=BOT.CTR
                         TR=TOP RIGHT,TL=TOP LEFT,TC=TOP CENTER)
   FORMAT


PAGE NUMBERS
   POSITION        TR
   FORMAT          P     (D=DIGITS ONLY, H=WITH HYPHENS, P=PAGE     NNN)


PAGE HEADING
   HEADING
   POSITION              (C=CENTER, L=LEFT JUSTIFY, R=RIGHT JUSTIFY)


-----------------------------------------------------------------------
IDEAL: RPT PAGE HEADING    RPT SALESRPT (001) TEST    SYS: DEV FILL-IN

FIELD NAME, LITERAL, FUNCTION              COLUMN
OR ARITHMETIC EXPRESSION                   W
                                           ID TAB EDIT PATTERN  COMMAND
                                           TH
------------------------------------------ -- --- ------------- ------
RPT-AREA.CURRENT-DATE                      08 +10 XX/XX/XX       000010
'CUSTOMER SALES BY EQUIPMENT NO '          30 +20 _____  000020
_____ __ L01 _____  000030
'WARE-HOUSE  '                             12 +20 _____  000040
RPT-AREA.WARE-HOUSE                        10 +02 _____  000050
'EQUIPMENT NO'                             12 +20 _____  000040
RPT-AREA.EQUIP-NO                          02 +02 _____  000050
RPT-AREA.EQUIP-NAME                        02 +20 _____  000060
_____ __ ___ _____  000070
_____ __ ___ _____  000080
_____ __ ___ _____  000090
_____ __ ___ _____  000100
_____ __ ___ _____  000110


-----------------------------------------------------------------------
IDEAL: RPT DETAIL DEFN.    RPT SALESRPT (001) TEST      SYS:DEV
```

```
FIELD NAME, LITERAL        SORT  BREAK  FUNCTION COLUMN
FUNCTION, OR               L A   L S I  T M M A  H W
ARITHMETIC EXPRESSION      V /   V K N  O A I V  D ID TAB EDIT PATTERN
                           L D   L P D  T X N G  G TH
------------------------   - -   - - -  - - - -  - -- --- -------------
========== TOP ==========  = =   = = =  = = = =  = == === =============
RPT-AREA.WAREHOUSE         1 A   1 P N  _ _ _ _  _ __ ___ _____
RPT-AREA.EQUIP-NO          2 A   2 P N  _ _ _ _  _ __ ___ _____
RPT-AREA.CUST-NO           3 A   _ _ _  _ _ _ _  U __ ___ _____
RPT-AREA.QUANTITY          _ _   _ _ _  S _ _ _  U __ ___ _____
_____    - -   - - -  - - - -  - -- ___ _____
_____    - -   - - -  - - - -  - -- ___ _____
======== BOTTOM =========  = =   = = =  = = = =  = == === =============


--------------------------------------------------------------------------
IDEAL: RPT COLUMN HEADINGS   RPT SALESRPT (001) TEST      SYS: DEV
FIELD NAME, LITERAL        COLUMN
FUNCTION OR                H W
ARITHMETIC EXPRESSION      D ID TAB HEADINGS
                          G TH
------------------------   - -- --- ------------------------------------
========== TOP ==========  = == === ====================================
RPT-AREA.WAREHOUSE         _ __ ___ _____
RPT-AREA.EQUIP-NO          _ __ ___ _____
RPT-AREA.CUST-NO           U __ ___ CUST-NO
RPT-AREA.QUANTITY          U __ ___ QUANTITY
_____    - __ ___ _____
_____    - __ ___ _____
======== BOTTOM =========  = == === ====================================
```

9

Batch and On-Line Services

In Chapter 3, we introduced the PROCESS menu, which contained the IDEAL services of COMPILE, RUN, SUBMIT, EXECUTE, and PRODUCE REPORT. In this chapter we will discuss the use of these functions in more detail.

But first, we will begin by discussing the actual functioning of the IDEAL environment.

IDEAL Sign-On Environment

The IDEAL environment is in reality a CICS (CUSTOMER INFOR-MATION CONTROL SERVICE) transaction. Therefore, we begin by signing on to the CICS region with the command:

```
CSSN PS PASSWORD NAME NAME
```

The underlined words are your CICS name and password. We then begin the IDEAL-CICS transaction by typing

```
IDEAL
```

which will bring up the IDEAL SIGNON screen (Figure 9-1) into which we will enter our IDEAL 3-character ID and password.

After IDEAL verifies that the user is authorized to use the product, it checks the table that contains the user's authorization

```
IIIIIIII    DDDDDD      EEEEEEE      AAAAA        LL  TM

IIIIIIII    DDDDDDD     EEEEEEE     AAAAAA        LL

   II      DD    DD     EE         AA    AA       LL

   II      DD    DD     EEEEEEE    AAAAAAAA       LL

   II      DD    DD     EEEEEEE   AAAAAAAAA       LL

   II      DD    DD     EE         AA    AA       LL

IIIIIIIII  DDDDDDDDD    EEEEEEE     AA      AA    LLLLLLLL

IIIIIIIII  DDDDDDDDD    EEEEEEE     AA      AA    LLLLLLLL
```

ADR/IDEAL (TM) IS A PRODUCT OF APPLIED DATA RESEARCH, INC.

USE OF THIS SYSTEM BY UNAUTHORIZED PERSONS IS STRICTLY PROHIBITED.

                   PLEASE TYPE IN YOUR USER ID _____
                                  PASSWORD>   <

ENTER: SIGN ON   PA 2 OR CLEAR: OFF

Figure 9-1   IDEAL Sign-On Screen.

level. This table takes the form shown in Figure 9-2 and is maintained by the IDEAL administrator.

For a user to be valid, at least one of these privilege levels must be chosen:

IDEAL ADMINISTRATOR — With this selection the user has global authority for all of the IDEAL functions, including all of the privileges of the other levels. The IDEAL administrator usually controls all of the SIGNON privileges and the setting of the global parameters.

PRINT ADMINISTRATOR — This level allows the user access to and control of all of the members of the output library. The print administrator can define remote printers to the IDEAL system.

DATAVIEW ADMINISTRATOR — Has the authority to define and catalog IDEAL DATAVIEWs. This function is usually handled by the database administrator.

IDEAL USER — This is the most common privilege; it allows sign-on and the privileges that are specified in the table on the lower half of the screen.

The first column specifies which system the user is allowed to access. As we stated earlier, an IDEAL session in a CICS region can be split into several smaller systems. Each system has its own set of

```
-------------------------------------------------------------------------
IDEAL: USER DEFINITION                          SYS: DEV   FILL-IN


PERSON NAME        _____    IDEAL USER ID ___
FULL NAME          _____
PASSWORD           _____
IDENTIFICATION  _____
ORG. UNIT          _____
DATE CREATED       _____
IDEAL PRIVILEGES:  MARK AT LEAST 1 WITH A "X" TO ENABLE IDEAL SIGNON


(_) IDEAL ADMINISTRATOR (ALLOWS USE OF ANY IDEAL FACILITY)
(_) PRINT ADMINISTRATOR (ALLOWS CONTROL OF PRINTING FACILITY + SIGNON)
(_) DVW  ADMINISTRATOR (ALLOWS CATALOGING DATAVIEW DEFINITIONS+SIGNON)
(_) IDEAL USER          (ALLOWS SIGNON AND ALL NON-PRIVILEGED FACILITIY)


ASSIGNED       INDICATE AT LEAST 1 ASSIGNED SYSTEM):
SYSTEM(S)      CONTROL  UPDATE  READ   UPDATE-PNL  UPDATE-RPT  RUN-PROD
   ____          ( _ )   ( _ )  ( _ )  ( _ )        ( _ )       ( _ )
   ____          ( _ )   ( _ )  ( _ )  ( _ )        ( _ )       ( _ )
   ____          ( _ )   ( _ )  ( _ )  ( _ )        ( _ )       ( _ )
   ____          ( _ )   ( _ )  ( _ )  ( _ )        ( _ )       ( _ )
-------------------------------------------------------------------------
```

Figure 9-2   User Definition Fill-in.

libraries (program, panel, report). However, every sub-system within a region shares the DATADICTIONARY and the database files connected to that region. It is also possible to connect certain physical files to specific sub-systems.

The rest of the columns specify what the user can do within the region. This includes

1. CONTROL — the ability to do everything except the running of production programs.
2. UPDATE — the ability to change program, panel, and report definitions.
3. READ — the ability to only read program, panel, and report definitions.
4. UPDATE-PNL — the ability to update panel definitions.
5. UPDATE-RPT — the ability to update report definitions.

6. RUN-PROD — The ability to run programs that are marked to production.

This facility gives us a great deal of flexibility in controlling access to the IDEAL environment. For example, if we had a single CICS region, we could define two sets of databases, one with production data and the other with test data. We can then define three sub-systems, one for production (PRD), one for staging new programs to production (STG), and one for development work (DEV).

We would then establish one person as the IDEAL administrator, and give him total access to all three sub-systems. This will probably be a senior applications programmer, a production control administrator (PCA), or a systems programmer.

We would then set the DBA (database administration) up with DATAVIEW administration authority.

The programming staff would then be set up with the ability to update programs in DEV and STG, and run production programs:

```
(_) IDEAL ADMINISTRATOR (ALLOWS USE OF ANY IDEAL FACILITY)

(X) PRINT ADMINISTRATOR (ALLOWS CONTROL OF PRINTING FACILITY + SIGNON)

(_) DVW   ADMINISTRATOR (ALLOWS CATALOGING DATAVIEW DEFINITIONS+SIGNON)

(X) IDEAL USER          (ALLOWS SIGNON AND ALL NON-PRIVILEGED FACILITIY)
```

ASSIGNED SYSTEM(S)	CONTROL	UPDATE	READ	UPDATE-PNL	UPDATE-RPT	RUN-PROD
	INDICATE AT LEAST 1 ASSIGNED SYSTEM):					
PRD	(_)	(_)	(X)	(_)	(_)	(X)
STG	(X)	(_)	(_)	(_)	(_)	(X)
DEV	(X)	(_)	(_)	(_)	(_)	(X)
----	(_)	(_)	(_)	(_)	(_)	( )
____	(_)	(_)	(_)	(_)	(_)	(_)
____	(_)	(_)	(_)	(_)	(_)	(_)

By setting them up this way they can do program maintenance in DEV and STG. They can also do problem review by being able to read the programs that are in production, and run them. We also can set them up to view all of the output library members so that they can see output messages from abending programs. (We will discuss how this is done later in this chapter.)

We would then set the corporate users up with a table such as:

```
(_) IDEAL ADMINISTRATOR (ALLOWS USE OF ANY IDEAL FACILITY)

(_) PRINT ADMINISTRATOR (ALLOWS CONTROL OF PRINTING FACILITY + SIGNON)

(_) DVW   ADMINISTRATOR (ALLOWS CATALOGING DATAVIEW DEFINITIONS + SIGNO
```

```
(X) IDEAL USER          (ALLOWS SIGNON AND ALL NON-PRIVILEGED FACILITI

ASSIGNED        INDICATE AT LEAST 1 ASSIGNED SYSTEM):
SYSTEM(S)    CONTROL   UPDATE   READ    UPDATE-PNL   UPDATE-RPT   RUN-PROD
   PRD       ( _ )     ( _ )   ( X )   ( _ )        ( _ )        ( X )
   STG       ( _ )     ( _ )   ( X )   ( _ )        ( _ )        ( X )
   DEV       ( _ )     ( _ )   ( _ )   ( _ )        ( _ )        ( X )
   ___       ( _ )     ( _ )   ( _ )   ( _ )        ( _ )        ( _ )
   ___       ( _ )     ( _ )   ( _ )   ( _ )        ( _ )        ( _ )
   ___       ( _ )     ( _ )   ( _ )   ( _ )        ( _ )        ( _ )
```

This will allow them to run their production programs. We can also allow some of our more sophisticated users the ability to view source code in the PRD system so that they can better understand its function. We can also give them read authority in the STG system for production sign-off review.

When the review and verification of the sign-on procedure is completed, IDEAL will execute the users special SIGNON member, which we saw in Chapter 3.

Through this facility we can

1. Select the system in which we wish to begin processing.
2. Select the physical files we wish to use.
3. Set the physical number of command lines.
4. Set the disposition and destination of any outputs that are generated by the IDEAL services.

When this has been executed, IDEAL will show us its primary menu, from which we can begin processing. This processing will be done in the following order:

1. Commands in the MAIN DISPLAY AREA
2. Commands on the COMMAND LINE
3. Entered MENU selections.
4. PF-Keys.
5. ENTER key

Output Library Environments

One of the services provided by the IDEAL language is the control of data sets created by IDEAL functions. This includes listings created by a PRINT command, compiler listings and error messages, reports generated by programs, etc.

We can then set ENVIRONMENTAL commands to control the destination and the disposition of these outputs. For destination, we can send them to a previously defined system printer:

```
SET OUTPUT DESTINATION SYSTEM (PRINTER-NAME)
```

or we can keep it as a member of a library that IDEAL maintains as part of its services:

```
SET OUTPUT DESTINATION LIBRARY
```

This library is established for each IDEAL region, and is controlled by having each output member assigned a sequential number as it is created. We can then view the accumulated listing of members with the following commands.

1. DISPLAY OUTPUT OWN STATUS (or DISPLAY OUTPUT STATUS) — displays a listing of all of the OUTPUT MEMBERS created under the user's ID.
2. DISPLAY OUTPUT ALL STATUS — displays a listing of all of the output members in the region.
3. DISPLAY OUTPUT 'NAME' STATUS — displays all outputs with a certain name.

The name field is populated as follows:

1 — Compile output, the name of the program being compiled
2 — List statement, the name of the creating program
3 — Report output, the name of the report
4 — Print command, designated as 'PRTLIST'
5 — PF-Key 3 print, designated as 'PRSCREEN'

These commands display an output listing that looks like that shown in Figure 9-3.

The first field that we see is the output number, which uniquely identifies the output member. The next field shows the three-character ID of the user who created the member. We then see the name of the output and the number of copies that were created. The next three fields show the results of the output destination and disposition choices. We can then see the date and time at which the member was created. The RT column shows the number of days that the

```
------+---+--------+--+---+-----+-----+--------+----+--+---------------
OUTPUT UID OUTPUT   CP DES DEST  DISP  DATE      TIME RT DESCRIPTION
NUMBER     NAME     YS TYP NAME        REQUEST   REQT
------+---+--------+--+---+-----+-----+--------+----+--+---------------
  223  EHP BLPGMLR1 01 LIB         HOLD  XX/XX/XX XXXX 02 COMPILE LISTING
  225  EHP BLPGMLR1 01 LIB         HOLD  XX/XX/XX XXXX 02 LIST STATEMENT
  226  EHP BLRPMLR1 01 LIB         HOLD  XX/XX/XX XXXX 02 REPORT BLRPMLR1
  227  EHP PRTLIST  01 SYS RMT25 PRINT  XX/XX/XX XXXX 02 IDEAL PRINT SER
  228  EHP PRSCREEN 01 SYS RMT25 PRINT  XX/XX/XX XXXX 02 MAIN MENU
```

Figure 9-3   Output Listing Example.

member will be retained in the library until it is purged by the system.

In this example we can see each of the basic types of output that will normally be encountered during program development.

We began by compiling the program BLPGMLR1, and when the compile was successful, we ran it on-line. The program produced both list statements (output number 225) and a report (output number 226). We then changed the output disposition and destination, and printed a copy of the program with the PRINT command (output number 227) and with the PF3 function. These two printouts were routed directly to the system printer labeled RMT25.

Output Status

An IDEAL output library member can have one of nine statuses:

CRTIN — Member is in the process of being created. This is seen most often on compile outputs while the compiler is running.

PRINT — Member is in the process of being printed. For example if we request a screen print with PF-3, the output will have this status until it comes out on the printer.

READY — Output is available for printing or display.

HOLD — Output is being held.

QHELD — The entire output queue is on hold.

KEEP — The output member is ready to be printed, and a copy will be kept in the output library.

LEAVE — The output member status retained after the PRINT command is executed.

PRINTED — Output has already been printed, but is retained for

future viewing.
RELEASE — Output is available for display, and will be deleted after it is displayed.

However, the ones that we will work with the most are the RELEASE, KEEP, and HOLD statuses. One of these options must be set when an IDEAL process service is executed. This is done with the command:

```
SET OUTPUT DISPOSITION (RELEASE)
                       (KEEP)
                       (HOLD)
```

This must be done because the processing of the output member is determined by the combination of this selection and the printer destination. When the output destination is set to the library, the following will happen to each of the output dispositions.

RELEASE — Output is placed in the library for browsing by the user at the terminal. The output member is deleted after it is displayed or printed.
HOLD — Output is placed in the library for furthur browsing. The output will be retained after it has been viewed, but it cannot be re-routed to the printer.
KEEP — Output is placed in the library for browsing at the terminal, and will be retained after it is viewed. The output can be selected for printing with the command:

```
PRINT OUTPUT (IDENTIFIER) (DESTINATION)
             (STATUS)
```

where

IDENTIFIER — identifies the output member we wish to print. This can be the specific number, a group of outputs with the same name, all of the outputs, or all of the outputs that belong to this user (OWN).
STATUS — is a substitute for the identifier command, and prints the status of all of the session options.
DESTINATION — identifies the printer that we wish to use.

If the output destination has been set up to be a system-defined printer, the following rules will be observed:

RELEASE: The output is sent to a batch job which routes it directly to a system printer. a copy is not placed in the output library.
HOLD: The output is placed in the library where it is held until the user releases it with the alter command. The output is then placed in a batch job, which routes it to the selected printer. A copy is retained in the library.
KEEP: The output is placed in the output library and sent to the printer in a batch job.

After an output library member has been created, we can view it with the command:

```
DISPLAY OUTPUT (NUMBER)
               (NAME)
```

With the NUMBER clause, we will see the contents of the specific member that we select. With the NAME command, we will see the contents if only one member has this name. If more than one member has this name we will get a listing of those members.

We can then browse through the output member, with either PF keys or command lines. These commands are

```
SCROLL FORWARD     (CURSOR    PAGE    N PAGES    N LINES)
SCROLL +
PF-KEY 8

SCROLL BACKWARD    (CURSOR    PAGE    N PAGES    N LINES)
SCROLL -
PF-KEY 7

SCROLL TOP
PF-KEY 10

SCROLL BOTTOM
PF-KEY 11

SCROLL RIGHT
PF-KEY 5

SCROLL LEFT
PF-KEY 4
```

With these commands we can navigate through the output member. We can scroll backward or forward, using the frame or cursor defaults, or we can go a specified number of pages or lines. We can also go right, left, top, or bottom with these simple commands.

We can also bring a certain line to the top of the display area with the command

```
POS (LINE-NUMBER)
```

or we can use the FIND command to locate a specified string, and bring that line to the top of the screen.

It is also possible to change the status of an output member. This is done with the command

```
ALTER OUTPUT (IDENTIFIER) DISPOSITION (RELEASE)
                                      (HOLD)
                                      (KEEP)
```

In this way we can change, for example, a status from HOLD to KEEP to allow printing, or a RELEASE status to HOLD to allow it to be retained by the user after he has viewed it. With the ALTER command we can also change the number of copies or the retention period of the library member.

It is also possible to change the destination of a certain output member. This command is

```
ALTER OUTPUT (IDENTIFIER) DESTINATION (SYSTEM NAME)
                                      (LIBRARY)
```

With this command we can change the printer to which an output member is pointed. We can also change it from a printer to the library and back again.

It is necessary to clean out the library from time to time. This is done with the command

```
DELETE OUTPUT (NUMBER)
              (NAME)
```

For this command to work, the status must be set to either HOLD or RELEASE.

Processing Commands

Now that we have learned how to control the output environments, we can begin processing with the IDEAL service facilities. We will begin our session by setting our output status.

```
SET OUTPUT DISPOSITION HOLD
SET OUTPUT DESTINATION LIBRARY
```

This selection will send all of our outputs to the library with a HOLD status. This allows us the best level of control. We can either reroute to the printer if needed, or we can delete them when we are done with them.

We will then write a simple program called BLPGMLR1 and compile it.

Since we are sending all of our output to the library, we do not need to have any part of the program code in the output listing. Therefore we have set the session option to put only the error messages in the output, and to highlight the errors in the source code in the program library.

Thus we will only use the command: COMPILE BLPGMLR1

We can then issue the command

```
DISPLAY OUTPUT STATUS
```

which would show us that the output member is being created.

```
------+---+--------+--+---+-----+-----+--------+----+--+---------------
OUTPUT UID OUTPUT   CP DES DEST  DISP  DATE      TIME RT DESCRIPTION
NUMBER     NAME     YS TYP NAME        REQUEST   REQT
------+---+--------+--+---+-----+-----+--------+----+--+---------------
  223 EHP BLPGMLR1 01 LIB        CRTIN XX/XX/XX XXXX 02 COMPILE LISTING
```

When we have a clean compile, we can print a copy to review before we begin our testing. To do this, we can execute a member that contains the following instructions:

```
SET OUTPUT DISPOSTITION RELEASE
SET OUTPUT DESTINATION SYSTEM RMT25
PRINT PGM BLPGMLR1
SET OUTPUT DISPOSITION HOLD
SET OUTPUT DESTINATION LIB
```

Here we have opened the output window and routed a copy of the program to the printer RMT25. We then reset our output selection to continue to route the outputs to the library. We could then show the following output display:

```
------+---+--------+--+---+-----+-----+--------+----+--+--------------
OUTPUT UID OUTPUT   CP DES DEST  DISP  DATE       TIME RT DESCRIPTION
NUMBER     NAME     YS TYP NAME        REQUEST    REQT
------+---+--------+--+---+-----+-----+--------+----+--+--------------
   223 EHP BLPGMLR1 01 LIB         HOLD XX/XX/XX XXXX 02 COMPILE LISTING
   227 EHP PRTLIST  01 SYS RMT25 PRINT XX/XX/XX XXXX 02 IDEAL PRINT SER
```

until the data is actually printed.

We will then begin our testing. When we run under this setup, all of our LIST statements will go to one member, which will have the name of the highest controlling program encountered in the run. All of the report output will have the name of the report.

```
OUTPUT UID OUTPUT   CP DES DEST  DISP  DATE       TIME RT DESCRIPTION
NUMBER     NAME     YS TYP NAME        REQUEST    REQT
------+---+--------+--+---+-----+-----+--------+----+--+--------------
   225 EHP BLPGMLR1 01 LIB         HOLD XX/XX/XX XXXX 02 LIST STATEMENT
   226 EHP BLRPMLR1 01 LIB         HOLD XX/XX/XX XXXX 02 REPORT BLRPMLR1
```

It should be noted that when an on-line program is run in IDEAL, even if it is a "batch" program (long running, or creates a report instead of using a panel), that the terminal will be "locked out" until the program is finished.

To avoid this terminal lock-up, IDEAL has provided a way to run jobs in the background rather than in the foreground environment with standard IBM-OS (or DOS) Job Control Language (JCL) streams.

This can and should be done for a number of reasons:

1. A report that contains a sort must be run in batch to allow for the allocation of sort work space.
2. A large job running on-line will tie up a terminal for the duration of its run.
3. Batch jobs are cheaper to run than on-line programs because there is less system overhead.
4. It is possible to run batch jobs when the online system is shut down. This allows for the protection of the data while a long

batch job is running. It also reduces the possibility of data contention problems between programs.

An example of a job stream that can run an IDEAL batch program is as follows:

```
//JOB
//RUNIDEAL  EXEC IDLBATCH
//IDEAL.SYSIN DD *
   SIGNON PERSON XXX PASSWORD XXXXXXXX
   SELECT SYSTEM PRD
   COMPILE PROGRAM1
   OFF
/*
```

IDLBATCH is the name of the PROC that we installed when the IDEAL language was delivered. This batch procedure simulates a user logging onto the system. In fact the output that results from a batch run contains copies of screens used by IDEAL during its operations.

For this reason we must provide a SIGNON-ID which has the same security requirements as an on-line session. We must also provide a selection of the sub-system that we wish to work on. We can then execute the same PRINT, COMPILE, DUP, and other execute processes that we have on-line.

In this example, the job will log onto the system, select the PRD system, and compile the last version of PROGRAM1 that it finds there. The compile listing will then be placed in the output library of user XXX.

In order to run a program in batch, it is neccessary to add another command that designates the file table that the program will use. A *file table* is a listing of the physical definitions of the database files that the program plans to use. The file table takes care of all of the neccessary file opens, allocations, and closes. These file tables are usually maintained by the DBA. The command is

```
SET RUN FILETABLE PGFTPRG1
```

With this command, we can have access to the databases listed in the filetable PGFTPRG1.

We can also override IDEAL's default to route output to the output library through the use of the disposition and destination clauses.

```
//JOB
//RUNIDEAL  EXEC IDLBATCH
//IDEAL.SYSIN DD *
  SIGNON PERSON XXX PASSWORD XXXXXXXX
  SELECT SYSTEM PRD
  SET OUTPUT DESTINATION SYSTEM RMT16
  SET OUTPUT DISPOSITION RELEASE
  SET RUN FILETABLE PGFTPRG1
  RUN PROGRAM1
  OFF
/*
```

When the destination is set to library, or the default is taken, then the output members function in the same way that they did in on-line. However, when the destination is a system printer, then only the disposition release is available.

By reviewing the batch JCL contents we can see some things that we can do to gain additional facilities from the system. The IDEAL batch procedure (IDLBATCH) contains the following data definition (DD) names:

STEPLIB — points to the CA-supplied software libraries, DBA-supplied file table libraries, and to any COBOL application LOAD-LIB accessed by the IDEAL program.

SYSPRINT — receives the listing of the IDEAL batch session. This especially includes the screens that print as if we were in an on-line session.

COMPLIST — receives the output of compile listings that are made in the batch session.

RUNLIST — receives the output of list statements that were used in the program

PRTLIST — receives the output of any print service commands issued during the batch session.

REPORT — this statement is the destination of report output generated by the PRODUCE command during a program run in batch. The DD name needs to be the same as the report name that is to be produced.

This gives us better control over our batch processing than we had with the default values. For example, we can route important update reports to an OS dataset for archiving, backup, or reprinting. We can also create output files for sending to off-site data centers. To have these datasets accessed by the system, it is important that we override the normal setup with these commands, which are placed in the SYSIN card:

```
SET OUTPUT DESTINATION SYSTEM RMT16
SET OUTPUT DISPOSITION RELEASE
```

Without these overrides, the output will go to the IDEAL libraries instead of to our datasets.

```
//JOB
//RUNIDEAL  EXEC IDLBATCH
//IDEAL.PRTLIST DD SYSOUT=A
//IDEAL.SYSIN DD *
  SIGNON PERSON XXX PASSWORD XXXXXXXX
  SELECT SYSTEM PRD
  SET OUTPUT DESTINATION SYSTEM RMT16
  SET OUTPUT DISPOSITION RELEASE
  PRINT PGM PROGRAM3
  OFF
/*

//JOB
//RUNIDEAL  EXEC IDLBATCH
//IDEAL.COMPLIST DD SYSOUT=A
//IDEAL.SYSIN DD *
  SIGNON PERSON XXX PASSWORD XXXXXXXX
  SELECT SYSTEM PRD
  SET OUTPUT DESTINATION SYSTEM RMT16
  SET OUTPUT DISPOSITION RELEASE
  COMPILE PGM PROGRAM3
  OFF
/*

//JOB
//RUNIDEAL  EXEC IDLBATCH
//IDEAL.BLRPMLR1 DD DSN=OA.AI386250.INVOICE,
//      DISP=(NEW,KEEP),
//      UNIT=TAPE,
//      DCB=(RECFM=FB,BLKSIZE=800,LRECL=80)
//IDEAL.SYSIN DD *
  SIGNON PERSON XXX PASSWORD XXXXXXXX
  SELECT SYSTEM PRD
  SET OUTPUT DESTINATION SYSTEM RMT16
  SET OUTPUT DISPOSITION RELEASE
```

```
RUN PGM BLPGMLR1
OFF
/*
```

We can also add another DD to our JCL which will contain any QSAM files that we wish to either read into or write out from our IDEAL program. The DD name consists of the 3-character file name and the 3-character database ID. This card takes the place of a file table entry for this database.

We can also include DD statements for each of the program libraries.

```
//IDDEVSRC  DD   DSN= DEV SYSTEM SOURCE LIBRARY
//IDDEVPNL  DD   DSN= DEV SYSTEM PANEL  LIBRARY
//IDDEVOBJ  DD   DSN= DEV SYSTEM OBJECT LIBRARY
```

By including these datasets in our batch JCL, we have the ability to use the entity level IDEAL editor commands. These include the commands that duplicate members both between systems and inside systems. We can also string DELETE commands together. In this way we can do mass updates to the source libraries in batch, rather than in the more expensive and time consuming on-line mode.

```
//JOB
//RUNIDEAL  EXEC IDLBATCH
//IDEAL.SYSIN DD *
  SIGNON PERSON XXX PASSWORD XXXXXXXX
  SELECT SYSTEM PRD
  SET OUTPUT DESTINATION SYSTEM RMT16
  SET OUTPUT DISPOSITION RELEASE
  DUP PGM PROGRAM1 SYS DEV NEW PROGRAM2
  DUP PGM PROGRAM2
  DISPLAY PNL PANEL2 FAC
  DELETE PNL PANEL2 V 2
  OFF
/*
```

We can also use this facility to produce report facsimiles, and route them to a printer in the same way that they will be routed when they are used in production. For example, suppose that we wished to create a facsimile of the report BLRPMLR1 as used by program BLPGMLR1.

```
//JOB
//RUNIDEAL   EXEC IDLBATCH
//IDEAL.BLRPMLR1 DD SYSOUT=A
//IDEAL.SYSIN    DD *
   SIGNON PERSON XXX PASSWORD XXXXXXXX
   SELECT SYSTEM PRD
   SET OUTPUT DESTINATION SYSTEM RMT16
   SET OUTPUT DISPOSITION RELEASE
   PRODUCE REPORT BLRPMLR1 FOR PROGRAM BLPGMLR1
   DETAIL 99 MAXLINES 99
   OFF
/*
```

With this setup, we would produce 99 lines of output, which should show the execution of all of the defined report features.

Another batch facility that we have available to us in version 1.4 of IDEAL is the ability to manipulate return codes.

The function $RETURN-CODE can be placed anywhere in the IDEAL program to allow the program to communicate with the operating system. This allows the program to tell the operating system that it has abended. This $RETURN-CODE will then be passed as a user return code to the operating system, allowing it to skip other steps in the job stream. In addition, if we have multiple RUN statements within the same IDEAL step, we can use the $RETURN-CODE to avoid processing.

```
//JOB
//RUNIDEAL   EXEC IDLBATCH
//IDEAL.BLRPMLR1 DD SYSOUT=A
//IDEAL.SYSIN    DD *
   SIGNON PERSON XXX PASSWORD XXXXXXXX
   SELECT SYSTEM PRD
   SET OUTPUT DESTINATION SYSTEM RMT16
   SET OUTPUT DISPOSITION RELEASE
   RUN BLPGMLR1
   IF $RETURN-CODE EQ 0
      RUN BLPGMLR2
   ENDIF
   OFF
/*
```

If program BLPGMLR1 returns a non-zero return code, the IF statement will avoid the processing if BLPGMLR2.

IDEAL Run Environment Manipulation

There are a number of options that we can set that affect the way that a program will function when it is run. For example, the command

```
SET RUN UPDATE N
```

will cause the database to not be updated during the run. This can be useful when making multiple tests with the same data in that it keeps us from having to reset the data between tests. The only problem comes when we try to run a program with a FOR NEW under this option. When this occurs, an *invalid reference of field* abend can occur.

Another option is the QUIT IDEAL command. When a program that is running under this option ends, the entire IDEAL session will be ended. This option can be particularly useful when combined with a high-level menu program. We could set up the users SIGNON member thus:

```
SELECT SYSTEM PRD
SET COMMAND LINE 0
SET RUN QUITIDEAL YES
RUN MAINMENU
SET ENVIRONMENT FINAL-ID PGMOFF
```

When the user signs on, the SIGNON member is executed which places him in the production system and removes access to any command lines. We then tell IDEAL to terminate the session when the next application program ends. That application program is called MAINMENU here, and consists entirely of SELECT statements and menu screen processing.

```
<<MAINMENU>> PROCEDURE
  REFRESH  MAINPNL
  TRANSMIT MAINPNL
  LOOP UNTIL $PF2(MAINPNL)
        SELECT MAINPNL.SELECTION
            WHEN 'CU' CALL CUSTMANT
            WHEN 'EQ' CALL EQMAINT
            WHEN 'KT' CALL KITMAINT
        ENDSELECT
        TRANSMIT MAINPNL
```

```
    ENDLOOP
ENDPROC
```

The MAINPNL looks like this:

```
ABC COMPANY - WAREHOUSE AND ORDER SYSTEM
        MAIN PROCESSING MENU

    SELECT DESIRED OPTION __

'CU' CUSTOMER NUMBER MAINTENANCE
'EQ' EQUIPMENT VALUE MAINTENANCE
'KT' KIT CONTENTS MAINTENANCE
```

When this MAINMENU program is executed, the users will not be able to execute any function that is not precoded into the menu program. They can also not get into the other IDEAL functions because they do not have a command line or access to the IDEAL menus. When they make a selection, the designated program is called and executed. When it is completed, control is returned to the MAINMENU program, which requests another selection. When this program is done, the IDEAL session is terminated because of the QUIT IDEAL command.

The FINAL-ID command tells IDEAL the name of the transaction to use instead of the normal OFF command. In this case it is a transaction called PGMOFF, which will terminate the CICS session.

Another option that we can set is the number of copies of the library output that will be produced. The default value is 1, but it can be changed through the command SET OUTPUT COPIES N, with "N" being the number of copies desired.

It is also possible to change the linkage between a dataview and a physical database ID. For example, let's say that we were making a change to the layout of the equipment dataview and wanted to do some parallel testing. We would define the new database layout in another part of the database with a new physical database ID. We would then run the test of the original database. When this is completed, we would issue the command:

```
ASSIGN DATAVIEW EQUIPMENT DBID 010
```

which would change the physical linkage for all programs being run during this IDEAL session. When we log-off, the original definition will be restored. It is also possible to limit this reassignment to a specific program occurrence. This command is

```
ALTER PROGRAM EQUIPMNT VERSION LAST DATAVIEW EQUIPMENT DBID 010
```

The program EQUIPMNT will look at the new physical DBID for the remainder of the session, until it is changed again, or until the RESET command is issued: RESET DATAVIEW EQUIPMENT.

The ASSIGN DATAVIEW command can also be coded in the procedure section of an application program. It is the same as above, except that it remains in effect only for the duration of the program run.

In this same way it is possible to alter the destination of a certain report. For example, let's say that we have a program that generates shipment orders. These forms tell how much of each item is to go into each shipment. We can then change the PRINTER-ID that the report goes to so that each warehouse gets the output on their local printer.

```
SELECT SHIPMENT-DWN.SHIPPING-WHSE
    WHEN '01' ASSIGN REPORT SHIPMENT DESTINATION SYSTEM RMT01
    WHEN '02' ASSIGN REPORT SHIPMENT DESTINATION SYSTEM RMT02
    WHEN '03' ASSIGN REPORT SHIPMENT DESTINATION SYSTEM RMT03
    WHEN '04' ASSIGN REPORT SHIPMENT DESTINATION SYSTEM RMT04
    WHEN '05' ASSIGN REPORT SHIPMENT DESTINATION SYSTEM RMT05
    WHEN '06' ASSIGN REPORT SHIPMENT DESTINATION SYSTEM RMT06
ENDSELECT
```

The rest of this command is

```
ASSIGN REPORT NAME (TO ALTNAME)
        DESTINATION (LIBRARY)
                    (SYSTEM XXXX)
                    (NETWORK XXXXX)
                    COPIES N
        DISPOSITION (DISP)
        MAXLINES M
        DESCRIPTION 'STRING'
```

where

NAME — is the DATADICTIONARY name of the report.
LIBRARY — means assignment to the output library.
SYSTEM — means assignment to a system printer.
NETWORK — means assignment to a network printer destination.
DISP — is the disposition of the output.

```
IIIIIIII     DDDDDD      EEEEEEE       AAAAA        LL   TM

IIIIIIII     DDDDDDD     EEEEEEE      AAAAAA        LL

   II       DD    DD     EE          AA    AA       LL

   II       DD    DD     EEEEEEE     AAAAAAAA       LL

   II       DD    DD     EEEEEEE     AAAAAAAAA      LL

   II       DD    DD     EE          AA    AA       LL

IIIIIIII    DDDDDDDDD    EEEEEEE     AA    AA       LLLLLLLL

IIIIIIII    DDDDDDDDD    EEEEEEE     AA    AA       LLLLLLLL
```

IDEAL HAS BEEN SIGNED OFF

Figure 9-4   IDEAL Sign-Off Screen.

M — is the maximumn lines to be assigned.
'STRING' — is an override value that will appear in the description field on the output status display.

The final service that we need to discuss is the sign-off. The OFF command brings up the screen shown in Figure 9-4. When this comes up, we will hit the clear key and enter either the command OFFON, which will bring up a new IDEAL SIGNON screen, or the command CSSF LOGOFF, which will end the CICS session.

Conclusions

In this chapter, we have seen three ways to run applications in IDEAL, on-line, batch, and on-line from a MENU DRIVE program. We have also discussed how to manipulate the environment through site, session, and program options to get the full power from the language. In addition, we have seen how to maintain and manipulate output datasets so that we can control their processing.

The next chapter, errors and error routines, will show us how to deal with any abends that running these programs can produce.

Exercises

1. List the four authorization levels, and the privileges of each.
2. List the six system control options.
3. What are the groupings that we can use when requesting the output status screen?

4. What will be the description placed by IDEAL on the status screen for an output report?
5. What are the three most common output statuses?
6. What will happen to an output member with a RELEASE status after it has been viewed? How can this be prevented?
7. What are the reasons for running IDEAL programs in batch?
8. Why must we provide a SIGNON ID when running batch?
9. What is the purpose of the batch file table?
10. Why do we need a file table to run in batch, but not on-line?
11. What are the DD names for the the following outputs:

    a. Compiler listings
    b. Program list statements
    c. IDEAL batch session screens
    d. Print service commands
    e. IDEAL generated reports

12. You are running an IDEAL batch job and your output reports are going to the library instead of to the datasets that you set up. What are some of the possible problems that you need to look for?
13. What commands can be used in IDEAL on-line that cannot be used in IDEAL batch?
14. What is the problem with setting the update option to N? What PDL command can we use that might serve us better?
15. If we needed to print off an output that was in HOLD status, what commands would we need to issue?
16. What are two ways that we can route printout from a report to a particular printer?
17. What are the three levels at which we can change the linkage between a dataview and a physical database?
18. What is the function of the FINAL-ID command?

Exercises — Answers

1. List the four authorization levels, and the privileges of each.

IDEAL ADMINISTRATOR — With this selection the user has global authority for all of the IDEAL functions, including all of the privileges of the other levels. The IDEAL administrator usually controls all of the SIGNON privileges and the setting of the global parameters.

PRINT ADMINISTRATOR — This level allows the user access and control of all of the members of the output library. The print administrator can also define remote printers to the system.

DATAVIEW ADMINISTRATOR — has the authority to define and catalog IDEAL dataviews. This function is usually handled by the database administrator.

IDEAL USER — This is the most common privilege, and allows SIGNON and the privileges that are specified in the table on the lower half of the screen.

2. List the six system control options.

   1. CONTROL — The ability to do every thing, except for the running of PRODUCTION programs.
   2. UPDATE — The ability to change program, panel, and report definitions.
   3. READ — The ability to only read program, panel, and report definitions.
   4. UPDATE-PNL — The ability to update panel definitions.
   5. UPDATE-RPT — The ability to update report definitions.
   6. RUN-PROD — The ability to run programs that are marked to production.

3. What are the groupings that we can use when requesting the output status screen?

```
DISPLAY OUTPUT STATUS
DISPLAY OUTPUT NAME
DISPLAY OUTPUT USR
DISPLAY OUTPUT ALL
```

4. What will be the description placed by IDEAL on the status screen for an output report?

   The name on the report following the literal 'REPORT'. This will occur unless the description is overriden.

5. What are the three most common output statuses?

```
HOLD, KEEP, RELEASE
```

6. What will happen to an output member with a RELEASE status after it has been viewed? How can this be prevented?

The output member will be deleted. This can be avoided by issuing the command ALTER OUTPUT (NUM) DISPOSITION KEEP either before or while viewing the output.

7. What are the reasons for running IDEAL programs in batch?

   1. A report that contains a sort must be run in batch to allow for the allocation of sort work space.
   2. A large job running on-line will tie up a terminal for the duration of its run. Thus we free up resources running batch.
   3. Batch jobs are cheaper to run than on-line programs because there is less system overhead.
   4. It is possible to run batch jobs when the on-line system is shut down. This allows for the protection of the data while a long batch job is running. It also reduces the possibility of data contention problems between programs.

8. Why must we provide a SIGNON ID when running batch?

   IDEAL goes through the SIGNON process when it begins the batch process. One of the reasons for this is to check the security and privilege levels. Another is to gain access to the output library.

9. What is the purpose of the batch file table?

   The batch file table contains a listing of the files that will be used during the run, and their physical definitions. This data is used to OPEN and CLOSE the files at the begining of the run.

10. Why do we need a file table to run in batch, but not on-line?

   IDEAL itself serves as the on-line file table. Each of the files are defined and opened when IDEAL is brought up, and they are closed when the transaction is ended.

11. What are the DD names for the the following outputs:

   a. Compiler listings — COMPLIST
   b. Program list statements — RUNLIST
   c. IDEAL batch session screens — SYSPRINT
   d. Print service commands — PRTLIST

e. IDEAL generated reports — REPORT DATADICTIONARY NAME

12. You are running an IDEAL batch job and your output reports are going to the library instead of to the datasets that you set up. What are some of the possible problems that you need to look for?

We could have one of two problems. Either the report DD name is not being recognized because of a spelling problem, or the IDEAL commands:

```
SET OUTPUT DESTINATION SYSTEM RMTXX
SET OUTPUT DISPOSITION RELEASE
```

are not found or are not being executed.

13. What commands can be used in IDEAL on-line that cannot be used in IDEAL batch?

Any IDEAL command that can be executed from a command line can be executed in batch.

14. What is the problem with setting the update option to N? What PDL command can we use that might serve us better?

IDEAL will get an *invalid reference of field* error if it tries to execute a FOR NEW statement. A better way to do this is to have the program execute a BACKOUT command at the end of the test run.

15. If we needed to print off an output that was in HOLD status, what commands would we need to issue?

```
ALTER OUTPUT (IDENTIFIER) STATUS KEEP
ALTER OUTPUT (IDENTIFIER) DESTINATION SYSTEM RMTXX
PRINT OUTPUT (IDENTIFIER)
```

16. What are two ways that we can route printout from a report to a particular printer?

The ASSIGN REPORT command
Place the report in a dataset and use an IEBGENER to print it.

17. What are the three levels at which we can change the linkage between a dataview and a physical database?

```
SESSION LEVEL UNTIL LOGOFF
SESSION LEVEL FOR A PARTICULAR PROGRAM UNTIL LOGOFF
PROGRAM LEVEL FOR THE LENGTH OF THE PROGRAM RUN
```

18. What is the function of the FINAL-ID command?

To execute another CICS transaction instead of processing the OFF command.

10

Errors and Error Processing

Every once in a while, a situation occurs in which IDEAL is unable to continue processing a request. This can happen when running a program or processing IDEAL components with the menu screens. When this happens IDEAL automatically produces a series of *diagnostic messages* which the programmer can use to fix the problem. In this chapter we will discuss how to use and control these diagnostic messages. We will begin with the program *run-time errors*, and then deal with IDEAL *internal errors*.

IDEAL Run-Time Abends

When an IDEAL program gets a run-time error, the following IDEAL functions are populated and are available to the program:

$ERROR-NAME — contains the name of the FIELD, SUB-SCRIPT, DATAVIEW, PROCEDURE, or PROGRAM that is in error.

$ERROR-VALUE — returns the value of the erroneous field (where appropriate).

$ERROR-PGM — the name of the abending program.

$ERROR-PROC — the name of the abending procedure within the program.

$ERROR-STMT — the statement number where the error occurred.

$ERROR-DESCRIPTION — returns a statement that describes the error.

$ERROR-CLASS — returns a three-character code that identifies the error class. This can be any one of nine classes:

1. NUM — Invalid numeric data
2. ARI — Arithmetic function error
3. REF — Reference error
4. SUB — Subscript error
5. DVW — Dataview error
6. PGM — Program error
7. SEQ — Sequence error
8. MIS — Miscellaneous error
9. SYS — Systems error

$ERROR-TYPE — returns a three-character code that, when combined with the ERROR CLASS, can furthur define the error. These are:

NUMERIC — A numeric field contains invalid numeric data.

1. NUM — Numeric field contains invalid numeric data.

ARITHMETIC — The processing of a numeric manipulation command has failed.

1. OFL — An overflow condition has occurred.
2. SQR — Program attempted to find the square root of a negative number.
3. UNS — An attempt has been made to move a signed number to an unsigned numeric field.
4. DVZ — Program attempted to divide by zero.
5. EXP — Program attempted to use a non-integer, or a number greater than 999, as an exponent.

REFERENCE — The program tried to reference a field that is not available to it.

1. REF — An attempt has been made to reference a field that has not been established in the program.
2. UPD — Program attempted to update a field that is not allowed to update.
3. PIU — Program attempted to pass a parameter as input to a subroutine which has defined it as update.

4. PAT — An attribute of a parameter in the calling program does not match the attributes in the called program.
5. PNO — The number of positional parameters exceeds the number allowed by IDEAL.

SUBSCRIPT — A subscript is outside of the bounds of its table.

1. SUB — The subscript is less than one, or greater than the number of occurrences of the table.
2. ODO — The ODO value exceeds the maximimn allowed.
3. GRP — The number of occurrences of a table that is being passed to a subroutine is different than the number in the called program.
4. SST — The start parameter of a substring is less than one or the length parameter is less that zero.

DATAVIEW — An error has occurred while trying to process a database request.

1. DVW — Only type available.

PROGRAM — The structure of the program is internally conflicting.

1. IQP — Quit statement has been used incorrectly.
2. PRO — Program attempted to recursively enter an active procedure (or to call the procedure that is already in control).
3. PGM — A program attempted to call itself

SEQUENCE — Invalid sequence of PDL commands

1. FOR — Attempted to nest for statements that call the same dataview.
2. DEL — Attempted to delete a non-update dataview, or a delete is outside of a FOR statement.
3. ADB — A program has issued an ASSIGN command for an active dataview
4. ARS — A program has issued an ASSIGN command for an active report.

Miscellaneous

1. SDV — Program tried to read a sequential dataset in an online mode.

2. DTE — Invalid value was returned through the $TIME or $DATE functions.
3. ARP — Invalid disposition was assigned for a report.
4. PNL — Panel name is invalid.
5. BPA — Use of a panel attempted in a batch job.

System

1. CVR — System error has occurred.
2. SYS — Serious system error has occurred.

IDEAL takes the value of these functions and produces an output that looks like this:

```
ERROR OCCURRED
CLASS=ARI   TYPE=OFL
DESCRIPTION:       1-IDAETERR02E - NUMERIC OVERFLOW
PROGRAM=BLPGBLER  PROCEDURE=ERROR-DISPLAYS      STATEMENT=000200
NAME:             WK-TOO-SMALL
```

Here we can see an example of an arithmetic overflow error. The class and the type fields contain the values that were stored in the functions $ERROR-CLASS and $ERROR-TYPE, respectively. The description field is generated by the system to aid in program debugging. The next line tells the programmer the program, procedure, and the statement number where the error occurred. The last line shows the name of the overflowing field.

In addition to these basic functions, there are three other functions that are available when a particular abend occurs. When a subscript error occurs, the function $SUBSCRIPT-POSITION is available, and contains the value of the offending subscript. The automatic display would look like this:

```
ERROR OCCURRED
CLASS=SUB  TYPE=SUB       RETURN CODE = 12
DESCRIPTION:       1-IDAETERR13E - INVALID SUBSCRIPT
PROGRAM=BLPGBLER  PROCEDURE=ERROR-DISPLAYS      STATEMENT=000500
NAME:             WK-SUBSR
VALUE:            +                    TYPE=P,   HEX=000C
SUBSCRIPT         1
```

When a database error occurs ($ERROR-TYPE = DVW), the functions of $ERROR-DVW-STATUS and $ERROR-INTERNAL-DVW-

STATUS are available. The display for this abend takes the following form:

```
ERROR OCCURRED
CLASS=DVW  TYPE=DVW      RETURN CODE = 12
DESCRIPTION:     1-IDAETERR17E - DVW ERROR
PROGRAM=BLPGLD01  PROCEDURE=BLD-BILL-HEAD      STATEMENT=002115
DATA-VIEW STATUS  10
```

The $ERROR-DVW-STATUS is the simple form of the database error listing and can be one of the following values:

I1 — End of volume was reached when processing a sequential dataview (or dataset).

I2 — Errors were found in the data of the record just read from the database.

I3 — Record integrity problem; another user has control of the record that we just tried to update.

I4 — More than 16 sequential files are in use by this program.

I5 — Missing DD statement for a sequential dataset.

I6 — The actual record length of the sequential file is different than the defined dataview.

I9 — The length of the right-hand operand of the CONTAINS statement is longer than the left-hand clause.

A more complete and useful set of codes is available through the $ERROR-INTERNAL-DVW-STATUS function. These codes are

```
01 - INVALID REQUEST COMMAND
02 - INVALID TABLE NAME
03 - INVALID KEY NAME
04 - INVALID RECORD ID
05 - TABLE NOT OPEN
06 - TABLE NOT OPEN FOR UPDATE
07 - DATA AREA FULL
08 - INDEX FULL
09 - REQUEST NOT PRECEDED BY PREREQUISITE REQUEST
10 - DUPLICATE MASTER KEY NOT ALLOWED
11 - MASTER KEY HAS BEEN MODIFIED
12 - READING AN ALREADY DELETED RECORD
13 - INTERNAL ERROR
14 - NO RECORD FOUND OR NO KEY FOUND
15 - EXCLUSIVE CONTROL INTERLOCK
17 - INPUT/OUTPUT ERROR
```

```
18 — EXCLUSIVE CONTROL DUPLICATE
19 — END OF FILE
20 — CONTROL AREA / KEY ELEMENT BUFFER TOO SMALL
21 — ERROR IN COMPRESS/EXPAND ROUTINE
22 — ELEMENT NAME NOT FOUND
23 — ELEMENT SECURITY CODE VIOLATION
24 — EXCLUSIVE CONTROL EVENTS EXCEEDED
25 — INVALID DATABASE ID
26 — INSUFFICIENT CONTROL AREA BUFFER SPACE
27 — GETIT BLOCK SIZE TOO SMALL
28 — LOG AREA BLOCK SIZE TOO SMALL
29 — EOF DURING LOGLB COMMAND
30 — TABLE NOT OPEN FOR THIS COMMAND
31 — KEY LENGTH INCONSISTENCY
36 — USER VIEW NOT OPEN
37 — INVALID ADDRESS
38 — PREVIOUS LOGGING ERROR
39 — CANNOT PROCESS OLD REQUEST
40 — SAVE TASK AREA EXTENSION TOO SMALL
41 — NOT ENOUGH EXTRA BUFFERS IN MASTER LIST
42 — NOT ENOUGH SEQUENTIAL EXTENSIONS IN MASTER LIST
43 — NO VALID INDEX
46 — TABLE ALREADY OPEN FOR UPDATE
47 — CANNOT OPEN DB
51 — INVALID MIX OF JOBS INCLUDING DB UTILITIES
52 — RECOVERY FILE OPEN/CLOSE FAILURE
54 — INSUFFICIENT OPEN TABLE BUFFER SPACE
55 — BAD USER REQUIREMENTS TABLE
56 — BAD MASTER LIST
57 — BAD RWTSA ADDRESS
58 — TABLE NOT LOADED
60 — DB CANNOT OPEN THE LOG AREA
63 — BAD DEVICE TYPE
65 — DD STATEMENT MISSING
66 — MULTI-VOLUMN OPEN FAILURE
67 — CXX INTERLOCK
68 — MULTI-USER FACILITY IS NOT UP
69 — TABLE HAS NO CURRENT INDEX
70 — BLOCK LENGTH TOO SMALL
71 — CMS OPEN FAILURE
72 — INVALID DATA AREA CONTROL BLOCK
74 — OS OPEN ALLOCATION ERROR
76 — OPEN ERROR
78 — FBA BLOCK OR EXTENT ERROR
```

```
79 — CXX WRONG RELEASE
80 — DATACOM/D-NET ERROR
81 — DATACOM/D-NET ERROR
82 — DB SVC PROGRAM PSW-KEY ERROR
83 — SVC INTEGRITY ERROR
84 — MULTI-TASKING ERROR
85 — INSUFFICIENT TASKS
86 — THE MULTI-USER FACILITY HAS ABENDED
87 — SECURITY VIOLATION DURING OPEN
88 — DATABASE HAS BEEN DISABLED
91 — COMPOUND BOOLEAN SELECTION FACILITY ERROR
92 — SET SELECTION INTERRUPT
93 — ATTEMPT TO POSITION PAST END/BEG-OF-SET
```

As we can see, these codes not only apply to IDEAL, but to the entire DATACOM environment. The fact is that many of these errors either cannot occur in, or cannot be controlled by IDEAL. A copy of the full *DATACOM Error Message Manual* should be available to you. We will discuss those error codes that can occur in IDEAL later in this chapter.

After it has displayed the diagnostic messages in the program's output area (which will go to the same place as the program's LIST statements), the program will execute a database backout and will issue a QUIT RUN command.

IDEAL will then issue a warning message that the program has ended. If we were running on-line, the message will appear in bold print at the top of the screen. If we are running in batch, the message will appear on the psuedo-screen that contains the RUN PROGRAM statement. However, a batch program running under IDEAL release 1.3 would send a normal return code to the operating system, which would send a 0000 completion code to the JES message log. Under 1.4, IDEAL will send the value in return code to the operating system.

To issue an abending message to the operating system or for any other reason, IDEAL has provided a way to override the default processing. This is done through the <<ERROR>> PROCEDURE.

The <<ERROR>> PROCEDURE can be placed anywhere in the program and has the appearance of a normal procedure. However, it cannot be called by the program, but only by the system, when it encounters an IDEAL error. Thus the statements

```
DO ERROR
QUIT ERROR
```

are invalid, because they try to take processing control away from the system. In addition, if a DO statement is executed from an error procedure, control will pass to the new procedure but will not return to the error procedure. Processing will end with the execution of the last statement of the called procedure.

All other PDL statements are available to the ERROR PROCE-DURE. An error procedure that would imitate the default processing would look like this:

```
<<ERROR>> PROCEDURE
  LIST ERROR
  BACKOUT
  QUIT RUN
ENDPROC
```

This procedure would list the standard error messages, perform a database backout, and end the program. Let's suppose that we are running an IDEAL batch program, and wanted to alert the operating system that an IDEAL abend has occurred. Under release 1.4 we would set the operator $RETURN-CODE to any special value we need to see, or allow it to retain its default value of 12. Under 1.3 we need to execute a COBOL program with the following command:

```
SET RETURN-CODE = PR-RETURN-CODE
```

where RETURN-CODE is the special COBOL register, and PR-RETURN-CODE is the value that we populated in our <<ERROR>> procedure.

```
<<ERROR>> PROCEDURE
  LIST ERROR
  BACKOUT
  MOVE '4444' TO PR-RETURN-CODE
  CALL CBLABEND USING PR-RETURN-CODE
  QUIT RUN
ENDPROC
```

With this processing the IBM user return code for the job would be 4444. We could then use the standard IBM JCL facilities to stop the run or to execute or avoid certain steps in the JOB stream.

(Please refer to Chapter 6 for a more detailed explanation of how to call a COBOL subroutine.)

We can, of course, be more specific about the type of error that we have.

```
<<ERROR>> PROCEDURE
  LIST ERROR
  BACKOUT
  IF $ERROR-TYPE = 'DVW'
     MOVE $ERROR-INTERNAL-DVW-STATUS TO PR-RETURN-CODE
  ELSE
     MOVE '4444' TO PR-RETURN-CODE
  ENDIF
  CALL CBLABEND USING PR-RETURN-CODE
  QUIT RUN
ENDPROC
```

This will show us the dataview status in the return code, if a dataview error occurred.

We can use the error routine not only to tell us where we failed in the program, but where we were in the database. For example, let's say that we were running a program that was reading a flat file and loading out a record to the customer database.

```
<LOAD-CUST-DATA> PROCEDURE
  FOR EACH CUST-INPUT
           ADD 1 TO CT-CUST-INPUT
           DO EDIT-CUST-DATA
           IF CUST-DATA-VALID
              DO ISRT-CUST-REC
           ENDIF
  ENDFOR
ENDPROC
```

```
<<ERROR>> PROCEDURE
  LIST ERROR
  LIST 'INPUT RECORD ' CT-CUST-INPUT
  LIST CUST-INPUT.CUST-NO
  BACKOUT
  MOVE '4444' TO PR-RETURN-CODE
  CALL CBLABEND USING PR-RETURN-CODE
  QUIT RUN
ENDPROC
```

Here we will see the record that we abended on, and some of the data that we were processing with. By examining this record we can determine the coding changes that are needed to bypass or correct this problem. This would allow us to prevent the abend and finish processing.

The ERROR PROCEDURE can also be used to recover from an otherwise fatal error and to continue processing. For example, let's say we are reading the CUST-EQUIP database to determine sales by customer. As part of the calculation, we wish to see the percent of cost per sales.

```
<CUST-SALES> PROCEDURE
  <CUST-EQUIP>
  FOR EACH CUST-EQUIP-DVW
          MOVE CUST-EQUIP-DVW.CUST-NO     TO RPT-CUST-NO
          MOVE CUST-EQUIP-DVW.PART-NO     TO RPT-PART-NO
          MOVE CUST-EQUIP-DVW.SALES       TO RPT-SALES
          MOVE CUST-EQUIP-DVW.COST        TO RPT-COST
          SET WK-MARGIN-PCT = RPT-COST / RPT-SALES
          SET RPT-MARGIN = $EDIT(WK-MARGIN-PCT,PIC='ZZ9.99')
          PRODUCE CUSTRPT
  ENDFOR
ENDPROC


<<ERROR>> PROCEDURE
  LIST ERROR
  IF $ERROR-TYPE = 'OFL'
     MOVE 'OVRFLW' TO RPT-MARGIN
     PRODUCE CUSTRPT
     PROCESS NEXT CUST-EQUIP
  ELSE
     IF $ERROR-TYPE = 'DVW'
        MOVE $ERROR-INTERNAL-DVW-STATUS TO PR-RETURN-CODE
     ELSE
        MOVE '4444' TO PR-RETURN-CODE
     ENDIF
     CALL CBLABEND USING PR-RETURN-CODE
     QUIT RUN
  ENDIF
ENDPROC
```

Here the program will place the message 'OVRFLW' in the margin percentage field if it encounters a situation where the cost is much greater than 999 times the price. This will allow the report to continue the process with the next record and not stop with an abend.

IDEAL Error Codes Discussion

Because IDEAL handles most of the background details of the processing for you through the compiler and compound Boolean selection, there are only a few of the DATACOM error codes that you are likely to encounter. In addition, many of the remaining codes are problems that are encountered because of the database or the status of events in the environment. In this section we will discuss only those codes that can be affected and eliminated by the programmer.

```
01 - INVALID REQUEST COMMAND
```

The actual DB command as translated by IDEAL is in error.

This is not supposed to happen, and the only occurrence that we have seen was when the file table for the program was set up incorrectly.

```
05 - TABLE NOT OPEN
```

The program is trying to access a database that is not opened.

Since IDEAL handles all of the opens and closes for you it means that it cannot recognize the requested database. This can be caused by one of three events:

1. The program's resource table is pointing to an old or a non-production version of the dataview. Change the resource table and recompile the program.
2. We are running a batch job and the database to which we referred is not in the associated file table. Add the database to the file table.
3. The file table is pointing to the wrong physical database. Change the file table.

```
09 - REQUEST NOT PROCEEDED BY PREREQUISITE REQUEST
```

This is another problem that should not happen in IDEAL. The only time that we have seen it happen was in a program that was trying to update a different occurrence of a record than the one the FOR statement had control over.

```
10 - DUPLICATE MASTER KEY NOT ALLOWED
```

The program has tried to add a record to the database, but a record with the same master key already exists. Add a WHEN DUPLICATE clause to your FOR statement.

```
11 - MASTER KEY HAS BEEN MODIFIED
```

The program has tried to change the master key of the record.
To change the key

1. The record must be read into the program with a FOR statement.
2. Create a new record with a FOR NEW statement and an alternate dataview for the same record.
3. Copy the data in the old record into the new record.
4. Put the new key into the new record.
5. ENDFOR on the FOR NEW.
6. Delete the old record.
7. ENDFOR the old record.

```
<CHNG-KEY> PROCEDURE
   FOR FIRST OLD-RECORD-DVW
       FOR NEW NEW-RECORD-DVW
           MOVE OLD-RECORD-DVW TO NEW-RECORD-DVW BY NAME
           MOVE NEW-KEY       TO NEW-RECORD-DVW.MASTER-KEY
       ENDFOR
       DELETE OLD-RECORD-DVW
   ENDFOR
ENDPROC


14 - NO RECORD FOUND OR NO KEY FOUND
```

Actually this should not occur either, and is covered by the WHEN NONE clause.

```
25 - INVALID DATABASE ID
```

The file table is pointing to the wrong physical database.

```
30 - TABLE NOT OPEN FOR THIS COMMAND
```

The file table does not contain the file that the program needs.

```
36 - USER VIEW NOT OPEN
```

The file table does not contain the file that the program needs.

```
65 — DD STATEMENT MISSING
```

This occurs when we are running a QSAM file into or out of the program, and we have not included it in the JCL. This is either an oversight or a misspelling.

IDEAL Internal Errors

An IDEAL internal error will occur whenever IDEAL itself, and not the program being run, is unable to complete a task. This can happen not only during program execution, but while we are doing other IDEAL functions. When an internal error occurs, it usually means that a portion of the background system is unavailable or has overflowed.

If we are processing on-line and an internal error occurs, a prompting message will appear under the command line. This message will have the following form:

```
#T-R-PPXXXXXXXXS — "TEXT"
```

where

#T — The asynchronous task number (compiles only)
R — Number of the region on the screen where the error occurred
PP — The product which abended
ID — IDEAL
SC — Session control
XXXXXXXX — The error message identification
S — The message severity code

A — ACTION — Operator must perform a specific action
C — CRITICAL — Notify the CA representative
D — DIRECTIVE — Carry out an action other than console reply.
E — ERROR — Error occurred that does not terminate processing
I — INFORMATION — No action required.
T — TERMINATE — Processing is terminated.
W — WARNING — Condition may lead to unexpected or unpredictable results.

"TEXT" — A literal that describes the error message

An example of this can be found in the message:

```
1-SCSCERRP99E - INTERR: INTERNAL SYSTEM ERROR
```

Here we see that the error occurred in the first region on our screen. The problem was found in the IDEAL product (ID), and the severity code of (E) caused the job to be terminated. We can then go into the *IDEAL Messages and Codes* manual to see the explanation. The entry for the error code ADERRP02E is

```
ADERRP02  INTERNAL SYSTEM ERROR
          EXPLANATION: AN UNEXPECTED CONDITION WAS DETECTED
          WITHIN IDEAL.
          CORRECTIVE ACTION: CONSULT DATACOM/DB DOCUMENTATION
          FOR EXPLANATION OF THE DB RETURN CODE.
```

Another tool that we have when we are processing on-line is the DISPLAY ERROR command. This command displays a screen of data for the error that has just occurred. This screen has the following format:

```
MESSAGE NUMBER        MESSAGE TEXT

_____   _____
                            NAME    VER   OFFSET DATE      TIME
SVRC=____  FUNC=____   RC=__   PGM=_____ ___ - _____ __/__/__ __:__

         NAME      VER OFFSET
CALPGM=_____ ___ _____ CURRACT=___ ACTTYP=___ USER=_____ ERRID=____

DFSCMND=_____  QUALIFIER=_____

SYS=_____ ENTTYP=_____ ENTNAM=_____ ENTVER=_____ ENTSTAT=_____

PANEL-NAME=_____ VER=_____ SUB-SYS=_____
LIB=_____     MEM=_____

LOGMSG: _____
```

where

Message number and message text are the same as appeared in the message line

SRVC — The internal service detecting the error

CMP — Compiler
DSF — Datadictionary service facility
LBN — Linked bundle (storage management)
LOG — General log message
PMS — Panel management service
PSS — Print subsystem
SCF — Session control facility
VLS — Virtual library system
VPE — Virtual processing environment

FUNC — The function being performed by the service.
RC — The return code from the service
PGM — The PGM in control when the error is detected. This includes the program name, version, and the offset into the program.
CALPGM — Identifier of the calling program
CURRACT — The current activity

AD — General service commands
AE — Application execution
CM — Compiler
DE — Working-data/Parameter editing
ED — General editing
PD — Panel definition facility
PM — Panel management services
PS — Print subsystem
RP — Report editing
SC — Session control

ACTTYP — The type or mode of activity

D — Display
E — Edit
U — Utility

USER — The three-character user-ID
ERRID — 1- to 10-character string returned by the program detecting the error. This may be blank.
DSFCMND — Used only in a DFS error. This is the command sent to DFS that created the error.
QUALIFIER — Used only in a DFS error. the DFS user request

area qualifier passed to DFS.

SYS — 3-character short system ID currently selected

ENTTYP — Current datadictionary entity type

ENTNAM — Current datadictionary entity name

ENTVER — Current datadictionary entity version

ENTSTAT — Current datadictionary entity status

PANEL-NAME — The current panel name and version

SUB-SYS — PDF error only, the current panel subsystem

LIB — 8-character DD name for VLS library in question

MEM — 24-character VLS member name

LOGMSG — Optional message written to the system log by the
program detecting the error

The display for this particular error appeared as

```
***** START OF       ERROR LOG ON XX/XX/XX   AT    XX:XX:XX      *****
0-SCSCERRP99E - INTERR: INTERNAL SYSTEM ERROR
SRVC=LOG FUNC=        RC=        PGM=SCBTINIT02.30-17FA XX/XX/XX  XX:XX
CALPGM=                   CURACT= ACTTYP= USER=   ERRID=SCBTIN05E
SYS=     ENTTYP=    ENTNAM=            ENTVER=        ENTSTAT=
LOGMSG:      ERROR AT DD INITIALIZATION    INO 011


*****      END OF       ERROR LOG ON XX/XX/XX     AT    XX:XX:XX *****
```

Which may or may not do any good. In most cases the best thing to
do when an internal error occurs is to look at what is happening, and
try to decide what part of IDEAL is either missing or has abended.

For example, if we are trying to compile a program and an internal error occurs, the display error command could result in the display:

```
***** START OF       ERROR LOG ON XX/XX/XX   AT    XX:XX:XX      *****
0-CMGENP99E - F INTERNAL ERROR: MESSAGE TEXT NOT FOUND
SRVC=LOG FUNC=        RC=        PGM=SCBTINIT02.30-17FA XX/XX/XX  XX:XX
CALPGM=                   CURACT= ACTTYP= USER=   ERRID=SCBTIN05E
SYS=     ENTTYP=    ENTNAM=            ENTVER=        ENTSTAT=
LOGMSG:      ERROR AT DD INITIALIZATION    INO 011


*****      END OF       ERROR LOG ON XX/XX/XX     AT    XX:XX:XX *****
```

Which is not very informative. At this point, we would need to
remember that we are compiling a program, and that there are size
limits on a program. This limit is the fact that an IDEAL program is

made up of blocks and that an *object module* can only have 230 blocks. These block value assignments are

```
SUBPROGRAM          1
READ DATAVIEW       2
UPDATE DATAVIEW     3
LEVEL 1 PARAMETER   1
REPORT              1
PANEL               2
```

There is also a limit to the variable tables in the compiler. This includes the procedure names, working storage variables, parameter variables, dataview field names, etc. This would result in the error display:

```
***** START OF       ERROR LOG ON XX/XX/XX    AT    XX:XX:XX    *****
0-CMGENP99E - LOGMSG: BLOCK LENGTH EXCEEDS 32000 TYPE A
SRVC=LOG FUNC=          RC=        PGM=SCBTINIT02.30-17FA XX/XX/XX  XX:XX
CALPGM=                 CURACT= ACTTYP= USER=   ERRID=SCBTIN05E
SYS=     ENTTYP=    ENTNAM=              ENTVER=     ENTSTAT=
LOGMSG:      ERROR AT DD INITIALIZATION   INO 011


*****      END OF      ERROR LOG ON XX/XX/XX    AT    XX:XX:XX  *****
```

Thus we would need to look at each of these areas for a problem, make adjustments to the program, and try again.

An internal error will occur if a portion of IDEAL is missing.

```
***** START OF       ERROR LOG ON XX/XX/XX    AT    XX:XX:XX    *****
0-CMGENP99E - INTERR: MESSAGE DOES NOT EXIST
SRVC=VLS FUNC=SCAN      RC=008    PGM=SC00MSGP02.30-0BBE XX/XX/XX  XX:XX
CALPGM=SC00MSGP02.30-0D9C CURACT= ACTTYP= USER=   ERRID=SCBTIN05E
SYS=     ENTTYP=    ENTNAM=              ENTVER=     ENTSTAT=
LIB=ADRLIB     MEM=IDAEMSGE
LOGMSG:      ERROR AT DD INITIALIZATION   INO 011


*****      END OF      ERROR LOG ON XX/XX/XX    AT    XX:XX:XX  *****
```

This message was received when an IDEAL batch program was being run. In batch, the error display appears at the top of the "log-on panel" display.

In this case, a review of the JCL showed that we tried to run in an IDEAL region that was closed at the time. Therefore, the multiuser facility was not available, and the JOB abended.

To be fair, IDEAL does occasionally tell what happened.

```
***** START OF        ERROR LOG ON XX/XX/XX    AT    XX:XX:XX    *****

0-CMGENP99E - INTERR: DATABASE FILE TABLE BLFTR00X CANNOT BE FOUND

SRVC=VPE FUNC=$DBC      RC=005     PGM=AETDVW   01.3 -AA6E XX/XX/XX   XX:XX

CALPGM=                      CURACT=AE ACTTYP=U USER=EHP ERRID=

SYS=PRD ENTTYP=PGM  ENTNAM=BLPGSLRP      ENTVER=000     ENTSTAT=PROD

LIB=ADRLIB       MEM=IDAEMSGE


*****        END OF        ERROR LOG ON XX/XX/XX     AT    XX:XX:XX  *****
```

But for the most part, an internal error can usually be solved only by reviewing the environment that is being used, and not through reliance on the error diagnostic display.

Conclusions

In this chapter we have seen the two types of errors that we are liable to encounter in our processing, *program* and *internal*. We have also seen some methods and information that can be used to solve these problems.

However, the best way to solve any debugging problem is through instinct and experience. We hope that the exercises for this chapter will help you gain that experience.

Exercises

1. What are the IDEAL error functions and their values?
2. What will normally happen when an IDEAL program abends?
3. What is the name of the procedure that will be executed during an IDEAL abend to override the normal abend function?
4. Why can't we have a quit from or a call to this paragraph?
5. What would be the class and type of the following errors?

   a. Subscript out of bounds.
   b. Invalid numeric data.
   c. Division by zero.
   d. Subroutine tries to update a non-update parm.

e. An assign statement was issued for a report that has already been started.

f. A dataview status of 10 has been encountered.

6. What is the difference between $ERROR-DVW-STATUS and $ERROR-INTERNAL-DVW-STATUS?

7. If we are running in IDEAL batch and a program without an error routine abends, what return code will be seen by the operating system?

8. What should we look for if one of the following DVW statuses is encountered?

```
07 -
08 -
11 -
15 -
46 -
51 -
65 -
88 -
```

9. Why are internal errors harder for IDEAL to deal with?

10. Using the *IDEAL Error Messages and Codes* manual, find the meaning and corrective action for the following error codes.

```
ADERRP31
ADERRP57
ADERRP62
```

Exercises — Answers

1. What are the IDEAL error functions and their values?

$ERROR-NAME — contains the name of the field, subscript, dataview, procedure, or program that is in error.

$ERROR-VALUE — returns the value of the erroneous field, where appropriate.

$ERROR-PGM — the name of the abending program.

$ERROR-PROC — the name of the abending procedure within the program

$ERROR-STMT — shows the statement number where the error occured.

$ERROR-CLASS — returns a three-character code that identifies the error class.

$ERROR-TYPE — returns a three-character code that when combined with the error class can furthur define the error.

$ERROR-DESCRIPTION — returns a statement that describes the error.

$SUBSCRIPT-POSITION — shows position of a subscript in error.

$ERROR-DVW-STATUS — simplified database error listing.

$ERROR-INTERNAL-DVW-STATUS — more inclusive list of DVW errors.

2. What will normally happen when an IDEAL program abends?

   Program will list out the error diagnostics, do a database back-out, and end the program.

3. What is the name of the procedure that will be executed during an IDEAL abend to override the normal abend function?

   <<ERROR>> PROCEDURE

4. Why can't we have a quit from or a call to this paragraph?

   The ERROR PROCEDURE really contains instructions to the operating system, not to the program, as to what should be done if an abend occurs. Thus it is controlled by IDEAL and not by the program.

5. What would be the class and type of the following errors?

   a. Subscript out of bounds.
   b. Invalid numeric data.
   c. Division by zero.
   d. Subroutine tries to update a non-update parm.
   e. An assign statement was issued for a report that has already been started.
   f. A dataview status of 10 has been encountered.

	Class	Type
a.	SUB	SUB
b.	NUM	NUM
c.	ARI	DVZ

d.   REF   UPD
e.   SEQ   ARS
f.   DVW   DVW

6. What is the difference between $ERROR-DVW-STATUS and $ERROR-INTERNAL-DVW-STATUS?

    The $ERROR-INTERNAL-DVW-STATUS deals with the entire range of problems that can occur within the DATACOM/DB-DC environment.

7. If we are running in IDEAL batch and a program without an error routine abends, what return code will be seen by the operating system?

    0000

8. What should we look for if one of the following DVW statuses is encountered?

    07 — DATA AREA FULL

    The physical space allocated to the database is full, and we have tried to add another record. Have the DBA either reorganize the database or increase the available space.

    08 — INDEX FULL

    The physical space allocated to the database index is full. Have the DBA either reorganize the index or allocate more space.

    11 — MASTER KEY HAS BEEN MODIFIED

    We have tried to move a new value to a key field of a DVW under a FOR FIRST or FOR EACH statement. The line number clause will point to the ENDFOR statement.

    15 — EXCLUSIVE CONTROL INTERLOCK

    Two jobs tried to get exclusive control on the same record; the abending program was waiting for the first program to release it but timed out.

46 — TABLE ALREADY OPEN FOR UPDATE

File table problem.

51 — INVALID MIX OF JOBS INCLUDING DB UTILITIES

The database utilities require the databases be closed. Check when they will be reopened and run your job again.

65 — DD STATEMENT MISSING

The QSAM file does not have a corresponding DD statement. Check the spelling on the DDNAME statement in your JCL.

88 — DATABASE HAS BEEN DISABLED

The DBA has closed the database that you need for some kind of maintenance. Check when it will be reopened and reschedule your job.

9. Why are internal errors harder for IDEAL to deal with?

When an internal error occurs, IDEAL itself has been interrupted. Thus it may have trouble, depending on the problem, determining its position and, hence, the true nature of the problem.

10. Using the *IDEAL Error Messages and Codes* manual, find the meaning and corrective action of the following error codes.

ADERRP31 MAIN PNL NOT FOUND

Explanation: The requested panel does not exist in the current panel library.
Corrective action: Verify the integrity of the VLS library.

ADERRP57 INTERR: NUMBER OF SIMULTANEOUS OUTPUTS EXCEEDS MAX OF 16

Explanation: Only 16 output members can be created simultaneously by a single user. An error occurred when the 17th member was opened.
Corrective action: Redesign the application to have fewer reports open at one time.

```
ADERRP62   OUTPUT LIB DIRECTORY IS FULL
```

Explanation: The output LIB INDEX is full. No more outputs can be added to the library.

Corrective action: Delete any unneeded outputs. If the problem is frequent, enlarge the library, reinitialize it, and assign a higher number of maximum number of simultaneous output files.

11

Structured Coding Techniques

Up to this point we have discussed all of the different components of an IDEAL program. We have also discussed the database IDEAL uses, and how to build FOR statements that effectively and efficiently access that database. Throughout this study, we have seen that IDEAL takes care of a lot of the mundane and detail work for us. We have also seen that the commands, LOOP — ENDLOOP, IF — ENDIF, FOR — ENDFOR, etc. all seem to have been created with the principles of structured program design in mind.

One would think that structured code would be the natural result of these simple commands and inherent structure. Sadly, this is not the case. We have seen a great many "spaghetti" IDEAL programs that were nearly impossible to fix or modify. We are not sure how this was done, but throughout the development of these programs the programmers were heard to complain about the many deficiencies of the language.

The purpose of this chapter is to discuss some of the structured coding techniques that we have found useful in our work, in the hope that they will be useful to the reader. We will begin our discussion with some of the basic concepts of program design so that we will have a clear basis for our discussion.

The best way to judge the structure of a program is through the concepts of coupling and cohesion.

The term *coupling* refers to the measure of the strength of the connection between modules of program code. The level of coupling between two modules can be measured in the amount of understanding we must have about one module to be able to understand the function of another.

There are three levels of coupling. These are

1. DATA COUPLING: This is the most desirable form of coupling, wherein data is passed to a module to begin the processing of that module or to return control to the calling module.
2. CONTROL COUPLING: This is the second level of coupling, and is not acceptable as data coupling. In this type of coupling a flag is passed up or down the program hierarchy to control the processing of the receiving module.
3. PATHOLOGICAL COUPLING: As its name infers, this is the worst type of coupling. The first module may extract some data from the second, change it, or branch to some specific instruction in the second or an entirely different module, based on some control.[1]

The opposite of coupling is *cohesion*. Whereas coupling is a measure of the independence of modules, cohesion is the measure of the glue that binds modules together.

There are seven levels of cohesion, which are defined as:

1. FUNCTIONAL — This is the best in that everything that is done in the module contributes directly to the accomplishment of a single task.
2. SEQUENTIAL — This serves as a gateway to other functions in the system. Typically, a sequentially cohesive module starts one module, regains control from it when it is done, and passes some data on to a third module. Thus it serves as a control point in the system.
3. COMMUNICATIONAL — This happens when separate functions that work on common data are grouped in the same module.
4. PROCEDURAL — This type of cohesion is present when modules are grouped together because they follow the flow of control of the program. This type of cohesion often occurs when programs are coded from traditional flow charts.
5. TEMPORAL — This happens when functions are grouped together merely because they happen at the same time.
6. LOGICAL — This type of coupling means that functions are grouped together simply because they do similar functions to the same data. The choice of the logic path to be followed is based on a control character that is set somewhere else in the system.

7. COINCIDENTAL — The modules just happen to be together
because of some arbitrary decision.[2]

In our discussion of structure in IDEAL, we will define a module
as being the verb, its corresponding end statement, and the interven-
ing code. With this definition, we can see five modules in the following example:

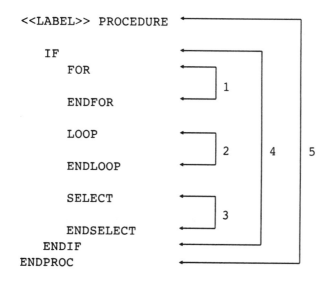

```
<<LABEL>> PROCEDURE

    IF
        FOR

        ENDFOR

        LOOP

        ENDLOOP

        SELECT

        ENDSELECT
    ENDIF
ENDPROC
```

We can give this definition because these structures are the basic
"building blocks" of an IDEAL program. An analysis of their combination and usage will give us a measure of the structure of the
resulting program.

In the rest of this chapter we will examine how the levels of coupling and cohesion relate to the different procedure language constructs, and how these constructs can be combined to produce structured programs.

The basic structure by itself is an example of the best level of both
coupling and cohesion.

```
FOR FIRST CUSTOMER-DVW
     WHERE CUSTOMER-DVW.CUST-NO = WK-CUST-NO
          MOVE CUSTOMER-DVW.CITY TO PANELNM.CITY
     WHEN  NONE
          MOVE $SPACES            TO PANELNM.CITY
ENDFOR
```

This statement is functionally cohesive because it handles a specific task, the population of the panel field labeled CITY. It is also an example of data coupling because a piece of data is input to the module (the field WK-CUST-NO), and a piece of information is returned from it (the population of PANELNM.CITY).

If we expand this structure to call another module, when we find the dataview, we can see an example of sequential cohesion between the FOR statement and the LOAD-CUST-DATA module.

```
FOR FIRST CUSTOMER-DVW
    WHERE CUSTOMER-DVW.CUST-NO = WK-CUST-NO
          DO LOAD-CUST-DATA
    WHEN   NONE
          MOVE $SPACES            TO PANELNM.CITY
ENDFOR


<<LOAD-CUST-DATA>> PROCEDURE
  MOVE CUSTOMER-DVW.CITY TO PANELNM.CITY
ENDPROC
```

The FOR statement starts the LOAD-CUST-DATA module. When it is completed, control will return to the FOR statement.

We can also expand this example to see this cohesion better:

```
FOR FIRST CUSTOMER-DVW
    WHERE CUSTOMER-DVW.CUST-NO = WK-CUST-NO
          DO LOAD-CUST-DATA
          DO SET-PANEL-ATTRS
    WHEN   NONE
          DO CLEAR-CUST-DATA
ENDFOR


<<LOAD-CUST-DATA>> PROCEDURE
  MOVE CUSTOMER-DVW.CITY TO PANELNM.CITY
ENDPROC


<<SET-PANEL-ATTRS>> PROCEDURE
  SET ATTR 'PSL' TEMP ON PANELNM.CITY
ENDPROC


<<CLEAR-CUST-DATA>> PROCEDURE
  MOVE $SPACES TO PANELNM.CITY
ENDPROC
```

Here the results of the FOR statement serve as the gateway to the subordinate paragraphs. If the record is found, the first two modules are executed. If the record is not found, we will call CLEAR-CUST-DATA.

We can also see sequential cohesion to be the basis of the SELECT statement. For example, in the main drive routine of an on-line program

```
SELECT PANELNM.OPTION
        WHEN 'A'  DO ADD-RECORD
        WHEN 'D'  DO DELETE-RECORD
        WHEN 'U'  DO UPDATE-RECORD
        WHEN 'V'  DO VIEW-RECORD
        WHEN NONE DO INVALID-OPTION
ENDSELECT
TRANSMIT PANELNM
```

a flag (PANELNM.OPTION) is passed to the driving module, which in turn calls other modules. These modules in turn invoke other functions. The VIEW-RECORD procedure will contain a FOR statement, which can have a panel load procedure. Control will then return to the end of the SELECT statement, and the TRANSMIT command will be executed.

An example of communicational cohesion can be seen in the following piece of code:

```
LOOP UNTIL PASS-BACK-OK
        DO
        DO
        DO
        TRANSMIT
        DO CHECK-BOTTOM
    ENDLOOP
ENDPROC

<<CHECK-BOTTOM>> PROCEDURE
  SELECT FIRST
    WHEN OEPLPPI.ORDER-QTY > 0
        MOVE
        MOVE
        SET PASS-BACK-OK = TRUE
    WHEN OEPLPPI.MENU-CODE > $SPACES
        MOVE
        IF
```

```
         ELSE
         ENDIF
         SET PASS-BACK-OK = TRUE
    WHEN OEPLPPI.NEXT-PART-NO > $SPACES
         REFRESH OEPLPPI
         SET PASS-BACK-OK = FALSE
    WHEN WK-REQ-PARTNO NE OEPLPPI.PART-NUMBER
         MOVE
         SET PASS-BACK-OK = FALSE
    WHEN $PF2 OR $PF14
         SET PASS-BACK-OK = TRUE
    WHEN OEPLPPI.QTY-ORDERED > 0
     AND OEPLPPI.PO-NUMBER    > $SPACES
         SET PASS-BACK-OK = TRUE
    WHEN OEPLPPI.QTY-ORDERED = 0
     AND OEPLPPI.PO-NUMBER    > $SPACES
         SET OEPLPPI.MESSAGE = 'ENTER ORDERING QTY'
         SET PASS-BACK-OK = FALSE
    WHEN OEPLPPI.QTY-ORDERED > 0
     AND OEPLPPI.PO-NUMBER    = $SPACES
         SET OEPLPPI.MESSAGE = 'ENTER CUSTOMER PO NO'
         SET PASS-BACK-OK = FALSE
    WHEN NONE
         SET PASS-BACK-OK = TRUE
    ENDSELECT
```

Here the SELECT FIRST contains not only different ways to escape from the loop, but options for processing within the LOOP statement, based on different pieces of data. This type of logic is difficult to understand, let alone debug. To bring it to a more acceptable level of cohesion, we would begin by separating the data editing and the loop escape functions. We will place the simple loop escape clauses into the LOOP statement itself:

```
LOOP UNTIL PASS-BACK-OK
        OR $PF2 OF $PF14
        OR OEPLPPI.MENU-CODE > $SPACES
        OR (OEPLPPI.ORDER-QTY > 0 AND OEPLPPI.PO-NUMBER > $SPACES)
        DO
        DO
        DO
        TRANSMIT
        DO CHECK-BOTTOM
    ENDLOOP
```

```
    DO  SET-RETURN
ENDPROC


<<CHECK-BOTTOM>>  PROCEDURE
   SET PASS-BACK-OK = FALSE
   SELECT
      WHEN  OEPLPPI.NEXT-PART-NO > $SPACES
            REFRESH OEPLPPI
      WHEN  WK-REQ-PARTNO NE OEPLPPI.PART-NUMBER
            MOVE
            SET PASS-BACK-OK = FALSE
      WHEN  OEPLPPI.QTY-ORDERED = 0
        AND OEPLPPI.PO-NUMBER    > $SPACES
            SET OEPLPPI.MESSAGE = 'ENTER ORDERING QTY'
            SET PASS-BACK-OK = FALSE
      WHEN  OEPLPPI.QTY-ORDERED > 0
        AND OEPLPPI.PO-NUMBER    = $SPACES
            SET OEPLPPI.MESSAGE = 'ENTER CUSTOMER PO NO'
            SET PASS-BACK-OK = FALSE
   ENDSELECT
ENDPROC


<<SET-RETURN>>  PROCEDURE
   :FROM ABOVE SELECT 'WHEN OEPLPPI.MENU-CODE > $SPACES'
   MOVE
   IF
   ELSE
   ENDIF
ENDPROC
```

Now the entire purpose of the CHECK-BOTTOM routine is to edit the data as it comes back to the program for the next loop. The escape from the loop has been isolated into the LOOP statement. The work that was done to prepare for the return of control to the calling program is removed from the loop module, and placed into a separate paragraph. Thus each of the three modules (the LOOP, the SELECT, and SET-RETURN) are functionally cohesive, which improves the overall structure of the entire program.

An example of procedural cohesion can be seen in this program:

```
FOR EACH   CUST-ORDER-LINE
      WHERE CUST-ORDER-LINE.SHIPPING-WHSE = WK-ENTERING-WHSE
            FOR FIRST COR-HEADER-READ
                WHERE COR-HEADER-READ.ORDER-CNTL-NO
```

```
                        = CUST-ORDER-LINE.ORDER-CNTL-NO
            FOR FIRST INV-MASTER
                WHERE INV-MASTER.WHSE-NO    = COR-HEADER-READ.WHSE-NO
                  AND INV-MASTER.CATALOG-NO = CUST-ORDER-LINE.CATALOG-NO
                    DO TRY-TO-COMMIT
                    IF STOCK-RELEASED
                        IF #LAST-ORDR-CNTL = 'NEWORD'
                        ELSE
                            CALL OEPGDATA USING INPUT #LAST-ORD-CNTL
                        ENDIF
                        SET ...
                    ENDIF
                WHEN  NONE
                        SET ATTR 'H' TEMP ON ...
                        SET ATTR 'PSH' TEMP ON ...
                        BACKOUT
                        QUIT PROCEDURE
            ENDFOR
                WHEN  NONE
                        SET ATTR 'H' TEMP ON ...
                        SET ATTR 'PSH' TEMP ON ...
                        BACKOUT
                        QUIT PROCEDURE
            ENDFOR
            SET ATTR 'H' TEMP ON ...
            SET ATTR 'PSH' TEMP ON ...
            BACKOUT
            QUIT PROCEDURE
        ENDFOR
        IF #NO-RELEASED > 0
            DO ...
            SET
        ENDIF
        IF #LAST-ORD-CNTL = 'NEW-ORD'
            CALL OEPGDATE USING INPUT CUST-ORDER-LINE.ORDER-CNTL-NO
        ENDIF
    ENDPROC
```

Here we see that the consecutive FOR statements are linked together procedurally. The execution of the subordinate FOR statement is directly affected by the result of the FOR statement above it, and control flows within the module based on those results. We can also see in this code an example of control coupling. The function of the subordinate FOR statement is determined by the value of a field which is populated above it.

Thus, to understand the subordinate FOR, we need to understand not only how processing reached this point but how the passed data fields were populated.

To return this to a better structural level, we can begin rebuilding it by isolating the basic modules and extracting them from the main structure. The purpose of the call to the CUST-ORDER-HDR was to validate its presence. The purpose of the call to the INV-MASTER file was to obtain inventory values and to validate its presence. We can then remove these structures from the main drive paragraph, which would give us the following code:

```
FOR EACH   CUST-ORDER-LINE
       WHERE CUST-ORDER-LINE.SHIPPING-WHSE = WK-ENTERING-WHSE
             DO GET-COR-HEAD
              IF FG-PROCEED
                  DO GET-INV-MAST
                IF FG-PROCEED
                    DO TRY-TO-COMMIT
                  IF STOCK-RELEASED
                      IF #LAST-ORDR-CNTL = 'NEWORD'
                      ELSE
                         CALL OEPGDATA USING INPUT #LAST-ORD-CNTL
                      ENDIF
                      SET ...
                  ENDIF
              ENDFOR
      IF FG-PROCEED
         IF #NO-RELEASED > 0
            DO ...
            SET
         ENDIF
      ENDIF
      IF FG-PROCEED
         IF #LAST-ORD-CNTL = 'NEW-ORD'
            CALL OEPGDATE USING INPUT CUST-ORDER-LINE.ORDER-CNTL-NO
         ENDIF
      ENDIF
     ENDPROC

   <<GET-COR-HDR>> PROCEDURE
      FOR FIRST COR-HEADER-READ
          WHERE COR-HEADER-READ.ORDER-CNTL-NO
```

```
                       = CUST-ORDER-LINE.ORDER-CNTL-NO
       WHEN   NONE
              SET FG-PROCEED FALSE
              SET ATTR 'H' TEMP ON ...
              SET ATTR 'PSH' TEMP ON ...
              BACKOUT
     ENDFOR
  ENDPROC



  <<GET-INV-MST>> PROCEDURE
    FOR FIRST INV-MASTER
        WHERE INV-MASTER.WHSE-NO    = COR-HEADER-READ.WHSE-NO
          AND INV-MASTER.CATALOG-NO = CUST-ORDER-LINE.CATALOG-NO
        WHEN   NONE
              SET FG-PROCEED FALSE
              SET ATTR 'H' TEMP ON ...
              SET ATTR 'PSH' TEMP ON ...
              BACKOUT
     ENDFOR
  ENDPROC
```

Here we have built two functionally cohesive modules and improved the main module to be sequentially cohesive. This is because the main module is now a gateway to the lower modules instead of being the decision maker. We still have control coupling as we are using a flag for control, but we have definitely improved the cohesion levels.

This allows us to more easily understand and modify the main module, and separates the functions into individual components.

The problem of procedural cohesion is worsened with the liberal usage of QUIT and PROCESS NEXT statements. This not only reduces the structure of the program, but it violates the rule of having only one entrance and one exit from a procedure.

```
FOR EACH   PRC-SPLDTL-READ
    WHERE PRC-SPLDTL-READ.CATALOG-NO = WK-CTLG-NO
          IF PRC-SPLDTL-READ.CUST-NO = WK-CUST-NO
          ELSE
              IF PRC-SPLDTL-READ.PRICE-TYPE-CD = 'P'
                  IF PRC-SPLDTL-READ.MARKET    = 'MKT' OR SPACES
                  ELSE
                      PROCESS NEXT
                  ENDIF
```

```
            ELSE
                PROCESS NEXT
            ENDIF
          ENDIF
          IF PRC-SPLDTL-READ.BEG-DATE <= QTY
              AND PRC-SPLDTL-READ.END-QTY >= QTY
          ELSE
              PROCESS NEXT
          ENDIF
          DO COMPARE
   ENDFOR


   <<COMPARE>> PROCEDURE
    IF PRC-SPLDTL-READ.PRICE-TYPE-CD = 'C'
       IF #PRICE-TYPE-CD              = 'P' OR 'Q'
           DO GET-JUL-DATE
           IF S-J-DATE
              DO REPLACE
              QUIT-COMPARE
           ELSE
              QUIT-COMPARE
           ENDIF
       ENDIF
       IF PRC-SPLDTL-READ.DESCEND-DATE <= #DESCEND-DATE
           DO GET-JUL-DATE
           IF S-J-DATE
              DO REPLACE
              QUIT-COMPARE
           ELSE
              QUIT-COMPARE
           ENDIF
       ELSE
           QUIT COMPARE
       ENDIF
    ENDIF
```

In this example we can see the need to understand the function of the entire program to be able to understand any single function. This is because there is no clear or consistent path to the lower modules.

To improve this code, we will begin with the compare paragraph.

```
   <<COMPARE>> PROCEDURE
    IF PRC-SPLDTL-READ.PRICE-TYPE-CD = 'C'
       IF #PRICE-TYPE-CD              = 'P' OR 'Q'
```

```
        DO GET-JUL-DATE
        IF S-J-DATE
           DO REPLACE
        ENDIF
     ELSE
        IF PRC-SPLDTL-READ.DESCEND-DATE <= #DESCEND-DATE
           DO GET-JUL-DATE
           IF S-J-DATE
              DO REPLACE
           ENDIF
        ENDIF
     ENDIF
  ENDIF
```

By replacing one of the ENDIF clauses with an ELSE clause, and allowing the natural fall-through of the program to occur, we improve the readability of the program. We can also see that we improve the cohesion of the two branches of the second IF by isolating them. We also reduce the amount of coupling between the two because they are now independent of each other. We do not have to follow the QUIT in the top leg to understand how we got to the bottom leg.

We can make a similar adjustment to the drive paragraph:

```
FOR EACH   PRC-SPLDTL-READ
    WHERE PRC-SPLDTL-READ.CATALOG-NO       = WK-CTLG-NO
          IF PRC-SPLDTL-READ.BEG-DATE     <= QTY
             AND PRC-SPLDTL-READ.END-QTY >= QTY
             IF PRC-SPLDTL-READ.CUST-NO    = WK-CUST-NO
                DO COMPARE
             ELSE
                IF PRC-SPLDTL-READ.PRICE-TYPE-CD = 'P'
                   IF PRC-SPLDTL-READ.MARKET      = 'MKT' OR SPACES
                      DO COMPARE
                   ENDIF
                ENDIF
             ENDIF
          ENDIF

ENDFOR
```

The purpose of this paragraph is to call the compare paragraph if the working storage field QTY is within the range, and either the CUST-NO matches or the MARKET matches and we have a "P" type record. Since the QTY check affects both types of records, we can move it from the bottom to the top of the structure. This way we will not need to make the CUST or MARKET comparison unless the QTY is in the range. We then have improved the structure of the program by again making each basic structure independent of the other structures, by looking for a specific occurrence to be present instead of using PROCESS NEXTs to eliminate invalid conditions.

In temporal cohesion several functions are related together because they occur at the same time. For example, we could have an order entry program that updates the appropriate inventory records after all of the lines of the order have been entered. This is an example of the improper use of the FOR EACH statement. The program

```
FOR EACH   ORDER-LINE
      WHERE ORDER-LINE.ORDER-NUMBER = WK-ORDER-NUMBER
            DO UPDATE-INV-REC
ENDFOR
```

will still have only one input to the structure. But it will have multiple update outputs, which have nothing to do with each other except that they are all ready to be processed at the same time. To make this structure functionally cohesive, we would change the program to update the inventory record when each individual line, and not the entire order, is completed.

Another problem with temporal cohesion in an on-line system, pointed out by this example, is that it can threaten the integrity of the database. By waiting until all of the lines on the order are processable, another order may be able to slip in and obtain the inventory that we were expecting to find.

This is not to say that all uses of the FOR EACH statement are wrong. But it is important to make sure that the data which is linking the records together is functionally, and not temporally, cohesive. In the program

```
FOR EACH   ORDER-LINE
      WHERE ORDER-LINE.ORDER-NUMBER = WK-ORDER-NUMBER
            DO DISPLAY-LINES
ENDFOR
```

we are displaying all of the lines of the order for the operator's review. It is functionally cohesive because the ORDER-NUMBER that is sent to the data links all of the records of the order together so that they can be displayed. The WK-ORDER-NUMBER is the single input, and the population of the display screen the single task.

In logical cohesion we have separate functions performed by the same piece of code. For example, our inventory relief is normally done at the primary warehouse. However, if we shipped from another warehouse, we must relieve inventory there and make a note of the demand on the primary record.

```
IF SHIPMENT.WAREHOUSE = PRIMARY-WHSE
    MOVE SHIPMENT.WAREHOUSE TO CALL-WHSE
    DO UPDATE-INV-MST
ELSE
    MOVE SHIPMENT.WAREHOUSE TO CALL-WHSE
    DO UPDATE-INV-MST
    MOVE PRIMARY-WHSE TO CALL-WHSE
    DO UPDATE-INV-MST
  ENDIF
ENDPROC
```

Here we are trying to do both types of inventory updates with the same piece of code. If a change is made to one of the update procedures, then a change must be made to the update module, the calling module, and possibly to the other update procedure, thus complicating the problem.

We can also see this as an example of pathological control coupling. The function of the second paragraph is controlled by the values in the calling paragraph. In this example, those values are set somewhere else. Thus to understand what the update module is doing, we must not only understand what the calling module is doing, but how the values of shipping and primary warehouse were set.

To improve this situation, we need to make the following changes:

```
IF SHIPMENT.WAREHOUSE = PRIMARY-WHSE
    DO UPDATE-PRIM-WHSE
ELSE
    DO UPDATE-PRIM-WHSE
    DO UPDT-SPLIT-WHSE
  ENDIF
ENDPROC

<<UPDATE-PRIM-WHSE>> PROCEDURE
  FOR FIRST INV-MASTER
      WHERE INV-MASTER.WARE-HOUSE = PRIMARY-WHSE
```

```
          AND INV-MASTER.PART-NO     = ORDER-LINE.PART-NO
               SET INV-MASTER.QUANTITY-AVAIL
                  = INV-MASTER.QUANTITY-AVAIL - ORDER-LINE.QUANTITY
     ENDFOR
   ENDPROC


   <<UPDT-SPLIT-WHSE>> PROCEDURE
     FOR FIRST INV-MASTER
          WHERE INV-MASTER.WARE-HOUSE = SHIPMENT.WAREHOUSE
            AND INV-MASTER.PART-NO     = ORDER-LINE.PART-NO
                 SET INV-MASTER.QTY-SPLIT
                    = INV-MASTER.QTY-SPLIT       + ORDER-LINE.QUANTITY
     ENDFOR
   ENDPROC
```

Here we have changed each of the two update paragraphs to be functionally cohesive, as they each have one input and a single purpose, which produces a single output. We have also changed their relationship with the calling module to be data coupling instead of external content. This is because the function of the update paragraphs is not controlled by the values of the primary and shipping warehouses. The identity of the records that are processed are changed, but what is done to them is always consistent from record to record.

Conclusions

From the discussion in this chapter, we can see that the key to obtaining a good level of structure is to ensure that each individual module is functionally or sequentially cohesive. For example, an inquiry FOR statement module should only include the population of fields from that one record. The WHEN clauses of a SELECT statement should all relate to an overall function (editing of input, loop escape, option processing). The selection clause of a FOR EACH command should be based on something other than timing.

When we concentrate on writing programs with these levels of cohesion, we will have the benefits of

1. more easily read and understood code
2. more easily modified programs
3. more efficient processing
4. better database integrity

Exercises

1. What are the seven levels of cohesion?
2. What are the three levels of coupling?
3. Why are these concepts important?

Exercises — Answers

1. What are the seven levels of cohesion?

   a. FUNCTIONAL — This is the best in that everything that is done in the module contributes directly to the accomplishment of a single task.
   b. SEQUENTIAL — This serves as a gateway to other functions in the system. Typically, a sequentially cohesive module starts one module, regains control from it when it is done, and passes some data on to a third module. It serves as a control point in the system.
   c. COMMUNICATIONAL — This happens when separate functions that work on common data are grouped in the same module.
   d. PROCEDURAL — This type of cohesion is present when modules are grouped together because they follow the flow of control of the program. This type of cohesion occurs when programs are coded from traditional flow charts.
   e. TEMPORAL — This happens when functions are grouped together merely because they happen at the same time.
   f. LOGICAL — This type of coupling means that functions are grouped together simply because they do similar functions to the same data. The choice of the logic path to be followed is based on a control character that is set somewhere else in the system.
   g. COINCIDENTAL — The modules just happen to be together because of some arbitrary decision.

2. What are the three levels of coupling?

   a. DATA COUPLING — This is the most desirable form of coupling, wherein data is passed to a module to begin the processing of that module, or to return control to the calling module.
   b. CONTROL COUPLING — This is the second level of coupling, and is not as acceptable as data coupling. In this

type of coupling a flag is passed up or down the program hierarchy to control the processing of the receiving module.

c. PATHOLOGICAL COUPLING — This is, as its name infers, the worst type of coupling. The first module may extract some data from the second, change it, or branch to some specific instruction in the second or an entirely different module, based on some control.

3. Why are these concepts important?

Through these concepts we have a basis from which to judge the structure of a module.

Notes

1. David King, *Current Practices in Software Development*, Yourdon Press, New York, New York, 1984, pp. 21–23.
2. Ibid. Pp. 20–21

12

IDEAL Case Study

Now that we have made a detailed study of the different features of the IDEAL language, we can discuss how they can be combined to create an intricate system. In this example, we will be building a basic freight processing system for our distribution company.

In this company, each order from the customer can be broken into one or more shipments from the warehouse, depending on the availability of the material that was ordered. Each shipment is represented on the database by a shipment-header record and a series of shipment lines. The shipment-header record contains the information that is held in common by all of the lines.

SHIPMENT-HEADER
ORDER-NO	The number that uniquely identifies the order
SHIPMENT-NO	The number that uniquely identifies the shipment
SHIPPING-WHSE	The warehouse from which the equipment was shipped
CUST-NO	The customer who ordered the material
CUST-SHIP-TO	The address where it was sent
DATE-SHIPPED	The date it left the warehouse
CARRIER-CD	The code for the trucker who carried it
FREIGHT-CHARGE	The portion of the total freight charge that is allocated to this order

SHIPMENT-WEIGHT   Total calculated weight of shipment

The shipment lines contain the data that is unique to each of the items that were ordered.

SHIPMENT-LINE

ORDER-NO	The number that uniquely identifies the order
SHIPMENT-NO	The number that uniquely identifies the shipment
LINE-NO	The number that uniquely identifies the line
EQUIPMENT-NO	The material that was shipped
QTY-SHIPPED	The number of units that were shipped
QTY-EXPECTED	The number of units that we expect to ship
LINE-WEIGHT	Total calculated weight of line

Multiple shipments can be sent to the same place on the same truck. These shipments are grouped together under what is called a *bill of lading*. To track these bill of lading groups, we will create three more database tables. These are the BOFL-HEADER, the BOFL-SHIPMENT, and the BOFL-LINE records. The BOFL-HEADER record again contains the data which is common to all of the shipments:

BOFL-HEADER

BILL-LADING-NO	The number that uniquely identifies the bill of lading
CARRIER-CD	The code for the trucker who carried it
FREIGHT-CHARGE	Total charge for the movement of the material on the bill of lading
CALCULATED-WGT	Calculated total weight of the material
SCALE-WGT	The actual physical weight of the material, measured on a scale in the warehouse
PRINT-IND	This flag tells the print program to select this record for processing
EXTRACT-IND	This flag tells the extract program to select this record for processing
EXTRACT-DATE	The date the record was extracted to be sent to a third party for processing

The BOFL-SHIPMENT record shows a list of the shipments that are covered by this bill of lading.

BOFL-SHIPMENT

BILL-LADING-NO	Number that uniquely identifies the bill of lading
ORDER-NO	The number that uniquely identifies the order
SHIPMENT-NO	The number that uniquely identifies the shipment

ORDER-NO and SHIPMENT-NO are the same fields that appear on the SHIPMENT HEADER. This means that they are "foreign keys" on this record.

The BOFL-LINE record contains a listing of the FREIGHT CLASSes of the EQUIPMENT that was shipped and how much material in that class was shipped, measured in pounds.

BOFL-LINE

BILL-LADING-NO	The number that uniquely identifies the bill of lading
FREIGHT-CLASS	freight class of the material being shipped
WEIGHT	How much material of this class was on the truck, in pounds

The assignment of freight class is dependent on the equipment's size, weight, density, value, etc. This is because freight charges in a truck are dependent not only on weight but on how much physical room the material takes up on the truck. While 1000 pounds of styrofoam does not weigh more than 1000 pounds of bricks, the trucker must charge more per pound to cover the entire cost of moving the load of styrofoam because he or she cannot carry as much total weight.

Because freight class and weight are attributes of the equipment being shipped, we can add these fields to the equipment database. We will also add a domain table containing freight class and the description of each freight class.

The calculation of the freight charge is dependent on

1. The freight class of the material being shipped
2. The distance between the shipping point and the destination

3. The weight of the material
4. Any negotiated discount we get from the carrier

To make our calculations, we will store this data in a series of database tables. The freight rate table was computed for us by another company which (for a fee) keeps track of the different rates. We then get that data from them on a tape and load it into our system.

FRT-RATE-RCD

SHIPPING-WHSE	The warehouse from which the material was sent
FREIGHT-CLASS	The freight class of the material being shipped
SHIP-TO-ZIP	The first three characters of the zip code of the destination address
WEIGHT-BREAK	The break point amount (Anything lower than this amount and higher than the amount on the last record read, gets this rate.)
RATE	The amount to charge per 100 pounds of shipment

We will also have a carrier domain table containing the CARRIER-CD, the CARRIER-NAME, and the DISCOUNT percentage from the standard rate that we have negotiated with this carrier.

This system will then have the following functions:

- Provide for the security of the entire on-line system.
- Provide a means of maintaining the carrier and freight-rate domain tables on line.
- Group shipments together into bills of lading, computing their total weight and freight charges.
- Enter the QTY-SHIPPED into SHIPMENT-LINES that were generated by another part of the system.
- Allocate the charges from the bill of lading evenly among the shipment records, based on their part of the total charge.
- Print the bill of lading documents.
- Extract the bill of lading records and send a dataset to a third party for processing.
- Provide a report showing how much business we are doing with each carrier.
- Provide a means of updating the freight-rate tables from a tape file, and produce a report of changes.

We can now discuss how IDEAL can be used to deal with each of these challenges.

Provide for the Security of the Entire On-Line System

The key to ensuring the security of any DP system is to provide as many levels of security as possible. While no system is foolproof, one may be able to make it so hard for unauthorized people to get into the system that they will go and bother someone else.

The first layer of security must be physical security around the site, and around the terminals with access to the machine where the system resides.

The second layer of security will be the standard CICS and IDEAL sign-ons. These facilities will only allow those with a recognizable log-on ID to access the system. We can further augment this layer by the way we define the ID to IDEAL. When we recall our discussion in Chapter 9 of the ID-FILL-IN screen:

```
------------------------------------------------------------------------------
IDEAL: USER DEFINITION                                 SYS: DEV    FILL-IN


PERSON NAME      _____      IDEAL USER ID  ____

FULL NAME        _____

PASSWORD         _____

IDENTIFICATION   _____

ORG. UNIT        _____

DATE CREATED     _____

IDEAL PRIVILEGES:  MARK AT LEAST 1 WITH A "X" TO ENABLE IDEAL SIGNON


(_) IDEAL ADMINISTRATOR (ALLOWS USE OF ANY IDEAL FACILITY)

(_) PRINT ADMINISTRATOR (ALLOWS CONTROL OF PRINTING FACILITY + SIGNON)

(_) DVW  ADMINISTRATOR (ALLOWS CATALOGING DATAVIEW DEFINITIONS+SIGNON)

(_) IDEAL USER          (ALLOWS SIGNON AND ALL NON-PRIVILEGED FACILITIY)


ASSIGNED      INDICATE AT LEAST 1 ASSIGNED SYSTEM):

SYSTEM(S)    CONTROL  UPDATE   READ    UPDATE-PNL  UPDATE-RPT  RUN-PROD
  ___        ( _ )    ( _ )   ( _ )   ( _ )        ( _ )        ( _ )
  ___        ( _ )    ( _ )   ( _ )   ( _ )        ( _ )        ( _ )
  ___        ( _ )    ( _ )   ( _ )   ( _ )        ( _ )        ( _ )
  ___        ( _ )    ( _ )   ( _ )   ( _ )        ( _ )        ( _ )
------------------------------------------------------------------------------
```

we will see that the ID can be limited in what it can do. If we set up most of the IDs to be IDEAL users, with only RUN-PROD privledges, we will limit their ability to only running production status programs. They will not be able to view or change any of the source code in the system.

A third layer of security can be built using the IDEAL SIGNON member. When the user logs into the IDEAL system, their SIGNON member is automatically executed. To provide additional system security, we can build the member so that it will not allow the ID to display a command line area. We can then tell it to run a MENU program, and when the menu program is completed, we can automatically sign off of IDEAL.

```
SET COMMAND LINE 0
SET RUN QUIT IDEAL Y
SET $FINAL-ID 'QUIT'
RUN MAINMENU
OFF
```

Here IDEAL will remove the user from the system as soon as the MAINMENU program is ended. To provide additional security, we can restrict the menu options that the user will see on the screen. We can do this by either building multiple menu screens and putting them in different IDs according to usage, or building a dynamic menu program.

For this feature, we would build one domain table that contains a listing of user IDs and the menu options that they can use, and another that shows the menu options and their descriptions. The MENU program would then use the $USER-ID function to access these domain tables.

```
<<LOAD-MENU-SCRN>> PROCEDURE
   MOVE $PANEL-GROUP-OCCURS(MENUPNL) TO WK-PANEL-LIMIT
   MOVE 00                           TO WK-PANEL-SUBSR
   MOVE $USER-ID                     TO WK-USER-ID
   FOR EACH  ACCESS-RECORD
       WHERE ACCESS-RECORD.USER-ID = WK-USER-ID
           FOR EACH  MENU-RECORD
               WHERE MENU-RECORD.MENU-OPTION = ACCESS-RECORD.MENU-OPTION
                   ADD 1 TO WK-PANEL-SUBSR
                   IF WK-PANEL-SUBSR LE WK-PANEL-LIMIT
                      DO LD-MENU-OPTION
```

```
                    ENDIF
                ENDFOR
        ENDFOR
    ENDPROC
```

The LD-MENU-OPTION procedure would then move the menu option and its description to the MENUPNL screen.

The user would enter the requested option, and the menu program would check the ACCESS domain table, giving or denying access to the requested program based on the result.

```
FOR FIRST ACCESS-RECORD
    WHERE ACCESS-RECORD.USER-ID     = WK-USER-ID
      AND ACCESS-RECORD.MENU-OPTION = MENUPNL.SELECTION
          MOVE 'Y' TO FG-ACCESS-FG            :ACCESS IS ALLOWED
    WHEN  NONE
          MOVE 'N' TO FG-ACCESS-FG
          FOR FIRST MENU-RECORD
              WHERE MENU-RECORD.MENU-OPTION = ACCESS-RECORD.MENU-OPTION
                    MOVE 'ACCESS DENIED'         TO MENUPNL.MESSAGE
                WHEN  NONE
                    MOVE 'OPTION DOES NOT EXIST' TO MENUPNL.MESSAGE
          ENDFOR
ENDFOR
```

The program will then only call the requested program if there is an access record for this combined user ID and selection.

With these layers of security, we limit access to those who

1. can gain physical access to the computer terminals.
2. have a valid CICS log-on.
3. have a valid IDEAL password and log-on.
4. are authorized to run IDEAL production programs.
5. are authorized to use the specific application.

Provide a Means of Maintaining the Carrier and Freight-Rate Tables

The programs that are used to maintain the carrier and freight-rate tables are entries in the menu-option database, and are called from the main menu.

Since each carrier table record completely describes a single carrier, we will do all of the maintenance to it with one on-line panel and program. The panel definition for this option is as follows:

```
IDEAL: PANEL PARAMETERS     PNL CARRPNL  (001) TEST     SYS: DEV FILL-IN


START       FIELD SYMBOL ^ NEW     FIELD SYMBOL +
END         FIELD SYMBOL ; DELETE FIELD SYMBOL *
REPEATING GROUP SYMBOL @


INPUT  FILL CHARACTER   S (S=SPACE, L=LOWVAL, Z=ZEROES, U=_,OTHER=ITSELF
OUTPUT FILL CHARACTER   U (S=SPACE, L=LOWVAL, Z=ZERORS, U=_,OTHER=ITSELF
NON-DISPLAY CHARACTER   S (S=SPACE, OTHER=AS SPECIFIED)
ERROR FILL CHARACTER    * (AS SPECIFIED)
CASE TRANSLATION        U (U=UPPER, M=MIXED)


REQUIRED                N (Y=YES, N=NO)
ERROR HANDLING          B (N=NONE, *=FILL W/ERRORFILL, H=HIGH INTENSITY,
                          (B=BOTH: H IF ILLEGAL VALUE & * IF REQ MISSING


PANEL WIDTH             080 (A VALUE BETWEEN 80 and 236)
PF1=HELP, PF3=CLARIFY   Y (Y=YES, N=NO)
PF7=SCR -, PF8=SCR+     N (N=NO, Y=OPT Y, Z=OPT Z)
  PF10=SCR TOP, PF11=SCR BOT    (OPTION Y)
  PF10=SCR LEFT,PF11=SCR RIGHT (OPTION Z)
EDIT-RULE ERROR PROC    C (C=CLARIFY COMMAND, A=APPLICATION)
PROCESS APPL ON SCROLL N (Y=YES,N=NO)
HELP PANEL NAME   _____   VERSION ___
PREFIX PANEL NAME _____   VERSION ___
SUFFIX PANEL NAME _____   VERSION ___
------------------------- B O T T O M -----------------------------
```

```
IDEAL: PANEL LAYOUT      PNL CARRPNL  (001) TEST     SYS: DEV FILL-IN
START:     END: ;     NEW: +     DELETE: *     REPEAT: @
....+....1....+....2....+....3....+....4....+....5....+....6....+...7..
   +_____ ;    +CARRIER CODE DATABASE MAINTENANCE PROGRAM;

  +OPTION; +_; +(A=ADD V=VIEW U=UPDATE D=DELETE);

  +CARRIER CODE; +__ ;
  +CARRIER NAME; +_____ ;
```

```
+DISCOUNT PCT; +_____;


+MESSAGE;        +_____;
```

```
============================B O T T O M==================================
```

```
------------------------------------------------------------------------
IDEAL: FIELD SUMMARY TABLE    PNL CARRPNL  (001) TEST  SYS: DEV FILL-IN
========================================================================
    ^_____;    ^CARRIER CODE DATABASE MAINTENANCE PROGRAM;
    1              2
    ^OPTION;       ^_; ^(A=ADD V=VIEW U=UPDATE D=DELETE);
    3              4   5
........................................................................
SEQ LV FIELD NAME       ATTR   T LEN  IN.DP OCC COMMENTS
--- -- --------------- ------ - ---- ----- --- ------------------------
 1  2 CURRENT-DATE     PSL    X   8
 2  2                  PSL    X  38            CARRIER CODE DATABASE MA
 3  2                  PSL    X   6            OPTION
 4  2 OPTION           UALEC  X   1
 5  2                  PSL    X  30            (A=ADD V=VIEW U=UPDATE D
 6  2                  PSL    X  12            CARRIER CODE
 7  2 CARRIER-CD       UALE   X   2
 8  2                  PSL    X  14            CARRIER NAME
 9  2 CARRIER-NAME     UALE   X  10
10  2                  PSL    X   5            DISCOUNT PCT
11  2 DISCOUNT-PCT     UNL    N   5    5
16  2                  PSL    X   7            MESSAGE
17  2 MESSAGE          PSL    X  41
```

The program would be as follows:

```
<<CARRIER>> PROCEDURE
  REFRESH  CARRPNL        : REFRESHES THE PANEL
  MOVE $DATE('MM/DD/YY') TO CARRPNL.CURRENT-DATE
  TRANSMIT CARRPNL        : TRANSMIT THE PANEL TO INITIALIZE MAIN LOOP
  LOOP UNTIL $PF2(CARRPNL) : PROCESS UNTIL USER HITS PFKEY 2
        SELECT CARRPNL.OPTION
```

```
                    WHEN 'A'  DO EDIT-INPUT
                              DO ADD-RECORD
                    WHEN 'D'  DO DELETE-RECORD
                    WHEN 'U'  DO EDIT-INPUT
                              DO UPDATE-RECORD
                    WHEN 'V'  DO VIEW-RECORD
                    WHEN NONE DO INVALID-SELECT
                  ENDSELECT
                  TRANSMIT CARRPNL
          ENDLOOP
      ENDPROC


      :*********************************************************************
      :**THIS PARAGRAPH EDITS THE INPUT TO MAKE SURE THAT THE DISCOUNT    **
      :**PERCENTAGE AND THE CARRIER NAME HAVE BEEN ENTERED.               **
      :*********************************************************************
      <<EDIT-INPUT>> PROCEDURE
        MOVE 'Y'            TO FG-INPUT-CORR
        IF CARRPNL.CARRIER-NAME LE $SPACES
           MOVE $LOW        TO CARRPNL.CARRIER-NAME
           SET ATTR 'UAHE' ON CARRPNL.CARRIER-NAME
           MOVE 'N'         TO FG-INPUT-CORR
        ELSE
           SET ATTR 'UALE' ON CARRPNL.CARRIER-NAME
        ENDIF

        IF CARRPNL.DISCOUNT-PCT EQ 00000
           SET ATTR 'UNH'  ON CARRPNL.DISCOUNT-PCT
           MOVE 'N'         TO FG-INPUT-CORR
        ELSE
           SET ATTR 'UNL'  ON CARRPNL.DISCOUNT-PCT
        ENDIF

        IF FG-INPUT-CORR = 'N'
           MOVE 'CORRECT HIGHLIGHTED FIELDS' TO CARRPNL.MESSAGE
        ENDIF
      ENDPROC


      :*********************************************************************
      :**THIS PARAGRAPH ADDS THE EDITED RECORD TO THE DATABASE.          **
      :*********************************************************************
      <<ADD-RECORD>> PROCEDURE
        IF FG-INPUT-CORR = 'Y'
```

```
      FOR NEW CARRIER-RCD
          MOVE CARRPNL.CARRIER-CD            TO CARRIER-RCD.CARRIER-CD
          MOVE CARRPNL.CARRIER-NAME          TO CARRIER-RCD.CARRIER-NAME
          MOVE CARRPNL.DISCOUNT-PCT          TO CARRIER-RCD.DISCOUNT-PCT
          MOVE 'CARRIER ADDED'               TO CARRPNL.MESSAGE
      WHEN DUPLICATE
          MOVE 'CARRIER ALREADY EXISTS'      TO CARRPNL.MESSAGE
      ENDFOR
   ENDIF
 ENDPROC


:*********************************************************************
:**THIS PARAGRAPH DELETES THE REQUESTED RECORD FROM THE DATABASE.   **
:*********************************************************************
<<DELETE-RECORD>> PROCEDURE
  FOR FIRST CARRIER-RCD
      WHERE CARRIER-RCD.CARRIER-CD          EQ CARRPNL.CARRIER-CD
          DELETE CARRIER-RCD
          MOVE 'CARRIER DELETED              TO CARRPNL.MESSAGE
      WHEN  NONE
          MOVE 'CARRIER NOT FOUND'          TO CARRPNL.MESSAGE
  ENDFOR
ENDPROC


:*********************************************************************
:**THIS PARAGRAPH ADDS THE EDITED DATA TO THE RECORD ON THE DATABASE.**
:*********************************************************************
<<UPDATE-RECORD>> PROCEDURE
  IF FG-INPUT-CORR = 'Y'
     FOR FIRST CARRIER-RCD
         WHERE CARRIER-RCD.CARRIER-CD       EQ CARRPNL.CARRIER-CD
             MOVE CARRPNL.CARRIER-NAME  TO CARRIER-RCD.CARRIER-NAME
             MOVE CARRPNL.DISCOUNT-PCT  TO CARRIER-RCD.DISCOUNT-PCT
             MOVE 'CARRIER UPDATED'     TO CARRPNL.MESSAGE
         WHEN  NONE
             MOVE 'CARRIER NOT FOUND'   TO CARRPNL.MESSAGE
     ENDFOR
  ENDIF
ENDPROC


:*********************************************************************
:**THIS PARAGRAPH DISPLAYS THE REQUESTED RECORD ON THE SCREEN.      **
:*********************************************************************
<<VIEW-RECORD>> PROCEDURE
```

```
FOR FIRST CARRIER-RCD
    WHERE CARRIER-RCD.CARRIER-CD        EQ CARRPNL.CARRIER-CD
          MOVE CARRIER-RCD.CARRIER-NAME TO CARRPNL.CARRIER-NAME
          MOVE CARRIER-RCD.DISCOUNT-PCT TO CARRPNL.DISCOUNT-PCT
          MOVE 'CARRIER FOUND           TO CARRPNL.MESSAGE
    WHEN NONE
          MOVE $LOW                     TO CARRPNL.CARRIER-NAME
          MOVE 00000                    TO CARRPNL.DISCOUNT-PCT
          MOVE 'CARRIER NOT FOUND'      TO CARRPNL.MESSAGE
    ENDFOR
ENDPROC


:********************************************************************
:**THIS PARA INFORMS THE USER THAT THEY HAVE CHOSEN AN INVALID OPTION**
:********************************************************************
<INVALID-SELECT> PROCEDURE
    MOVE 'INVALID OPTION'               TO CARRPNL.MESSAGE
ENDPROC


============================B O T T O M============================
```

All of this is relatively straightforward.

The program to maintain the freight-rate table is a little more complicated because the basic "unit of work" is made up of a series of records, rather than a single record. Here the unit of work is made up of records with the same SHIPPING-WHSE, FREIGHT-CLASS, and SHIP-TO-ZIP. We will then have a repeating group on our panel for each of the weight-break changes.

The panel definition screens would be populated as follows:

```
-----------------------------------------------------------------------
IDEAL: PANEL PARAMETERS    PNL FRTRATE  (001) TEST    SYS: DEV FILL-IN


START     FIELD SYMBOL ^ NEW    FIELD SYMBOL +
END       FIELD SYMBOL ; DELETE FIELD SYMBOL *
REPEATING GROUP SYMBOL @


INPUT  FILL CHARACTER  S (S=SPACE, L=LOWVAL, Z=ZEROES, U= ,OTHER=ITSELF
OUTPUT FILL CHARACTER  U (S=SPACE, L=LOWVAL, Z=ZERORS, U=_,OTHER=ITSELF
NON-DISPLAY CHARACTER  S (S=SPACE, OTHER=AS SPECIFIED)
ERROR FILL CHARACTER   * (AS SPECIFIED)
CASE TRANSLATION       U (U=UPPER, M=MIXED)


REQUIRED               N (Y=YES, N=NO)
```

```
ERROR HANDLING         B (N=NONE, *=FILL W/ERRORFILL, H=HIGH INTENSITY,
                          (B=BOTH: H IF ILLEGAL VALUE & * IF REQ MISSING


PANEL WIDTH          080 (A VALUE BETWEEN 80 and 236)
PF1=HELP, PF3=CLARIFY   Y (Y=YES, N=NO)
PF7=SCR -, PF8=SCR+    N (N=NO, Y=OPT Y, Z=OPT Z)
  PF10=SCR TOP, PF11=SCR BOT   (OPTION Y)
  PF10=SCR LEFT,PF11=SCR RIGHT (OPTION Z)
EDIT-RULE ERROR PROC   C (C=CLARIFY COMMAND, A=APPLICATION)
PROCESS APPL ON SCROLL N (Y=YES,N=NO)
HELP PANEL NAME    _____    VERSION ___
PREFIX PANEL NAME _____    VERSION ___
SUFFIX PANEL NAME _____    VERSION ___
-------------------------- B O T T O M --------------------------------
```

```
IDEAL: PANEL LAYOUT       PNL FRTRATE  (001) TEST    SYS: DEV FILL-IN
START: ^   END: ;     NEW: +     DELETE: *     REPEAT: @
....+....1....+....2....+....3....+....4....+....5....+....6....+...7..
   +_____;    +FREIGHT RATE DATABASE MAINTENANCE PROGRAM;

  +OPTION; +_; +(A=ADD V=VIEW U=UPDATE D=DELETE);

  +SHIPPING-WHSE +___; +                            ;
  +FREIGHT-CLASS;+___; +                            ;
  +SHIP-TO-ZIP ; +___;

 +-------------------  -------------------  -------------------;
 +WEIGHT IN  RATE PER  WEIGHT IN  RATE PER  WEIGHT IN  RATE PER;
 + POUNDS    POUND     POUNDS     POUND     POUNDS     POUND ;
  @_____;  @_____;  @_____;  @_____;  @_____;  @_____;

  +MESSAGE;     +_____;




========================B O T T O M================================


-----------------------------------------------------------------------
IDEAL: FIELD SUMMARY TABLE    PNL FRTRATE  (001) TEST  SYS: DEV FILL-IN
=======================================================================
```

```
^_____;      ^FREIGHT RATE DATABASE MAINTENANCE PROGRAM;
1               2
^OPTION;         ^_;  ^(A=ADD V=VIEW U=UPDATE D=DELETE);
3               4    5
.................................................................
SEQ LV FIELD NAME      ATTR   T LEN  IN.DP OCC COMMENTS
--- -- ------------- ------ - ---- ----- --- ---------------------
 1  2 CURRENT-DATE     PSL    X   8
 2  2                  PSL    X  38           CARRIER CODE DATABASE MA
 3  2                  PSL    X   6           OPTION
 4  2 OPTION           UALEC  X   1
 5  2                  PSL    X  30           (A=ADD V=VIEW U=UPDATE D
 6  2                  PSL    X  12           SHIPPING WHSE
 7  2 SHIPPING-WHSE    UALE   X   3
 8  2 WHSE-NAME        PSL    X   3
 9  2                  PSL    X  14           FREIGHT CLASS
10  2 FREIGHT-CLASS    UALE   X   3
11  2 FRT-CLS-DESC     PSL    X   3
10  2                  PSL    X   5           SHIP-TO-ZIP
11  2 SHIP-TO-ZIP      UNL    N   3
13  2                  PSL    X  80           WEIGHT IN    RATE PER   W
14  2                  PSL    X  80           POUNDS       POUND      P
15  2                                      9
16   3 WEIGHT-COL-1    UNL    N   7
17   3 RATE-COL-1      UNL    N   5
18   3 WEIGHT-COL-2    UNL    N   7
19   3 RATE-COL-2      UNL    N   5
20   3 WEIGHT-COL-3    UNL    N   7
21   3 RATE-COL-3      UNL    N   5
22  2                  PSL    X   7           MESSAGE
23  2 MESSAGE          PSL    X  41
```

```
_____

    _____      FREIGHT RATE DATABASE MAINTENANCE PROGRAM


    OPTION      (A=ADD V=VIEW U=UPDATE D=DELETE)


    SHIPPING-WHSE   ___
    FREIGHT-CLASS   ___
    SHIP-TO-ZIP     ___


    --------------------  --------------------  --------------------
    WEIGHT IN   RATE PER  WEIGHT IN   RATE PER  WEIGHT IN   RATE PER
     POUNDS      POUND     POUNDS      POUND     POUNDS      POUND
```

```
————————        ——————        ————————        ——————        ————————        ——————
————————        ——————        ————————        ——————        ————————        ——————
————————        ——————        ————————        ——————        ————————        ——————
————————        ——————        ————————        ——————        ————————        ——————
————————        ——————        ————————        ——————        ————————        ——————
————————        ——————        ————————        ——————        ————————        ——————
————————        ——————        ——————        ——————        ————————        ——————
————————        ——————        ————————        ——————        ————————        ——————
————————        ——————        ————————        ——————        ————————        ——————

MESSAGE            _____
===========================B  O  T  T  O  M==================================
```

The program will have the same basic structure as the CARRIER
program, except for the addition of the repeating group on the panel,
and the fact that since this is now a more complex data group, we
want to make sure that the data is viewed before the record is updated or deleted.

```
<<FRTRATE>> PROCEDURE
  REFRESH  FRTRATE          : REFRESHES THE PANEL
  MOVE $DATE('MM/DD/YY') TO FRTRATE.CURRENT-DATE
  TRANSMIT FRTRATE          : TRANSMIT THE PANEL TO INITIALIZE MAIN LOOP
  LOOP UNTIL $PF2(FRTRATE) : PROCESS UNTIL USER HITS PFKEY 2
          MOVE 'Y'    TO FG-INPUT-CORR
          SELECT FRTRATE.OPTION
            WHEN 'A'  DO EDIT-INPUT
                      DO ADD-RECORD-SEC
            WHEN 'D'  DO CHECK-VIEW
                      DO DELETE-RECORD
            WHEN 'U'  DO EDIT-INPUT
                      DO CHECK-VIEW
                      DO UPD-RECORD-SEC
            WHEN 'V'  DO REFRESH-FRTRATE
                      DO EDIT-INPUT
                      DO VIEW-RECORD
            WHEN NONE DO INVALID-SELECT
          ENDSELECT
          IF FRTRATE.OPTION NOT EQ 'V'
             DO RESET-LAST-VIEW
          ENDIF
          TRANSMIT FRTRATE
      ENDLOOP
  ENDPROC
```

```
:*********************************************************************
:**THIS AREA EDITS THE INPUT TO MAKE SURE THAT A VALID SHIPPING WHSE,**
:**FREIGHT CLASS, AND ZIP-CODE HAVE BEEN ENTERED                    **
:*********************************************************************
<<EDIT-INPUT>> PROCEDURE
  IF FRTRATE.SHIPPING-WHSE LE $SPACES
     SET ATTR 'UAHE'        ON FRTRATE.SHIPPING-WHSE
     MOVE $LOW              TO FRTRATE.SHIPPING-WHSE
     MOVE 'N'               TO FG-INPUT-CORR
     MOVE 'ENTER WHSE'      TO FRTRATE.WHSE-NAME
  ELSE
     FOR FIRST WAREHOUSE-RCD
        WHERE WAREHOUSE-RCD.WHSE-NO       EQ FRTRATE.SHIPPING-WHSE
              MOVE WAREHOUSE-RCD.WHSE-NAME TO FRTRATE.WHSE-NAME
              SET ATTR 'UALE'             ON FRTRATE.SHIPPING-WHSE
        WHEN  NONE
              MOVE 'N'                    TO FG-INPUT-CORR
              MOVE 'NOT FOUND'            TO FRTRATE.WHSE-NAME
              SET ATTR 'UAHE'             ON FRTRATE.SHIPPING-WHSE
     ENDFOR
  ENDIF


  IF FRTRATE.FREIGHT-CLASS LE $SPACES
     MOVE $LOW             ON FRTRATE.FREIGHT-CLASS
     SET ATTR 'UAHE'       ON FRTRATE.FREIGHT-CLASS
     MOVE 'N'              TO FG-INPUT-CORR
     MOVE 'ENTER FRT CLS'  TO FRTRATE.FRT-CLS-DESC
  ELSE
     FOR FIRST FRT-CLASS-RCD
        WHERE FRT-CLASS-RCD.FREIGHT-CLASS     EQ FRTRATE.FREIGHT-CLASS
              MOVE FRT-CLASS-RCD.DESCRIPTION TO FRTRATE.FRT-CLS-DESC
              SET ATTR 'UALE'               ON FRTRATE.FREIGHT-CLASS
        WHEN  NONE
              MOVE 'NOT FOUND'              TO FRTRATE.FRT-CLS-DESC
              SET ATTR 'UAHE'               ON FRTRATE.FREIGHT-CLASS
              MOVE 'N'                      TO FG-INPUT-CORR
     ENDFOR
  ENDIF


  IF FRTRATE.SHIP-TO-ZIP LE $SPACES
     MOVE $LOW        TO FRTRATE.SHIP-TO-ZIP
     SET ATTR 'UAHE' ON FRTRATE.SHIP-TO-ZIP
     MOVE 'N'         TO FG-INPUT-CORR
  ELSE
```

```
        SET ATTR 'UALE' ON FRTRATE.SHIP-TO-ZIP
    ENDIF


  IF FG-INPUT-CORR = 'N'
      MOVE 'CORRECT HIGHLIGHTED FIELDS' TO FRTRATE.MESSAGE
  ENDIF
ENDPROC


:****************************************************************************
:**THIS AREA ADDS THE EDITED RECORD TO THE DATABASE            **
:****************************************************************************
<<ADD-RECORD-SEC>> PROCEDURE
  IF FG-INPUT-CORR = 'Y'
      MOVE $SPACES                TO FRTRATE.MESSAGE
      DO INT-CHK-WEIGHT
      LOOP UNTIL FG-PROC-COMP = 'Y'
              DO SEL-CHK-WEIGHT
              DO ADD-RECORD
      ENDLOOP
      IF FRTRATE.MESSAGE = $SPACES
         MOVE 'RATE TABLE ADDED' TO FRTRATE.MESSAGE
      ENDIF
  ENDIF
ENDPROC


<<ADD-RECORD>> PROCEDURE
  FOR   NEW FRTRATE-RCD
          MOVE FRTRATE.SHIPPING-WHSE        TO FRTRATE-RCD.SHIPPING-WHSE
          MOVE FRTRATE.FREIGHT-CLASS        TO FRTRATE-RCD.FREIGHT-CLASS
          MOVE FRTRATE.SHIP-TO-ZIP          TO FRTRATE-RCD.SHIP-TO-ZIP
          MOVE WK-CHK-WEIGHT                TO FRTRATE-RCD.WEIGHT
          MOVE WK-CHK-RATE                  TO FRTRATE-RCD.RATE
    WHEN DUPLICATE
     ·   BACKOUT
         MOVE 'RATE TABLE ALREADY EXISTS' TO FRTRATE.MESSAGE
  ENDFOR
ENDPROC


:****************************************************************************
:**THIS AREA DELETES THE REQUESTED RECORD FROM THE DATABASE        **
:****************************************************************************
<<DELETE-RECORD>> PROCEDURE
  IF FG-INPUT-CORR = 'Y'
      FOR FIRST FRTRATE-RCD
```

```
            WHERE FRTRATE-RCD.SHIPPING-WHSE     EQ FRTRATE.SHIPPING-WHSE
              AND FRTRATE-RCD.FREIGHT-CLASS     EQ FRTRATE.FREIGHT-CLASS
              AND FRTRATE-RCD.SHIP-TO-ZIP       EQ FRTRATE.SHIP-TO-ZIP
                  DELETE FRTRATE-RCD
            WHEN  NONE
                  MOVE 'RATE TABLE NOT FOUND'  TO FRTRATE.MESSAGE
        ENDFOR
        IF FRTRATE.MESSAGE = $SPACES
           MOVE 'RATE TABLE DELETED'            TO FRTRATE.MESSAGE
        ENDIF
     ENDIF
  ENDPROC


  :***********************************************************************
  :**THIS AREA MOVES THE EDITED DATA TO THE RECORD ON THE DATABASE      **
  :***********************************************************************
  <<UPD-RECORD-SEC>> PROCEDURE
    IF FG-INPUT-CORR = 'Y'
       MOVE $SPACES                    TO FRTRATE.MESSAGE
       DO INT-CHK-WEIGHT
       LOOP UNTIL FG-PROC-COMP = 'Y'
               DO SEL-CHK-WEIGHT
               DO UPDATE-RECORD
       ENDLOOP
       IF FRTRATE.MESSAGE = $SPACES
          MOVE 'RATE TABLE UPDATED' TO FRTRATE.MESSAGE
       ENDIF
     ENDIF
  ENDPROC


  <<UPDATE-RECORD>> PROCEDURE
    FOR EACH   FRTRATE-RCD
        WHERE FRTRATE-RCD.SHIPPING-WHSE     EQ FRTRATE.SHIPPING-WHSE
          AND FRTRATE-RCD.FREIGHT-CLASS     EQ FRTRATE.FREIGHT-CLASS
          AND FRTRATE-RCD.SHIP-TO-ZIP       EQ FRTRATE.SHIP-TO-ZIP
          AND FRTRATE-RCD.WEIGHT            EQ FRTRATE.WK-CHK-WEIGHT
             MOVE WK-CHK-RATE               TO FRTRATE-RCD.RATE
         WHEN  NONE
               MOVE 'RATE TABLE NOT FOUND' TO FRTRATE.MESSAGE
      ENDFOR
  ENDPROC


  :***********************************************************************
  :** PARA REFRESHES THE PANEL, AND THEN RESTORES THE HEADER FIELDS ON **
```

```
:** THE DISPLAY                                              **
:******************************************************************
<<REFRESH-FRTRATE>> PROCEDURE
  MOVE FRTRATE.SHIPPING-WHSE          TO WK-LAST-VIEW.SHIPPING-WHSE
  MOVE FRTRATE.FREIGHT-CLASS          TO WK-LAST-VIEW.FREIGHT-CLASS
  MOVE FRTRATE.SHIP-TO-ZIP            TO WK-LAST-VIEW.SHIP-TO-ZIP
  REFRESH FRTRATE
  MOVE WK-LAST-VIEW.SHIPPING-WHSE     TO FRTRATE.SHIPPING-WHSE
  MOVE WK-LAST-VIEW.FREIGHT-CLASS     TO FRTRATE.FREIGHT-CLASS
  MOVE WK-LAST-VIEW.SHIP-TO-ZIP       TO FRTRATE.SHIP-TO-ZIP
  MOVE $DATE('MM/DD/YY')              TO FRTRATE.CURRENT-DATE
ENDPROC


:******************************************************************
:**THIS AREA DISPLAYS THE REQUESTED RECORD ON THE SCREEN        **
:******************************************************************
<<VIEW-RECORD-SEC>> PROCEDURE
  MOVE 1                              TO WK-COLUMN
  MOVE 0                              TO WK-SUBSR
  MOVE $PANEL-GROUP-OCCURS(FRTRATE)   TO WK-LIMIT
  DO REFRESH-FRTRATE
  FOR EACH  FRTRATE-RCD
      WHERE FRTRATE-RCD.SHIPPING-WHSE  EQ FRTRATE.SHIPPING-WHSE
        AND FRTRATE-RCD.FREIGHT-CLASS  EQ FRTRATE.FREIGHT-CLASS
        AND FRTRATE-RCD.SHIP-TO-ZIP    EQ FRTRATE.SHIP-TO-ZIP
            DO LD-PANEL-TABLE
            MOVE 'RATE TABLE FOUND    TO FRTRATE.MESSAGE
      WHEN  NONE
            MOVE 'RATE TABLE NOT FOUND' TO FRTRATE.MESSAGE
  ENDFOR
ENDPROC


:==================================================================
:== PARA LOADS THE DATA FROM THE RECORD INTO THE CORRECT ENTRY==
:== OF THE PANEL                                            ==
:==================================================================
<<LD-PANEL-TABLE>> PROCEDURE
  ADD 1 TO WK-SUBSR
  IF WK-SUBSR GT WK-LIMIT
     ADD  1 TO WK-COLUMN
     MOVE 1 TO WK-SUBSR
  ENDIF
  SELECT
    WHEN WK-COLUMN = 1
```

```
        MOVE FRTRATE-RCD.WEIGHT TO FRTRATE.WEIGHT-COL-1(WK-SUBSR)
        MOVE FRTRATE-RCD.RATE   TO FRTRATE.RATE-COL-1  (WK-SUBSR)
    WHEN WK-COLUMN = 2
        MOVE FRTRATE-RCD.WEIGHT TO FRTRATE.WEIGHT-COL-2(WK-SUBSR)
        MOVE FRTRATE-RCD.RATE   TO FRTRATE.RATE-COL-2  (WK-SUBSR)
    WHEN WK-COLUMN = 3
        MOVE FRTRATE-RCD.WEIGHT TO FRTRATE.WEIGHT-COL-3(WK-SUBSR)
        MOVE FRTRATE-RCD.RATE   TO FRTRATE.RATE-COL-3  (WK-SUBSR)
  ENDSELECT
ENDPROC


:************************************************************************
:**THIS PARA INFORMS THE USER THAT THEY HAVE CHOSEN AN INVALID OPTION**
:************************************************************************
<<INVALID-SELECT>> PROCEDURE
  MOVE 'INVALID OPTION'                   TO CARRPNL.MESSAGE
ENDPROC


:************************************************************************
:**THESE PARAGRAPHS ARE CALLED FROM MORE THAN ONE OF THE MAIN DRIVE  **
:**ROUTINES                                                          **
:************************************************************************


:==================================================================
:== PARA INITIALIZES THE PANEL READ ROUTINE                 ==
:==================================================================
<<INT-CHK-WEIGHT>> PROCEDURE
  MOVE $PANEL-GROUP-OCCURS(FRTRATE) TO WK-LIMIT
  MOVE 1                            TO WK-COLUMN    :COLUMN COUNTER
  MOVE 0                            TO WK-SUBSR     :ROW COUNTER
  MOVE 'N'                          TO FG-PROC-COMP
ENDPROC


:==================================================================
:== PARA SELECTS THE COMPARISON WEIGHT, READING TOP TO BOTTOM,==
:== THROUGH EACH COLUMN                                      ==
:==================================================================
<<SEL-CHK-WEIGHT>> PROCEDURE
  ADD 1 TO WK-SUBSR
  IF WK-SUBSR GT WK-LIMIT
     ADD  1 TO WK-COLUMN
     MOVE 1 TO WK-SUBSR
  ENDIF
```

```
SELECT
   WHEN WK-COLUMN = 1
         MOVE FRTRATE.WEIGHT-COL-1(WK-SUBSR) TO WK-CHK-WEIGHT
         MOVE FRTRATE.RATE-COL-1  (WK-SUBSR) TO WK-CHK-RATE
   WHEN WK-COLUMN = 2
         MOVE FRTRATE.WEIGHT-COL-2(WK-SUBSR) TO WK-CHK-WEIGHT
         MOVE FRTRATE.RATE-COL-2  (WK-SUBSR) TO WK-CHK-RATE
   WHEN WK-COLUMN = 3
         MOVE FRTRATE.WEIGHT-COL-3(WK-SUBSR) TO WK-CHK-WEIGHT
         MOVE FRTRATE.RATE-COL-3  (WK-SUBSR) TO WK-CHK-RATE
   WHEN WK-COLUMN = 4
         MOVE 'Y' TO FG-PROC-COMP
         MOVE 0000000                          TO WK-CHK-WEIGHT
         MOVE 00000                            TO WK-CHK-RATE
   ENDSELECT


   IF WK-CHK-WEIGHT = 0000000    :CHECKS FOR LAST TABLE ENTRY
       MOVE 'Y' TO FG-PROC-COMP
   ENDIF
ENDPROC


:==================================================================
:== THIS AREA CHECKS TO SEE IF RECORD BEING UPDATED WAS THE   ==
:== LAST ONE VIEWED                                          ==
:==================================================================
<<CHECK-VIEW>> PROCEDURE
   IF  WK-LAST-VIEW.SHIPPING-WHSE = FRTRATE.SHIPPING-WHSE
   AND WK-LAST-VIEW.FREIGHT-CLASS = FRTRATE.FREIGHT-CLASS
   AND WK-LAST-VIEW.SHIP-TO-ZIP   = FRTRATE.SHIP-TO-ZIP
       DO CHECK-WEIGHTS
   ELSE
       MOVE 'N'        TO FG-INPUT-CORR
       MOVE 'RECORD MUST BE VIEWED BEFORE UPDATE' TO FRTRATE.MESSAGE
   ENDIF
ENDPROC


:==================================================================
:== PARA CHECKS TO SEE IF THE WEIGHT BREAKS HAVE BEEN CHANGED ==
:== SINCE THE LAST VIEW. TO CHANGE THE WEIGHT BREAK STRUCTURE ==
:== THE RECORDS MUST BE DELETED AND READDED                  ==
:==================================================================
```

```
<<CHECK-WEIGHTS>> PROCEDURE
  DO INT-CHK-WEIGHT
  FOR EACH  FRT-RATE-RCD
     WHERE FRT-RATE-RCD.SHIPPING-WHSE = FRTRATE.SHIPPING-WHSE
       AND FRT-RATE-RCD.FREIGHT-CLASS = FRTRATE.FREIGHT-CLASS
       AND FRT-RATE-RCD.SHIP-TO-ZIP   = FRTRATE.SHIP-TO-ZIP
          DO SEL-CHK-WEIGHT
          IF WK-CHK-WEIGHT NOT EQ FRT-RATE-RCD.WEIGHT
             MOVE 'N'                          TO FG-INPUT-CORR
             MOVE 'WEIGHT BREAKS HAVE CHANGED' TO FRTRATE.MESSAGE
          ENDIF
  ENDFOR
ENDPROC


:****************************************************************************
:*THIS PARA RESETS THE FIELDS THAT ARE CHECKED FOR THE LAST REC VIEWED*
:****************************************************************************
<<RESET-LAST-VIEW>> PROCEDURE
  MOVE $SPACES   TO WK-LAST-VIEW.SHIPPING-WHSE
  MOVE $SPACES   TO WK-LAST-VIEW.FREIGHT-CLASS
  MOVE $SPACES   TO WK-LAST-VIEW.SHIP-TO-ZIP
ENDPROC
=============================B O T T O M=================================
```

In this program we see an example of how to handle multiple columns in an IDEAL panel repeating group. We should also note that the EDIT-INPUT paragraph was used to populate the WHSE-NAME and FRT-CLS-DESC during the view option to save coding. The use of the working storage field FG-INPUT-CORR instead of a flag field is just an idiosyncrasy of the author.

Group Shipments Together into Bills of Lading, Computing Their Total Weight and Freight Charges

The purpose of this program will be to enter the bill-of-lading header data and the shipment records that are included in this bill of lading, and to compute the freight weights and charges.

The coding for the input of the header data and the shipment numbers is similar to what we have already seen, and we will save it for an exercise at the end of this chapter. The code that does interest us at this point is the table processing that is used to compute the BOFL-HEADER.CALCULATED-WGT, and the distribution of the resulting freight charge to the different invoices.

```
<<PROC-LINE-INPUT>> PROCEDURE
  DO COMPUTE-WGHTS
  DO COMPUTE-CHRGS
  DO ALLOC-CHARGS
ENDPROC


:*****************************************************************************
:**THIS AREA READS EACH SHIPMENT HEADER RECORD RELATED TO THE BILL OF**
:**LADING, COMPUTES THE LINE WEIGHT, THE SHIPMENT WEIGHT, AND THE    **
:**TOTAL WEIGHT FOR THE BILL OF LADING                             **
:*****************************************************************************
<<COMPUTE-WGHTS>> PROCEDURE
  DO INIT-TABLE-AREA
  FOR EACH   BOFL-SHIPMENT
      WHERE BOFL-SHIPMENT.BILL-LADING-NO  = BOFL-HEADER.BILL-OF-LADING
      FOR FIRST SHIPMENT-HEADER
          WHERE SHIPMENT-HEADER.ORDER-NO     = BOFL-SHIPMENT.ORDER-NO
            AND SHIPMENT-HEADER.SHIPMENT-NO = BOFL-SHIPMENT.SHIPMENT-NO
                DO PROC-SHIP-LINES
      ENDFOR
  ENDFOR
  DO PROC-BOFL-LINS
ENDPROC


:=================================================================
:== PARA INITIALIZES THE FIRST RECORD IN THE TABLE TO BE 999  ==
:== WHICH IS DEFINED IN OUR SYSTEM TO BE 'UNKNOWN FRT CLASS'  ==
:=================================================================
<<INIT-TABLE-AREA>> PROCEDURE
  MOVE 0 TO WK-BOFL-WEIGHT
  MOVE 0 TO WK-SUBSR
  MOVE 1 TO WK-TBL-REC-USED
  MOVE '999' TO WK-FRTCLS-TBL.FREIGHT-CLASS(1)
  MOVE 00000 TO WK-FRTCLS-TBL.WEIGHT       (1)
ENDPROC


:=================================================================
:== AREA PROCESSES THE SHIPMENT LINES, GETTING LINE WEIGHT AND==
:== SHIPMENT WEIGHT                                          ==
:=================================================================
<<PROC-SHIP-LINES>> PROCEDURE
  MOVE 00000 TO SHIPMENT-HEADER.SHIPMENT-WEIGHT
  FOR EACH   SHIPMENT-LINE
      WHERE SHIPMENT-LINE.ORDER-NO      = SHIPMENT-HEADER.ORDER-NO
```

```
                 AND SHIPMENT-LINE.SHIPMENT-NO = SHIPMENT-HEADER.SHIPMENT-NO
                     DO GET-EQUIP-RCD
                     DO CALC-LIN-WEIGHT
                     DO UPDT-FRTCLS-TBL
          ENDFOR
       ENDPROC


   :================================================================
   :== PARA GETS THE UNIT WEIGHT AND FREIGHT CLASS FROM THE      ==
   :== EQUIPMENT MASTER RECORD FROM THIS PART                    ==
   :================================================================
   <<GET-EQUIP-RCD>> PROCEDURE
       FOR FIRST EQUIPMENT-RCD
          WHERE EQUIPMENT-RCD.EQUIP-NO = SHIPMENT-LINE.EQUIP-NO
                 MOVE EQUIPMENT-RCD.WEIGHT        TO WK-EQUIP-WGT
                 MOVE EQUIPMENT-RCD.FREIGHT-CLASS TO WK-FREIGHT-CLS
                 IF WK-FREIGHT-CLS                LE $SPACES
                    MOVE '999'                    TO WK-FREIGHT-CLS
                 ENDIF
             WHEN  NONE
                 MOVE 00000                       TO WK-EQUIP-WGT
                 MOVE '999'                       TO WK-FREIGHT-CLS
          ENDFOR
       ENDPROC


   :================================================================
   :== PARA CALCULATES LINE WEIGHT AS QTY-SHIPPED TIMES UNIT SHIP==
   :== WEIGHT. IT THEN ACCUMULATES THE SHIPMENT AND BOL WEIGHTS  ==
   :================================================================
   <<CALC-LIN-WEIGHT>> PROCEDURE
     SET SHIPMENT-LINE.LINE-WEIGHT        = SHIPMENT-LINE.QTY-SHIPPED
                                          * WK-EQUIP-WGT
     SET SHIPMENT-HEADER.SHIPMENT-WEIGHT = SHIPMENT-HEADER.SHIPMENT-WEIGHT
                                          + SHIPMENT-LINE.LINE-WEIGHT
     SET WK-BOFL-WEIGHT                   = WK-BOFL-WEIGHT
                                          + SHIPMENT-LINE.LINE-WEIGHT
   ENDPROC


   :================================================================
   :== PARA ADDS THE FREIGHT CLASS AND WEIGHT TO THE BOL LINE    ==
   :== TABLE IN WORKING STORAGE                                  ==
   :================================================================
   <<UPDT-FRTCLS-TBL>> PROCEDURE
     MOVE 0    TO WK-SUBSR
```

```
       MOVE 'N' TO FG-TABLE-UPDT
       LOOP VARYING WK-SUBSR FROM 1 BY 1
               UNTIL WK-SUBSR GT WK-TBL-RECS-USED
                   DO SRCH-FRTCLS-TBL
       ENDLOOP
       IF FG-TABLE-INPUT = 'N'
          MOVE WK-FREIGHT-CLS TO WK-FRTCLS-TBL.FREIGHT-CLASS(WK-SUBSR)
          MOVE SHIPMENT-LINE.LINE-WEIGHT
                           TO WK-FRTCLS-TBL.WEIGHT      (WK-SUBSR)
          ADD 1 TO WK-TBL-REC-USED
       ENDIF
    ENDPROC


    :----------------------------------------------------------------
    :-- PARA SEARCHES TABLE TO SEE IF THE FREIGHT CLASS ALREADY   --
    :-- EXISTS IN THE TABLE.                                      --
    :----------------------------------------------------------------
    <<SRCH-FRTCLS-TBL>> PROCEDURE
      IF WK-FREIGHT-CLS = WK-FRTCLS-TBL.FREIGHT-CLASS(WK-SUBSR)
         MOVE 'Y' TO FG-TABLE-UPDT
         ADD SHIPMENT-LINE.LINE-WEIGHT
          TO WK-FRTCLS-TBL.WEIGHT(WK-SUBSR)
      ENDIF
    ENDPROC


    :================================================================
    :== PARA READS THE WORKING STORAGE TABLE AND CREATES THE BOFL ==
    :== LINE RECORDS, ONE FOR EACH TABLE ENTRY                    ==
    :================================================================
    <<PROC-BOFL-LINS>> PROCEDURE
      MOVE 0 TO WK-SUBSR
      LOOP VARYING WK-SUBSR FROM 1 BY 1
              UNTIL WK-SUBSR GREATER THAN WK-TBL-REC-USED
                  IF WK-FRTCLS-TBL.WEIGHT(WK-SUBSR) GT 0
                      DO BLD-LINE-RCD
                  ENDIF
      ENDLOOP
    ENDPROC


    <<BLD-LINE-RCD>> PROCEDURE
      FOR NEW BOFL-LINE
          MOVE BLHEADER.BILL-LADING-NO        TO BOFL-LINE.BILL-LADING-NO
          MOVE WK-FRTCLS-TBL.WEIGHT(WK-SUBSR)   TO BOFL-LINE.WEIGHT
          MOVE WK-FRTCLS-TBL.FREIGHT-CLASS(WK-SUBSR)
```

```
                 TO BOFL-LINE.FREIGHT-CLASS
        ENDFOR
      ENDPROC


      :************************************************************
      :**THIS AREA COMPUTES THE FREIGHT CHARGES BASED ON CARRIER DISCOUNT, **
      :**RATE BY WEIGHT FOR THE FREIGHT CLASS                           **
      :**TOTAL WEIGHT FOR THE BILL OF LADING                            **
      :************************************************************
      <<COMPUTE-CHRGS>> PROCEDURE
        MOVE 00000.00 TO WK-BOFL-CHARGE
        DO GET-CARRIER-RCD
        LOOP VARYING WK-SUBSR FROM 1 BY 1
               UNTIL WK-SUBSR GT WK-TBL-RCD-USED
                    DO FIND-RATE-TBL
                    DO COMP-CHARGES
        ENDLOOP
        DO UPDT-BOFL-HDR
      ENDPROC


      :================================================================
      :== PARA GETS THE CARRIER DISCOUNT FROM CARRIER RCD, BASED ON ==
      :== INPUT DATA FROM THE HEADER SCREEN                        ==
      :================================================================
      <<GET-CARRIER-RCD>> PROCEDURE
        FOR FIRST CARRIER-RCD
            WHERE CARRIER-RCD.CARRIER-CD        EQ BLHEADER.CARRIER-CD
                 MOVE CARRIER-RCD.DISCOUNT-PCT TO WK-DISCOUNT-PCT
            WHEN  NONE
                 MOVE 00000                    TO WK-DISCOUNT-PCT
        ENDFOR
      ENDPROC


      :================================================================
      :== PARA GETS THE FRT RATE RCD WITH THE PROPER WEIGHT BREAK.  ==
      :== OTHER INPUT COMES FROM BOFL HEADER INPUT SCREEN (BLHEADER)==
      :================================================================
      <<FIND-RATE-TBL>> PROCEDURE
        MOVE WK-FRTCLS-TBL.FREIGHT-CLASS(WK-SUBSR) TO WK-FREIGHT-CLS
        MOVE 00000                              TO WK-PREV-WEIGHT
        MOVE 00000                              TO WK-RATE
        FOR EACH  FRTRATE-RCD
            WHERE FRTRATE-RCD.SHIPPING-WHSE EQ BLHEADER.SHIPPING-WHSE
              AND FRTRATE-RCD.FREIGHT-CLASS EQ WK-FREIGHT-CLS
```

```
        AND FRTRATE-RCD.SHIP-TO-ZIP   EQ BLHEADER.SHIP-TO-ZIP
            IF  FRTRATE-RCD.WEIGHT   GE WK-FRTCLS-TBL.WEIGHT(WK-SUBSR)
            AND WK-PREV-WEIGHT       LE WK-FRTCLS-TBL.WEIGHT(WK-SUBSR)
                MOVE FRTRATE-RCD.RATE       TO WK-RATE
            ENDIF
            MOVE FRTRATE-RCD.WEIGHT       TO WK-PREV-WEIGHT
   ENDFOR
ENDPROC


:===================================================================
:== PARA COMPUTES THE ACTUAL LINE CHARGES, AND INCREMENTS THE ==
:== BOL HEADER TOTAL CHARGES. RATE IS BY HUNDRED WEIGHT       ==
:===================================================================
<<COMP-CHARGES>> PROCEDURE
   SET WK-CLS-CHARGE  = (WK-FRTCLS-TBL.WEIGHT(WK-SUBSR) / 100)
                      * WK-RATE
                      * (WK-DISCOUNT-PCT / 100)
   SET WK-BOFL-CHARGE = WK-BOFL-CHARGE
                      + WK-CLS-CHARGE
ENDPROC


:===================================================================
:== PARA SETS THE CAL WEIGHT, CHARGES, ON THE BOFL HEADER RCD ==
:===================================================================
<<UPDT-BOFL-HDR>> PROCEDURE
   FOR FIRST BOFL-HEADER
       WHERE BOFL-HEADER.BILL-LADING-NO = BLHEADER.BILL-LADING-NO
             MOVE WK-BOFL-WEIGHT TO BOFL-HEADER.CALCULATED-WGT
             MOVE WK-BOFL-CHARGE TO BOFL-HEADER.FREIGHT-CHARGE
   ENDFOR
ENDPROC


:*********************************************************************
:**THIS AREA ALLOCATES THE FREIGHT CHARGES TO THE DIFFERENT SHIPMENTS**
:**FOR INVOICING BY TOTAL WEIGHT.                                  **
:*********************************************************************
<<ALLOC-CHARGS>> PROCEDURE
   FOR EACH  BOFL-SHIPMENT
       WHERE BOFL-SHIPMENT.BILL-LADING-NO   = BLHEADER.BILL-OF-LADING
       FOR FIRST SHIPMENT-HEADER
           WHERE SHIPMENT-HEADER.ORDER-NO     = BOFL-SHIPMENT.ORDER-NO
           AND SHIPMENT-HEADER.SHIPMENT-NO = BOFL-SHIPMENT.SHIPMENT-NO
               DO COMP-FRT-ALLOC
       ENDFOR
```

```
    ENDFOR
  ENDPROC


  <<COMP-FRT-ALLOC>> PROCEDURE
    SET SHIPMENT-HEADER.FREIGHT-CHARGE = BOFL-HEADER.FREIGHT-CHARGE
                                 * (SHIPMENT-HEADER.SHIPMENT-WEIGHT
                                  / BOFL-HEADER.CALCULATED-WEIGHT)
  ENDPROC
```

Print the Bill-of-Lading Documents

The bill-of-lading document is a special form that serves as both a freight manifest and a freight bill. The basic form used by our example company follows:

```
                        BILL OF LADING              NO.


                                CARRIER

        ADDRESS TO:             FROM:







                                TOTAL CHARGE
===========================================================================
  CLASS     DESCRIPTION      WEIGHT  CLASS     DESCRIPTION      WEIGHT
```

TOTAL WEIGHT

When filled in, it would look like this:

```
                  BILL OF LADING              NO. AA11001212


    ADDRESS TO:                    FROM:


    W.T DOOR MANUFACTURERS         IDEAL MANUFACTURING CO. - WHSE 01
    1201 INDUSTRIAL PARKWAY        7225 LEMON AVENUE
    DALLAS, TX                     AMBLER, PA
    76100                          19002


    CARRIER: G0701 ORANGE FREIGHT INC    TOTAL CHARGE    24.75
    =====================================================================
    CLASS      DESCRIPTION      WEIGHT   CLASS      DESCRIPTION      WEIGHT
    100   LADDER, ALUM W/WOOD    10.5    500   DOOR FRAMES - WOOD    200.0
    600   COPPER CABLE, ELEC     13.3    650   DOOR HANDLES - BRASS    5.1
    700   SILICA GEL              1.0




                             TOTAL WEIGHT           229.9
```

As was discussed in the chapter on the report definition facility of IDEAL (Chapter 8), the product is not very flexible. While major enhancements are planned for future releases, it is still challenging to produce a very complicated report. In fact, if this form was any more complicated it would be our recommendation to write this program in another language.

However, since this book is on IDEAL, we will give it a shot. The program name and the report name will be BOLPRINT. We will begin with the PARM area of the report definition.

```
------------------------------------------------------------------------
IDEAL: RPT PARAMETERS          RPT BOLPRINT (001) TEST         SYS: DEV


LINES PER PAGE ON PRINTOUT          24  ( 1 THRU 250)
REPORT WIDTH                        080 (40 THRU 230)
SPACING BETWEEN LINES               1   ( 1 THRU 3)
SPACING BETWEEN COLUMNS             01  ( 0 THRU 66 OR A=AUTOMATIC)
SUMMARIES ONLY                      N   (Y=YES,N=NO)
COLUMN HEADINGS DESIRED             Y   (Y=YES,N=NO)
COLUMN HEADINGS INDICATION          U   (U=UNDERSCORE,N=NONE,D=DASHES)
CONTROL BREAK HEADING               N   (Y=YES,N=NO)
CONTROL BREAK FOOTING               N   (Y=YES,N=NO)
GROUP CONTINUATION AT TOP OF PAGE   N   (Y=YES,N=NO)
ANNOTATED COUNT IN CONTROL FOOTINGS N   (Y=YES,N=NO)
REPORT FINAL SUMMARY TITLE          N   (Y=YES,N=NO)
  SPACING BEFORE SUMMARY            1   (1 THRU 9 = LINES,P=NEW PAGE)
  TITLE       _____


DATE
  POSITION        TL    (NO=NONE,BR=BOT.RIGHT,BL=BOT.LEFT,BC=BOT.CTR
                         TR=TOP RIGHT,TL=TOP LEFT,TC=TOP CENTER)
  FORMAT        MM/DD/YY


PAGE NUMBERS
  POSITION        NO
  FORMAT          H     (D=DIGITS ONLY, H=WITH HYPHENS, P=PAGE    NNN)


PAGE HEADING
  HEADING         _____
  POSITION        C     (C=CENTER, L=LEFT JUSTIFY, R=RIGHT JUSTIFY)
```

We should note here that, since we have a special form, we have changed entries for the report width and number of lines per page. In addition we have turned off all of the standard header codes so that we could control everything with the HDR screen fill-in.

```
------------------------------------------------------------------------
IDEAL: RPT PAGE HEADING    RPT BOLPRINT (001) TEST    SYS: DEV FILL-IN


FIELD NAME, LITERAL, FUNCTION             COLUMN
OR ARITHMETIC EXPRESSION                  W
                                          ID TAB EDIT PATTERN  COMMAND
                                          TH
------------------------------------------------------  --  ---  ---------------  -------
```

RPT-AREA.BILL-OF-LADING	10 062	_____	000020
_____	__ L03	_____	000030
RPT-AREA.SHP-ADDR-NAME	30 005	_____	000040
RPT-AREA.WAREHOUSE-NAME	30 039	_____	000050
_____	__ L01	_____	000060
RPT-AREA.SHP-STREET-NAME	30 005	_____	000070
RPT-AREA.WHS-STREET-NAME	30 039	_____	000080
_____	__ L01	_____	000090
RPT-AREA.SHP-CITY-STATE	30 005	_____	000100
RPT-AREA.WHS-CITY-STATE	30 039	_____	000110
_____	__ L01	_____	000120
RPT-AREA.SHP-ZIP-CODE	10 010	_____	000130
RPT-AREA.WHS-ZIP-CODE	10 039	_____	000140
_____	__ L02	_____	000150
RPT-AREA.CARRIER-NO	06 011	_____	000160
RPT-AREA.CARRIER-NAME	20 017	_____	000170
RPT-AREA.FREIGHT-CHARGE	10 065	ZZZZZZ9.99	000180
_____	__ ___	_____	000190

By using the line eject feature in the TAB column, we are able to define different types of lines on the report header.

The detail definition screen will be entered as follows:

```
------------------------------------------------------------------------

IDEAL: RPT DETAIL DEFN.      RPT BOLPRINT (001) TEST       SYS:DEV


FIELD NAME, LITERAL          SORT  BREAK  FUNCTION COLUMN
FUNCTION, OR                 L A   L S I  T M M A  H W
ARITHMETIC EXPRESSION        V /   V K N  O A I V  D ID TAB EDIT PATTERN
                             L D   L P D  T X N G  G TH
-------------------------    - -   - - -  - - - -  - -- --- -------------
========== TOP ==========    = =   = = =  = = = =  = == === =============
RPT-AREA.BILL-OF-LADING      _ _   1 P N  _ _ _ _  _ 10 ___ _____
RPT-AREA.FREIGHT-CLASS-1     _ _   _ _ _  _ _ _ _  N 03 002 _____
RPT-AREA.DESCRIPTION-1       _ _   _ _ _  _ _ _ _  N 20 009 _____
RPT-AREA.WEIGHT-1            _ _   _ _ _  _ _ _ _  N 06 029 ZZZZZ.Z
RPT-AREA.FREIGHT-CLASS-2     _ _   _ _ _  _ _ _ _  N 03 040 _____
RPT-AREA.DESCRIPTION-2       _ _   _ _ _  _ _ _ _  N 20 045 _____
RPT-AREA.WEIGHT-2            _ _   _ _ _  _ _ _ _  N 06 065 ZZZZZ.Z
======== BOTTOM =========    = =   = = =  = = = =  = == === =============
```

Here we turned off the column headings, because they are already printed on the form. We also defined the bill of lading as a page break field, so that when it changes IDEAL will calculate the total

weight and place it in the appropriate box. To get the vertical alignment of the total field right, we will have to make sure that we
produce 25 lines on every page, even if some of the lines are blank.
This is why we suppressed all of the digits in the edit pattern of the
weight field.

We will then code the following program.

```
:*****************************************************************
:**THIS PROGRAM PRINTS THOSE BILL OF LADING RECORDS WHERE THE PRINT  **
:**INDICATOR IS EQUAL TO Y.                                          **
:*****************************************************************
<<BOLPRINT>> PROCEDURE
  FOR EACH BOFL-HEADER
        IF BOFL-HEADER.PRINT-IND = 'Y'
            DO LOAD-HDR-DATA
            DO GET-CARRIER-RCD
            DO GET-SHIP-TO
            DO PROCESS-LINES
            MOVE 'N' TO BOFL-HEADER.PRINT-IND
        ENDIF
  ENDFOR
ENDPROC


:*****************************************************************
:**PARA LOADS DATA FROM BOFL-HEADER ONTO THE REPORT              **
:*****************************************************************
<<LOAD-HDR-DATA>> PROCEDURE
  MOVE BOFL-HEADER.BILL-OF-LADING TO RPT-AREA.BILL-OF-LADING
  MOVE BOFL-HEADER.FREIGHT-CHARGE TO RPT-AREA.FREIGHT-CHARGE
  MOVE BOFL-HEADER.CARRIER-CD     TO RPT-AREA.CARRIER-CD
ENDPROC


:*****************************************************************
:**PARA GETS THE CARRIER NAME FROM THE CARRIER DOMAIN TABLE      **
:*****************************************************************
<<GET-CARRIER-RCD>> PROCEDURE
  FOR FIRST CARRIER-RCD
        WHERE CARRIER-RCD.CARRIER-CD      EQ BOFL-HEADER.CARRIER-CD
                MOVE CARRIER-RCD.CARRIER-NAME TO RPT-AREA.CARRIER-NAME
        WHEN  NONE
                MOVE $SPACES                  TO RPT-AREA.CARRIER-NAME
  ENDFOR
ENDPROC
```

```
;**********************************************************************
;**PARA FINDS THE FIRST SHIPMENT RECORD, TO GET THE SHIP POINT      **
;**********************************************************************
<<GET-SHIP-TO>> PROCEDURE
  FOR FIRST BOFL-SHIPMENT
       WHERE BOFL-SHIPMENT.BILL-LADING-NO  = BOFL-HEADER.BILL-OF-LADING
       FOR FIRST SHIPMENT-HEADER
           WHERE SHIPMENT-HEADER.ORDER-NO    = BOFL-SHIPMENT.ORDER-NO
             AND SHIPMENT-HEADER.SHIPMENT-NO = BOFL-SHIPMENT.SHIPMENT-NO
                 DO GET-SHIP-ADDR
                 DO GET-WHSE-ADDR
       ENDFOR
  ENDFOR
ENDPROC


;====================================================================
;== PARA GETS THE DELIVERY ADDRESS FROM THE CUSTOMER MST FILE ==
;====================================================================
<<GET-SHIP-ADDR>> PROCEDURE
  FOR FIRST CUST-ADDRESS
       WHERE CUST-ADDRESS.CUST-NO       EQ SHIPMENT-HEADER.CUST-NO
         AND CUST-ADDRESS.CUST-SHIP-TO EQ SHIPMENT-HEADER.CUST-SHIP-TO
             DO LD-SHIPTO-ADDR
       WHEN  NONE
             MOVE $SPACES                 TO RPT-AREA.SHP-ADDR-NAME
             MOVE $SPACES                 TO RPT-AREA.SHP-STREET-NAME
             MOVE $SPACES                 TO RPT-AREA.SHP-CITY-STATE
             MOVE $SPACES                 TO RPT-AREA.SHP-ZIP-CODE
    ENDFOR
ENDPROC


;====================================================================
;== PARA LOADS THE DELIVERY ADDRESS FROM THE CUSTOMER MST FILE==
;== NOTE:                                                     ==
;==  1) HOW THE COMBINED USE OF THE $SUBSTR AND $EDIT COMMANDS==
;== ALLOWS US TO POPULATE THE ZIP CODE FIELD WITH AN EDIT MASK==
;== ONLY WHEN IT HAS THE NEW NINE CHARACTER ZIP CODE         ==
;==  2) HOW THE COMBINED USE OF THE $STRING AND $TRIM COMMANDS==
;== ALLOWS US TO FLOAT THE STATE FIELD AND ITS COMMA TO THE  ==
;== END OF THE STATE FIELD OF THE ADDRESS                    ==
;====================================================================
<<LD-SHIPTO-ADDR>> PROCEDURE
  MOVE CUST-ADDRESS.NAME                  TO RPT-AREA.SHP-ADDR-NAME
```

```
    MOVE CUST-ADDRESS.STREET-ADDRESS           TO RPT-AREA.SHP-STREET-NAME
    IF $SUBSTR(ADDRESS.ZIP-CODE,START=6,LENGTH=4) = $SPACES
       MOVE CUST-ADDRESS.ZIP-CODE              TO RPT-AREA.SHP-ZIP-CODE
    ELSE
       MOVE $EDIT(CUST-ADDRESS.ZIP-CODE,PIC='XXXX-XXXX')
                                               TO RPT-AREA.SHP-ZIP-CODE
    ENDIF
    MOVE $STRING($TRIM(CUST-ADDRESS.CITY,RIGHT=' '),', ',
                      CUST-ADDRESS.STATE) TO RPT-AREA.SHP-CITY-STATE
ENDPROC


:=================================================================
:== PARA GETS THE SHIP FROM ADDRESS OF THE SHIPPING WHSE      ==
:=================================================================
<<GET-WHSE-ADDR>> PROCEDURE
  FOR FIRST WHSE-ADDRESS
       WHERE WHSE-ADDRESS.WHSE-NO       EQ SHIPMENT-HEADER.SHIPPING-WHSE
             DO LD-WHSE-ADDR
       WHEN  NONE
             MOVE $SPACES               TO RPT-AREA.WHS-ADDR-NAME
             MOVE $SPACES               TO RPT-AREA.WHS-STREET-NAME
             MOVE $SPACES               TO RPT-AREA.WHS-CITY-STATE
             MOVE $SPACES               TO RPT-AREA.WHS-ZIP-CODE
  ENDFOR
ENDPROC


:=================================================================
:== PARA LOADS THE ADDRESS OF THE SHIPPING WHSE AS SHIP FROM  ==
:=================================================================
<<LD-WHSE-ADDR>> PROCEDURE
  MOVE WHSE-ADDRESS.NAME                TO RPT-AREA.WHS-ADDR-NAME
  MOVE WHSE-ADDRESS.STREET-ADDRESS     TO RPT-AREA.WHS-STREET-NAME
  IF $SUBSTR(WHSE-ADDRESS.ZIP-CODE,START=6,LENGTH=4) = $SPACES
     MOVE WHSE-ADDRESS.ZIP-CODE        TO RPT-AREA.WHS-ZIP-CODE
  ELSE
     MOVE $EDIT(WHSE-ADDRESS.ZIP-CODE,PIC='XXXXX-XXXX')
                                       TO RPT-AREA.WHS-ZIP-CODE
  ENDIF
  MOVE $STRING($TRIM(WHSE-ADDRESS.CITY,RIGHT=' '),', ',
                    WHSE-ADDRESS.STATE) TO RPT-AREA.WHS-CITY-STATE
ENDPROC


:*****************************************************************
:**PARA PRINTS THE LINES ON THE FORM                          **
```

```
;************************************************************************
<<PROCESS-LINES>> PROCEDURE
  MOVE 0 TO WK-RECORD-CNT
  MOVE 0 TO WK-SIDE-IND
  MOVE 0 TO WK-TTL-WEIGHT
  FOR EACH  BOFL-LINE
      WHERE BOFL-LINE.BILL-OF-LADING = BOFL-HEADER.BILL-OF-LADING
            ADD 1 TO WK-RECORD-CNT
            IF WK-RECORD-CNT = 31
               DO CAUSE-PAGE-BRK
            ENDIF
            ADD 1 TO WK-SIDE-IND
            DO GET-FRT-CLASS
            DO LD-LINE-DATA
            IF WK-SIDE-IND = 2
               MOVE 0 TO WK-LINE-IND
               PRODUCE BOLPRINT
            ENDIF
  ENDFOR
  DO COMPLETE-FORM
  DO WRITE-TOTAL
ENDPROC


;==================================================================
;==PARA CAUSES THE PROGRAM TO SKIP THE TOTALS LINE AND START   ==
;==PROCESSING A NEW PAGE                                       ==
;==================================================================
<<CAUSE-PAGE-BRK>> PROCEDURE
  MOVE 1            TO WK-RECORD-CNT
  MOVE $SPACES      TO RPT-AREA.FREIGHT-CLASS-1
  MOVE $SPACES      TO RPT-AREA.DESCRIPTION-1
  MOVE 00000.0      TO RPT-AREA.WEIGHT-1
  MOVE $SPACES      TO RPT-AREA.FREIGHT-CLASS-2
  MOVE $SPACES      TO RPT-AREA.DESCRIPTION-2
  MOVE 00000.0      TO RPT-AREA.WEIGHT-2
  PRODUCE BOLPRINT
ENDPROC


;==================================================================
;==PARA GETS THE FREIGHT CLS DESCRIPTION FROM THE DOMAIN TABLE==
;==================================================================
<<GET-FRT-CLASS-1>> PROCEDURE
  FOR FIRST FRT-CLASS
      WHERE FRT-CLASS.FREIGHT-CLASS      EQ BOFL-FREIGHT-CLASS
```

```
            IF WK-SIDE-IND = 1
                MOVE FRT-CLASS.DESCRIPTION TO RPT-AREA.DESCRIPTION-1
            ELSE
                MOVE FRT-CLASS.DESCRIPTION TO RPT-AREA.DESCRIPTION-2
            ENDIF
        WHEN  NONE
            IF WK-LINE-IND = 1
                MOVE $SPACES              TO RPT-AREA.DESCRIPTION-1
            ELSE
                MOVE $SPACES              TO RPT-AREA.DESCRIPTION-2
            ENDIF
    ENDFOR
ENDPROC


:==================================================================
:==PARA MOVES LINE DATA FROM BOFL LINE RECORD TO REPORT AREA   ==
:==================================================================
<<LD-LINE-DATA-1>> PROCEDURE
    ADD BOFL-LINE.WEIGHT              TO WK-TTL-WEIGHT
    IF WK-SIDE-IND = 1
        MOVE BOFL-LINE.FREIGHT-CLASS     TO RPT-AREA.FREIGHT-CLASS-1
        MOVE BOFL-LINE.WEIGHT            TO RPT-AREA.WEIGHT-1
    ELSE
        MOVE BOFL-LINE.FREIGHT-CLASS     TO RPT-AREA.FREIGHT-CLASS-2
        MOVE BOFL-LINE.WEIGHT            TO RPT-AREA.WEIGHT-2
    ENDIF
ENDPROC


:==================================================================
:==PARA MAKES SURE THAT THERE ARE 15 DETAIL LINES ON EACH PAGE==
:==================================================================
<<COMPLETE-FORM>> PROCEDURE
    IF WK-SIDE-IND = 1
        MOVE $SPACES                 TO RPT-AREA.FREIGHT-CLASS-2
        MOVE $SPACES                 TO RPT-AREA.DESCRIPTION-2
        MOVE 00000                   TO RPT-AREA.WEIGHT-2
        PRODUCE BOLPRINT
        ADD 1 TO WK-RECORD-CNT
    ENDIF
    IF WK-RECORD-CNT LT 30
        LOOP UNTIL WK-RECORD-CNT GT 30
                ADD 2                TO WK-RECORD-CNT
                MOVE $SPACES         TO RPT-AREA.FREIGHT-CLASS-1
```

```
                MOVE $SPACES          TO RPT-AREA.DESCRIPTION-1
                MOVE 00000            TO RPT-AREA.WEIGHT-1
                MOVE $SPACES          TO RPT-AREA.FREIGHT-CLASS-2
                MOVE $SPACES          TO RPT-AREA.DESCRIPTION-2
                MOVE 00000            TO RPT-AREA.WEIGHT-2
                PRODUCE BOLPRINT
        ENDLOOP
    ENDIF
  ENDPROC



  :====================================================================
  :==PARA WRITES OUT THE TOTAL WEIGHT LINE                          ==
  :====================================================================
  <<WRITE-TOTAL>> PROCEDURE
    MOVE $SPACES          TO RPT-AREA.FREIGHT-CLASS-1
    MOVE $SPACES          TO RPT-AREA.DESCRIPTION-1
    MOVE 00000            TO RPT-AREA.WEIGHT-1
    MOVE $SPACES          TO RPT-AREA.FREIGHT-CLASS-2
    MOVE $SPACES          TO RPT-AREA.DESCRIPTION-2
    MOVE WK-TTL-WEIGHT    TO RPT-AREA.WEIGHT-2
    PRODUCE BOLPRINT
  ENDPROC
```

By filling in the last part of the form with blank lines, we cause the report writer to place the total amount on the bottom of the form.

Extract the Bill-of-Lading Records and Send a Dataset to a Third Party for Processing

This facility is similar to the last program that we looked at, in that it uses an IF statement against the PRINT-IND to select the records that were to be printed. This program will use the EXTRANT-IND.

To use a QSAM file for extracting data, we will have to define it to the DATADICTIONARY as a *non-database* file. The dataview name would then be entered into the resource table of the program. The DDNAME in the JCL that is used to run this program will be the three-character database ID in the DATADICTIONARY, followed by three zeroes.

The QSAM file fields are:

```
BOFL-EXTRACT
    BILL-OF-LADING
    CARRIER-CD
    CUST-NO
    SHIPPING-WHSE
    SHIP-TO-ZIP
    FREIGHT-CLASS
    WEIGHT
```

We can then write the following program.

```
:**************************************************************************
:**PROGRAM EXTRACTS THOSE RECORDS WHERE THE EXTRACT-IND IS SET TO Y  **
:**AND SENDS THEM ON A QSAM TAPE TO A THIRD PARTY FOR PROCESSING      **
:**************************************************************************
<<BLEXTRACT-PGM>> PROCEDURE
  FOR EACH BOFL-HEADER
        IF BOFL-HEADER.EXTRACT-IND = 'Y'
            DO GET-SHIP-TO
            DO PROCESS-LINES
            MOVE $DATE('YYMMDD') TO BOFL-HEADER.EXTRACT-DATE
            MOVE 'N'             TO BOFL-HEADER.EXTRACT-IND
        ENDIF
  ENDFOR
ENDPROC


:**************************************************************************
:**PARA FINDS THE FIRST SHIPMENT RECORD, TO GET THE SHIP POINT       **
:**************************************************************************
<<GET-SHIP-TO>> PROCEDURE
  FOR FIRST BOFL-SHIPMENT
      WHERE BOFL-SHIPMENT.BILL-LADING-NO  = BOFL-HEADER.BILL-OF-LADING
      FOR FIRST SHIPMENT-HEADER
          WHERE SHIPMENT-HEADER.ORDER-NO     = BOFL-SHIPMENT.ORDER-NO
            AND SHIPMENT-HEADER.SHIPMENT-NO = BOFL-SHIPMENT.SHIPMENT-NO
                MOVE SHIPMENT-HEADER.CUST-NO        TO WK-CUST-NO
                MOVE SHIPMENT-HEADER.SHIPPING-WHSE TO WK-SHIP-WHSE
                DO GET-SHIP-ADDR
          WHEN  NONE
                MOVE $SPACES                        TO WK-CUST-NO
                MOVE $SPACES                        TO WK-SHIP-WHSE
                MOVE $SPACES                        TO WK-ZIP-CODE
```

```
            ENDFOR
         ENDFOR
      ENDPROC


      :==================================================================
      :== PARA GETS THE DELIVERY ADDR ZIP-CD FROM THE CUST MST FILE ==
      :==================================================================
      <<GET-SHIP-ADDR>> PROCEDURE
         FOR FIRST CUST-ADDRESS
               WHERE CUST-ADDRESS.CUST-NO        EQ SHIPMENT-HEADER.CUST-NO
                 AND CUST-ADDRESS.CUST-SHIP-TO EQ SHIPMENT-HEADER.CUST-SHIP-TO
                     MOVE CUST-ADDRESS.ZIP-CODE      TO WK-ZIP-CODE
               WHEN  NONE
                     MOVE $SPACES                    TO WK-ZIP-CODE
         ENDFOR
      ENDPROC


      :**********************************************************************
      :**PARA GETS LINE FOR EXTRACTING                                    **
      :**********************************************************************
      <<PROCESS-LINES>> PROCEDURE
         FOR EACH  BOFL-LINE
               WHERE BOFL-LINE.BILL-OF-LADING = BOFL-HEADER.BILL-OF-LADING
                     DO LOAD-EXTC-DATA
         ENDFOR
      ENDPROC


      :==================================================================
      :==PARA MOVES LINE DATA FROM BOFL LINE RECORD TO OUTPUT AREA   ==
      :==================================================================
      <<LOAD-EXTC-DATA>> PROCEDURE
         FOR NEW BOFL-EXTRACT
               MOVE BOFL-HEADER.BILL-OF-LADING TO BOFL-EXTRACT.BILL-OF-LADING
               MOVE BOFL-HEADER.CARRIER-CD     TO BOFL-EXTRACT.CARRIER-CD
               MOVE WK-CUST-NO                 TO BOFL-EXTRACT.CUST-NO
               MOVE WK-SHIP-WHSE               TO BOFL-EXTRACT.SHIPPING-WHSE
               MOVE WK-SHIP-TO-ZIP             TO BOFL-EXTRACT.SHIP-TO-ZIP
               MOVE BOFL-LINE.FREIGHT-CLASS    TO BOFL-EXTRACT.FREIGHT-CLASS
               MOVE BOFL-LINE.WEIGHT           TO BOFL-EXTRACT.WEIGHT
         ENDFOR
      ENDPROC
```

Produce a Report Showing How Much Business We Are Doing with Each Carrier

This report will be used in negotiations with our freight carriers when we discuss volume discount contracts. These are the discounts that appear in the carrier file.

The program will get this data from the BOFL-HEADER record. Since the CARRIER-CD is not a key to this file, we will have to use the sort feature of the report definition facility. We will begin with the PARM screen of the CRRUSAGE report.

```
------------------------------------------------------------------------
IDEAL: RPT PARAMETERS              RPT CRRUSAGE (001) TEST        SYS: PRD


LINES PER PAGE ON PRINTOUT        60  ( 1 THRU 250)
REPORT WIDTH                      133 (40 THRU 230)
SPACING BETWEEN LINES             1   ( 1 THRU 3)
SPACING BETWEEN COLUMNS           01  ( 0 THRU 66 OR A=AUTOMATIC)
SUMMARIES ONLY                    N   (Y=YES,N=NO)
COLUMN HEADINGS DESIRED           Y   (Y=YES,N=NO)
COLUMN HEADINGS INDICATION        U   (U=UNDERSCORE,N=NONE,D=DASHES)
CONTROL BREAK HEADING             N   (Y=YES,N=NO)
CONTROL BREAK FOOTING             N   (Y=YES,N=NO)
GROUP CONTINUATION AT TOP OF PAGE N   (Y=YES,N=NO)
ANNOTATED COUNT IN CONTROL FOOTINGS N (Y=YES,N=NO)
REPORT FINAL SUMMARY TITLE        N   (Y=YES,N=NO)
  SPACING BEFORE SUMMARY          1   (1 THRU 9 = LINES,P=NEW PAGE)
  TITLE      _____


DATE
  POSITION        NO     (NO=NONE,BR=BOT.RIGHT,BL=BOT.LEFT,BC=BOT.CTR
                          TR=TOP RIGHT,TL=TOP LEFT,TC=TOP CENTER)
  FORMAT          _____


PAGE NUMBERS
  POSITION        TR
  FORMAT          P      (D=DIGITS ONLY, H=WITH HYPHENS, P=PAGE    NNN)


PAGE HEADING
  HEADING         _____
  POSITION        C      (C=CENTER, L=LEFT JUSTIFY, R=RIGHT JUSTIFY)
```

Here we have gone back to standard size paper. We will also let the Report Writer facility handle the page numbers. The application program will populate the date field. We will then define the header screen so that the carrier information appears on the report header.

```
-----------------------------------------------------------------------
IDEAL: RPT PAGE HEADING     RPT CRRUSAGE (001) TEST     SYS: DEV FILL-IN


FIELD NAME, LITERAL, FUNCTION                COLUMN

OR ARITHMETIC EXPRESSION                     W

                                             ID TAB EDIT PATTERN   COMMAND
                                             TH
-----------------------------------------    -- --- ------------- ------
'CARRIER USAGE REPORT FOR THE MONTH OF'      38 052 _____ 000010
RPT-AREA.RPT-DATE                            16 +01 _____ 000020
_____    __ L01 _____ 000030
RPT-AREA.CARRIER-CD                           06 020 _____ 000040
RPT-AREA.CARRIER-NAME                         30 028 _____ 000050
_____    __ ___ _____ 000060
_____    __ ___ _____ 000070
_____    __ ___ _____ 000080
_____    __ ___ _____ 000090
```

Since CARRIER-CD is not a key field on the BOFL-HEADER database, we will use the SORT feature of the Report Writer facility to get the report data into the proper order. We will also cause the report to page break on CARRIER-CD. To do this we will define CARRIER-CD on the DETAIL screen, but we will not print it on the detail line. We will then be able to use it as the primary break field and as a sort key.

```
-----------------------------------------------------------------------
IDEAL: RPT DETAIL DEFN.     RPT CRRUSAGE (001) TEST       SYS:DEV


FIELD NAME, LITERAL       SORT  BREAK  FUNCTION COLUMN

FUNCTION, OR              L A   L S I  T M M A  H W

ARITHMETIC EXPRESSION     V /   V K N  O A I V  D ID TAB EDIT PATTERN

                         L D   L P D  T X N G  G TH
-----------------------   - -   - - -  - - - -  - -- --- --------------
========== TOP ========== = =   = = =  = = = =  = == === ==============
RPT-AREA.CARRIER-CD       1 A   1 P N  _ _ _ _  N 06 ___ _____
RPT-AREA.SHIPPING-WHSE    2 A   2 1 G  _ _ _ _  U 03 ___ _____
RPT-AREA.BILL-LADING NO   3 A   _ _ _  _ _ _ _  U 10 ___ _____
```

```
RPT-AREA.FREIGHT-CHARGE     _ _  _ _ _   S _ _ _   U 09 ___  Z,ZZZ,ZZ9
RPT-AREA.CALUCLATED-WGT      _ _  _ _ _   S _ _ _   U 06 ___  ZZ,ZZ9
RPT-AREA.SCALE-WEIGHT        _ _  _ _ _   S _ _ _   U 06 ___  ZZ,ZZ9
RPT-AREA.EXTRACT-DATE        _ _  _ _ _ _ _ _ _     U 08 ___  _____
======== BOTTOM =========   = =  = = =  = = = =  = == === =============
```

We will use the SHIPPING-WHSE as a secondary sort key, and a secondary break field. The field will only print when its value changes. We will also use the BILL-LADING-NO as a tertiary sort key. Whenever the value of the CARRIER-CD or SHIPPING-WHSE changes, a summary line will be written showing the totals of FREIGHT-CHARGE, CALCULATED-WGT, and SCALE-WEIGHT.

The column heading fill-in screen would look like this:

```
------------------------------------------------------------------------
IDEAL: RPT COLUMN HEADINGS    RPT CRRUSAGE (001) TEST      SYS: DEV
FIELD NAME, LITERAL         COLUMN
FUNCTION OR                 H W
ARITHMETIC EXPRESSION       D ID TAB HEADINGS
                            G TH
------------------------- - -- --- ------------------------------------
========== TOP ========== = == === ==================================
RPT-AREA.CARRIER-CD         N 06 ___  _____
RPT-AREA.SHIPPING-WHSE      U 03 ___  /SHP/WHS/
RPT-AREA.BILL-LADING-NO     U 10 ___  /  BILL OF /LADING NO/
RPT-AREA.FREIGHT-CHARGE     U 09 ___  / FREIGHT/ CHARGE/
RPT-AREA.CALCULATED-WGT     U 06 ___  /CALCUL/WEIGHT/
RPT-AREA.SCALE-WEIGHT       U 06 ___  /ACTUAL/WEIGHT/
RPT-AREA.EXTRACT-DATE       U 08 ___  /REPORT/ DATE/
======== BOTTOM ========= = == === ==================================
```

The program will take current system date, compute the previous month, and compare that date to the BOFL-HEADER.EXTRACT-DATE to select the report records. The program will also accept a parameter input to override the compare date. This will be used in a rerun situation, for example when a report is lost and has to be regenerated.

We will complete the PARM screen for this program as one of the exercises at the end of this chapter. The working-storage and procedure areas of program CRRUSAGE will appear as follows:

```
LEVEL FIELD NAME        T I CH/DG OCCUR VALUE/COMMENT/DEP ON/COPY
1     WK-NUMERIC-YY      U Z   4
1     WK-NUMERIC-MM      U Z   2
```

```
1       WK-EXTRACT-DATE
 2        WK-EXTRACT-YEAR
  3         EXTRACT-CENT      X      2
  3         EXTRACT-YR        X      2
 2        EXTRACT-MM          X      2
1       WK-OVERRIDE-DT
 2        EXTRACT-YR          X      2
 2        EXTRACT-MM          X      2
1       WK-RPT-MONTH          X     10
1       RPT-AREA
 2        CARRIER-CD          X      6
 2        SHIPPING-WHSE       X      3
 2        BILL-LADING-NO      X     10
 2        FREIGHT-CHARGE      N      7.2
 2        CALCULATED-WGT      N      5
 2        SCALE-WEIGHT        N      5
 2        EXTRACT-DATE        X      8
 2        RPT-DATE            X     16
 2        CARRIER-NAME        X     30


:*************************************************************************
:**THIS PROGRAM WILL SELECT THE BILL OF LADING RECORDS FOR EITHER THE**
:**LAST MONTH OR A PARAMETER SELECTED MONTH, AND REPORT ON HOW MUCH   **
:**BUSINESS WE DID WITH EACH OF OUR FREIGHT CARRIERS                  **
:*************************************************************************
<<CRRUSAGE>> PROCEDURE
   MOVE PRM-OVERRIDE-DT TO WK-OVERRIDE-DT :THIS IS THE PARAMETER
                                         :SUPPLIED OVERRIDE DATE
    DO SET-EXTRACT-DT
    DO SET-REPORT-DT
    FOR EACH BOLF-HEADER
        IF  BOFL-HEADER.EXTRACT-YR = WK-EXTRACT-DATE.EXTRACT-YR
        AND BOFL-HEADER.EXTRACT-MM = WK-EXTRACT-DATE.EXTRACT-MM
            DO GET-SHIP-WHSE
            DO GET-CARRIER-RCD
            DO LOAD-RPT-LINE
            PRODUCE CRRUSAGE
        ENDIF
    ENDFOR
ENDPROC


:*************************************************************************
:**THIS AREA SETS THE REPORT EXTRACT DATE FROM THE LAST CURRENT MONTH**
:**OR THE PARAMETER SELECTED MONTH.                               **
```

```
;*********************************************************************
<<SET-EXTRACT-DT>> PROCEDURE
  IF WK-OVERRIDE-DT GT $SPACES            :USE PARAMETER DATE
      MOVE WK-OVERRIDE-DT.EXTRACT-YR TO WK-EXTRACT-DT.EXTRACT-YR
      MOVE WK-OVERRIDE-DT.EXTRACT-MM TO WK-EXTRACT-DT.EXTRACT-MM
    ELSE                                  :FIND LAST MONTH
      MOVE $YEAR                 TO WK-NUMERIC-DT.NUMERIC-YR
      MOVE $MONTH                TO WK-NUMERIC-DT.NUMERIC-MM
      IF WK-NUMERIC-DT.NUMERIC-MM = 1         :IF THIS IS JANUARY
          MOVE 12 TO WK-NUMERIC-DT.NUMERIC-MM :USE DECEMBER OF LAST YEAR
          SUB 1 FROM WK-NUMERIC-DT.NUMERIC-YR
        ELSE
          SUB 1 FROM WK-NUMERIC-DT.NUMERIC-MM :USE PREVIOUS MONTH THIS YR
      ENDIF
                                          :MOVE DATE FROM NUMERIC TO
                                          :ALPHANUMERIC FIELDS
      MOVE $EDIT(WK-NUMERIC-DATE.NUMERIC-MM,PIC='99')
        TO WK-EXTRACT-DT.EXTRACT-MM
      MOVE $EDIT(WK-NUMERIC-DATE.NUMERIC-YR,PIC='9999')
        TO WK-EXTRACT-DT.EXTRACT-YEAR
  ENDIF
ENDPROC


;*********************************************************************
;**THIS PARA STRINGS THE LITERAL FOR THE EXTRACT MONTH WITH THE      **
;**EXTRACT DATE TO FORM THE REPORT DATE                              **
;*********************************************************************
<<SET-REPORT-DT>> PROCEDURE
  MOVE $DATE('MONTH',DATE=WK-EXTRACT-DT.EXTRACT-MM) TO WK-RPT-MONTH
  MOVE $STRING(WK-RPT-MONTH,', ',WK-EXTRACT-DT.EXTRACT-YY)
    TO RPT-AREA.RPT-DATE
ENDPROC



;*********************************************************************
;**THIS PARA GETS THE SHIPPING WHSE FROM THE FIRST SHIPMENT RECORD   **
;**THAT IS RELATED TO THIS BILL OF LADING RECORD                     **
;*********************************************************************
<<GET-SHIP-WHSE>> PROCEDURE
  FOR EACH  BOFL-SHIPMENT
      WHERE BOFL-SHIPMENT.BILL-LADING-NO  = BOFL-HEADER.BILL-OF-LADING
      FOR FIRST SHIPMENT-HEADER
          WHERE SHIPMENT-HEADER.ORDER-NO     = BOFL-SHIPMENT.ORDER-NO
            AND SHIPMENT-HEADER.SHIPMENT-NO = BOFL-SHIPMENT.SHIPMENT-NO
```

```
                MOVE SHIPMENT-HEADER.SHIPPING-WHSE
                    TO RPT-AREA.SHIPPING-WHSE
        ENDFOR
    ENDFOR
ENDPROC


:***********************************************************************
:**THIS PARA GETS THE CARRIER NAME FROM THE CARRIER DOMAIN TABLE     **
:***********************************************************************
<<GET-CARRIER-RCD>> PROCEDURE
  FOR FIRST CARRIER-RCD
      WHERE CARRIER-RCD.CARRIER-CD       EQ BOFL-HEADER.CARRIER-CD
            MOVE CARRIER-RCD.CARRIER-NAME TO RPT-AREA.CARRIER-NAME
        WHEN  NONE
            MOVE $SPACES                 TO RPT-AREA.CARRIER-NAME
    ENDFOR
ENDPROC


:***********************************************************************
:**THIS PARA MOVES THE DATA FROM THE BOFL-HEADER TO THE REPORT LINE  **
:***********************************************************************
<<LOAD-RPT-LINE>> PROCEDURE
    MOVE BOFL-HEADER.CARRIER-CD     TO RPT-AREA.CARRIER-CD
    MOVE BOFL-HEADER.BILL-LADING-NO TO RPT-AREA.BILL-LADING-NO
    MOVE BOFL-HEADER.FREIGHT-CHARGE TO RPT-AREA.FREIGHT-CHARGE
    MOVE BOFL-HEADER.CALCULATED-WGT TO RPT-AREA.CALCULATED-WGT
    MOVE BOFL-HEADER.SCALE-WEIGHT   TO RPT-AREA.SCALE-WEIGHT
    MOVE $EDIT(BOFL-HEADER.EXTRACT-DATE,PIC='XX/XX/XX')
                                    TO RPT-AREA.EXTRACT-DATE
ENDPROC
```

Provide a Means of Updating the Freight-Rate Tables from a Tape File and Produce a Report of Changes

In this next example, we will read in a tape from the vendor who maintains our freight-rate tables, and produce a report of the expected changes by comparing it to our current freight-rate database.

The input file will be defined in the DATADICTIONARY as another QSAM file, and it will have the following fields:

```
FREIGHT-UPDT
  SHIPPING-WHSE
  FREIGHT-CLASS
```

```
SHIP-TO-ZIP

WEIGHT-BREAK

RATE
```

We will read this file into the program, and load each group of records with the same SHIPPING-WHSE, FREIGHT-CLASS, and SHIP-TO-ZIP into a table. We will then get the corresponding FREIGHT-RATE database records and load them into a similar table. We will compare the two tables, and print out a report if there are any differences.

The input dataset must be sorted into the proper sequence before the IDEAL program reads it because IDEAL does not have a way to sort incoming records from a QSAM file.

The detail section of the report definition is as follows:

```
------------------------------------------------------------------------

IDEAL: RPT DETAIL DEFN.    RPT FRTUPDT  (001) TEST       SYS:DEV


FIELD NAME, LITERAL        SORT  BREAK  FUNCTION COLUMN

FUNCTION, OR               L A   L S I  T M M A  H W

ARITHMETIC EXPRESSION      V /   V K N  O A I V  D ID TAB EDIT PATTERN

                          L D   L P D  T X N G  G TH

-------------------------  - -   - - -  - - - -  - --  ---  --------------

========== TOP ==========  = =   = = =  = = = =  = ==  ===  ==============

RPT-AREA.SHIPPING-WHSE     _ _   1 P G  _ _ _ _  U 03  ___  _____

RPT-AREA.FREIGHT-CLASS     _ _   2 1 G  _ _ _ _  U 03  ___  _____

RPT-AREA.SHIP-TO-ZIP       _ _   3 1 G  _ _ _ _  U 03  ___  _____

RPT-AREA.CURRENT-WGT       _ _   _ _ _  _ _ _ _  U 09  ___  Z,ZZZ,ZZ9

RPT-AREA.CURRENT-RATE      _ _   _ _ _  _ _ _ _  U 06  ___  ZZ,ZZ9

RPT-AREA.UPDATE-WEIGHT     _ _   _ _ _  _ _ _ _  U 09  ___  Z,ZZZ,ZZ9

RPT-AREA.UPDATE-RATE       _ _   _ _ _  _ _ _ _  U 06  ___  ZZ,ZZ9

RPT-AREA.CHANGE-TYPE       _ _   4 1 G  _ _ _ _  U 20  ___  _____

======== BOTTOM =========  = =   = = =  = = = =  = ==  ===  ==============
```

Since the records are sorted before they come into the program, we will not need the sort feature. We will page-break on SHIPPING-WHSE. Also FREIGHT-CLASS, SHIP-TO-ZIP, and CHANGE-TYPE will only print when one of their values changes.

The working storage will look like this:

```
LEVEL FIELD NAME         T I CH/DG OCCUR VALUE/COMMENT/DEP ON/COPY

1     RPT-AREA

  2     SHIPPING-WHSE    X      3
```

2	FREIGHT-CLASS	X	3		
2	SHIP-TO-ZIP	X	3		
2	CURRENT-WGT	X	7		
2	CURRENT-RATE	X	5		
2	UPDATE-WEIGHT	X	7		
2	UPDATE-RATE	X	5		
2	CHANGE-TYPE	X	20		
1	WK-SUBSR	N	3		
1	WK-LIMIT	N	3	50	
1	WK-CURR-TABLE			50	:TABLE FOR CURRENT DB REC
2	CURR-WEIGHT	N	7		
2	CURR-RATE	N	5		
1	WK-UPDT-TABLE			50	:TABLE FOR UPDATE RECORDS
2	UPDT-WEIGHT	N	7		
2	UPDT-RATE	N	5		
1	FG-FIRST-TIME	X	1	'Y'	
1	FG-WGT-CHANGE	X	1		
1	FG-RATE-CHANGE	X	1		
1	WK-UPDT-TBL-USE	N	3		
1	WK-CURR-TBL-USE	N	3		

Note that we have set up the two tables with 50 occurrences each. The FG-FIRST-TIME will be used to initialize the HOLD fields on the first input record.

The program will look like this:

```
:*********************************************************************
<<FRTUPDT>> PROCEDURE
  FOR EACH FREIGHT-UPDT
          IF FG-FIRST-TIME = 'Y'
             DO SET-NEXT-LOOP
          ENDIF
          IF  FREIGHT-UPDT.SHIPPING-WHSE = RPT-AREA.SHIPPING-WHSE
          AND FREIGHT-UPDT.FREIGHT-CLASS = RPT-AREA.FREIGHT-CLASS
          AND FREIGHT-UPDT.SHIP-TO-ZIP   = RPT-AREA.SHIP-TO-ZIP
          ELSE
             DO GROUP-BREAK
          ENDIF
          DO LOAD-UPDT-TABLE
  ENDFOR
  DO GROUP-BREAK                      :PROCESS THE LAST GROUP OF RECORDS
ENDPROC
```

```
:**************************************************************************
:**THIS PARA LOADS THE INPUT FILE INTO THE UPDATE TABLE                 **
:**************************************************************************
<<LOAD-UPDT-TABLE>> PROCEDURE
  ADD 1                      TO                          WK-SUBSR
  MOVE FREIGHT-UPDT.WEIGHT TO WK-UPDT-TABLE.UPDT-WEIGHT(WK-SUBSR)
  MOVE FREIGHT-UPDT.RATE    TO WK-UPDT-TABLE.UPDT-RATE  (WK-SUBSR)
  ADD  1                       TO WK-UPDT-TBL-USE
ENDPROC


:**************************************************************************
:**THIS AREA IS EXECUTED WHEN A DATA BREAK OCCURS                       **
:**************************************************************************
<<GROUP-BREAK>> PROCEDURE
  DO LOAD-CURR-TABLE
  DO COMPARE-TABLES
  IF FG-WGT-CHANGE  = 'Y'
  OR FG-RATE-CHANGE = 'Y'
     DO PRODUCE-RPT
     DO UPDATE-FRT-TBL
  ENDIF
  DO SET-NEXT-LOOP
ENDPROC


:=========================================================================
:==PARA FINDS THE CORRESPONDING FREIGHT-RATE RECORDS AND LOADS==
:===THEM INTO THEIR TABLE                                    ==
:=========================================================================
<<LOAD-CURR-TABLE>> PROCEDURE
  MOVE 0 TO WK-SUBSR
  FOR EACH   FRT-RATE-RCD
     WHERE FRT-RATE-RCD.SHIPPING-WHSE = FREIGHT-UPDT.SHIPPING-WHSE
        AND FRT-RATE-RCD.FREIGHT-CLASS = FREIGHT-UPDT.FREIGHT-CLASS
        AND FRT-RATE-RCD.SHIP-TO-ZIP   = FREIGHT-UPDT.SHIP-TO-ZIP
           ADD 1 TO WK-SUBSR
           MOVE FRT-RATE-RCD.WEIGHT TO CURR-WEIGHT(WK-SUBSR)
           MOVE FRT-RATE-RCD.RATE   TO CURR-RATE  (WK-SUBSR)
  ENDFOR
  MOVE WK-SUBSR TO WK-CURR-TBL-USE
ENDPROC


:=========================================================================
:==PARA COMPARES THE TWO FREIGHT RATE TABLES, IF TABLES HAVE A==
:===DIFFERENT NUMBER OF RECORDS, THEN THEY ARE AUTOMATICALLY   ==
```

```
:==DIFFERENT                                                       ==
:=================================================================
<<COMPARE-TABLES>> PROCEDURE
  MOVE 'N' TO FG-RATE-CHANGE
  MOVE 'N' TO FG-WGT-CHANGE
  IF WK-CURR-TBL-USE NE WK-UPDT-TBL-USE
     MOVE 'Y' TO FG-WGT-CHANGE
  ELSE
     LOOP VARYING WK-SUBSR FROM 1 BY 1
            UNTIL WK-SUBSR GT WK-UPDT-TBL-USE
                IF WK-CURR-WEIGHT(WK-SUBSR) NE WK-UPDT-WEIGHT(WK-SUBSR)
                   MOVE 'Y' TO FG-WGT-CHANGE
                ENDIF
                IF WK-CURR-RATE(WK-SUBSR)   NE WK-UPDT-RATE(WK-SUBSR)
                   MOVE 'Y' TO FG-RATE-CHANGE
                ENDIF
     ENDLOOP
ENDPROC



:=================================================================
:==AREA PRODUCES THE CHANGE REPORT FROM THE TWO TABLES       ==
:=================================================================
<<PRODUCE-RPT>> PROCEDURE
  DO REPORT-REASON
  LOOP VARYING WK-SUBSR FROM 1 BY 1
          UNTIL WK-SUBSR GT WK-CURR-TBL-USE
            AND WK-SUBSR GT WK-UPDT-TBL-USE
                DO REPORT-LINES
    ENDLOOP
ENDPROC



:-----------------------------------------------------------------
:--PARA SETS THE CHANGE TYPE THAT IS BEING REPORTED          --
:-----------------------------------------------------------------
<<REPORT-REASON>> PROCEDURE
  MOVE 0 TO WK-SUBSR
  IF FG-WGT-CHANGE = 'Y'
     MOVE 'WEIGHT BREAKS HAVE CHANGED' TO RPT-AREA.CHANGE-TYPE
  ELSE
     IF FG-RATE-CHANGE = 'Y'
        MOVE 'RATES HAVE CHANGED'       TO RPT-AREA.CHANGE-TYPE
     ENDIF
```

```
      ENDIF
   ENDPROC


:---------------------------------------------------------------
:--PARA MOVES DATA FROM THE TABLES TO THE REPORT. IF ONE TABLE--
:--IS SHORTER THAN THE OTHER, ITS SIDE WILL BE ZERO FILLED    --
:---------------------------------------------------------------
<<REPORT-LINES>> PROCEDURE
   IF WK-SUBSR LE WK-CURR-TBL-USE
      MOVE WK-CURR-TABLE.CURR-WEIGHT(WK-SUBSR) TO RPT-AREA.CURRENT-WGT
      MOVE WK-CURR-TABLE.CURR-RATE  (WK-SUBSR) TO RPT-AREA.CURRENT-RATE
   ELSE
      MOVE 0000000                       TO RPT-AREA.CURRENT-WGT
      MOVE 00000                         TO RPT-AREA.CURRENT-RATE
   ENDIF

   IF WK-SUBSR LE WK-UPDT-TBL-USE
      MOVE WK-UPDT-TABLE.CURR-WEIGHT(WK-SUBSR) TO RPT-AREA.UPDATE-WGT
      MOVE WK-UPDT-TABLE.CURR-RATE  (WK-SUBSR) TO RPT-AREA.UPDATE-RATE
   ELSE
      MOVE 0000000                       TO RPT-AREA.UPDATE-WGT
      MOVE 00000                         TO RPT-AREA.UPDATE-RATE
   ENDIF
   PRODUCE FRTUPDT
ENDPROC


:***************************************************************************
:**THIS PARA UPDATES THE DB TABLES WITH INPUT DATA                      **
:***************************************************************************
<<UPDATE-FRT-TBL>> PROCEDURE
:THIS PARAGRAPH WILL BE CODED AS PART OF THE EXERCISES AT THE END OF
:THIS CHAPTER
ENDPROC


:***************************************************************************
:**THIS PARA RESETS THE COMPARISON FIELDS FOR THE NEXT LOOP            **
:***************************************************************************
<<SET-NEXT-LOOP>> PROCEDURE
   MOVE 'N'                     TO FG-FIRST-TIME
   MOVE FREIGHT-UPDT.SHIPPING-WHSE TO RPT-AREA.SHIPPING-WHSE
   MOVE FREIGHT-UPDT.FREIGHT-CLASS TO RPT-AREA.FREIGHT-CLASS
   MOVE FREIGHT-UPDT.SHIP-TO-ZIP   TO RPT-AREA.SHIP-TO-ZIP
   MOVE 0 TO WK-SUBSR
   MOVE 0 TO WK-CURR-TBL-USE
```

```
MOVE 0 TO WK-UPDT-TBL-USE
ENDPROC
```

Conclusions

In reviewing this case study, we can see a number of IDEAL's strong points:

1. The ability to write highly structured programs through the use of structured constructs such as the FOR, LOOP, and SELECT.
2. The ability to code simple report programs through the use of the report definition fill-in screens.
3. The ease of use of the panel definition facility.
4. The availability of the IDEAL internal features such as $DATE, $EDIT, $TRIM, and $STRING.
5. The ability to read and write external QSAM files.
6. The ability to easily document code, thus making the program easier to read and understand.
7. The ability to enhance standard security facilities.
8. Enhanced readability through name concatination.

The exercises at the end of this chapter are further challenges based on this case study, and use information from throughout the entire text.

Exercises

1. What facility can you use to dynamically assign a printer to the BILL OF LADING print program, based on the shipping warehouse? How would this be coded?
2. Design the panel for the bill-of-lading header input.
3. Design the panel for the bill of lading/shipment relationships.
4. Write the BILL-OF-LADING header input program.
5. Why did we use an IF statement instead of a WHERE statement in the extract programs?
6. Code the parm area of CRRUSAGE.

```
LEVEL FIELD NAME      T I CH/DG OCCUR U M COMMENTS/DEP ON/COPY

_____ _____ _ _ _____ _____ _ _ _____

_____ _____ _ _ _____ _____ _ _ _____
```

7. What will the run statement look like?
8. Add a second report to CRRUSAGE, comparing CALCU-
   LATED-WGT to the SCALE-WGT, sorting by SHIPPING-
   WHSE and BILL-LADING-NO.

```
--------------------------------------------------------------------
IDEAL: RPT PARAMETERS              RPT ACCURACY (001) TEST        SYS: DEV
LINES PER PAGE ON PRINTOUT         60  ( 1 THRU 250)
REPORT WIDTH                       132 (40 THRU 230)
SPACING BETWEEN LINES              1   ( 1 THRU 3)
SPACING BETWEEN COLUMNS            01  ( 0 THRU 66 OR A=AUTOMATIC)
SUMMARIES ONLY                     N   (Y=YES,N=NO)
COLUMN HEADINGS DESIRED            Y   (Y=YES,N=NO)
COLUMN HEADINGS INDICATION         U   (U=UNDERSCORE,N=NONE,D=DASHES)
CONTROL BREAK HEADING              N   (Y=YES,N=NO)
CONTROL BREAK FOOTING              N   (Y=YES,N=NO)
GROUP CONTINUATION AT TOP OF PAGE  N   (Y=YES,N=NO)
ANNOTATED COUNT IN CONTROL FOOTINGS N  (Y=YES,N=NO)
REPORT FINAL SUMMARY TITLE         N   (Y=YES,N=NO)
  SPACING BEFORE SUMMARY           1   (1 THRU 9 = LINES,P=NEW PAGE)
  TITLE         _____

DATE
  POSITION         TL     (NO=NONE,BR=BOT.RIGHT,BL=BOT.LEFT,BC=BOT.CTR
                          TR=TOP RIGHT,TL=TOP LEFT,TC=TOP CENTER)
  FORMAT           YY/MM/DD
PAGE NUMBERS
  POSITION         TR
  FORMAT           P      (D=DIGITS ONLY, H=WITH HYPHENS, P=PAGE     NNN)


PAGE HEADING
  HEADING          _____
  POSITION         C      (C=CENTER, L=LEFT JUSTIFY, R=RIGHT JUSTIFY)



--------------------------------------------------------------------
IDEAL: RPT PAGE HEADING      RPT ACCURACY (001) TEST    SYS: DEV FILL-IN

FIELD NAME, LITERAL, FUNCTION                COLUMN
OR ARITHMETIC EXPRESSION                     W
                                             ID TAB EDIT PATTERN  COMMAND
                                             TH
_____ __ ___ _____ _____
_____ __ ___ _____ 000020
```

```
_____ __ ___ _____ 000030
_____ __ ___ _____ 000040
_____ __ ___ _____ 000050
_____ __ ___ _____ 000060
```

```
----------------------------------------------------------------------

IDEAL: RPT DETAIL DEFN.     RPT ACCURACY (001) TEST       SYS:DEV

FIELD NAME, LITERAL         SORT  BREAK  FUNCTION COLUMN

FUNCTION, OR                L A   L S I  T M M A  H W

ARITHMETIC EXPRESSION       V /   V K N  O A I V  D ID TAB EDIT PATTERN

                            L D   L P D  T X N G  G TH

--------------------------  - -   - - -  - - - -  - -- --- -------------

========== TOP ==========   = =   = = =  = = = =  = == === =============

_____   - -   - - -  - - - -  - -- --- _____

_____   - -   - - -  - - - -  - -- --- _____

_____   - -   - - -  - - - -  - -- --- _____

_____   - -   - - -  - - - -  - -- --- _____

_____   - -   - - -  - - - -  - -- --- _____

_____   - -   - - -  - - - -  - -- --- _____

======== BOTTOM =========   = =   = = =  = = = =  = == === =============
```

9. What coding changes would you make to program CRRUSAGE to produce a report that will inform the user that the peogram did not find any records to process?

10. Code the update paragraphs for program FRTUPDT.

Exercises — Answers

1. What facility can you use to dynamically assign a printer to the BILL OF LADING print program, based on the shipping warehouse? How would this be coded?
   We can dynamically change the output destination in the program with a SELECT statement based on the SHIPPING-WHSE.

```
SELECT SHIPMENT-HEADER.SHIPPING-WHSE
    WHEN '01' ASSIGN REPORT BOLPRINT DESTINATION SYSTEM RMT01
    WHEN '02' ASSIGN REPORT BOLPRINT DESTINATION SYSTEM RMT02
    WHEN '03' ASSIGN REPORT BOLPRINT DESTINATION SYSTEM RMT03
    WHEN '04' ASSIGN REPORT BOLPRINT DESTINATION SYSTEM RMT04
```

```
        WHEN '05' ASSIGN REPORT BOLPRINT DESTINATION SYSTEM RMT05
        ENDSELECT
```

2. Design the panel for the bill-of-lading header input.

```
------------------------------------------------------------------------
IDEAL: PANEL PARAMETERS     PNL BLHEADER (001) TEST    SYS: DEV FILL-IN
START      FIELD SYMBOL ^ NEW    FIELD SYMBOL +
END        FIELD SYMBOL ; DELETE FIELD SYMBOL *
REPEATING GROUP SYMBOL @


INPUT  FILL CHARACTER  S (S=SPACE, L=LOWVAL, Z=ZEROES, U=_,OTHER=ITSELF
OUTPUT FILL CHARACTER  U (S=SPACE, L=LOWVAL, Z=ZERORS, U=_,OTHER=ITSELF
NON-DISPLAY CHARACTER  S (S=SPACE, OTHER=AS SPECIFIED)
ERROR FILL CHARACTER   * (AS SPECIFIED)
CASE TRANSLATION       U (U=UPPER, M=MIXED)


REQUIRED               N (Y=YES, N=NO)
ERROR HANDLING         B (N=NONE, *=FILL W/ERRORFILL, H=HIGH INTENSITY,
                          (B=BOTH: H IF ILLEGAL VALUE & * IF REQ MISSING


PANEL WIDTH           80 (A VALUE BETWEEN 80 AND 236)
PF1=HELP, PF3=CLARIFY   Y (Y=YES, N=NO)
PF7=SCR -, PF8=SCR+     N (N=NO, Y=OPT Y, N=OPT N)
  PF10=SCR TOP, PF11=SCR BOT      (OPTION Y)
  PF10=SCR LEFT,PF11=SCR RIGHT    (OPTION Z)
EDIT-RULE ERROR PROC    C  (C=CLARIFY COMMAND, A=APPLICATION)
PROCESS APPL ON SCROLL N  (Y=YES, N=NO)
HELP PANEL NAME   _____  VERSION ___
PREFIX PANEL NAME _____  VERSION ___
SUFFIX PANEL NAME _____  VERSION ___
-------------------------- B O T T O M --------------------------------
```

```
------------------------------------------------------------------------
IDEAL: PANEL LAYOUT       PNL BLHEADER (001) TEST    SYS: DEV FILL-IN
START:      END: ;     NEW: +      DELETE: *      REPEAT: @
....+....1....+....2....+....3....+....4....+....5....+....6....+...7..
   +_____; +BILL OF LADING HEADER MAINTENANCE;

  +OPTION; +_; +(A=ADD V=VIEW U=UPDATE D=DELETE);

  +BILL OF LADING NUMBER  +_____;
  +CARRIER CODE;          +_____;
  +ACTUAL SCALE WEIGHT;   +_____;  +IN POUNDS;
```

```
+CALCULATED WEIGHT;        +_____;   +IN POUNDS;
+FREIGHT-CHARGE;           +_____;
+PRINT INDICATOR;          +_;
+EXTRACT INDICATOR/DATE +_; +_____;


+MESSAGE;       +_____;
```

```
-------------------------- B O T T O M -----------------------------


-----------------------------------------------------------------------
IDEAL: FIELD SUMMARY TABLE    PNL BLHEADER (001) TEST  SYS: DEV FILL-IN
=======================================================================
    +_____;     +BILL OF LADING HEADER MAINTENANCE;
    1              2
    ^OPTION;       ^_; ^(A=ADD V=VIEW U=UPDATE D=DELETE);
    3              4   5
.........................................................................
SEQ LV FIELD NAME       ATTR   T LEN  IN.DP OCC COMMENTS
--- -- --------------- ------ - ---- ----- --- -----------------------
  1  2 CURR-DATE        PSL    X   8
  2  2                  PSL    X  38            CUSTOMER DATABASE MAINTE
  3  2                  PSL    X   6            OPTION
  4  2 OPTION           UALE   X   1
  5  2                  PSL    X  30            (A=ADD V=VIEW U=UPDATE D
  6  2                  PSL    X  14            BILL OF LADING
  7  2 BILL-LADING-NO   UALE   X  10
  8  2                  PSL    X  12            CARRIER CODE
  9  2 CARRIER-CD       UALE   X   6
 10  2                  PSL    X  19            ACTUAL SCALE WEIGHT
 11  2 SCALE-WEIGHT     UNLE   N   6   4.1
 12  2                  PSL    X  17            CALCULATED WEIGHT
 13  2 CALCULATED-WGT   PSL    N   6   4.1
 14  2                  PSL    X  14            FREIGHT-CHARGE
 15  2 FREIGHT-CHARGE   PSL    N   7   4.2
 16  2                  PSL    X  15            PRINT INDICATOR
 17  2 PRINT-IND        PSL    X   1
 18  2                  PSL    X  22            EXTRACT INDICATOR/DATE
 19  2 EXTRACT-IND      PSL    X   1
 20  2 EXTRACT-DATE     PSL    X   8
 21  2                  PSL    X   7            MESSAGE
 22  2 MESSAGE          PSH    X  41
```

Note that the calculated values (CALCULATED-WGT and FREIGHT-CHARGE) and the system control fields (PRINT-IND, EXTRACT-IND, and EXTRACT-DATE) are protected and that they are grouped together in the lower part of the screen. They are required to be on this screen so that the user can view them, but they cannot be updated.

3. Design the panel for the bill of lading/shipment relationships.

One of the easiest solutions is to add the relationship input to the BLHEADER screen.

```
IDEAL: PANEL LAYOUT        PNL BLHEADER (001) TEST      SYS: DEV FILL-IN
START: ^    END: ;      NEW: +      DELETE: *      REPEAT: @
....+....1....+....2....+....3....+....4....+....5....+....6....+...7..
    +_____;     +BILL OF LADING HEADER MAINTENANCE;


    +OPTION; +_; +(A=ADD V=VIEW U=UPDATE D=DELETE);


    +BILL OF LADING NUMBER  +_____;
    +CARRIER CODE;          +_____;
    +ACTUAL SCALE WEIGHT;   +_____;    +IN POUNDS;


 @_____@__; @_____@__; @_____@__; @_____@__; @_____@__; @_____@__;


    +CALCULATED WEIGHT;     +_____;    +IN POUNDS;
    +FREIGHT-CHARGE;        +_____;
    +PRINT INDICATOR;       +_;
    +EXTRACT INDICATOR/DATE +_; +_____;


    +MESSAGE;       +_____;

-------------------------- B O T T O M --------------------------
```

```
_____        BILL OF LADING HEADER MAINTENANCE


   OPTION        (A=ADD V=VIEW U=UPDATE D=DELETE)


   BILL OF LADING NUMBER    _____
   CARRIER CODE             _____
   ACTUAL SCALE WEIGHT      _____        IN POUNDS
```

```
____ __   ____ __   ____ __   ____ __   ____ __   ____ __
____ __   ____ __   ____ __   ____ __   ____ __   ____ __
____ __   ____ __   ____ __   ____ __   ____ __   ____ __
____ __   ____ __   ____ __   ____ __   ____ __   ____ __
```

```
CALCULATED WEIGHT        _____      IN POUNDS

FREIGHT-CHARGE           _____

PRINT INDICATOR          _

EXTRACT INDICATOR/DATE   _   _____

       .

MESSAGE         _____


---------------------------- B O T T O M -----------------------------


------------------------------------------------------------------------
IDEAL: FIELD SUMMARY TABLE   PNL BLHEADER (001) TEST  SYS: DEV FILL-IN
========================================================================
   +_____;    +BILL OF LADING HEADER MAINTENANCE;
   1              2
  ^OPTION;        ^_; ^(A=ADD V=VIEW U=UPDATE D=DELETE);
   3              4  5
.........................................................................
SEQ LV FIELD NAME       ATTR   T LEN  IN.DP OCC COMMENTS
--- -- --------------   ------ - ----  ----- --- ------------------------
  1  2 CURR-DATE        PSL    X   8
  2  2                  PSL    X  38             CUSTOMER DATABASE MAINTE
  3  2                  PSL    X   6             OPTION
  4  2 OPTION           UALE   X   1
  5  2                  PSL    X  30             (A=ADD V=VIEW U=UPDATE D
  6  2                  PSL    X  14             BILL OF LADING
  7  2 BILL-LADING-NO   UALE   X  10
  8  2           ,      PSL    X  12             CARRIER CODE
  9  2 CARRIER-CD       UALE   X   6
 10  2                  PSL    X  19             ACTUAL SCALE WEIGHT
 11  2 SCALE-WEIGHT     UNLE   N   6   4.1
 12  2                                        4
 13  3 ORDER-CNTL-CL1   UALE   X   6
 14  3 SHIPMENTNO-CL1   UALE   X   2
 15  3 ORDER-CNTL-CL2   UALE   X   6
 16  3 SHIPMENTNO-CL2   UALE   X   2
 17  3 ORDER-CNTL-CL3   UALE   X   6
 18  3 SHIPMENTNO-CL3   UALE   X   2
 19  3 ORDER-CNTL-CL4   UALE   X   6
```

```
20  3 SHIPMENTNO-CL4   UALE   X    2
21  3 ORDER-CNTL-CL5   UALE   X    6
22  3 SHIPMENTNO-CL5   UALE   X    2
23  3 ORDER-CNTL-CL6   UALE   X    6
24  3 SHIPMENTNO-CL6   UALE   X    2
25  2                  PSL    X   17           CALCULATED WEIGHT
26  2 CALCULATED-WGT   PSL    N    6    4.1
27  2                  PSL    X   14           FREIGHT-CHARGE
28  2 FREIGHT-CHARGE   PSL    N    7    4.2
29  2                  PSL    X   15           PRINT INDICATOR
30  2 PRINT-IND        PSL    X    1
31  2                  PSL    X   22           EXTRACT INDICATOR/DATE
32  2 EXTRACT-IND      PSL    X    1
33  2 EXTRACT-DATE     PSL    X    8
34  2                  PSL    X    7           MESSAGE
35  2 MESSAGE          PSH    X   41
```

4. Write the BILL-OF-LADING header input program.

```
<<BLHEADER>>
  REFRESH  BLHEADER
  MOVE $DATE('MM/DD/YY') TO BLHEADER.CURR-DATE
  TRANSMIT BLHEADER
  LOOP UNTIL $PF2(BLHEADER)
       SELECT BLHEADER.OPTION
          WHEN 'V'  DO VIEW-BLHEADER
          WHEN 'I'  MOVE 'N'                TO FG-UPDATE-COMP
                    LOOP UNTIL $PF2(BLHEADER)
                       OR FG-UPDATE-COMP
                       OR BLHEADER.BILL-LADING-NO NE WK-BILL-LADING
                       OR BLHEADER.OPTION       NE 'I'
                          DO EDIT-INPUT
                          TRANSMIT BLHEADER
                          DO ADD-BLHEADER
                    ENDLOOP
          WHEN NONE DO INVALID-OPTION
       ENDSELECT
       TRANSMIT BLHEADER
  ENDLOOP
ENDPROC


:***********************************************************************
:** THIS PARAGRAPH VIEWS THE REQUESTED BOL HEADER              **
:***********************************************************************
```

```
<<VIEW-BLHEADER>> PROCEDURE

  DO REF-BLHEADER

  FOR FIRST BOFL-HEADER

      WHERE BOFL-HEADER.BILL-LADING NO       EQ BLHEADER.BILL-LADING-NO

             MOVE BOFL-HEADER.CARRIER-CD      TO BLHEADER.CARRIER-CD

             MOVE BOFL-HEADER.SCALE-WEIGHT    TO BLHEADER.SCALE-WEIGHT

             MOVE BOFL-HEADER.CALCULATED-WGT  TO BLHEADER.CALCULATED-WGT

             MOVE BOFL-HEADER.FREIGHT-CHARGE  TO BLHEADER.FREIGHT-CHARGE

             MOVE BOFL-HEADER.PRINT-IND       TO BLHEADER.PRINT-IND

             MOVE BOFL-HEADER.EXTRACT-IND     TO BLHEADER.EXTRACT-IND

             MOVE BOFL-HEADER.EXTRACT-DATE    TO BLHEADER.EXTRACT-DATE

             MOVE 'RECORD FOUND'              TO BLHEADER.MESSAGE

             DO GT-BOL-ORD-TBL

      WHEN  NONE

             MOVE $SPACES                     TO BLHEADER.CARRIER-CD

             MOVE 0000.0                      TO BLHEADER.SCALE-WEIGHT

             MOVE 0000.0                      TO BLHEADER.CALCULATED-WGT

             MOVE 0000.00                     TO BLHEADER.FREIGHT-CHARGE

             MOVE $SPACES                     TO BLHEADER.PRINT-IND

             MOVE $SPACES                     TO BLHEADER.EXTRACT-IND

             MOVE $SPACES                     TO BLHEADER.EXTRACT-DATE

             MOVE 'NO RECORD FOUND'           TO BLHEADER.MESSAGE

  ENDFOR

ENDPROC



:========================================================================
:== THIS PARAGRAPH REFRESHES THE HEADER SCREEN                        ==
:========================================================================
<<REF-BLHEADER>> PROCEDURE

  MOVE BLHEADER.BILL-LADING-NO TO WK-BILL-LADING

  REFRESH BLHEADER

  MOVE WK-BILL-LADING           TO BLHEADER.BILL-LADING-NO

  MOVE $DATE('MM/DD/YY')        TO BLHEADER.CURR-DATE

ENDPROC



:========================================================================
:== THIS PARAGRAPH GETS THE RELATED BOL SHIPMENT RECORDS             ==
:========================================================================
<<GT-BOL-ORD-TBL>> PROCEDURE

  MOVE 1 TO BLHEADER.SUBSR

  MOVE 0 TO BLHEADER.COLUMN

  FOR EACH  BOFL-SHIPMENT

      WHERE BOFL-SHIPMENT.BILL-LADING-NO     EQ BLHEADER.BILL-LADING-NO

            IF BLHEADER-SUBSR LE 4
```

```
                    DO LD-BOL-ORD-TBL
              ELSE
                    MOVE 'MORE SHIPMENT RECORDS AVAILABLE'
                                             TO BLHEADER.MESSAGE
              ENDIF
         WHEN  NONE
              MOVE 'NO SHIPMENT RECS FOUND'  TO BLHEADER.MESSAGE
      ENDFOR
   ENDPROC


   :=========================================================================
   :== THIS PARAGRAPH LOADS THE RELATED BOL SHIPMENT RECORDS          ==
   :=========================================================================
   <<LD-BOL-ORD-TBL>> PROCEDURE
      MOVE BOFL-SHIPMENT.ORDER-NO     TO WK-ORDER-NO
      MOVE BOFL-SHIPMENT.SHIPMENT-NO TO WK-SHIPMENT-NO
      ADD 1 TO BLHEADER-COLUMN
      SELECT BLHEADER-COLUMN
      WHEN 1 MOVE WK-ORDER-NO    TO BLHEADER.ORDER-CNTL-CL1(BLHEADER-SUBSR)
             MOVE WK-SHIPMENT-NO TO BLHEADER.SHIPMENTNO-CL1(BLHEADER-SUBSR)
      WHEN 2 MOVE WK-ORDER-NO    TO BLHEADER.ORDER-CNTL-CL2(BLHEADER-SUBSR)
             MOVE WK-SHIPMENT-NO TO BLHEADER.SHIPMENTNO-CL2(BLHEADER-SUBSR)
      WHEN 3 MOVE WK-ORDER-NO    TO BLHEADER.ORDER-CNTL-CL3(BLHEADER-SUBSR)
             MOVE WK-SHIPMENT-NO TO BLHEADER.SHIPMENTNO-CL3(BLHEADER-SUBSR)
      WHEN 4 MOVE WK-ORDER-NO    TO BLHEADER.ORDER-CNTL-CL4(BLHEADER-SUBSR)
             MOVE WK-SHIPMENT-NO TO BLHEADER.SHIPMENTNO-CL4(BLHEADER-SUBSR)
      WHEN 5 MOVE WK-ORDER-NO    TO BLHEADER.ORDER-CNTL-CL5(BLHEADER-SUBSR)
             MOVE WK-SHIPMENT-NO TO BLHEADER.SHIPMENTNO-CL5(BLHEADER-SUBSR)
      WHEN 6 MOVE WK-ORDER-NO    TO BLHEADER.ORDER-CNTL-CL6(BLHEADER-SUBSR)
             MOVE WK-SHIPMENT-NO TO BLHEADER.SHIPMENTNO-CL6(BLHEADER-SUBSR)
             MOVE 0             TO BLHEADER-COLUMN
             ADD  1             TO BLHEADER-SUBSR
      ENDSELECT
   ENDPROC


   :***********************************************************************
   :** THIS PARAGRAPH EDITS THE INPUTTED INFORMATION              **
   :** NOTE THAT WE SET THE ATTRIBUTE TEMPORARILY TO PROTECT WHEN THE  **
   :** DATA PASSES THE EDIT TO KEEP THE USER FROM CHANGING IT AFTER    **
   :** IT HAS BEEN VERIFIED AS CORRECT. THE PROGRAM THEN GIVES THE USER**
   :** THE OPPORTUNITY TO REVIEW THE DATA BEFORE THE UPDATE IS APPLIED **
   :***********************************************************************
   <<EDIT-INPUT>> PROCEDURE
      MOVE BLHEADER.BILL-LADING-NO           TO WK-BILL-LADING
```

```
    MOVE 'Y'                              TO FG-INPUT-CORR
    MOVE 'N'                              TO FG-UPDATE-COMP
    IF BLHEADER.CARRIER-CD                EQ $SPACES
       MOVE $LOW                          TO BLHEADER.CARRIER-CD
       SET ATTR 'UAHE'                    ON BLHEADER.CARRIER-CD
       MOVE 'N'                           TO FG-INPUT-CORR
       MOVE 'ENTER CARRIER-CD'            TO BLHEADER.MESSAGE
    ELSE
       FOR FIRST CARRIER-RCD
           WHERE CARRIER RCD.CARRIER-CD   EQ BLHEADER.CARRIER-CD
                 SET ATTR 'PSL' TEMP      ON BLHEADER.CARRIER-CD
           WHEN  NONE
                 SET ATTR 'UAHE'          ON BLHEADER.CARRIER-CD
                 MOVE 'N'                 TO FG-INPUT-CORR
                 MOVE 'INVALID CARRIER-CD' TO BLHEADER.MESSAGE
       ENDFOR
    ENDIF


    IF BLHEADER.SCALE-WEIGHT EQ 0
       SET ATTR 'UNH'                     ON BLHEADER.SCALE-WEIGHT
       MOVE 'N'                           TO FG-INPUT-CORR
       MOVE 'ENTER SCALE WEIGHT'          TO BLHEADER.MESSAGE
    ELSE
       SET ATTR 'PSL' TEMP                ON BLHEADER.SCALE-WEIGHT
    ENDIF


    IF BLHEADER.ORDER-CNTL-CL1(1) EQ $SPACES
       SET ATTR 'UAHE'                    ON BLHEADER.ORDER-CNTL-CL1(1)
       MOVE 'N'                           TO FG-INPUT-CORR
       MOVE 'ENTER ORDER NUMBERS'         TO BLHEADER.MESSAGE
    ELSE
       SET ATTR 'PSL' TEMP                ON BLHEADER.ORDER-CNTL-CL1(1)
    ENDIF


    IF FG-INPUT-CORR = 'Y'
       MOVE 'PRESS PF4 TO APPLY INPUT'    TO BLHEADER.MESSAGE
    ENDIF
ENDPROC


:*********************************************************************
:**THIS PARAGRAPH ADDS THE INPUTED DATA TO THE FILE              **
:*********************************************************************
<<ADD-BLHEADER>> PROCEDURE
  IF FG-INPUT-CORR           = 'Y'
```

```
    AND $PF4(BLHEADER)
    AND BLHEADER.OPTION          = 'I'
    AND BLHEADER.BILL-LADING-NO = TO WK-BILL-LADING
        FOR NEW BOFL-HEADER
            DO LD-BOLF-HEADER
            DO PROC-BOLF-SHIP
            DO PROC-LINE-INPUT :WRITTEN IN CHAPTER 12
            MOVE 'Y' TO FG-UPDATE-COMP
        ENDFOR
    ENDIF
ENDPROC


:*********************************************************************
:**THIS PARAGRAPH POPULATES THE NEW BOFL-HEADER RECORD            **
:*********************************************************************
<<LD-BOLF-HEADER>> PROCEDURE
  MOVE BLHEADER.BILL-LADING-NO     TO BOFL-HEADER.BILL-LADING-NO
  MOVE BLHEADER.CARRIER-CD         TO BOFL-HEADER.CARRIER-CD
  MOVE BLHEADER.SCALE-WEIGHT       TO BOFL-HEADER.SCALE-WEIGHT
  MOVE BLHEADER.CALCULATED-WGT     TO BOFL-HEADER.CALCULATED-WGT
  MOVE BLHEADER.FREIGHT-CHARGE     TO BOFL-HEADER.FREIGHT-CHARGE
  MOVE 'Y'                         TO BOFL-HEADER.PRINT-IND
  MOVE 'Y'                         TO BOFL-HEADER.EXTRACT-IND
  MOVE $SPACES                     TO BOFL-HEADER.EXTRACT-DATE
ENDPROC


:*********************************************************************
:**THIS AREA BUILDS THE BOFL SHIPMENT RECORDS FROM THE SCREEN DATA  **
:*********************************************************************
<<PROC-BOLF-SHIP>> PROCEDURE
  MOVE 0    TO BLHEADER-SUBSR
  LOOP VARYING BLHEADER-SUBSR FROM 1 BY 1
        UNTIL BLHEADER-SUBSR GT 4
        MOVE  0    TO BLHEADER-COLUMN
        LOOP  VARYING BLHEADER-COLUMN FROM 1 BY 1
              UNTIL BLHEADER-COLUMN GT 6
                    DO SELECT-FROM-SCR
                    IF WK-ORDER-NO GT $SPACES
                       DO BLD-BOFL-SHIP
                    ENDIF
        ENDLOOP
    ENDLOOP
  ENDPROC
```

```
<SELECT-FROM-SCR> PROCEDURE
   SELECT BLHEADER-COLUMN
   WHEN 1 MOVE BLHEADER.ORDER-CNTL-CL1(BLHEADER-SUBSR) TO WK-ORDER-NO
          MOVE BLHEADER.SHIPMENTNO-CL1(BLHEADER-SUBSR) TO WK-SHIPMENT-NO
   WHEN 2 MOVE BLHEADER.ORDER-CNTL-CL2(BLHEADER-SUBSR) TO WK-ORDER-NO
          MOVE BLHEADER.SHIPMENTNO-CL2(BLHEADER-SUBSR) TO WK-SHIPMENT-NO
   WHEN 3 MOVE BLHEADER.ORDER-CNTL-CL3(BLHEADER-SUBSR) TO WK-ORDER-NO
          MOVE BLHEADER.SHIPMENTNO-CL3(BLHEADER-SUBSR) TO WK-SHIPMENT-NO
   WHEN 4 MOVE BLHEADER.ORDER-CNTL-CL4(BLHEADER-SUBSR) TO WK-ORDER-NO
          MOVE BLHEADER.SHIPMENTNO-CL4(BLHEADER-SUBSR) TO WK-SHIPMENT-NO
   WHEN 5 MOVE BLHEADER.ORDER-CNTL-CL5(BLHEADER-SUBSR) TO WK-ORDER-NO
          MOVE BLHEADER.SHIPMENTNO-CL5(BLHEADER-SUBSR) TO WK-SHIPMENT-NO
   WHEN 6 MOVE BLHEADER.ORDER-CNTL-CL6(BLHEADER-SUBSR) TO WK-ORDER-NO
          MOVE BLHEADER.SHIPMENTNO-CL6(BLHEADER-SUBSR) TO WK-SHIPMENT-NO
ENDPROC


<BLD-BOFL-SHIP> PROCEDURE
   FOR NEW BOFL-SHIPMENT
          MOVE BLHEADER.BILL-LADING-NO TO BOFL-SHIPMENT.BILL-LADING-NO
          MOVE WK-ORDER-NO             TO BOFL-SHIPMENT.ORDER-NO
          MOVE WK-SHIPMENT-NO          TO BOFL-SHIPMENT.SHIPMENT-NO
   ENDFOR
ENDPROC


:******************************************************************
:**THIS PARAGRAPH IS EXECUTED WHEN THE USER CHOSES AN INVALID OPTION**
:******************************************************************
<<INVALID-OPTION>> PROCEDURE
   MOVE 'INVALID OPTION              TO BLHEADER.MESSAGE
ENDPROC
```

5. Why did we use an IF statement instead of a WHERE statement in the EXTRACT programs?

   Since the fields PRINT-IND and EXTRACT-IND are not defined as secondary keys, the use of a WHERE statement would have caused IDEAL to build a temporary index, causing the program to use more resources.

6. Code the PARM area of CRRUSAGE.

LEVEL	FIELD NAME	T	I	CH/DG	OCCUR	U	M	COMMENTS/DEP ON/COPY
1	P-EXTRACT-DATE	X		6		I	I	: OVERRIDE DATE AS PARM

```
_____  _____  _ _ _____  _____  _ _ _____
=========================B O T T O M====================================
```

7. What will the run statement look like?

```
RUN CRRUSAGE PARM '880606'
```

8. Add a second report to CRRUSAGE, comparing CALCU-LATED-WGT to the SCALE-WGT, sorting by SHIPPING-WHSE and BILL-LADING-NO.

```
------------------------------------------------------------------------
IDEAL: RPT PARAMETERS           RPT ACCURACY (001) TEST        SYS: DEV

LINES PER PAGE ON PRINTOUT         60  ( 1 THRU 250)
REPORT WIDTH                      132 (40 THRU 230)
SPACING BETWEEN LINES              1   ( 1 THRU 3)
SPACING BETWEEN COLUMNS            01  ( 0 THRU 66 OR A=AUTOMATIC)
SUMMARIES ONLY                     N   (Y=YES,N=NO)
COLUMN HEADINGS DESIRED            Y   (Y=YES,N=NO)
COLUMN HEADINGS INDICATION         U   (U=UNDERSCORE,N=NONE,D=DASHES)
CONTROL BREAK HEADING              N   (Y=YES,N=NO)
CONTROL BREAK FOOTING              N   (Y=YES,N=NO)
GROUP CONTINUATION AT TOP OF PAGE  N   (Y=YES,N=NO)
ANNOTATED COUNT IN CONTROL FOOTINGS N  (Y=YES,N=NO)
REPORT FINAL SUMMARY TITLE         N   (Y=YES,N=NO)
  SPACING BEFORE SUMMARY           1   (1 THRU 9 = LINES,P=NEW PAGE)
  TITLE        _____


DATE
  POSITION        TL    (NO=NONE,BR=BOT.RIGHT,BL=BOT.LEFT,BC=BOT.CTR
                         TR=TOP RIGHT,TL=TOP LEFT,TC=TOP CENTER)
  FORMAT          YY/MM/DD


PAGE NUMBERS
  POSITION        TR
  FORMAT          P     (D=DIGITS ONLY, H=WITH HYPHENS, P=PAGE    NNN)

PAGE HEADING
  HEADING         _____
  POSITION        C     (C=CENTER, L=LEFT JUSTIFY, R=RIGHT JUSTIFY)
```

```
------------------------------------------------------------------------

IDEAL: RPT PAGE HEADING     RPT ACCURACY (001) TEST    SYS: DEV FILL-IN


FIELD NAME, LITERAL, FUNCTION              COLUMN
OR ARITHMETIC EXPRESSION                   W
                                           ID TAB EDIT PATTERN   COMMAND
                                           TH


_____   __ ___  _____  _____
'BOL WEIGHT ACCURACY REPORT'               30 050  _____   000020
_____   __ L01  _____   000030
RPT-AREA.WHSE-NO                           03 010  _____   000040


------------------------------------------------------------------------

IDEAL: RPT DETAIL DEFN.     RPT ACCURACY (001) TEST         SYS:DEV


FIELD NAME, LITERAL      SORT  BREAK  FUNCTION COLUMN
FUNCTION, OR            L A   L S I  T M M A  H W
ARITHMETIC EXPRESSION   V /   V K N  O A I V  D ID TAB EDIT PATTERN
                       L D   L P D  T X N G  G TH
-------------------------  - -   - - -   - - - -   - -- ---  -------------
========= TOP ==========   = =   = = =   = = = =   = == ===  =============
RPT-AREA.WHSE-NO           1 A   1 P N   _ _ _ _   _ 03 ___  _____
RPT-AREA.CALCULATED-WGT    _ _   _ _ _   _ _ _ _   _ __ ___  ZZZZ9.9
RPT-AREA.SCALE-WGT         _ _   _ _ _   _ _ _ _   _ __ ___  ZZZZ9.9
======= BOTTOM =========   = =   = = =   = = = =   = == ===  =============
```

9. What coding changes would you make to program CRRUSAGE to produce a report that will inform the user that the peogram did not find any records to process?

We could add a flag to the program that would be set to true whenever a report line was produced. If no report lines were produced, the flag would retain its initial value of false. In this case we could execute the following parargaph:

```
<<NULL-REPORT>> PROCEDURE
   MOVE '******'     TO RPT-AREA.CARRIER-CD
   MOVE 'NULL REPORT' TO RPT-AREA.CARRIER-NAME
   MOVE '***'        TO RPT-AREA.SHIPPING-WHSE
   MOVE '**********' TO RPT-AREA.BILL-LADING-NO
   PRODUCE CRRUSAGE
   PRODUCE CRRUSAGE
   MOVE ' NO'        TO RPT-AREA.SHIPPING-WHSE
```

```
MOVE 'RECS FOUND'   TO RPT-AREA.BILL-LADING-NO
PRODUCE CRRUSAGE
MOVE '***'          TO RPT-AREA.SHIPPING-WHSE
MOVE '**********'   TO RPT-AREA.BILL-LADING-NO
PRODUCE CRRUSAGE
PRODUCE CRRUSAGE
```

This would produce the following partial report:

```
******   NULL REPORT


SHP   BILL OF     FREIGHT   CALCUL ACTUAL REPORT
WHS   LADING NO   CHARGE    WEIGHT WEIGHT DATE


____  _____  _____  _____ _____ _____
***   **********         0       0      0
***   **********         0       0      0
NO RECS FOUND            0       0      0
***   **********         0       0      0
***   **********         0       0      0


                         0       0      0
```

10. Code the update paragraphs for program FRTUPDT.

```
:***********************************************************************
:**THIS PARA UPDATES THE DB TABLES WITH INPUT DATA                   **
:***********************************************************************
<<UPDATE-FRT-TBL>> PROCEDURE
  MOVE 0 TO WK-SUBSR
  IF FG-WGT-CHANGE = 'Y'
     DO DELETE-FRT-TBL
  ENDIF
  LOOP VARYING WK-SUBSR FROM 1 BY 1
        UNTIL WK-SUBSR GT WK-UPDT-TBL-USE
              SELECT FIRST
                 WHEN FG-WGT-CHANGE  = 'Y' DO INSERT-FRT-TBL
                 WHEN FG-RATE-CHANGE = 'Y' DO UPDATE-FRT-TBL
              ENDSELECT
  ENDLOOP
ENDPROC


:=======================================================================
:== PARAGRAPH DELETES OLD WEIGHT STRUCTURE IN PREPERATION FOR         ==
:== INSERTING THE NEW STRUCTURE                                       ==
```

```
:=======================================================================
<<DELETE-FRT-TBL>> PROCEDURE
  FOR EACH   FRT-RATE-RCD
      WHERE FRT-RATE-RCD.SHIPPING-WHSE = RPT-AREA.SHIPPING-WHSE
        AND FRT-RATE-RCD.FREIGHT-CLASS = RPT-AREA.FREIGHT-CLASS
        AND FRT-RATE-RCD.SHIP-TO-ZIP   = RPT-AREA.SHIP-TO-ZIP
            DELETE FRT-RATE-RCD
  ENDFOR
ENDPROC


:=======================================================================
:==PARAGRAPH INSERTS NEW WEIGHT STRUCTURE INTO THE DATABASE          ==
:=======================================================================
<<INSERT-FRT-TBL>> PROCEDURE
  MOVE 0 TO WK-SUBSR
  FOR NEW    FRT-RATE-RCD
            ADD 1 TO WK-SUBSR
            MOVE RPT-AREA.SHIPPING-WHSE TO FRT-RATE-RCD.SHIPPING-WHSE
            MOVE RPT-AREA.FREIGHT-CLASS TO FRT-RATE-RCD.FREIGHT-CLASS
            MOVE RPT-AREA.SHIP-TO-ZIP   TO FRT-RATE-RCD.SHIP-TO-ZIP
            MOVE UPDT-WEIGHT(WK-SUBSR)   TO FRT-RATE-RCD.WEIGHT
            MOVE UPDT-RATE  (WK-SUBSR)   TO FRT-RATE-RCD.RATE
  ENDFOR
ENDPROC


:=======================================================================
:==PARAGRAPH UPDATES CURRENT WEIGHT STRUCTURE WITH NEW RATES         ==
:==WEIGHT BREAKS SHOULD LINE UP AUTOMATICALLY                        ==
:=======================================================================
<UPDATE-FRT-TBL> RPOCEDURE
  MOVE 0 TO WK-SUBSR
  FOR EACH  FRT-RATE-RCD
      WHERE FRT-RATE-RCD.SHIPPING-WHSE = FRTRATE.SHIPPING-WHSE
        AND FRT-RATE-RCD.FREIGHT-CLASS = FRTRATE.FREIGHT-CLASS
        AND FRT-RATE-RCD.SHIP-TO-ZIP   = FRTRATE.SHIP-TO-ZIP
            ADD 1 TO WK-SUBSR
            MOVE UPDT-RATE  (WK-SUBSR)  TO FRT-RATE-RCD.RATE
  ENDFOR
ENDPROC
```

IDEAL Edit Patterns

CATEGORY AND	DATA IN	EDIT	ALPHANUMERIC
MEANING	SOURCE	PATTERN	RESULT

===

Alphanumeric Data

X ALPHANUMERIC CHARACTER	STATE	X(5)	STATE
B BLANK SPACE	1234	BXXXX	1234
ANY OTHER CHARACTER	AB1234	XXX-XXX	AB1-234

Numeric Data

9	UNSUPRESSED NUMERIC	123	999	123
Z	ZERO SUPRESSION	V12**	ZZZ.99	.12
*	ASTERISK REPLACEMENT	1V23	**9.99	**1.23
,	COMMA	123456.78	ZZZ,ZZZ.99	123,456.99
/	SLASH	123083	99/99/99	12/30/83
B	BLANK SPACE	123083	99B99B99	12 30 83
0	ZERO	123	99900	12300
.	DECIMAL POINT	23V45	ZZZ.99	23.45
-	MINUS SIGN FIXED RIGHT	23V45	ZZZ.99-	23.45-
-	MINUS SIGN FIXED LEFT	23V45	-ZZZ.99	- 23.45
-	MINUS SIGN FLOATING	23V45	---Z.99	--23.45

```
+   PLUS SIGN FIXED RIGHT        23V45          ZZZ.99-          23.45+
+   PLUS SIGN FIXED LEFT         23V45          -ZZZ.99        +  23.45
+   PLUS SIGN FLOATING           23V45          ---Z.99         +23.45
CR  CREDIT SYMBOL               023V45          999.99CR        23.45CR
DB  CREDIT SYMBOL               023V45          999.99DB        23.45DB
$   DOLLAR SIGN FIXED           023V45          $999.99        $ 23.45
$   DOLLAR SIGN FLOATING        023V45          $$$$.99        $23.45
<>  ENCLOSED NEGATIVES IN <>    -23V45          <999.99>       <  23.45>
<>  ENCLOSED NEG IN <> FLOAT    -23V45          <<<<.99>        <23.45>
```

IDEAL Reserved Words

ACTION	DATAVIEW
ADD	DATE
ALARM	DBID
ALL	DESCRIPTION
ALPHANUMERIC	DESCENDING
ADD	DESTINATION
ANY	DISPOSITION
ASCENDING	DELETE
ASSIGN	DO
AT	DOWN
ATTR	DUPLICATE
ATTRIBUTE	EACH
ATTRIBUTES	EJECT
AUXLIST1	ELSE
AUXLIST2	ENDFOR
AUXLIST3	ENDIF
AUXLIST4	ENDLOOP
AUXLIST5	ENDSEL
AUXLIST6	ENDSELECT
AUXLIST7	ENDPROC
AUXLIST8	ENDPROCEDURE
AUXLIST9	ENSURE
BACKOUT	ERROR
BY	EQ
CALL	EQUAL
CHECKPOINT	EVERY
CLEAR	FALSE
COLOR	FIRST
CONTAINS	FOR
COPIES	FROM
CURSOR	GE

GREATER	RECEIVED
GT	REFRESH
HIGHLIGHT	REINPUT
HOME	RELEASE
IF	REPORT
INPUT	RESET
INVERT	RESPONSE
INVISIBLE	RUN
IS	SELECT
LE	SET
LESS	SKIP
LIBRARY	SUBTRACT
LIST	SYSTEM
LOOP	TEMP
LOWLIGHT	THAN
LT	THE
MAXLINES	THEN
MOVE	THRU
NAME	TIMES
NE	TO
NETWORK	TRANSFER
NEW	TRANSMIT
NEWPAGE	TRUE
NEXT	UNIQUE
NO	UNPR
NONE	UNPROTECTED
NOT	UNTIL
NOTIFY	USING
NUMERIC	UP
ON	UPDATE
OR	VARYING
ORDERED	WHEN
OTHER	WHERE
PAGE	WHILE
PANEL	WITH
PARMS	XHIGHLIGHT
POSITION	$ABS
PROC	$ACCOUNT-ID
PROCEDURE	$ALPHABETIC
PROCESS	$CHAR-TO-HEX
PRODUCE	$COUNT
PROGRAM	$CPU
PROTECTED	$CURSOR
QUIT	$DATE

$DAY

$DBCS ATTACH

$DBCS DETACH

$EDIT

$EMPTY

$ENTER KEY

$ERROR-CLASS

$ERROR-DESCRIPTION

$ERROR-DVW-DBID

$ERROR-DVW-STATUS

$ERROR-DVW-INTERNAL-TYPE

$ERROR-NAME

$ERROR-PGM

$ERROR-PROC

$ERROR-STMT

$ERROR-TYPE

$ERROR-VALUE

$EXP

$FILLER

$FINAL-ID

$FIXED-MASK

$FIX-MASK

$HEX-TO-CHAR

$HIGH

$INDEX

$INTERNAL-DATE

$INT-DATE

$KEY

$LENGTH

$LOW

$MAIN

$MONTH

$NUMBER

$NUMERIC

$PAD

$PANEL-ERROR

$PANEL-FIELD-ERROR

$PANEL-GROUP-OCCURS

$PF1 $PF01

$PF2 $PF02

$PF3 $PF03

$PF4 $PF04

$PF5 $PF05

$PF6 $PF06

$PF7 $PF07

$PF8 $PF08

$PF9 $PF09

$PF10 - $PF48

$RC

$RECEIVED

$REMAINDER

$RETURN-CODE

$ROUND

$SPACE $SPACES

$SQRT

$STRING

$SUBSCRIPT-POSITION

$SUBSTR

$TERMINAL-ID

$TIME

$TODAY

$TRANSACTION-ID

$TRANSLATE

$TRIM

$VERIFY

$VERIFY-DATE $VER-DATE

$WEEKDAY

$YEAR

$USER-ID

$USER-NAME

IDEAL Development Screen Examples

```
IDEAL: MAIN MENU          MEM EHP.SIGNON          SYS: DEV  MENU


ENTER DESIRED OPTION NUMBER ===  THERE ARE 9 OPTIONS IN THIS MENU:


1. PROGRAM                DEFINE AND MAINTAIN PROGRAMS

2. DATAVIEW               DISPLAY DATAVIEW DEFINITIONS

3. PDF                    PANEL DEFINITION FACILITY

4. RDF                    REPORT DEFINITION FACILITY

5. PROCESS                COMPILE, RUN, SUBMIT

6. DISPLAY                DISPLAY ENTITIES

7. PRINT                  PRINT ENTITIES

8. ADMINISTRATION         ADMINISTRATION FUNCTIONS

9. OFF                    END IDEAL SESSION
```

Figure B-1   Main Menu Screen.

```
IDEAL: XXXXXXX MAINTAINCE    XXX                        SYS: DEV   MENU


ENTER DESIRED OPTION NUMBER ==    THERE ARE  7 OPTIONS IN THIS MENU

   1. EDIT/DISPLAY       - EDIT OR DISPLAY A XXXXXXX

   2. CREATE             - CREATE A XXXXXXX

   3. PRINT              - PRINT A XXXXXXX

   4. DELETE             - DELETE A XXXXXXX

   5. MARK STATUS        - MARK PROGRAM STATUS TO PRODUCTION OR HISTORY

   6. DUPLICATE          - DUPLICATE XXXXXX TO NEXT VERSION OR NEW NAME

   7. DISPLAY INDEX      - DISPLAY INDEX OF XXXXXXX NAMES IN SYSTEM
```

Figure B-2   Entity Maintenance Menu.

```
IDEAL: EDIT/DISPLAY PROGRAM    PGM                SYS: DEV PROMPTER


EDIT/DISPLAY _ PROGRAM _____    VERSION LAST  PROC
             (1)          (2)              (3)   (4)
```

```
(1) E = EDIT     (2) NAME (3) NNN = VER. #  (4) IDE  = IDENTIFICATION
    D = DISPLAY              PROD (DISPLAY       RES  = RESOURCE TABLE
                                   ONLY)         PAR  = PARAMETER DEF
                            LAST                 WOR  = WORKING DATA
                                                 PROC = PROCEDURE
```

Figure B-3   EDIT Program Definition Prompt Screen.

```
IDEAL: EDIT/DISPLAY REPORT     RPT                SYS: DEV PROMPTER


EDIT/DISPLAY _ REPORT _____    VERSION LAST  DET
             (1)          (2)              (3)   (4)
```

```
(1) E = EDIT     (2) NAME (3) NNN = VER. #  (4) IDE = IDENTIFICATION
    D = DISPLAY              PROD (DISPLAY       PAR = PARAMETERS
                                   ONLY)         HEA = PAGE HEADING
                            LAST                 DET = DETAIL
                                                 COL = COLUMN HEADING
```

Figure B-4   EDIT Report Definition Prompt Screen.

```
IDEAL: EDIT/DISPLAY PANEL        PNL                    SYS: DEV PROMPTER

EDIT/DISPLAY _    PANEL _____   VERSION  LAST  LAY _____
           (1)              (2)              (3)   (4)      (5)

(1) E = EDIT    (2) NAME (3) NNN = VER. #  (4)IDE = IDENTIFICATION
    D = DISPLAY              PROD (DISPLAY     PAR = PARAMETERS
                                   ONLY)       LAY = LAYOUT
                            LAST              SUM = SUMMARY
                                             FIE = FIELD
                                             FAC = FACSIMILE
                                             IRU = INPUT RULES
                                             ORU = OUTPUT RULES

                                         (5)FIELD NAME
                                            OR NUMBER
                                            WHEN (4) is FIE
```

Figure B-5   EDIT Panel Definition Prompt Screen.

```
IDEAL: EDIT/DISPLAY PANEL          DVW       SYS:DEV    PROMPTER

  DISPLAY    DATAVIEW  _____   VERSION   LAST
                           (1)                     (2)

  (1) DATAVIEW NAME      (2) NNN = VER. #
                             PROD (DISPLAY
                             LAST
```

Figure B-6   DISPLAY DATAVIEW Prompt Screen.

```
IDEAL: CREATE              XXX                 SYS: DEV PROMPTER

CREATE   XXX    _____
         (1)     (2)

(1) PGM=PROGRAM (2) NAME
    PNL=PANEL
    RPT=REPORT
    SYS=SYSTEM
    USR=USER
```

Figure B-7   CREATE Prompt.

```
IDEAL: DELETE              XXX  (001) TEST      SYS: DEV PROMPTER


DELETE  XXX  _____   VERSION LAS
        (1)      (2)              (3)



(1) PGM=PROGRAM USR=USER DEFINITION   (2) NAME (3) VER.# ONLY
    PNL=PANEL   SYS=SYSTEM DEFINITION
    RPT=REPORT  OUT=OUTPUT
    SYS=SYSTEM
    USR=USER
```

Figure B-8   DELETE Prompt Screen.

```
IDEAL: MARK STATUS        XXX  (001) TEST      SYS: DEV PROMPTER


MARK STATUS   XXX  _____   VERSION LAST TO ____
              (1)      (2)                (3)      (4)



(1) PGM = PROGRAM (2) NAME (3) NNN = VER. # (4) PROD = PRODUCTION
    PNL = PANEL             PROD             HIST = HISTORY
    RPT = REPORT
    SYS = SYSTEM
    USR = USER
```

Figure B-9   MARK STATUS Prompt Screen.

```
IDEAL: DUPLICATE          XXX  (001) TEST      SYS: DEV PROMPTER


DUPLICATE XXX _____  VERSION LAST SYSTEM ___ TO _____ _____
          (1)      (2)              (3)      (4)     (5)    (6)



(1) PGM=PROGRAM (2) NAME (3) NNN=VER.# (4) ORIGIONAL    5-6:NEXT VERSION
    PNL=PANEL             LAST          SYSTEM ID           OR
    RPT=REPORT           PROD          (DEFAULT      "NEWNAME" NAME
    SYS=SYSTEM                          CURRENT)  (FOR PGM,PNL,
    USR=USER                                               RPT,MEM)
    MEM=MEMBER
```

Figure B-10   DUPLICATION Prompt Screen.

```
NAME          VER S DESCRIPTION                        CREATED   UPDATED
BLPGA000      001 T MANUAL INVOICE HEADER PROCES 11/18/83 04/10/84 NON-SHR
BLPGA000      002 T MANUAL INVOICE HEADER PROCES 04/10/84 04/10/84 NON-SHR
BLPGA007      001 T ADD INVOICE TO SALES HISTORY 01/25/84 05/09/84 NON-SHR
BLPGA007      002 T ADD INVOICE TO SALES HISTORY 02/02/84 02/16/84 NON-SHR
BLPGA007      003 T ADD INVOICE TO SALES HISTORY 12/16/84 05/30/84 NON-SHR
BLPGA007      004 T ADD INVOICE TO SALES HISTORY 05/30/84 08/22/84 NON-SHR
BLPGA107      001 T LINE DIRECTION PGM           11/18/83 04/10/84 NON-SHR
BLPGBLCU      001 T CLEANUP BILLING DB           07/03/85 09/13/85 NON-SHR
```

Figure B-11   INDEX Display Example.

```
IDEAL: DISPLAY INDEX        XXX  (001) TEST        SYS: DEV PROMPTER


DISPLAY INDEX ___  _____  VERSION ___
              (1)       (2)                  (3)


   RELATED TO ___  _____  VERSION ___
              (4)       (5)                  (6)
```

```
(1) PGM=PROGRAM   (2) ENTITY NAME    (3)  VERSION: NNN=VER.#
    PNL=PANEL                                  TEST
    RPT=REPORT                                 PROD
    SYS=SYSTEM                                 HIST
    USR=USER
    DVW=DATAVIEW
    MEM=MEMBER


(4) PGM=PROGRAM   (5) ENTITY NAME    (6)  VERSION: NNN=VER.#
    PNL=PANEL                                  TEST
    RPT=REPORT                                 PROD
    SYS=SYSTEM                                 HIST
    USR=USER
    DVW=DATAVIEW
```

Figure B-12   INDEX Display Prompt.

```
IDEAL: PROCESS PROGRAM    PGM XXXXXXXX (XXX) TEST      SYS:DEV MENU


ENTER DESIRED OPTION NUMBER ==   THERE ARE 3 OPTIONS IN THIS MENU


 1. COMPILE      - COMPILE A PROGRAM

 2. RUN          - RUN A PROGRAM ONLINE

 3. SUBMIT       - SUBMIT A MEMBER CONTAINING A BATCH JOBSTREAM

 4. EXECUTE      - EXECUTE A MEMBER CONTAINING IDEAL COMMANDS

 5. PRODUCE      - PRODUCE A REPORT FACSIMILE
```

Figure B-13   PROCESS Selection Menu Screen.

```
IDEAL: COMPILE PROGRAM          XXX              SYS:DEV  PROMPTER


COMPILE _____   VERSION   LAST
           (1)                (2)


IDE   N    EXD   N    BOD   N    ADV   Y    MEL   Y    PNL  N
      (3)        (4)        (5)        (6)        (7)


DESTINATION LIB _____ COPIES  1   NAME _____ DISP HOL
                (8)   (9)             (10)        (11)      (12)
-------------------------------------------------------------------
(1) PROGRAM NAME
(2) VERSION: NNN = VER.#, PROD, LAST
(3)-(9): COMPILER LISTING OPTIONS, Y=YES, N=NO
  (3) IDE = IDENTIFICATION
  (4) EXD = EXTERNAL DATA (DATAVIEWS, PANELS, REPORTS)
  (5) BOD = BODY (WORKING DATA, PARAMETERS, PROCEDURE)
  (6) ADV = ADVISORY MESSAGES
  (7) MEL = MARK ERROR LINES IN LIBRARY
  (8) PNL = PANEL LISTING F=FULL S=SHORT N=NO LISTING
(9)-(13):COMPILE LISTING DESTINATION INFORMATION:(11) #COPIES
(9) LIB=OUTPUT LIBRARY  (10) SYSTEM               (12) PRINTOUT NAME
    SYS=SYSTEM PRINTER       DESTINATION          (13) REL=RELEASE,
    NET=NETWORK PRINTER      NAME                      HOL=HOLD,KEE=KEEP
```

Figure B-14   COMPILATION Prompt Screen.

```
IDEAL: RUN PROGRAM              XXX              SYS:DEV  PROMPTER


RUN   _____   VERSION   LAST    UPDATE DB?   Y
        (1)                (2)                  (3)


PARAMETER _____
                   (4)


REPORT OPTIONS:
DEST LIB _____ COPIES  1  DISP HOL  MAXLINES _____ DESC _____
     (5)    (6)           (7)    (8)             (9)            (10)
------------------------------------------------------------------------
(1) PROGRAM NAME
(2) VERSION: NNN = VER.#, PROD, LAST
(3) UPDATE DB?: Y=YES, N=NO
(4) USER PARAMETER TO THE APPLICATION PROGRAM (MUST BE IN QUOTES)
(5) LIB = OUTPUT LIBRARY   (6) SYSTEM      (7) # COPIES (8) REL=RELEASE
    SYS = SYSTEM PRINTER        PRINTER NAME               HOL=HOLD
    NET = NETWORK PRINTER                                  KEE=KEEP
(9) MAXIMUM LINES PER REPORT       (10) DESCRIPTION (MUST BE IN QUOTES)
NOTE: OUTPUT NAMES WILL BE THE SAME AS REPORT NAMES
```

Figure B-15   RUN PROGRAM Prompt Screen.

```
IDEAL: SUBMIT MEMBER     PGM XXXXXXXX (XXX) TEST  SYS:DEV PROPMTER

SUBMIT _____
     (MEMBER NAME)
```

Figure B-16   SUBMIT MEMBER Screen.

```
IDEAL: EXECUTE MEMBER     PGM XXXXXXXX (XXX) TEST  SYS:DEV PROPMTER


EXECUTE _____     USER _____
          (1)               (2)


    (1)  MEMBER NAME
    (2)  USER NAME
```

Figure B-17   EXECUTE MEMBER Screen.

```
IDEAL: PRODUCE FACSIMILE          RPT                    SYS:DEV  PROMPTER


PRODUCE RPT    _____
               (1)


FOR PROGRAM    _____   VERSION    LAST
               (2)                   (3)


DETAIL ____
       (4)


REPORT OPTIONS:
DEST LIB _____ COPIES  1  DISP HOL  MAXLINES _____  DESC _____
     (5)   (6)            (7)    (8)            (9)            (10)
```

```
(1) REPORT NAME
(2) NAME OF PROGRAM WHOSE RESOURCE TABLE CONTAINS THIS REPORT
(3) VERSION: NNN = VER.#, PROD, LAST
(4) NUMBER OF OUTPUT RECORDS TO BE PRODUCED
(5) LIB = OUTPUT LIBRARY   (6) SYSTEM      (7) # COPIES (8) REL=RELEASE
    SYS = SYSTEM PRINTER        PRINTER NAME             HOL=HOLD
    NET = NETWORK PRINTER                                KEE=KEEP
(9) MAXIMUM LINES PER REPORT       (10) DESCRIPTION (MUST BE IN QUOTES)
NOTE: OUTPUT NAMES WILL BE THE SAME AS REPORT NAMES
```

Figure B-18   PRODUCE REPORT FACSIMILE.

```
IDEAL: PRINT MENU              XXX XXXXXXXX (XXX) TEST SYS:DEV    MENU

 ENTER DESIRED OPTION NUMBER ==     THERE ARE 4 OPTIONS IN THIS MENU


  1.PRINT OCCURANCE    PRINT A SPECIFIC PGM,PNL,RPT,DVW,USR,SYS,MEM,OUT
  2.PRINT OPTIONS      PRINT CURRENT SESSIONS OPTIONS
  3.PRINT DESTINATION PRINT CURRENT PRINT DESTINATIONS
  4.PRINT INDEX        PRINT INDEX OF PGMS,PNLS,RPTS,DVWS,SYS,USRS,MEMS
```

Figure B-19   PRINT MENU.

```
IDEAL: PRINT OCCURANCE    XXX XXXXXXXX (XXX) TEST SYS:DEV   PROMPTER


 PRINT  ___  _____    VERSION LAST
          (1)      (2)                  (3)



 DEST LIB _____ COPIES 1  NAME _____ DISP HOL DESC _____
      (4)    (5)            (6)       (7)        (8)          (9)
```

```
(1) PGM=PROGRAM  SYS=SYSTEM DEFN (2)NAME (3)NNN  (4) DESTINATION

    PNL=PANEL    USR=USER DEFN.              PROD  LIB=OUTPUT LIBRARY

    RPT=REPORT   MEM=MEMBER                  LAST  SYS=SYSTEM PRINTER

    DVW=DATAVIEW OUT=OUTPUT

(5) DESTINATION NAME  (6)COPIES  (7) NAME OF OUTPUT (8) DISPOSITION

                                                       REL=RELEASE

(9) DESCRIPTION (MUST BE IN QUOTES)                    KEE=KEEP

                                                       HOL=HOLD
```

Figure B-20   PRINT OCCURENCE Prompt Screen.


```
IDEAL: ADMINISTRATION MAINT      MENU


ENTER DESIRED OPTION NUMBER ===      THERE ARE 5 OPTIONS IN THIS MENU


  1. USER              - DEFINE AND MAINTAIN USER DEFINITIONS

  2. SYSTEM            - DEFINE AND MAINTAIN SYSTEM DEFINITIONS

  3. DDOL              - ENTER DATADICTIONARY ONLINE (FOR DD MAINT.)

  4. CATALOG DATAVIEW  - CATALOG DATAVIEWS

  5. UTILITY           - MISCELLANEOUS UTILITIES
```

Figure B-21   ADMINISTRATION MAINTENANCE MENU.

C

IDEAL Environmental SET Statements

IDEAL has a series of SET commands that are used to define the environment that is being used. These commands are also used to set panel and report definition defaults. In this appendix we will define and examine the syntax of these different commands. Most of these commands are established by the site's IDEAL administrator and are executed when the IDEAL session is established, but they can be overridden by a user at any time. These overrides affect only that user's session.

Environmental SET Commands

The environmental commands can be subdivided into groups. These are COMMAND AREA, SCROLLING, EDITOR, OUTPUT, COMPILE, and RUN options.

Command Area Options

As we saw in Chapter 3, it is possible for us to arrange the basic screen with a number of SET commands.

1. SET COMMAND COMMENT X

This command establishes the character that will be used to mark the beginning of a comment string. Anything to the right of this character is treated as a comment.

2. SET COMMAND DELIMITER X
It is possible to string multiple commands on a single command line. This can be done by placing the character identified with this statement between the commands. If the command

SET COMMAND DELIMITER ;

was issued, we could then write

DEL OUT 52;RUN BLPGA107;D OUT STA

These commands would then be executed sequentially, which would delete output number 52, run program BLPGA107, and when it was completed show the output status screen instead of the screen we were on when the command was issued.

3. SET COMMAND LINE n
This allows us to have from 0 to 5 command lines displayed on the screen. The "n" is the desired number of lines.

4. SET COMMAND REPEAT X
IDEAL remembers the last successful command that it issued. This makes it possible for us to repeat the command without retyping it. This is done by keying in the character defined in this command as the REPEAT command, and hitting the ENTER button.

5. SET COMMAND RESHOW X
Like the REPEAT command, we can cause IDEAL to display the last command that was executed. We can then modify the part of the command that must be changed and enter it again. This is particularly helpful if we are doing multiple occurrences of the same command. This command designates the character that is used to execute the reshow.

6. SET COMMAND RESHOW (OFF)
                    (ON)
We can cause IDEAL to automatically execute the reshow. However the default is OFF.

7. SET COMMAND SEPARATOR X

This command defines the character that is to be used to separate the command area and the display area of the screen.

8. SET COMMAND DATEFOR x

This command sets up the default date format. The choices are

A — American format (MM/DD/YY)
E — European format (DD/MM/YY)
I — International (YY/MM/DD)

We have seen the scrolling commands throughout the text. These commands apply to scrolling through output, panels, and while editing or displaying entities. We can either scroll from the position of the cursor, or for an entire frame. The command that makes this selection is

SET SCROLL (FRAME)
           (CURSOR)

Some commands define the editing environment.

1. SET BOUNDS num-1, (MAX)
                     (num-2)

This command limits the area that the FIND and the CHANGE commands will operate in. The area will begin on line num-1, and go either to the bottom of the displayed entity or to line number num-2.

2. SET EDIT CASE (UPPER)
                 (MIXED)

This command establishes the entered text as either mixed or upper case.

3. SET EDIT CONTEXT n

This command establishes the number of context lines that appear above and below the input window.

4. SET EDIT HIGHLIGHT (OFF   )
                      (ERRORS)

This command controls the option that allows the compiler to highlight in the source code those lines that are in error.

5. SET EDIT MARGIN (RIGHT)
            (LEFT)
   This command controls which side of the screen the sequence numbers and command area will appear on.

6. SET EDIT MULTIPLIER (RIGHT)
                (LEFT)
   This command controls which side of the line command we will place the number that causes multiple execution of the line command.

7. SET VERSION (nnn   )
            (LAST   )
            (PRODUCTION)
   This command establishes what the default version will be when we enter the EDIT or the DISPLAY commands.

We discussed the OUTPUT options in Chapter 9, but we will review the syntax of these commands here.

1. SET OUTPUT DESTINATION (SYSTEM name)
                    (LIBRARY   )
   With this command we can route output to the output library for storage, or directly to a system printer that is defined to IDEAL.

2. SET OUTPUT DISPOSITION (HOLD   )
                    (RELEASE)
                    (KEEP   )
   Here we establish the status that the output will have while it waits in the output library. For a furthur definition we will refer you to the discussion in Chapter 9.

3. SET OUTPUT COPIES num
   This command defines how many copies of the output from a program run will be created.

4. SET OUTPUT RETENTION nnn
   This command defines the number of days that an output member will be retained.

5. SET OUTPUT MAXLINES nnnnnn
   This command defines the maximum number of lines that can be put in an output member.

6. SET OUTPUT WIDTH nnn

    This command defines the output line width, up to 240 spaces.

The COMPILE options are used to determine what will be included in the output of a compiler run. These commands also set what the default values will be on the COMPILE PROCESS screen.

1. SET COMPILE IDE (Y)
                   (N)

    Includes identification and resource information on the compiler listing.

2. SET COMPILE EXD (Y)
                   (N)

    Includes external definitions (dataviews, panel definitions,) on the compiler listing.

3. SET COMPILE BOD (Y)
                   (N)

    Includes the body of the program (working data, parameter data, report definitions) on the compiler listing.

4. SET COMPILE ADV (Y)
                   (N)

    Includes compiler advisory messages on the compiler listing.

5. SET COMPILE MEL (Y)
                   (N)

    Highlights lines in the original source library that the compiler found to be in error.

6. SET COMPILE REF (FULL)
                   (SHORT)
                   (NO)

    Controls the inclusion of a compiler cross reference in the compiler output source listing during a batch compile.

7. SET COMPILE PANEL (FULL)
                     (SHORT)
                     (NO)

    Controls the inclusion of the panel definition in the compiler output source listing.

The RUN options are used to assist and to control program execution.

1. SET RUN UPDATE   (Y)
                    (N)

   This causes commands that would normally update the database to be ignored during the run.

2. SET RUN LOOPLIMIT nnnnnnnnn

   This command is used in the test environment, and controls the number of times that the IDEAL program will execute a FOR or a LOOP construct. It is used to avoid excess looping when a program is being debugged.

3. SET RUN FILETABLE name

   The file table identifies the databases that will be used during an IDEAL batch run. This command defines the name of the file table to be used.

4. SET RUN QUITIDEAL (Y)
                      (N)

   If this command is set, then the IDEAL session will be terminated when the program is completed.

5. SET RUN CLEAR (QUITSHOW)
                 (RESHOW)

   This command allows us to hit the clear key to end an IDEAL program. If the QUITSHOW option is set, then the QUITIDEAL command takes over. If QUITIDEAL is Y, the IDEAL session is terminated. If QUITIDEAL is N, the main menu is displayed. If the RESHOW option is chosen, the current screen is redisplayed.

   We have not seen this command interrupt a program loop.

6. SET ENVIRONMENT ACCOUNT-ID

   Each ACCOUNT-ID corresponds to a CICS transaction id that must be entered in the CICS PCT (program control table). This entry can then be used for system tuning.

7. SET ENVIRONMENT FINAL-ID xxxx

   We can also have another CICS transaction take over when our IDEAL application is completed. This could be some kind of clean-up or master menu program. The xxxx is the identity of this transaction.

Panel Definition SET Commands

The panel definition SET commands are used to establish the default values that appear on the PARM screen. These can be used to establish and enforce site coding standards. We can see most of these when we recall the PARM screen of the panel definition facility.

```
IDEAL: PANEL PARAMETERS    PNL CUSTMANT (001) TEST    SYS: DEV FILL-IN


START      FIELD SYMBOL ^ NEW    FIELD SYMBOL +

END        FIELD SYMBOL ; DELETE FIELD SYMBOL *

REPEATING GROUP SYMBOL @


INPUT  FILL CHARACTER  S (S=SPACE, L=LOWVAL, Z=ZEROES, U=_,OTHER=ITSELF

OUTPUT FILL CHARACTER  U (S=SPACE, L=LOWVAL, Z=ZERORS, U=_,OTHER=ITSELF

NON-DISPLAY CHARACTER  S (S=SPACE, OTHER=AS SPECIFIED)

ERROR FILL CHARACTER   * (AS SPECIFIED)

CASE TRANSLATION       U (U=UPPER, M=MIXED)


REQUIRED               N (Y=YES, N=NO)

ERROR HANDLING         B (N=NONE, *=FILL W/ERRORFILL, H=HIGH INTENSITY,
                         (B=BOTH: H IF ILLEGAL VALUE & * IF REQ MISSING


PANEL WIDTH           80 (A VALUE BETWEEN 80 AND 236)

PF1=HELP, PF2=RETURN   Y (Y=YES, N=NO)

PF7=SCR -, PF8=SCR+    Y (N=NO, Y=OPT Y, Z=OPT Z)

  PF10=SCR TOP, PF11=SCR BOT    (OPTION Y)

  PF10=SCR LEFT, PF11=SCR RIGHT (OPTION Z)

EDIT-RULE ERROR PROC   C (C=CLARIFY COMMAND, A=APPLICATION)

PROCESS APPL ON SCROLL N (Y=YES, N=NO)


HELP PANEL NAME    _____  VERSION ___

PREFIX PANEL NAME  _____  VERSION ___

SUFFIX PANEL NAME  _____  VERSION ___


--------------------------- B O T T O M --------------------------------
```

1. SET PANEL (STARTSYM char)   start of field symbol
            (ENDSYM   char)   end of field symbol
            (DELSYM   char)   delete field sysbol
            (NEWSYM   char)   new field symbol
            (REPSYM   char)   repeat field symbol

Defines the default values of the characters that are used when we are working on the panel layout screen.

2. SET PANEL LAYOUT CASE (UPPER)
                            (MIXED)

Determines if the information entered during the layout function is to be accepted in whatever case it's in, or if it should be changed to upper case.

3. SET PANEL SCROLL (FRAME)
                       (CURSOR)

Establishes how the scroll will function when we are working in the layout and summary tables of the panel definition facility.

4. SET PANEL INFILL (SPACES   )
                     (LOWVALUES)
                     (ZERO   )
                     (UNDERSCORE)
                     (x   )

Establishes the default input fill character.

5. SET PANEL OUTFILL (SPACES   )
                      (LOWVALUES)
                      (UNDERSCORE)
                      (x   )

Establishes the default output fill character.

6. SET PANEL LAYOUTCASE (UPPER)
                        (MIXED)

Determines if the data entered into the fields by the user will be accepted in the entered case or will be translated to upper case.

7. SET PANEL NULLFIELD (SPACES   )
                        (LOWVALUES)
                        (INFILL   )

Determines the input fill character when the entire field is set to nulls.

8. SET PANEL DECIMAL (PERIOD)
                      (COMMA)

Establishes the default symbol that will represent a decimal point.

9. SET PANEL PF13   (YES)
                    (NO)

Establishes if PF keys 13 and 15 are to be used by the application.

10. SET PANEL PF781011 (NO)
                       (YES)
                       (Z)

Establishes standard key assignments for PF keys 7, 8, 10, and 11.

	YES	Z	NO
PF KEY 7 / 19	— SCROLL DOWN	SCROLL DOWN	NO SCROLLING
PF KEY 8 / 20	— SCROLL UP	SCROLL UP	NO SCROLLING
PF KEY 10 / 22	— SCROLL TOP	SCROLL LEFT	NO SCROLLING
PF KEY 11 / 23	— SCROLL BOTTOM	SCROLL RIGHT	NO SCROLLING

11. SET PANEL ERRORHANDLING x
Establishes the default method of highlighting a field in error.

12. SET PANEL FIELD REQUIRED   (YES)
                               (NO)

Establishes if all fields on the panel are required to have a value entered into them.

13. SET PANEL WIDEOPTION (YES)
                         (NO)
Enables wide panel support.

14. SET PANEL WIDTH(*)
                    (nnn)

Sets the default panel width with a value either between 80 and 236 or the width of the current terminal screen (*).

Report Definition SET Commands

The report definition SET commands are similar to the panel definition SET commands in that they establish the default values for the fields on the parameter screen of the report definition facility. Again, we can view this PARM screen and then begin our discussion.

```
-----------------------------------------------------------------------
IDEAL: RPT PARAMETERS           RPT XXXXXXXX (XXX) XXXX        SYS: XXX


LINES PER PAGE ON PRINTOUT         XX  ( 1 THRU 250)
REPORT WIDTH                       XXX (40 THRU 230)
SPACING BETWEEN LINES              X   ( 1 THRU 3)
SPACING BETWEEN COLUMNS            XX  ( 0 THRU 66 OR A=AUTOMATIC)
SUMMARIES ONLY                     X   (Y=YES,N=NO)
COLUMN HEADINGS DESIRED            X   (Y=YES,N=NO)
COLUMN HEADINGS INDICATION         X   (U=UNDERSCORE,N=NONE,D=DASHES)
CONTROL BREAK HEADING              X   (Y=YES,N=NO)
CONTROL BREAK FOOTING              X   (Y=YES,N=NO)
GROUP CONTINUATION AT TOP OF PAGE  X   (Y=YES,N=NO)
ANNOTATED COUNT IN CONTROL FOOTINGS X  (Y=YES,N=NO)
REPORT FINAL SUMMARY TITLE         X   (Y=YES,N=NO)
  SPACING BEFORE SUMMARY           X   (1 THRU 9 = LINES,P=NEW PAGE)
  TITLE          _____


DATE
  POSITION          XX     (NO=NONE,BR=BOT.RIGHT,BL=BOT.LEFT,BC=BOT.CTR
                            TR=TOP RIGHT,TL=TOP LEFT,TC=TOP CENTER)
  FORMAT            XXXXXXXXXXXX


PAGE NUMBERS
  POSITION          XX
  FORMAT            H      (D=DIGITS ONLY, H=WITH HYPHENS, P=PAGE    NNN)


PAGE HEADING
  HEADING           XXXXXXXXXXXXXXXXXXXXXXXXXXXXXXXXXXXXXXXXXXXX
  POSITION          X      (C=CENTER, L=LEFT JUSTIFY, R=RIGHT JUSTIFY)
```

1. SET REPORT LINES   nn   RANGE   1-99
   Establishes the default number of lines on a report page.

2. SET REPORT WIDTH   nnn   RANGE 40-230
   Establishes the default width of a report page.

3. SET REPORT SPACING n   RANGE   1-3
   Establishes the default spacing between columns.

4. SET REPORT CONTHEAD   (Y)
                         (N)
   Establishes the default for CONTROL HEADING processing.

5. `SET REPORT CONTFOOT  (Y)`
                        `(N)`
    Establishes the default for CONTROL FOOTING processing.

6. `SET REPORT DATEFOR 'date-pattern'`
    Establishes the default format of the report date display.

7. `SET REPORT DATEPOS xx`
    Establishes the default position of the report date display.

8. `SET REPORT PAGEFMT x                    (H,D,P)`
    Establishes the default format of the page number display.

9. `SET REPORT PAGEPOS xx`
    Establishes the default position of the page number display.

Options Display

After the site administrator has established the default values, and at any subsequent time, we can display the different session options. This is done with the command:

`DISPLAY SESSION OPTIONS`

where OPTION is one of the following:

```
OUTPUT
DATAVIEW
EDIT
COMPILE
PANEL
DBID
REPORT
PROGRAM
ASSIGN
RUN
VERSION
ENVIRONMENT
```

Sample IDEAL On-Line Program

IDENTIFICATION: TIPGEMPV   VERSION: 001 STATUS: TEST

    PROGRAM TIPGEMPV
    DATE CREATED 09/19/86 DATE LAST MODIFIED 01/27/87

    RUN STATUS NON-SHARED
    SHORT DESCRIPTION MANUAL - EMPLOYEE VIEW
    DESCRIPTION:

        SEARCHES EMPLOYEE AND PAYROLL DATABASES BY FNTERED EMPLOYEE
        NUMBER AND DISPLAYS RETURNED DATA ON THE SCREEN.
        _____
        _____

RESOURCES: TIPGEMPV

DATAVIEW	VER	PANEL	VER	REPORT	VER	PROGRAM	VER	SYS
$ID-EMPLOYEE	0001	TIPLEMPV	0001					
$ID-PAYROLL	0001							

```
PARAMETER: TIPGEMPV


_____  _____  _____  _ _  _____  _____  _ _  _____
SEQ    LEVEL FIELD NAME        T I CH/DG OCCUR U M COMMENTS/DEP ON/COPY
_____  _____  _____  _ _  _____  _____  _ _  _____
            NO PARAMETERS FOR THIS PROGRAM


WORKING DATA: TIPGEMPV


_____  _____  _____  _ _  _____  _____  _____
SEQ    LEVEL FIELD NAME        T I CH/DG OCCUR COMMENTS/DEP ON/COPY
_____  _____  _____  _ _  _____  _____  _____
000100 1     WK-ALPHA-SSN      X     9


PROCEDURE: TIPGEMPV


_____
:*************************************************************************
:** THIS PROGRAM DISPLAYS THE INFORMATION FOR THE REQUESTED EMPLOYEE **
:** NUMBER FROM THE SCREEN                                           **
:*************************************************************************


<<TIPGEMPV>> PROCEDURE
  RESET     TIPLEMPV
  TRANSMIT TIPLEMPV
  LOOP UNTIL $PF2 OR $PF14
       DO GET-ID-EMPLOYEE
       DO GET-ID-PAYROLL
       TRANSMIT TIPLEMPV
  ENDLOOP
ENDPROC


:*************************************************************************
:** THIS AREA GETS THE ID-EMPLOYEE RECORD FOR THE REQUESTED EMPLOYEE **
:*************************************************************************


<<GET-ID-EMPLOYEE>> PROCEDURE
  FOR FIRST $ID-EMPLOYEE
       WHERE $ID-EMPLOYEE.NUMBER = TIPLEMPV.NUMBER
            DO LD-ID-EMPLOYEE
       WHEN   NONE
            MOVE $LOW                        TO TIPLEMPV.NAME
            MOVE $LOW                        TO TIPLEMPV.STREET-ADDRESS
```

```
             MOVE $LOW                            TO TIPLEMPV.CITY-ADDRESS
             MOVE $LOW                            TO TIPLEMPV.STATE-ADDRESS
             MOVE $LOW                            TO TIPLEMPV.ZIP-CODE-LOC
             MOVE $LOW                            TO TIPLEMPV.ALPHA-SSN
             MOVE 'EMPLOYEE RECORD NOT FOUND' TO TIPLEMPV.MESSAGE
      ENDFOR
  ENDPROC


  <<LD-ID-EMPLOYEE>> PROCEDURE
    MOVE $ID-EMPLOYEE.NAME                    TO TIPLEMPV.NAME
    MOVE $ID-EMPLOYEE.STREET-ADDRESS         TO TIPLEMPV.STREET-ADDRESS
    MOVE $ID-EMPLOYEE.CITY-ADDRESS           TO TIPLEMPV.CITY-ADDRESS
    MOVE $ID-EMPLOYEE.STATE-ADDRESS          TO TIPLEMPV.STATE-ADDRESS
    MOVE $ID-EMPLOYEE.ZIP-CODE-LOC           TO TIPLEMPV.ZIP-CODE-LOC
    MOVE $EDIT($ID-EMPLOYEE.SOCIAL-SECURITY,PIC='999999999')
                                             TO WK-ALPHA-SSN
    MOVE $EDIT(WK-ALPHA-SSN,PIC='XXX-XX-XXXX') TO TIPLEMPV.ALPHA-SSN
    MOVE $SPACES                             TO TIPLEMPV.MESSAGE
  ENDPROC


  :*********************************************************************
  :** THIS AREA GETS THE ID-PAYROLL RECORD FOR THE REQUESTED EMPLOYEE ***
  :** AND LOADS IT ONTO THE SCREEN. IF THE RECORD IS NOT FOUND , THE  ***
  :** SCREEN FIELDS ARE REINITIALIZED.                                ***
  :*********************************************************************


  <<GET-ID-PAYROLL>> PROCEDURE
    FOR FIRST $ID-PAYROLL
        WHERE $ID-PAYROLL.NUMBER = TIPLEMPV.NUMBER
              DO LD-ID-PAYROLL
        WHEN  NONE
              DO INT-ID-PAYROLL
    ENDFOR
  ENDPROC


  <<LD-ID-PAYROLL>> PROCEDURE
    MOVE $ID-PAYROLL.ACTIVITY-CODE      TO TIPLEMPV.ACTIVITY-CODE
    MOVE $ID-PAYROLL.ACTIVITY-STATUS    TO TIPLEMPV.ACTIVITY-STATUS
    MOVE $ID-PAYROLL.CURRENT-RATE       TO TIPLEMPV.CURRENT-RATE
    MOVE $ID-PAYROLL.YTD-WAGES          TO TIPLEMPV.YTD-WAGES
    MOVE $ID-PAYROLL.YTD-COMMISSION     TO TIPLEMPV.YTD-COMMISSION
    MOVE $ID-PAYROLL.YTD-TAX            TO TIPLEMPV.YTD-TAX
  ENDPROC
```

```
<<INT-ID-PAYROLL>> PROCEDURE
  MOVE $LOW                          TO TIPLEMPV.ACTIVITY-CODE
  MOVE $LOW                          TO TIPLEMPV.ACTIVITY-STATUS
  MOVE 0                             TO TIPLEMPV.CURRENT-RATE
  MOVE 0                             TO TIPLEMPV.YTD-WAGES
  MOVE 0                             TO TIPLEMPV.YTD-COMMISSION
  MOVE 0                             TO TIPLEMPV.YTD-TAX
  IF TIPLEMPV.MESSAGE GT $SPACES
     MOVE 'EMPLOYEE NUMBER NOT FOUND' TO TIPLEMPV.MESSAGE
  ELSE
     MOVE 'PAYROLL RECORD NOT FOUND ' TO TIPLEMPV.MESSAGE
  ENDIF
ENDPROC
```

```
IDEAL: PANEL PARAMETERS    PNL TIPLEMPV (001) TEST    SYS: DEV FILL-IN


START     FIELD SYMBOL ^ NEW    FIELD SYMBOL +
END       FIELD SYMBOL ; DELETE FIELD SYMBOL *
REPEATING GROUP SYMBOL @


INPUT  FILL CHARACTER  S (S=SPACE, L=LOWVAL, Z=ZEROES, U=_,OTHER=ITSELF
OUTPUT FILL CHARACTER  U (S=SPACE, L=LOWVAL, Z=ZERORS, U=_,OTHER=ITSELF
NON-DISPLAY CHARACTER  S (S=SPACE, OTHER=AS SPECIFIED)
ERROR FILL CHARACTER   * (AS SPECIFIED)
CASE TRANSLATION       U (U=UPPER, M=MIXED)


REQUIRED              N (Y=YES, N=NO)
ERROR HANDLING        B (N=NONE, *=FILL W/ERRORFILL, H=HIGH INTENSITY,
                         (B=BOTH: H IF ILLEGAL VALUE & * IF REQ MISSING


PANEL WIDTH           80 (A VALUE BETWEEN 80 AND 236)
PF1=HELP, PF2=CLARIFY  Y (Y=YES, N=NO)
PF7=SCR -, PF8=SCR+    N (N=NO, Y=OPT Y,  Z=OPT Z)
  PF10=SCR TOP, PF11=SCR BOT    (OPTION Y)
  PF10=SCR LEFT,PF11=SCR RIGHT  (OPTION Z)
EDIT-RULE ERROR PROC   C (C=CLARIFY COMMAND,  A=APPLICATION)
PROCESS APPL ON SCROLL N (Y=YES,N=NO)


HELP PANEL NAME    _____  VERSION ___
PREFIX PANEL NAME  _____  VERSION ___
SUFFIX PANEL NAME  _____  VERSION ___


-------------------------- B O T T O M --------------------------
```

```
IDEAL: PANEL LAYOUT        PNL TIPLEMPV (001) TEST     SYS: DEV FILL-IN
START: ^     END: ;     NEW: +      DELETE: *      REPEAT: @
....+....1....+....2....+....3....+....4....+....5....+....6....+...7..
                +EMPLOYEE INQUIRY PROGRAM;      EMPLOYEE NO;    +____;


   +_____;          +CURRENT RATE;     +_____;
   +_____;
   +_____; +,;+__;          +YTD FIGURE;
   +_____;                              +WAGES;        +_____;
                                        +COMMISSION;+_____;
   +_____;                        +TAXES;        +_____;



                                        +ACTIVITY CODE;  +_;
                                        +ACTIVITY STATUS;+_;


        +_____;




---------------------------- BOTTOM ------------------------------


--------------------------------------------------------------------------
IDEAL: FIELD SUMMARY TABLE   PNL TIPLEMPV (001) TEST  SYS: DEV FILL-IN
==========================================================================
                +EMPLOYEE INQUIRY PROGRAM;      EMPLOYEE NO;    +____;
                1                               2               3


   +_____;          +CURRENT RATE;     +_____;
..........................................................................
SEQ LV FIELD NAME     .ATTR   T LEN  IN.DP OCC COMMENTS
--- -- --------------- ------ - ---- ----- --- ------------------------
  1  2                 PSL    X  24            EMPLOYEE INQUIRY PROGRAM
  2  2                 PSL    X  11            EMPLOYEE NO
  3  2 NUMBER          UNL    X   5   5        _____
  4  2 NAME            PSL    X  23            _____
  5  2                 PSL    X  12            CURRENT RATE
  6  2 CURRENT-RATE    PSL    N  10   6.2      _____
  7  2 STREET-ADDRESS  PSL    X  23            _____
  8  2 CITY-ADDRESS    PSL    X  15            _____
  9  2                 PSL    X   1            ,
 10  2 STATE-ADDRESS   PSL    X   2            __
 11  2                 PSL    X  11            YTD FIGURES
```

```
12  2 ZIP-CODE-LOC     PSL    X    5                  _____
13  2                  PSL    X    5            WAGES
14  2 YTD-WAGES        PSL    N   10   6.2            _____
15  2                  PSL    X   10            COMMISSION
16  2 YTD-COMMISSION   PSL    N   10   6.2            _____
17  2 ALPHA-SSN        PSL    X   11                  _____
18  2                  PSL    X    5            TAXES
19  2 YTD-TAX          PSL    N   10   6.2            _____
20  2                  PSL    X   13            ACTIVITY CODE
21  2 ACTIVITY-CODE    PSL    X    1                  _____
22  2                  PSL    X   15            ACTIVITY STATUS
23  2 ACTIVITY-STATUS PSL     X    1                  _____
24  2 MESSAGE          PSH    X   60                  _____
```

IDEAL: EXTENDED FIELD DEFN.   PNL TIPLEMPV (001) TEST SYS:DEV FILL-IN

                               ^YTD WAGES; ^_____;
                                 13   14

....+....1....+....2....+....3....+....4....+....5....+....6....+....7.
FIELD NAME   YTD-WAGES

COMMENTS   _____
TYPE   N   (X=ALPHANUMERIC, N=NUMERIC, G=GROUP)
OCCURRENCES   __   (FOR GROUPS ONLY)
ATTRIBUTE   PSL (U=UNPROT H=HIGHLIGHT   A=327X ALPHA   )
                     (P=PROT   I=INVISIBLE   N=327X NUMERIC   )
                     (S=SKIP   L=LOWLIGHT   E=ENSURE RECIEVED)
                     (C=CURSOR   )
COLOR   N   (N=NEUTRAL, B=BLUE, R=RED, P=PINK, G=GREEN,)
                     (T=TURQUOISE, Y=YELLOW, W=WHITE/BLACK   )
EX HIGHLIGHTING N   (N=NONE, B=BLINK, R=REVERSE VIDEO, U=UNDERSCORE)
OUTPUT FILL CHAR U   (S=SPACES, L=LOWVAL, U=_, OTHER=ITSELF)
ERROR HANDLING *   (N=NONE, *=FILL *, H=HIGHLIGHT)
                     (B=BOTH: H IF ILLEGAL VALUE & * IF REQD IS MISSING
REQUIRED   N   (Y=YES, N=NO)
MUST-FILL   N   (Y=YES, N=NO)
MINIMUM VALUE   MAXIMUM VALUE
JUSTIFY INPUT   A   (N=NO, L=LEFT, R=RIGHT, A=ALIGN BY DECIMAL)

INPUT FILL CHAR S   (S=SPACES, L=LOWVAL, Z=ZEROES, U=_, OTHER=ITSELF)
VARIABLE DELIM _
CASE   U   (U=UPPER, M=MIXED)
EDIT PATTERN   ZZZZZ9.99-

```
IN.DP             6.2 (INTEGERS.DECIMALS)
MIN REQ DECIMALS 2    (VALID ONLY FOR TYPE=N AND JUSTIFY=A)
ALLOW DIGIT SEP  N    (Y=YES, N=NO)
ALLOW MINUS SIGN N    (Y=YES, N=NO)
ALLOW CURRENCY   N    (Y=YES, N=NO)
CHECK DIGIT      N    (N=NONE, T=MODULO 10, E=MODULO 11)
```

```
_____


                EMPLOYEE INQUIRY PROGRAM      EMPLOYEE NO      _____

_____          CURRENT RATE         _____
_____
_____    __          YTD FIGURE
_____                                 WAGES             _____
                                       COMMISSION        _____
_____                             TAXES             _____


                                ACTIVITY CODE        _
                                ACTIVITY STATUS      _

        _____
```

Sample IDEAL Report Program

```
IDENTIFICATION: TIPGEMPL          VERSION: 001 STATUS: TEST

    PROGRAM TIPGEMPL
    DATE CREATED 09/19/86   DATE LAST MODIFIED 01/27/87

    RUN STATUS NON-SHARED
    SHORT DESCRIPTION MANUAL - EMPLOYEE LIST
    DESCRIPTION:

        REPORTS ON CONTENTS AND INTEGRITY OF EMPLOYEE AND PAYROLL
        DATABASES.

        _____
        _____




RESOURCES: TIPGEMPL
```

DATAVIEW	VER	PANEL	VER	REPORT	VER	PROGRAM	VER	SYS
$ID-EMPLOYEE	0001			TIRPEMPL	00001			
$ID-PAYROLL	0001							

```
PARAMETER: TIPGEMPL


_____ _____ _____ _ _ _____ _____ _ _ _____
SEQ     LEVEL FIELD NAME        T I CH/DG OCCUR U M COMMENTS/DEP ON/COPY
------ ----- --------------- - - ----- ----- - - --------------------
             NO PARAMETERS FOR THIS PROGRAM


WORKING DATA: TIPGEMPL


_____ _____ _____ _ _ _____ _____ _____
SEQ     LEVEL FIELD NAME        T I CH/DG OCCUR COMMENTS/DEP ON/COPY
------ ----- --------------- - - ----- ----- ----------------------
000100 1     WK-ALPHA-SSN      X     9
000200
000300 1     RPT-AREA
000400 2       NUMBER          X     6
000500 2       NAME            X    24
000600 2       STREET-ADDRESS  X    24
000700 2       CITY-ADDRESS    X    25
000800 2       STATE-ADDRESS   X     2
000000 2       ZIP-CODE-LOC    X     5
001000 2       SOCIAL-SECURITY X    11
001100 2       ACTIVITY-CODE   X     4
001200 2       ACTIVITY-STATUS X     4
001300 2       CURRENT-RATE    X    10
001400 2       YTD-WAGES       X    10
001500 2       YTD-COMMISSION  X    10
001600 2       YTD-TAX         X    10
001700 2       FIL-COMMA       X     1
001800 2       FIL-WAGES       X    10       'YTD WAGES'
001900 2       FIL-COMM        X    10       'YTD COMM '
002000 2       FIL-TAXES       X    10       'YTD TAXES'
002100
002200


PROCEDURE: TIPGEMPL


_____
:************************************************************************
:** THIS PROGRAM AUDITS THE ADR SUPPLIED EMPLOYEE DATABASE BY READING**
:** EACH EMPLOYEE RECORD , JOINING IT TO THE CORRESPONDING PAYROLL   **
:** RECORD , AND PRINTING THE RESULTS.                              **
:************************************************************************
```

```
<<TIPGEMPL>> PROCEDURE
  FOR EACH $ID-EMPLOYEE
              DO LOAD-EMPL-DATA
              DO PAYROLL-DATA
              PRODUCE TIRPEMPL
        WHEN NONE
              DO NO-DATA-ERROR
              PRODUCE TIRPEMPL
  ENDFOR
ENDPROC


:************************************************************************
:** PARAGRAPH LOADS THE DATA FROM THE EMPLOYEE DB TO THE REPORT AREA **
:** NOTE THE USAGE OF THE TWO $EDIT COMMANDS TO MOVE THE NUMERIC DB  **
:** SSN TO THE EDITED ALPHA SSN ON THE REPORT.                      **
:************************************************************************


<<LOAD-EMPL-DATA>> PROCEDURE
  MOVE $ID-EMPLOYEE.NUMBER           TO RPT-AREA.NUMBER
  MOVE $ID-EMPLOYEE.NAME             TO RPT-AREA.NAME
  MOVE $ID-EMPLOYEE.STREET-ADDRESS   TO RPT-AREA.STREET-ADDRESS
  MOVE $ID-EMPLOYEE.CITY-ADDRESS     TO RPT-AREA.CITY-ADDRESS
  MOVE $ID-EMPLOYEE.STATE-ADDRESS    TO RPT-AREA.STATE-ADDRESS
  MOVE $ID-EMPLOYEE.ZIP-CODE-LOC     TO RPT-AREA.ZIP-CODE-LOC
  MOVE $EDIT($ID-EMPLOYEE.SOCIAL-SECURITY,PIC='999999999')
                                     TO WK-ALPHA-SSN
  MOVE $EDIT(WK-ALPHA-SSN,PIC='XXX-XX-XXXX')
                                     TO RPT-AREA.SOCIAL-SECURITY
ENDPROC



:************************************************************************
:** PARAGRAPH OBTAINS THE CORRESPONDING PAYROLL DB RECORD          **
:************************************************************************


<<PAYROLL-DATA>> PROCEDURE
  FOR FIRST $ID-PAYROLL
        WHERE $ID-PAYROLL.NUMBER = $ID-EMPLOYEE.NUMBER
              DO LOAD-PAYROLL
        WHEN  NONE
              DO PAYROLL-ERROR
  ENDFOR
ENDPROC
```

```
:*************************************************************************
:** PARAGRAPH LOADS THE PAYROLL DATA FROM THE DATABASE TO THE REPORT **
:*************************************************************************


<<LOAD-PAYROLL>> PROCEDURE
  MOVE $ID-PAYROLL.ACTIVITY-CODE            TO RPT-AREA.ACTIVITY-CODE
  MOVE $ID-PAYROLL.ACTIVITY-STATUS          TO RPT-AREA.ACTIVITY-STATUS
  MOVE $EDIT($ID-PAYROLL.CURRENT-RATE,PIC='ZZZ,ZZ9.99')
                                            TO RPT-AREA.CURRENT-RATE
  MOVE $EDIT($ID-PAYROLL.YTD-WAGES,PIC='ZZZ,ZZ9.99')
                                            TO RPT-AREA.YTD-WAGES
  MOVE $EDIT($ID-PAYROLL.YTD-COMMISSION,PIC='ZZZ,ZZ9.99')
                                            TO RPT-AREA.YTD-COMMISSION
  MOVE $EDIT($ID-PAYROLL.YTD-TAX,PIC='ZZZ,ZZ9.99')
                                            TO RPT-AREA.YTD-TAX
ENDPROC


:*************************************************************************
:** PARAGRAPH IS EXECUTED WHEN A PAYROLL RECORD IS NOT FOUND.        **
:*************************************************************************


<<PAYROLL-ERROR>> PROCEDURE
  MOVE $ID-PAYROLL.ACTIVITY-CODE            TO RPT-AREA.ACTIVITY-CODE
  MOVE $ID-PAYROLL.ACTIVITY-STATUS          TO RPT-AREA.ACTIVITY-STATUS
  MOVE $STRING('        0.00')              TO RPT-AREA.CURRENT-RATE
  MOVE $STRING('        0.00')              TO RPT-AREA.YTD-WAGES
  MOVE $STRING('        0.00')              TO RPT-AREA.YTD-COMMISSION
  MOVE $STRING('        0.00')              TO RPT-AREA.YTD-TAX
ENDPROC


:*************************************************************************
:** PARAGRAPH IS EXECUTED WHEN THE EMPLOYEE DATABASE IS EMPTY. MOVES **
:** A MESSAGE TO THE REPORT AREA THAT TELLS THE USER THE DATABASE IS **
:** EMPTY.                                                           **
:*************************************************************************


<<NO-DATA-ERROR>> PROCEDURE
  MOVE $SPACES                     TO RPT-AREA.NUMBER
  MOVE '***********************'   TO RPT-AREA.NAME
  MOVE 'NO EMPLOYEE RECS FOUND'    TO RPT-AREA.STREET-ADDRESS
  MOVE '***************'           TO RPT-AREA.CITY-ADDRESS
  MOVE '*'                         TO RPT-AREA.FIL-COMMA
  MOVE '**'                        TO RPT-AREA.STATE-ADDRESS
  MOVE $SPACES                     TO RPT-AREA.ZIP-CODE-LOC
```

```
    MOVE $SPACES                      TO RPT-AREA.SOCIAL-SECURITY
ENDPROC


------------------------------------------------------------------------

IDEAL: RPT PARAMETERS          RPT TIRPEMPL (001) TEST        SYS: DEV


LINES PER PAGE ON PRINTOUT          60  ( 1 THRU 250)
REPORT WIDTH                        132 (40 THRU 230)
SPACING BETWEEN LINES               1   ( 1 THRU 3)
SPACING BETWEEN COLUMNS             02  ( 0 THRU 66 OR A=AUTOMATIC)
SUMMARIES ONLY                      N   (Y=YES,N=NO)
COLUMN HEADINGS DESIRED             Y   (Y=YES,N=NO)
COLUMN HEADINGS INDICATION          U   (U=UNDERSCORE,N=NONE,D=DASHES)
CONTROL BREAK HEADING               N   (Y=YES,N=NO)
CONTROL BREAK FOOTING               N   (Y=YES,N=NO)
GROUP CONTINUATION AT TOP OF PAGE   N   (Y=YES,N=NO)
ANNOTATED COUNT IN CONTROL FOOTINGS N   (Y=YES,N=NO)
REPORT FINAL SUMMARY TITLE          N   (Y=YES,N=NO)
  SPACING BEFORE SUMMARY            2   (1 THRU 9 = LINES,P=NEW PAGE)
  TITLE          _____


DATE
  POSITION        TL     (NO=NONE,BR=BOT.RIGHT,BL=BOT.LEFT,BC=BOT.CTR
                          TR=TOP RIGHT,TL=TOP LEFT,TC=TOP CENTER)
  FORMAT          MM/DD/YY


PAGE NUMBERS
  POSITION        TR
  FORMAT          H      (D=DIGITS ONLY, H=WITH HYPHENS, P=PAGE    NNN)



PAGE HEADING
  HEADING         EMPLOYEE DATABASE AUDIT REPORT
  POSITION        C      (C=CENTER, L=LEFT JUSTIFY, R=RIGHT JUSTIFY)


------------------------------------------------------------------------

IDEAL: RPT PAGE HEADING     RPT TIRPEMPL (001) TEST    SYS: DEV FILL-IN


FIELD NAME, LITERAL, FUNCTION            COLUMN
OR ARITHMETIC EXPRESSION                 W
                                         ID TAB EDIT PATTERN  COMMAND
                                         TH
------------------------------------------- -- --- ------------- ------
_____ __ ___ _____ 000010
```

```
_____ __ ___ _____ ____ 000020
_____ __ ___ _____ ____ 000030
_____ __ ___ _____ ____ 000040
_____ __ ___ _____ ____ 000050
_____ __ ___ _____ ____ 000060
_____ __ ___ _____ ____ 000070
_____ __ ___ _____ ____ 000080
_____ __ ___ _____ ____ 000090
_____ __ ___ _____ ____ 000100
_____ __ ___ _____ ____ 000110
```

```
------------------------------------------------------------------------
IDEAL: RPT DETAIL DEFN.      RPT TIRPEMPL (001) TEST        SYS:DEV
```

FIELD NAME, LITERAL FUNCTION, OR ARITHMETIC EXPRESSION	SORT		BREAK			FUNCTION				COLUMN			EDIT PATTERN
	L V L	A / D	L V L	S K P	I N D	T O T	M A X	M I N	A V G	H D G	W I D T H	TAB	
========= TOP ==========	=	=	=	=	=	=	=	=	=	=	==	===	=============
RPT-AREA.NUMBER	_	_	_	_	_	_	_	_	_	U	06	+02	_____
RPT-AREA.NAME	_	_	_	_	_	_	_	_	_	U	24	+02	_____
RPT-AREA.ACTIVITY-CODE	_	_	_	_	_	_	_	_	_	U	04	+03	_____
RPT-AREA.ACTIVITY-STATUS	_	_	_	_	_	_	_	_	_	U	04	+02	_____
RPT-AREA.CURRENT-RATE	_	_	_	_	_	_	_	_	_	U	10	+02	_____
RPT-AREA.FIL-WAGES	_	_	_	_	_	_	_	_	_	N	10	+02	_____
RPT-AREA.YTD-WAGES	_	_	_	_	_	_	_	_	_	N	10	+02	_____
_____	_	_	_	_	_	_	_	_	_	_	__	L01	_____
RPT-AREA.STREET-ADDRESS	_	_	_	_	_	_	_	_	_	N	24	+10	_____
RPT-AREA.FILL-COMM	_	_	_	_	_	_	_	_	_	N	10	+27	_____
RPT-AREA.YTD-COMMISSION	_	_	_	_	_	_	_	_	_	N	10	+02	_____
_____	_	_	_	_	_	_	_	_	_	_	__	L01	_____
RPT-AREA.CITY-ADDRESS	_	_	_	_	_	_	_	_	_	N	15	+10	_____
RPT-AREA.FILL-COMMA	_	_	_	_	_	_	_	_	_	N	01	+01	_____
RPT-AREA.STATE-ADDRESS	_	_	_	_	_	_	_	_	_	N	02	+01	_____
RPT-AREA.ZIP-CODE-LOC	_	_	_	_	_	_	_	_	_	N	05	+01	_____
RPT-AREA.FIL-TAXES	_	_	_	_	_	_	_	_	_	N	10	+25	_____
RPT-AREA.YTD-TAXES	_	_	_	_	_	_	_	_	_	N	10	+02	_____
_____	_	_	_	_	_	_	_	_	_	_	__	L01	_____
RPT-AREA.SOCIAL-SECURITY	_	_	_	_	_	_	_	_	_	N	11	+10	_____
_____	_	_	_	_	_	_	_	_	_	_	__	L01	_____
======== BOTTOM =========	=	=	=	=	=	=	=	=	=	=	==	===	=============

```
------------------------------------------------------------------------
IDEAL: RPT COLUMN HEADINGS    RPT XXXXXXXX (XXX) XXXX       SYS: DOC
FIELD NAME, LITERAL         COLUMN
FUNCTION OR                 H W
ARITHMETIC EXPRESSION       D ID TAB HEADINGS
                            G TH
------------------------- - -- --- ------------------------------------
========= TOP ========== = == === ====================================
RPT-AREA.NUMBER             U 06 +02 NUMBER
RPT-AREA.NAME               U 24 +02 NAME / ADDRESS / SSN
RPT-AREA.ACTIVITY-CODE      U 04 +03 CODE
RPT-AREA.ACTIVITY-STATUS    U 04 +02 STAT
RPT-AREA.CURRENT-RATE       U 10 +02 CURR RATE
RPT-AREA.FIL-WAGES          N 10 +02 _____
RPT-AREA.YTD-WAGES          N 10 +02 _____
_____ _ __ L01 _____
RPT-AREA.STREET-ADDRESS     N 24 +10 _____
RPT-AREA.FILL-COMM          N 10 +27 _____
RPT-AREA.YTD-COMMISSION     N 10 +02 _____
_____ _ __ L01 _____
RPT-AREA.CITY-ADDRESS       N 15 +10 _____
RPT-AREA.FILL-COMMA         N 01 +01 _____
RPT-AREA.STATE-ADDRESS      N 02 +01 _____
RPT-AREA.ZIP-CODE-LOC       N 05 +01 _____
RPT-AREA.FIL-TAXES          N 10 +25 _____
RPT-AREA.YTD-TAXES          N 10 +02 _____
_____ _ __ L01 _____
RPT-AREA.SOCIAL-SECURITY    N 11 +10 _____
_____ _ __ L01 _____
======== BOTTOM ========= = == === ====================================
```

F

VLS Libraries and Production Implementation

Now that we have done all of this development work, we need to implement the program into the production system. Users and managers like to see this happen often, something about return on investment and productivity.

In this appendix we will discuss the process of moving programs from a developmental environment to a production environment. We will also discuss the relationships of the different internal libraries, and how they function together in the VLS environment. Some companies do not use the VLS libraries, choosing rather to use standard LOADLIBS, which became available with the 1.4 release of the language. This appendix is for those customers who choose to use VLS, or who started with an earlier version.

We will begin by defining an example environment.

The Environment

As we can see in Figure F-1, our sample distribution company has set up two separate CICS regions on its machine, one for controlled production processing and the other for program testing and development. Each region has its own separate set of data, residing in separate databases.

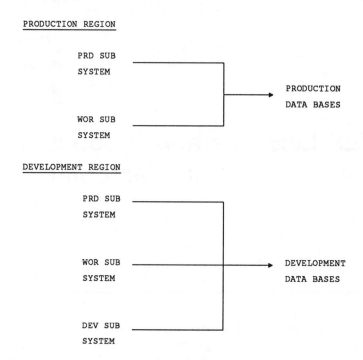

Figure F-1   Relationship of Subsystems to Databases.

Each region is in turn split into separate subsystems. The production region contains a PRD and a WOR subsystem. The development region contains PRD, WOR, and DEV subsystems.

Figure F-2 shows us the library relationships within each SUB-SYSTEM.

The first thing we notice is that, in addition to sharing the databases, each subsystem shares the DATADICTIONARY and the IDDVW library for that region.

The DATADICTIONARY contains

1. The subsystem's definitions
2. The user definitions and authorizations
3. The dataview definitions
4. An entry for and model of each panel definition
5. An entry for and model of each report definition
6. An entry for and model of each program definition
7. A listing of the relationships that are used to fill in the program resource table display

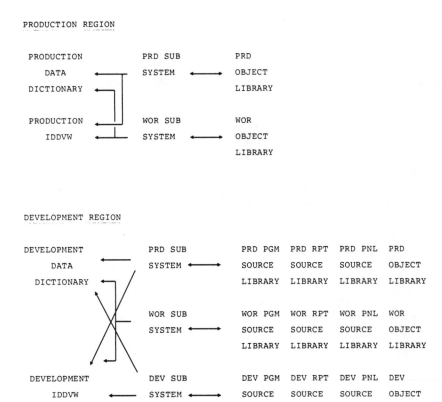

PRODUCTION REGION

```
PRODUCTION        PRD SUB          PRD
   DATA           SYSTEM           OBJECT
DICTIONARY                         LIBRARY

PRODUCTION        WOR SUB          WOR
   IDDVW          SYSTEM           OBJECT
                                   LIBRARY
```

DEVELOPMENT REGION

```
DEVELOPMENT       PRD SUB     PRD PGM   PRD RPT   PRD PNL   PRD
   DATA           SYSTEM      SOURCE    SOURCE    SOURCE    OBJECT
DICTIONARY                    LIBRARY   LIBRARY   LIBRARY   LIBRARY

                  WOR SUB     WOR PGM   WOR RPT   WOR PNL   WOR
                  SYSTEM      SOURCE    SOURCE    SOURCE    OBJECT
                             LIBRARY   LIBRARY   LIBRARY   LIBRARY

DEVELOPMENT       DEV SUB     DEV PGM   DEV RPT   DEV PNL   DEV
   IDDVW          SYSTEM      SOURCE    SOURCE    SOURCE    OBJECT
                             LIBRARY   LIBRARY   LIBRARY   LIBRARY
```

Figure F-2   Relationship of Subsystems to Libraries.

The IDDVW library contains the object modules for the dataview definitions.

We should then notice that each development subsystem contains four separate libraries. These are

1. PROGRAM SOURCE LIBRARY, which contains the procedure, working storage, and parameter components of the program.
2. REPORT DEFINITION SOURCE LIBRARY, which contains the parameter, heading, detail, and column definitions.
3. PANEL DEFINITION LIBRARY, which contains the parameter, layout, summary, and extended field definitions for the panel.

4. OBJECT LIBRARY, which contains the separate object modules for each of the following:

   a. program component
   b. report definition
   c. panel definition
   d. working data definition
   e. parameter data definition

These separate object modules are then combined into a single executable load module.

In contrast to these four libraries, Figure F-2 shows that the two production subsystems only point to an object library. The source code is stored in the development region only, and not in the production region. This was done to eliminate the possibility of writing and running untested code against the production databases, thus helping to protect the integrity of those databases.

An additional library that is not shown in the figures is the member or IDDAT library. This library is shared among all of the subsystems of a region.

Library Interaction

Now that we have defined this environment, we can take some examples to see how the different libraries work together.

We will begin with the basic example of the creation of a new program in the DEV subsystem of the development region. This new program has the following resource table fill-in:

```
-----------------------------------------------------------------------
IDEAL: RESOURCE TABLE        PGM PROGRAM1 (001) TEST        SYS: DEV
=======================================================================

   DATAVIEW        VERS    PANEL    VERS    REPORT   VERS  PROGRAM  VERS SYS

   DATAVIEW-1      0001    PANEL1   0001    REPORT1  0001  _____ ____ ___

   DATAVIEW-2      0001    _____   ____    _____  ____  _____ ____ ___


   _____      ____    _____   ____    _____  ____  _____ ____ ___
```

This new program PROGRAM1 requires the use of two dataviews (DATAVIEW-1 and DATAVIEW-2), a panel (PANEL1), and a report (REPORT1).

At this point it is important to note that the resource table does not really exist as we see it. It is a series of relationship pointers

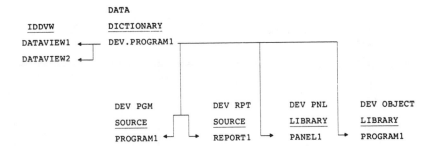

Figure F-3   Resources of Program1.

that are stored in the DATADICTIONARY. When we understand this concept, we can show the logical relationships in a form like Figure F-3.

Here we see the pointers from the DEV.PROGRAM1 program model in the DATADICTIONARY point to the DEV PGM source library, the DEV RPT source library, the DEV panel library, and the DEV object library.

We can then add to this figure by changing the resource table to look at SUBRUTN1 in the DEV subsystem.

```
.------------------------------------------------------------------------
IDEAL: RESOURCE TABLE        PGM PROGRAM1 (001) TEST      SYS: DEV

========================================================================

  DATAVIEW       VERS    PANEL   VERS    REPORT  VERS   PROGRAM  VERS SYS

DATAVIEW-1       0001  PANEL1    0001  REPORT1   0001  SUBRUTN1  0001 DEV

DATAVIEW-2       0001  _____  ____  _____  ____  _____  ____ ___

------------------  ____  _____  ____  _____  ____  _____  ____
```

The DEV subsystem does not have any entries in its resource table. When PROGRAM1 is recompiled, the pointers of Figure F-3 are changed as shown in Figure F-4. Here we see that the DATADICTIONARY entry for PGM PROGRAM1 now points to the entry for SUBRUTN1 in both the source library and the object library. This is in addition to the DATADICTIONARY pointers for program SUBRUTN1.

We can then add a production status subroutine to our example:

```
----------------------------------------------------------------------
IDEAL: RESOURCE TABLE        PGM PROGRAM1 (001) TEST      SYS: DEV
```

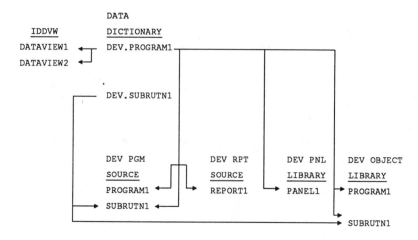

Figure F-4   Resources of Program1 with Subroutines.

```
==============================================================================
  DATAVIEW        VERS    PANEL   VERS    REPORT   VERS   PROGRAM   VERS SYS
  DATAVIEW-1      0001    PANEL1  0001    REPORT1  0001   SUBRUTN1  0001  ___
  DATAVIEW-2      0001    _____  ____    _____  ____   PRDSUBR1  0001  PRD

  _____    ____    _____  ____    _____  ____   _____   ____  ___
```

which in turn has the following resource table:

```
------------------------------------------------------------------------------
  IDEAL: RESOURCE TABLE          PGM PRDSUBR1 (001) PROD       SYS: PRD
==============================================================================
  DATAVIEW        VERS    PANEL   VERS    REPORT  VERS   PROGRAM   VERS SYS
  DATAVIEW-2      0001    PANEL3  0001    _____  ____   _____   ___ ___
  DATAVIEW-3      0001    _____  ____    _____  ____   _____   ____ ___

  _____    ____    _____  ____    _____  ____   _____   ____ ___
```

Again we see the pointers from the DATADICTIONARY entry for program PRD.PRDSUBR1 to the individual libraries. This time, however, the pointers are to the libraries in the PRD subsystem as opposed to the DEV subsystem. (See Figure F-5.)

In addition, when PROGRAM1 is compiled, the pointers for resources in PRDSUBR1 are included in its DATADICTIONARY entry. This includes a new pointer to DATAVIEW-3, and one to the PRD object library entry for PRDSUBR1. We are only able to point to

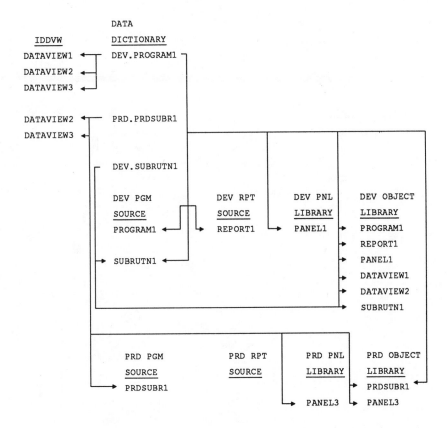

Figure F-5   Resources of Program1, with a Subroutine in PRD Subsystem.

program object modules in a different object library than the one we have. Because the panel named PANEL3 does not exist in the DEV system panel library, there is no pointer to it from PROGRAM1. Then, when program PROGRAM1 is executed, and panel PANEL3 is accessed by PRDSUBR1, a run-time error occurs.

To solve this problem, it is necessary to enter the DEV subsystem and, using the command

```
DUP PNL PANEL3 SYS PRD NEW PANEL3
```

copy the PANEL SOURCE and OBJECT from the PRD system to the DEV system. The pointers from PROGRAM1 are then connected

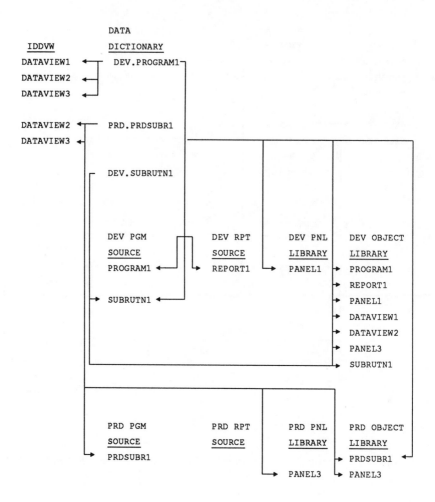

Figure F-6   Addition of Panel3 to Resources of Program1.

to the object module (as seen in Figure F-6), and the program can be executed.

Another frequent problem occurs when a program tries to use different versions of the same program. Let's say that a program calls two subroutines (SUBRUTN2 and SUBRUTN3). Each of these subroutines calls a common subroutine (SUBCOMMN). If the resource table of SUBRUTN2 points to the PROD version of SUBCOMMN, and SUBRUTN3 points to a new test version, a run-time error occurs when one of them is accessed. One of these subroutines must be changed and recompiled to allow processing to continue.

Production Implementation

Now that we have developed and tested our program in the development region and everyone has passed judgement on it, we need to move it to the production region. This is done through an ADR VLS utility called "TRANSPRT." This facility moves the load modules from one region to another. The rules for this facility are

1. All transportable modules must be marked to production status.
2. The facility can only move object modules, not source code.
3. The facility only works in corresponding subsystems (development PRD to production PRD, development WOR to production WOR).

Thus to transport our program to production, we need to move it from DEVELOPMENT.DEV to DEVELOPMENT.PRD, mark it to production status, and execute the transport utility. Simple, right?

Not quite.

To mark something to production status, we must first mark all of its subordinates to production status. We must then edit the resource table, type "PROD" into the version field of all of the entries, and recompile the program.

Thus to move our PROGRAM1 program to production, we need to do the following:

1. SELECT SYSTEM PRD
2. DUP PNL PANEL1 SYS DEV NEW PANEL1
3. DUP RPT REPORT1 SYS DEV NEW REPORT1
4. DUP PGM SUBRTN1 SYS DEV NEW SUBRTN1
5. MARK PNL PANEL1 V 1 PROD
6. MARK RPT REPORT1 V 1 PROD
7. MARK PGM SUBRTN1 V 1 PROD
8. DUP PGM PROGRAM1 SYS DEV NEW PROGRAM1
9. EDIT PGM PROGRAM1 RES
10. Type over the version numbers
11. COMPILE PROGRAM1

> 12. MARK PGM PROGRAM1 V 1 PROD
> 13. Execute the TRANSPORT

All of this is assuming that this is a new program, or that all of the previous versions of the programs, the panel, and the report have been marked to history status and deleted. If not, we have to find another way to move them from DEV to PRD, because the DUP facility will not work if the name already exists in the target system.

For this example, we will assume that PROGRAM1 version 3, PANEL1 version 1, and REPORT1 version 3 already exist in the PRD system.

We begin by comparing the resource tables of the DEV version with the resources in PRD. We see that the panel versions are the same, but the REPORT1 version number in DEV is a history version in PRD. If we were to try to bring the program over to PRD with this discrepancy, we would cause a DATADICTIONARY error. Thus we need to remove the REPORT1 entry from the resource table.

We then execute the following commands to move these entities to PRD.

> 1. SELECT SYSTEM PRD
> 2. DUP RPT REPORT1
> 3. EDIT RPT REPORT1
> 4. Physically enter the changes to the report definition
> 5. MARK RPT REPORT1 V 4 PROD
> 6. DUP PNL PANEL1
> 7. EDIT PNL PANEL1
> 8. Physcially enter the changes to the panel definition
> 9. MARK PNL PANEL1 V 2 PROD
> 10. DUP PGM SUBRTN1 SYS DEV NEW SUBRTN1
> 11. MARK PGM SUBRTN1 V 1 PROD
> 12. DUP PGM PROGRAM1 SYS DEV NEW DUMMYNM
>   (Duplicate program to a dummy name.)
> 13. DUP PGM PROGRAM1
> 14. EDIT PGM PROGRAM1
> 15. Remove all lines of code from PROC AREA
> 16. COPY DUMMYNM TOP BOTTOM TOP
> 17. EDIT PGM PROGRAM1 WOR
> 18. Remove all lines of code from WOR AREA
> 19. COPY DUMMYNM TOP BOTTOM TOP
> 20. EDIT PGM PROGRAM1 PARM

21. Remove all lines of code from PARM AREA
22. COPY DUMMYNM TOP BOTTOM TOP
23. EDIT PGM PROGRAM1 RES
24. Type over version numbers with PROD
25. COMPILE PROGRAM1
26. MARK PGM PROGRAM1 V 4 PROD
27. Execute transport facility
28. DELETE PGM DUMMYNM V 1

The transport facility unloads the object modules from the object library and loads them into the production region object library. The facility takes the entire executable load module over, including the object code for the associated reports, panels, and dataviews. Thus the definition of a new field in a development dataview will still be available to the transported program, even though the change has not been formally applied to the production dataview.

Because the transport facility only carries over executable load modules, the majority of IDEAL commands will not function, as they operate against the source code. The only commands that will work in the production region are

1. RUN
2. DEQUEUE
3. ALTER PROGRAM
4. ASSIGN DATAVIEW

any other command will receive a "not found" error.

Another tool that we do not have in the production region is the DISPLAY INDEX command, again because the source code from which the INDEX is built does not exist in the production region.

To substitute for this, IDEAL has provided the following commands:

```
DISPLAY INDEX MEMBER USER @I$OBJ
DISPLAY INDEX MEMBER USER @I$PNL
```

which show a listing of the contents of the program and panel object libraries, respectively. With this facility we can see the last time a piece of production code was changed, which can help us in problem determination. An example of this is shown in Figure F-7.

```
IDEAL: DISPLAY INDEX MEM     MEM                        SYS:WOR  DISPLAY


NAME                    RECS  DESCRIPTION               CREATED  UPDATED
============================== T O P ==================================
WORBLPGSHPT      PRDJA  93008 PROGRAM SYMBOL TABLE      10/21/87 10/21/87
WORBLPGSHPT      PRDTA  93008 OBJECT MODULE FOR PGM B   10/21/87 10/21/87
WORBLPGSHPT      PRDTB  93008 PROGRAM SYMBOL TABLE      10/21/87 10/21/87
WORBLPGSHVW      PRDJA  93008 PROGRAM SYMBOL TABLE      10/16/87 10/16/87
WORBLPGSHVW      PRDTA  93008 OBJECT MODULE FOR PGM B   10/16/87 10/16/87
WORBLPGSHVW      PRDTB  93008 PROGRAM SYMBOL TABLE      10/16/87 10/16/87
WORDAPGCFTR      PRDJA  93008 PROGRAM SYMBOL TABLE      11/26/87 11/26/87
WORDAPGCFTR      PRDTA  93008 OBJECT MODULE FOR PGM D   11/26/87 11/26/87
WORDAPGCFTR      PRDTB  93008 PROGRAM SYMBOL TABLE      11/26/87 11/26/87
```

Figure F-7   Index Display of Transported Programs.

Exercises

1. What libraries do subsystems share ?
2. What libraries are attached to a specific region?
3. What does the DATADICTIONARY contain?
4. Do reports accessed by a program in another subsystem need to be resident in the subsystem in which we are running? Why?
5. What happens when two subroutines call different versions of the same common module?
6. Can we transport directly from DEVELOPMENT.DEV to PRODUCTION.PRD?
7. In what direction of a program's hierarchy must we work when marking a program to production?
8. Is the Resource table stored as source code?
9. How can a change in a development dataview be found in production?
10. What command can we use to find out when a program was transported?

Exercises — Answers

1. What libraries do subsystems share ?

    a.   Databases
    b.   IDDVW — Dataview Object Library
    c.   IDDAT — Member Library

2. What libraries are attached to a specific region?

    a.   Program Source Library
    b.   Report Definition Source Library
    c.   Panel Definition Library
    d.   Object Library

3. What does the DATADICTIONARY contain?

    a.   The subsystem's definitions
    b.   The user definitions and authorizations
    c.   The dataview definitions
    d.   An entry for and model of each panel definition
    e.   An entry for and model of each report definition
    f.   An entry for and model of each program definition
    g.   A listing of the relationships that are used to fill in the program resource table display

4. Do reports accessed by a program in another subsystem need to be resident in the subsystem in which we are running? Why?

Yes, so that the DATADICTIONARY can establish a pointer to the report object module.

5. What happens when two subroutines call different versions of the same common module?

A run-time error occurs.

6. Can we transport directly from DEVELOPMENT.DEV to PRODUCTION.PRD?

No. We must transport across corresponding subsystems.

7. In what direction of a program's hierarchy must we work when marking a program to production?

We must start with the lowest module and work up.

8. Is the resource table stored as source code?

   No, the resource table display is built from datadictionary relationship pointers.

9. How can a change in a development dataview be found in production?

   If an object module with that change was transported.

10. What command can we use to find out when a program was transported?

    DISPLAY INDEX MEMBER USER @I$OBJ

Index